PREDICATES AND THEIR SUBJECTS

Studies in Linguistics and Philosophy

Volume 74

PREDICATES
AND THEIR SUBJECTS

by

SUSAN ROTHSTEIN
Bar-Ilan University, Ramat Gan, Israel

KLUWER ACADEMIC PUBLISHERS
DORDRECHT/BOSTON/LONDON

A catalogue record for this book is available from the Library of Congress.

ISBN 0-7923-6409-0

Published by Kluwer Academic Publishers,
PO Box 17, 3300 AA Dordrecht, The Netherlands.

Sold and distributed in North, Central and South America
by Kluwer Academic Publishers,
101 Philip Drive, Norwell, MA 02061, U.S.A.

In all other countries, sold and distributed
by Kluwer Academic Publishers,
PO Box 322, 3300 AH Dordrecht, The Netherlands

Printed on acid-free paper

Printed and bound in Great Britain by MPG Books, Bodmin, Cornwall

CONTENTS

INTRODUCTION

'Subject' is a concept which has been notoriously difficult for linguists to define. Keenan, in his 1976 article, lists some thirty odd properties which he identifies as properties which characterise subjects, as opposed to other arguments, but he admits that there is no combination of these properties which is necessary or sufficient to identify a particular NP in a sentence of a language as the subject of that sentence. It is not even clear that any one of these properties is necessary. The characteristics range over the syntactic, semantic and pragmatic domains, and include case-marking, being non-droppable from the sentence, and so on. Keenan gives what he calls a 'weak definition' of subject, which identifies the subject as the NP which has more of the properties on his list than any other NP in the sentence. Keenan does not explain what 'subject' is, nor why these properties should tend to concentrate themselves round a single NP, but the data he presents justifies the intuition that there is some point in attempting to define the notion.

Different syntactic theories, attempting to define 'subject', have approached the problem in different ways. In Relational Grammar (Perlmutter 1983, Perlmutter and Rosen 1984) and Lexical-Functional Grammar (Bresnan 1982a), 'subject' is the highest of a series of ranked grammatical relations, which are primitives in the theories. Other theories, in particular, Chomskyan approaches, have attempted to do without any grammatical relations which cannot be reduced to positions in a tree. 'Subject' is defined in hierarchical terms as the subject of a sentence, or in terms of its relation to Inflection. Thus the subject is the NP dominated by S or IP (=[NP,IP]) (Chomsky 1981), or the argument assigned Case by, or coindexed with, Inflection (Borer 1986, Fukui and Speas 1986, Fukui 1986, Speas 1986). A different approach is to define 'subject' in combinatorial terms as the last argument of the verb to be fed in: a good example of this is Dowty's (1982) treatment of grammatical relations within Montague's type theory (Montague 1970, 1973). The direct object is the argument which combines with the transitive verb to yield an intransitive verb, and the subject is the argument which combines with an intransitive verb to yield a syntactic expression of type t, a sentence. Generalized Phrase Structure Grammar (Gazdar, Klein, Pullum and Sag 1985) follows this approach also, and defines the subject as the "term which combines last of all with a verbal phrase to make a sentence" (p198,(36.i)). Williams (1980, 1983a,b, 1987) formulates a version of the 'last argument in' approach in terms of thematic roles, and tries to implement the argument-based definitions of 'subject' in an essentially government-binding syntactic framework.

I have been thinking, as a linguist, about what subjects are for nearly twenty years now. The central idea that I have been developing, which I first gave expression to in my dissertation in 1983, is that the subject argument is special because it is a structurally selected argument of a structurally defined constituent, and not a lexically selected argument of a lexical head (although a lexical head may constrain what can fill the subject position). The structurally defined constituent which selects the subject is what I called (in Rothstein 1983 and onward) a syntactic predicate. The syntactic predicate is the only non-lexical argument-selecting element in the sentence, and its single argument, its subject, thus has the properties which distinguish it from all other arguments. Syntactic predicates are structurally unsaturated in the Fregean sense: subject arguments are the syntactic elements which saturate these unsaturated entities.

A basic intuition underlying this idea is that the grammar requires a sentence (IP, element of type t, or however you want to phrase it) to be the outcome of an operation of functional application **whether or not there is any thematic reason to require it**. The pleonastic in (1) is necessary because the sentence must be the result of an operation of functional application, despite the fact that the VP looks like a thematically saturated constituent.

(1)   It seems that this sentence needs a subject.

It adds no information to the sentence, but we cannot use the VP to make the assertion in (1). The claim that I make is that it is the operation, or relation, between the VP and the pleonastic element, which is crucial for deriving the sentence-level expression. This means that the operation which gets us from VP to sentence level in (1) is the same operation that gets us from VP to sentence level in (2), where the subject is thematic:

(2)   Dafna is eating ice-cream.

In neither case is the operation driven by the properties of the verbal head.

The thematic operation of applying the VP *is eating ice-cream* to the external thematic argument of *eat* is made possible by, or takes a ride on, the syntactic operation of applying the syntactic VP predicate to the subject argument. This is what makes the agent the 'external argument' of the head. The obligatoriness of the subject position, and the independence of the subject-predicate relation from the head-argument thematic relations, explain a number of facts about the subject, in particular why it hosts pleonastics and why it is the landing site for NP-raising in passive and raising constructions.

This core idea is essentially what I published in my dissertation in 1983, although I didn't phrase it quite like this. I remember saying then that I thought that the central idea in my dissertation was probably right, but that it would take me fifteen years or so to understand enough to explain why. So this book is really an attempt to show what the original idea in my dissertation means, and to give a coherent syntactic and semantic account of how it can be worked out. It turns out that I made a fairly accurate assessment of how long it would take (although I am more sceptical now about the absolute 'rightness' of linguistic ideas than I was then). Other than that, in terms of content, the dissertation and the book have almost nothing in common.

I begin with a 'prologue' in chapter 1, in which I argue against 'ordinary language' attempts to give a non-grammatical definition of 'subject', and in which I review the basic grammatical arguments which show that the subject is the structurally prominent argument in a hierarchical syntactic structure. This chapter is really meant to 'clear the stage' for the show, and that is why it is not represented in the 'part' structure of the book. Chapters 2–5 constitute Part I of the book: the syntax of predication. In chapter 2 I set up the basics of the grammatical theory of predication and explain how the Fregean notion of unsaturatedness and saturatedness is given syntactic form. Syntactic predicates are the basic unsaturated constituents which must be saturated by arguments, and subjects are the arguments which saturate them. I argue that maximal projections of lexical heads are inherently unsaturated syntactic predicates, and I propose representing syntactic predicate saturation by syntactic coindexing. In chapter 3 I argue that it is this syntactic definition of subject as 'subject of a syntactic predicate' which explains the properties which subjects in English have, and I show that other attempts to define syntactic subjects in terms of case-assignment or labelled positions in a tree don't work. Chapter 4 examines in depth the thematic theory of predication developed by Edwin Williams in a series of papers (in particular 1980, 1983a,b, 1987). Williams, like me, defines 'subject' in terms of a predication relation, but he argues that the predication relation itself is to be defined in terms of thematic arguments: the subject of a predicate is the external thematic argument of the head of the predicate. Williams' theory is thus a syntactically expressed version of the 'distinguished thematic argument' or 'last argument in' theory. I show that, aside from the issue of pleonastics, which Williams doesn't deal with, this thematic theory gets into technical problems with raising to subject. What I show is that these problems stem from a basic incompatibility between a 'distinguished argument' theory of subjects and predicates on the one hand and a theory of raising and passive which relies on traces and syntactic chains. In other words, a thematic/distinguished argument theory of subjects commits you to a non-movement (i.e. non-trace) based account of passive and raising. Chapter 5 extends the account of the syntax of predication to cover a variety of different complex predication structures and contrasts clausal predication with different forms of adjunct predication.

Part II of the book deals with the semantics of predication. There is a semantic correlate of the syntactic idea that constituents are syntactic predicates independently of their thematic properties: the predicate status of VPs, indeed of all lexical (non-functionally headed) XPs is not derived from the argument properties of their heads. Heads which assign n thematic roles normally denote n-1 place functions which allow them to be applied to their internal arguments. Thus the translation of the head *read*, which assigns two thematic roles, is as in (3):

(3) read_V: $<Ag, \text{Th}> \rightarrow \lambda y \lambda e.\text{READ}(e) \wedge \text{Ag}(e) = x \wedge \text{Th}(e) = y$

(3) expresses that the verb exerts thematic restrictions on two participants, represented by the theme and the agent roles, but that only application to the theme role is triggered internally. VPs (and other lexical XPs) are saturated constituents of type $<e,t>$ (the type of sets of events) and they become semantic predicates by a rule of automatic predicate formation which applies at the VP level independent of the thematic properties of the head. If *read* is applied to the direct object *War and Peace*, then (4a) will be the translation of the VP, and the input to predicate formation. The result of predicate formation will be (4b).

(4)   a. $\lambda e.READ(e) \wedge Ag(e) = x \wedge Th(e) = $ War and Peace
      b. $\lambda x \lambda e.READ(e) \wedge Ag(e) = x \wedge Th(e) = $ War and Peace

The expression in (4a) is saturated, since it is of type $<e,t>$, but we can call it *implicitly unsaturated*, since it contains the free x variable, and thus encodes the information that no value has been supplied for the agent role. Predicate formation makes the expression into the *explicitly unsaturated* expression in (4b). Chapter 6 shows how to work out the semantic expression of the idea that predication is not a thematically dependent relation. Chapter 7 shows how the system explains the distribution of non-thematic arguments, in particular the distribution of pleonastics. Predicate formation applies to an XP whether or not it is implicitly unsaturated, and thus an XP may translate into an expression of the form $\lambda x.\alpha$, whether or not α contains a free x variable. I argue that pleonastics denote a minimal information object $\perp$. When predicate formation results in vacuous lambda abstraction, i.e. when it applies to an XP which is not implicitly unsaturated, a principle of Strong Compositionality, which requires that no semantic information is lost in the derivation, guarantees that the only possible subject is a pleonastic. The rest of chapter 7 is devoted to verifying the claim that pleonastics can appear only in subject position. In the process of discussing the semantics of predication, I compare my account with the semantic account of subjects in Dowty (1982), and with Chierchia's account of the predication relation (Chierchia 1984, 1986, 1989).

Part III discusses copular constructions, and in particular the syntax and semantics of identity sentences. The central point is that in a non-verbal predicational structure, the argument and predicate (let us call it 'AP' for simplicity, though it need not be adjectival) naturally form a predication relation, or small clause. Any additional elements, such as inflection or a copular verb, are required for non-predication related reasons, and requirements differ from language to language. In Hebrew, this results in matrix small clauses, and in English it results in small clause complements to verbs like *consider*. I show that identity sentences cannot be truly small, since they do not consist of an argument and inherent predicate, and thus do not naturally form a predication structure. While languages differ as to how they construct identity sentences, a minimal requirement is that a syntactic predication structure must be formed at the clausal level. I show that in Hebrew, matrix identity sentences require only the addition of a minimal inflectional node to create such a structure, while in English, a copular *be* is required. In each case, Inflection and *be* trigger type-shifting of the post-copula argument. Chapter 8 is devoted to the Hebrew data and chapter 9 discussed the English data. The theory of predication that I develop in this book is incompatible with an 'inverse' account of copular constructions, and in the second part of chapter 9 I argue against the inverse account.

Part IV consists of one long chapter. I start from an apparently minor problem in the small clause data. If complements to *consider* verbs can be small, and *be* is required only to create a predication structure, then the question is, why is (5) not grammatical?

(5)   *I consider Mary be Dr. Smith.

To be honest, I did my best for years to ignore this problem. When I finally came to terms with the fact that it wouldn't go away, and that maybe it wasn't so minor after all, I started work on what turned out to be chapter 10, and the reader will see that this is only a beginning. But it is where this book finished.

One further point: the actual writing – and rewriting – of the book took place over a period of over ten years, and the style and content reflect, I think, something of how my thinking has developed over that time. I am still resisting the temptation to rewrite it all from scratch, and also the temptation to explain how I would have done it differently if I were starting it now. The book was not intended as a personal intellectual history, but I think it ended up a little more like that than I expected.

A project of this length, spanning many years and three continents, collects many debts of gratitude along the way, and I want to mention at least some. I first started to think about this book as a coherent project when I was on sabbatical at MIT in the academic year 1990–1991. Among the people who I talked with that year were Sylvain Bromberger and the late George Boolos. I presented material from chapters 2–4 and chapter 8 during that year at Harvard, the University of Arizona at Tucson, Irvine, UCLA, the University of Pennsylvania, Syracuse University and at the Workshop on Hebrew at UQAM. All the audiences contributed in some way. Caroline Heycock and I talked about syntactic predication and reverse copula constructions at length (mainly in diners around Penn Station, which is as near to midway between Philadelphia and Boston as you can get). I wrote the draft of the first chapter in my parents' house (then in London) in the summer of 1991, when I couldn't come home for reasons to do with the tax year, and they provided excellent working conditions. My late uncle, Milton Rose, set up his printer for me there too.

In Israel I have talked at length with many people, in particular Anita Mittwoch, Edit Doron, Tali Siloni and Alex Grosu. Jonathan Fine has always been a supportive colleague, a ready informant and a willing and encouraging listener. I have talked a lot with my students over the years, in particular with Iris Elisha, Yael Greenberg and Daphna Heller and in particular about chapters 8 and 9. Yael and Daphna each took on aspects of the Hebrew pronominal copula in their MA theses, and I learned a lot from working with them. The Israeli linguistics community has over the years been a constant source of stimulation, and audiences at the annual conferences of the Israel Association for Theoretical Linguistics and at many departmental colloquia have been challenging and supportive. I presented material from chapter 6 at the Israel Association for Theoretical Linguistics in the annual conference in 1995, and from chapter 10, in the annual conference of the same association in 1997. I also presented material from chapter 10 at the Texas Linguistics Society meeting in March 1997, in a course at the LSA summer school at Cornell that Fred Landman and I taught together in 1997, at a department seminar at Tel Aviv University and at the Conference on Semantics at the Center for Advanced Studies of the Hebrew University of Jerusalem in December 1997. I presented material from chapters 8, 9 and 10 in courses at Bar-Ilan University in the spring of 1992 and the spring of 1998. I want to thank all the people mentioned here by name, and all the audiences for helpful comments and discussions.

There are also a number of 'anonymous' thank yous to be expressed. Parts of chapter 7 appeared in Linguistic Inquiry as Rothstein (1995a) and are reprinted here with permission. A version of chapter 10 appears in Natural Language Semantics 7 under the title "Finegrained structure in the eventuality domain: the semantics of predicative adjective phrases and *be*". I'd like to thank reviewers of both papers, especially the NLS reviewer who sent me twenty pages of thought-provoking discussion, and who later admitted to being Barbara Partee. Many thanks to two reviewers of the present manuscript, who gave me detailed and helpful comments which greatly improved the final version of the book. Thanks also to Polly Jacobson, who as series editor for SLAP gave me helpful comments on the manuscript.

Fred Landman and I first talked about the minimal information object (the 'bore at the party', as he called it) over dinner in Cafe Kaze in Tel Aviv in the spring of 1992. We have come a long way together since then. I want to thank him for reading and commenting on the whole manuscript, for long discussions on predication, predicates and semantic domains (the 'p.c.'s in the text should indicate something of how intense this was), for technical help in keeping track of my variables, and for helping to turn myself into a semanticist in the process. Also for many well-cooked dinners and much fun along the way.

The penultimate draft of the book was written in the year after our daughter Dafna was born. As anyone who has a small child in a not-so-big apartment will understand, working at home was impossible that year. Shlomit and Haim of Cafe Ditza kept the table next to the electricity outlet for me and my computer whenever I wanted it (three days a week during term time, five days a week in the semester break), and kept us supplied with coffee and electricity, and good-humoured encouragement. It is no exaggeration to say that it was invaluable. Meanwhile, Sara Aharon looked after Dafna at home with such competence and warmth that I had the mental space, at Cafe Ditza, to think about my book.

I thought I would end up by saying that although Dafna has been ever present since 1996, I couldn't really say that I had to thank her (since I am restricting myself to expressing professional thanks). But last week, she wandered into the study where our rather elderly printer was churning out pages of the book, and she started to take them out one by one and put them in a pile. So she gets a thank you too.

August 8, 1999
Tel Aviv

WHY 'SUBJECT' IS A GRAMMATICAL CONCEPT

1.1. Aristotelian assumptions

The traditional approach to subjects, predicates and predication is essentially pragmatic, and defines the subject in terms of a semantic/pragmatic predication relation explained in terms of 'aboutness'. As for the syntax, it proposes that the syntactic subject is the syntactic expression of the entity that the sentence is about, and a sentence is said to 'say something about its subject'. This subject-predicate relation has often been taken for granted as being in some sense 'given', and the subject and predicate are frequently assumed to be the basic semantic elements which a proposition is composed out of. Chapter 1 of this book reviews some of the issues that these assumptions raise, and aims to clear the ground for the discussion of grammatically or structurally grounded theories of predication which constitutes the bulk of this book. I am not, at this stage, interested in the question of which structural definitions of predicate, subject, and predication are to be preferred; rather I want to identify some of the difficulties which arise when we try to define these concepts pragmatically, and to show why we are led to search for purely structural definitions.

Aristotle defines 'proposition' recursively, relying on the distinction between subject and predicate: a composite proposition is composed of simple propositions, and a simple proposition "asserts or denies something of something". A proposition is "a statement, with meaning, as to the presence of something in a subject or its absence, in the present, past, or future, according to the divisions of time" ("On Interpretation" paragraph 5). He then goes on in the next paragraph to use the term 'predicate', stating that positive and negative propositions are contradictory "which have the same subject and predicate", but which differ as to whether it is affirmed that the predicate is present in the subject or denied." (paragraph 6).

This account makes explicit the intuitions about the workings of propositions, subjects and predicates which have governed much linguistic thought. Aristotle claims that the structure of a proposition is inherently bipartite, with only one part, the subject, being what later philosophers have called an 'argument', and the other part, the predicate, expressing a property. These elements are used in calculating the semantic value of the proposition: the proposition is true if the subject does have the property expressed by the predicate and

1

false otherwise. (The converse is true for what Aristotle calls a negative proposition or 'denial'.) Aristotle takes the distinction between arguments, which are naming expressions, and predicates, which are property expressions, as basic, and Strawson (1970) argues through the validity of this distinction.

As we can see, the Aristotelian analysis focuses on defining the structure of the proposition, rather than on defining the nature of subject and predicate expressions or the relation between them. The subject is the 'subject of a proposition', and it is implied that predication is defined in terms of the proposition too. A proposition simply is an instance of predication; a proposition expresses an affirmation and an affirmation is "the statement of a fact with regard to a subject" (paragraph 11); the fact, as we saw above, is whether a particular property is or is not present in the subject. This relation of 'presence' between a property and the denotation of an argument is taken to be primitive. The bipartite structure of the proposition follows from the fact that the predicate is a property, or one-place relation.

This story about the nature of propositions becomes more complex if we look at examples which contain more than one Noun Phrase (NP). Since the Aristotelian example propositions in "On Interpretation" all contain only one nominal expression, and the predicate is headed by a verb or adjective which contains no nominal or other referential expressions, the primacy of the subject in the propositions is self-evident. The question is whether the primacy of the 'subject' is maintained when it is no longer the only referential/argument element in the sentence. If we take a more complex proposition such as (1), the semantic primacy of the subject is less easy to establish.

(1)   Mary gave John a copy of War and Peace.

In (1), the subject of the proposition is, intuitively and for most grammarians, the NP *Mary*, while the predicate is the complex Verb Phrase (VP) *gave John a copy of War and Peace*, and this intuition is associated with the Aristotelian idea that the sentence is true because Mary has the property of having given John a copy of War and Peace. But this analysis of (1) doesn't reflect the way the world is; it reflects how we go about calculating the truth value of (1). The actual state of affairs that makes (1) true does not have to be described by the statement that Mary has the property of having given John a copy of War and Peace. It can easily be perceived and described as a situation or state of affairs in which John has the property that Mary gave him War and Peace for his birthday, or in which a copy of War and Peace has the property that Mary gave it to John for his birthday or one in which Mary, John and War and Peace stand in the relation that the first gave the second a copy of the third. When we assign the value true to (1) it is because the objects denoted by the three NPs stand in the ordered relation denoted by 'give' and if (1) is false, it can be because any one of the three arguments is 'responsible'. A, B and C are appropriate responses to a denial of the truth of the assertion in (1);

(2)   That's not true.   A.   It was Kathy.
                          B.   She gave him Anna Karenina.
                          C.   She gave Jane War and Peace.

If we calculate the truth value of (1) by checking whether the ordered GIVE relation denoted by *give* holds between Mary, John and War and Peace, then we are not necessarily assigning any inherent structure to the proposition. But if we calculate its truth value by seeing whether one NP has a particular, possibly complex property, then we are essentially assigning the proposition a binary structure – dividing it into subject and predicate. And if the NP chosen for this calculation is always and necessarily the same NP, the subject, then we are singling out one argument as prominent and essentially assigning a subject-predicate structure to the sentence.

However, if we look at states of affairs in the world, there doesn't seem to be any prima facie good reason for seeing them as centered round one individual, and that means that as soon as there is more than one NP in a sentence, the self-evident nature of the binary structure of the proposition disappears. If there is no language-independent reason for making an assertion about a state of affairs in terms of the property that one participant does or doesn't have, then the justification must come from the way language works. Then if we continue to adopt an Aristotelian approach which matches our intuitions that (1) is true if Mary has a particular property, we first need to justify in linguistic terms why we assign the proposition a binary structure, and then we need to show why the binary structure always makes the same argument prominent.

In principle these two steps can be independent; the proposition could have a binary structure, but it could be assigned in such a way that the subject could vary from sentence to sentence. This is what Geach claims in his discussion of subjects and propositions (Geach 1962). He adopts an Aristotelian definition of proposition, and applies it to sentences with more than one NP, without claiming that one particular NP is always going to be the subject. Thus he writes: "A predicate is an expression that gives us an assertion about something if we attach it to another expression for what we are making the assertion about. A subject of a sentence S is an expression standing for something that S is about, S itself being formed by attaching a predicate to that expression." (paragraph 17). However, the binary structure of the proposition does not mean that a specific NP will be the subject, only that there must be a subject. A proposition may be ambiguous between several different predications, with any of the nominal constituents in the proposition being the subject. He takes as an example sentence (3):

(3)   Peter struck Malchus

He writes as follows: "In 'Peter struck Malchus' the predicate is - - - *struck Malchus* if we take Peter as the subject and *Peter struck* - - - if we take Malchus." (paragraph 26) For Geach, the predicate says something about the subject, and this relation of 'saying something about', which we will call the 'aboutness' relation, is the crucial element in the predication relation. The semantic subject of the sentence is the element that the predicate says something about; the grammatical subject of a sentence is the NP which denotes this element. There is no constant structural relation between subject and predicate, and no way to determine which the subject is which doesn't depend on the context. Consequently, given a sentence out of context, there is no way to determine which proposition it expresses.

This leaves several questions unanswered. First, there appear to be deep-rooted intuitions that in a sentence such as (3), *Peter* is more obviously the subject. Geach ignores this intuition, but we may ask what the basis of it is, and whether he is right to ignore it. (The reader who doesn't have such intuitions will have to be convinced by the linguistic arguments alone.) Second, Geach does not explain why the best analysis of a proposition is binary. Since there is more than one NP in the sentence, why not say that the Aristotelian definition has to be extended and that in such situations the structure of the proposition is not binary but, in the case of (3), ternary? The proposition expressed by (3) is then true if the striking relation holds between the individuals denoted by *Peter* and *Malchus*, where the first NP is the first argument of the relation and the second NP is the second argument. In such an approach, what is central is not a predicate which expresses a property, but a predicator, such as *strike*, which expresses a relation.

The reason why Geach assumes that a proposition has a binary structure is because he sees the aboutness relation as central, and because he assumes that aboutness is a monadic relation between a one-place predicate expression and a single argument (see the citation from paragraph 17 above). The Aristotelian definition says that a proposition is true if the property expressed by the predicate inheres in the subject. Geach adds to this that the subject is the entity that the sentence is about (though he doesn't really explain what this aboutness relation actually is), and that it is this aboutness relation which dictates the binary structure of the proposition. 'Aboutness' is a pragmatic notion, there is nothing to prevent us from using it to assign different binary structures to propositions – counter to those intuitions which tell us that the sentence has an invariant subject.

It is important to see that the aboutness relation is an abstract linguistic relation; there is nothing about the world which makes it true that a proposition is 'about' a single element, rather than pairs of elements in a sentence like (2), or triples of elements in (1). This shows up very clearly in the case of symmetrical predicates. The examples in (4) are true under the same conditions, and yet Geach would claim that (4a) is 'about' John and Mary while (4b) is 'about' either John or Mary:

(4)   a. John and Mary first met in 1989.
      b. John first met Mary in 1989.

Geach's analysis, and any definition of subject which uses an aboutness relation, depends on our being able to give a coherent definition of what aboutness actually is, and showing how and whether it might explain the binary structure of the clause. This is the topic of the next section.

1.2. ABOUTNESS

I am going to follow Reinhart (1981) in using 'topic' for the argument of the aboutness relation, rather than subject. Reinhart (1981) clarifies the distinction between two kinds of topic; the sentence topic – which is the topic or subject in the Geachian sense of aboutness, and the discourse topic, which is the conversational topic or general area of discussion to which the speaker wishes to use the sentence to contribute information. Thus if (5) or (6) (Grice's example) is uttered in response to a request for a recommendation for Mr Morgan, the sentence topic is Mr Morgan but the discourse topic is something like Mr Morgan's scholarly ability:

(5)   Mr Morgan is a careful and knowledgeable researcher, but is somewhat lacking in originality.

(6)   Mr Morgan is very pleasant and has clear and legible handwriting.

Now, the hypothesis that we are exploring is that the binary structure of the proposition can be explained by positing an aboutness relation which a proposition expresses, which holds between a one-place predicate expression, the predicate, and a single argument expression, the subject. In the process of exploring this, we would like an explanation of what the aboutness relation actually is. In search of this, I am going to discuss at length the work of Strawson (1964, 1970), which is probably the fullest treatment of aboutness and subjecthood in the pragmatic tradition. We will see that aboutness, as it is used in this tradition, is not enough to give us the binary structure of a clause. I shall show that it emerges from Strawson's work that a proposition is normally about one of the arguments that it contains, rather than about ordered pairs or triples, but that there are propositions which have the same binary structure, but which do not appear to be about any argument that they contain.

Strawson initially follows the Geachian approach, assuming that a sentence can be divided into subject and predicate and that "In the case of a statement containing more that one, say two, referring expressions, it is to be open to us to cast one of these for the role of subject expression, while the other is regarded as absorbed into the predicate term, which is attached to the subject term to yield the statement as a whole." (p110) Thus Strawson apparently shares Geach's perception that the predication relation inherently involves aboutness, and that, as far as aboutness goes, any NP can be the subject – or topic – or the sentence. However, Strawson departs from Geach in assuming that in addition to the aboutness argument, there is always, also, a 'logical' or 'grammatical' subject, and this will be crucial later in the discussion.

Let us first discuss the 'aboutness' subject, which we will from now on refer to as the sentence topic, following Reinhart (1981). Strawson's exploration of aboutness involves reexamining the issues surrounding truth-value assignments to sentences containing non-referring definite descriptions such as 'the present King of France', such as (7):

(7)   The present King of France is bald.

Strawson's original position (Strawson 1950) was that a sentence such as (7) failed to have a truth-value, since the existential presupposition carried by the definite description, that there currently exists one and only one King of France, is not met. As Strawson puts it, "the question whether the statement is true or false doesn't arise because there is no King of France." (p112) To say it differently, he is essentially assuming that a truth-value of a proposition is calculated by checking whether the individual denoted by the subject does or does not have the property expressed by the predicate. Then, in (7) we cannot check the truth-value, since there is no individual which is the referent of the subject, whose properties we can check.

   In his 1964 paper, Strawson makes two points which bear on the discussion of aboutness and propositions. The first is that (7) also may sometimes be judged false. The truth-value gap occurs only when the sentence is 'about' the present King of France, that is to say, when the present King of France is the topic of the sentence, However, he claims, if (7) is supplied as an answer to "what bald notables are there?" our intuitions seem to be that (7) is false because the "antecedently introduced class" – the class of bald notables – fails to include the present King of France. In this case the topic of the sentence is 'bald notables', and not a particular French monarch. What we do to find the truth value is to check the members of the class of bald notables, to see whether the class of bald notables has the property that it includes the present King of France, and when he fails to appear in the set, we judge the sentence false. Whether the present King of France fails to appear because he isn't bald or because he doesn't exist is an irrelevant consideration. In a similar example, Strawson suggests that (8) is normally neither true or false:

(8)   The present King of France married again.

However, suppose we have introduced what he calls an "antecedent centre of interest", for example by a question like (9):

(9)   What important political events occurred recently?

As an answer to (9), (8) will be judged false, since the event that it asserts to have occurred didn't in fact occur. In such circumstances (8) is "a wrong answer to a question which does arise" and not "an answer to a question which doesn't arise." (p112). In Strawson's words the truth-value gap occurs because "a statement is assessed as putative information about its topic" (p115), and if there is no entity corresponding to the topic, then the question of whether the information is correct or incorrect will not arise. We can reformulate this more formally: the truth-value gap occurs only when the NP which lacks a referent is the topic of the sentence.

   This gives us a clear sense of what Strawson means by aboutness. A proposition p is about an individual i if we assess the truth-value of p by checking whether i has a particular property or not. The individual that p is about in this sense is the topic of p. If a proposition purports to be about an NP that has no reference, the proposition cannot be assigned a truth value since the necessary checking and calculation cannot take place. (Notice that the truth conditions for (7) remain the same whether the topic is the present King of France or the set of bald notables. The question is not what the truth conditions of p are, but how they are verified.) While the verification of a proposition usually centres around the referent of the subject NP, this need not be the case, as (8) and (9) and the discussion of bald notables show.

I am not going to discuss here whether Strawson's analysis of undefinedness and the truth-value gap, together with the theory of presuppositions that it implies, is correct or not. It rests on theoretical notions of how sets are defined and what it means for x to be a member of a set Y which many logicians, including Russell, would disagree with. But, as it is, it represents the most coherent attempt to work out what pragmatic 'aboutness' might be, and I am interested in whether it can be used as the basis for a pragmatic theory of subjecthood. As we will see, it can't.

For our discussion of the relation between the binary structure of the sentence and the definition of topic and 'aboutness subject', Strawson's crucial point is that (7) can be putative information about bald notables and (8) can be putative information about important political events even though neither is mentioned in the sentence. And in these cases the topics of the sentences, which give what we might call the focus of the verification, are not expressed in the sentences at all. But if these sentences are about objects which are not mentioned in the sentence, and if the sentence topic is not expressed in the sentence at all, then these sentences cannot have a binary structure derived from the aboutness relation. Our conclusion has to be that either the binary structure of the proposition is due to something else, or these propositions don't actually have a binary structure.

The second point which Strawson makes in connection with the theory of aboutness raises the issue of the distinction between sentence topic and grammatical subject. He claims that there is an asymmetry between grammatical subjects and objects which appears when we look at the way the truth-value gap works. If the grammatical subject is the topic, then (7) is frequently judged to have no truth-value. In the same situation, (10) is almost always judged as false:

(10)   I met the present King of France yesterday.

This is because the sentence is judged to be about me, and we can therefore check and see that it is not one of my properties that I met the present King of France yesterday without even asking whether this is because there is no present King of France or because I didn't get a ticket to the French Royal Garden Party. Minimally contrasting active and passive pairs make the same point. He claims that we are more likely to say that (11a) fails to have a truth value, while (11b) is easily interpreted as false:

(11)   a. The present King of France visited the exhibition yesterday.
      b. The exhibition was visited yesterday by the present King of France.

Strawson's claim that any NP can be the topic of the sentence, together with his account of how and where truth-value gaps occur, predicts that it should be as easy to evaluate (10) and (11b) as also as failing to have a truth-value. But he also claims that it is much harder to get such a reading than it is for (7) or (11a). This shows that his prediction is wrong, and that the property of being the grammatical subject affects the ease with which an argument can be interpreted as sentence topic. But this shows clearly that Strawson relies on a notion of grammatical subject which is distinct from topichood. If choice of topic is influenced by grammatical subjecthood, then here we have a second argument why the grammatical subject cannot be defined in terms of aboutness, and we reinforce the validity of the search for a definition of what the grammatical subject is. So, the asymmetry between subject and object in generating truth-value gaps is also a piece of objective evidence to support the intuition we mentioned in the discussion of Geach that the grammatical subject is a more likely candidate for the topic (aboutness subject) than any other NP. Strawson recognises explicitly that grammatical subject and topic are indeed different entities. He points out that "It often is the case that the placing of an expression at the beginning of a sentence in the position of grammatical subject serves, as it were, to announce the statement's topic." (p118). I take this to make the fairly non-controversial claim (see among others Reinhart (1981) and references cited there) that the unmarked case in English is that the sentence subject gives the sentence topic, and this brings us back to the question of what the grammatical subject is. Strawson (1964) does not give a definition of grammatical subject, relying on the "relatively precise senses of logic and grammar" (p114), and assuming the syntactic definition to be given. It is only in his 1974 essay "Subject and Predicate in Logic and Grammar" that he seriously attempts to give content to the term.

1.3. PIVOTS AND THE SEMANTIC PROMINENCE OF SUBJECTS

The explicit goal of the 1974 essay is to explore the syntactic realisation of semantic relations. The pragmatic issue of aboutness is not raised, nor are the conclusions of the 1964 paper. Strawson wants to "trace some formal characteristics of logic and its grammar to their roots in general features of thought and experience". (1974, page vii) I stress this because I discuss this part of Strawson's work here as an attempt (perhaps the most careful in the recent philosophical literature) to explain how grammatical notions are derived from semantic ones, and it is important to be clear that he does see grammatical structure as a 'clothing' for semantic structure.

    Strawson is committed to there being a grammatical notion of subject, and he is equally committed to there being a semantic basis for that notion. The essay starts from an essentially Aristotelian semantic concept of the proposition:

a sentence "specifies a type of substance-involving situation or state of affairs or possible fact"; (1974, p100). In the core case, the subject is the element in the sentence which specifies individual particulars, the predicate is the element which specifies general characteristics, and the state of affairs asserted to hold is that the particulars have the general characteristics. Clearly, this is only the core case, since not all subjects denote particulars, but Strawson's extension of the definition to more general cases doesn't concern us here.

What does concern us is his discussion of how his system deals with propositions whose main predicator is dyadic, rather than monadic. Strawson is committed to a bipartite proposition, and to the intuition that there is some basic notion of grammatical subject and that, contra Geach, we are not free to choose any argument of a predicator to be the subject of the sentence. Since he does not take the bipartite structure of the proposition to be a structural given, he needs, with a dyadic predicator, to find some justification for the sentence being about the properties of one of the arguments rather than the other. In other words, if the predicator is not monadic, and the predicate of the sentence is monadic, there must be some inherent semantic asymmetry in the argument structure of a predicator which makes one argument of a dyadic predicate primary. This primary argument will be the grammatical subject of a sentence, although Strawson never commits himself explicitly to what the relation between primary argument and subjecthood is, making do with the statement that "the notion of primacy is built into that of grammatical subject" (p138).

The notion of primacy that Strawson uses is that of a 'pivotal' argument of a predicator. The crucial fact, he claims, is that "it is essential to the sense of any non-symmetrical predicate dyadic relation-expression whatever, that it selects or picks out or applies to **one** of the terms it relates in a way in which it does not select or pick out or apply to the other." (p91) The issue is raised in the context of a discussion of what he calls 'term ordering', or the fact that sets of arguments of predicators are inherently ordered. Take the two examples in (12), where the arguments *John* and *Mary* appear in a different order in each case.

(12) a. John saw Mary.
      b. Mary saw John.

Strawson comments that, along with the fact that these sentences denote different propositions, there is some sense in which we feel that in the former *John* is the 'source' of the relation and *Mary* the object while in the latter example the converse is the case. He uses other metaphors to explain this: in (12a) *John* is the 'pivot' of the report; we look at the relation SEE (John, Mary) from the standpoint of John, and in (12b), Mary is the pivot and the report is from her standpoint. Strawson calls the pivot argument the 'primary' term and the other argument the 'secondary' term. And it is this notion of being the pivot of a relation which Strawson uses to justify the primacy of one argument, and the fact that this primary argument is the one which in traditional grammar is considered the subject. And it is this notion of 'primacy' which he uses to justify differing from Geach in accepting as basic the traditional intuition that we are not free to choose which argument is taken as the subject of the sentence.

The problem is, however, that it is not clear that there is any independent semantic basis for the notion of pivot, or primary argument. The test that Strawson uses is essentially a syntactic test and not a semantic one, and while he shows that one argument is prominent or 'primary', he does not show that this follows from an inherent semantic asymmetry. His intuitions are at least as well, if not better, explained by the claim that the sentence has a hierarchical internal structure, which makes one argument structurally prominent, and that the feeling that this argument is the pivot of the relation follows from this structural prominence, rather than the other way round. Let us see why.

Strawson's arguments for classifying the arguments of a dyadic predicator as primary and secondary are as follows.

Our intuitions are that an ordered relation is always presented from a certain 'point of view'. Changing the standpoint requires changing the ordered relation: "if we look at it [a two-itemed fact] from the standpoint of one [of its terms], we get one non-symmetrical relation, if we look at it from the standpoint of the other we get the converse relation." (p91) Relations come in pairs of converses: active and passive forms of a verb are the paradigmatic members of such a pair, while an example of a non-morphologically related pair is 'older/younger'. (13) and (14) are examples of such converse pairs:

(13)   a. John admires Mary.
       b. Mary is admired by John.

(14)   a. John is older than Mary.
       b. Mary is younger than John.

Strawson gives a test for discerning which is the primary term of a non-symmetrical relation. The sentences in (14) can be rewritten using the format in (15): (page 91)

(15)   Of the (unordered) pair, John and Mary, related by the age-difference relation, Mary is (the) younger/John is (the) older.

The 'preamble' here can be followed by two descriptions of the age-difference relation, the two members of a 'pair of converses', and in each case only one argument need be mentioned. This is identified as the primary argument. He generalises the format in (15) to (16):

(16)   Of the pair, a and b, related by the R–R' relation,
       (i) R ...
       (ii) R' ...

The test works equally well for active/passive pairs:

(17)   Of the pair, John and the egg, related by the *eat–be eaten* relation,
       (i) John eats.
       (ii) The egg is eaten.

If we use this test as illustrated here, it turns out that the primary argument is always the one realised in what is traditionally called subject position, what we consider to be the first of the ordered set of arguments of the predicator. Strawson tries to show that this test is not dependent on the properties of English syntax and that we can use some other formalism to capture the notion of primacy, but it turns out that only in English does the test correspond with some deep-felt intuitions. Other representations stipulate that one argument is primary, but only in the version given in (17) does the schema allow one to deduce on the basis of intuition which that argument is.

It is important to note that when Strawson introduces the concept of 'pivot', or primary argument, he is not identifying the pivot of a proposition, but the pivot of a relation. But, he uses this to justify maintaining the bipartite structure of the proposition. One of the terms of a relation is primary, and because of this, it will become the 'argument' of the proposition.

It then becomes clear, intuitively, why the grammatical subject is the default candidate for sentence topic. The pivot is always the grammatical subject of the sentence, and thus the relation expressed in the proposition will be presented from the 'standpoint' of the grammatical subject. While a sentence does not have to be 'about' the pivotal argument of a relation, it should be possible to tell a convincing story about how a proposition expressing a relation expresses it 'about' its primary argument.

The trouble is that one the one hand, the semantic metaphor of 'pivot' which Strawson uses (and he agrees that it is a metaphor) is not clear, and on the other, the test that he uses as evidence to support his point turns out to be a test which can easily be explained as a syntactic test and not a semantic test at all.

First, let us look at what the semantic basis of the pivot or primary argument isn't. It doesn't have its basis in a lexical relation, since neither the first argument in an ordered relation nor the pivot argument can be fully predicted on the basis of the semantics of the relations, and thus an attempt to derive the semantic basis of a primary argument from thematic structure is not going to succeed. Although there are many generalisations about how thematic arguments are syntactically realised, some of which Strawson discusses, and many of which have been discussed at length in many different places (see Gruber 1965, Jackendoff 1972, Dowty 1982, Baker 1988), it is not always predictable how lexical arguments are going to be syntactically realised, partly because it is not always clear what thematic classification these arguments are supposed to receive. The pair *please* and *like* both have two arguments, an experiencer and a 'cause', but they appear in different orders (saying that this is because *please* is a 'psych' verb and *like* isn't just begs the question), and the test in (16) identifies the cause as the pivot for *please* and the experiencer as the pivot for *like*. The converse holds for *is/are pleased* and *is/are liked*:

(18) a. This music pleases many people.
      b. Many people like this music.

(19)   a. Many people are pleased by this music.
       b. This music is liked by many people.

Furthermore, as Strawson discusses himself, there is a primary first argument even when there is no clear thematic distinction between the various arguments of a predicate. He discusses the primary arguments of predicates like *is younger than/is older than* precisely so as to avoid the suspicion that some aspect of thematic structure is making the first argument primary.

Second, Strawson does not want to identify the pivot argument with the sentence topic. Since the pivot argument must appear in the position of the grammatical subject, and the topic in the unmarked case also is the argument which appears in subject position, it is easy for a single argument to be subject, pivotal argument and topic. But, as he showed in his 1964 paper, the topic cannot be identified with either grammatical subject, nor, we see, with the pivot argument. Remember that, for him, *the present King of France* must be the grammatical subject in (11a), repeated here as (20), but it need not be the topic if it is introduced as an answer to the question "which notables visited the exhibition yesterday?":

(20)   The present King of France visited the exhibition yesterday.

But, the grammatical subject is still the pivot argument of the relation, since this is determined independently of the context in which the proposition is used, and thus independently of the factors which influence aboutness.

If we look closely at Strawson's test for identifying the pivot argument (as opposed to the intuition underlying the idea), it becomes clear that it is not really a semantic test at all. The test in (16), illustrated in (17), relies on the fact that it is usually, if not always, easier to drop non-subjects in sentences than it is subjects; in other words the subject is the 'least droppable' NP in the clause. (This is not true if we take pro-drop into account, but that is a very different phenomenon. A pro-drop language is one in which the verb is inflected for person, number and gender and which allows, or even prefers, a pronominal subject of the verb to be phonologically null, presumably because it is identified by the morphological inflection. Italian and Spanish are examples of pro-drop languages. But in these cases, the pronominal subject is recoverable from inflectional information explicitly available on the verb. Strawson's test does not make use of this kind of phonological argument dropping where the NP is recoverable, but uses genuine argument dropping, in which what is usually a two-place relation is expressed as a property.)

Since the subject is the least droppable NP in a sentence, a paraphrase which is constrained to express only one argument of the main relation of that sentence will have to express the argument realised in subject position. The question is why the subject is least droppable. It could be because the argument realised in this position is primary, but it could be because the subject position itself is the 'most' obligatory, and thus the argument which is expressed in subject position cannot be dropped. I shall argue that given the unclarity of the semantic notion of 'primary argument' and the good evidence that the subject position is obligatory, this latter explanation is a more plausible account of what is going on in (17) than an appeal to pivot arguments.

Let us see what the semantic explanation for the subject being non-droppable is. If we look at again at (17) and at a parallel example in (21), we see that Strawson's test involves attempting to intransitivise a dyadic relation.

(17)   Of the pair, John and the egg, related by the *eat–be eaten* relation,
    (i)   John eats.
    (ii)   The egg is eaten.

(21)   a.   Mary catches the ball.
    b.   Of the pair Mary and the ball related by the *catch- be caught* relation,
      (i)   Mary catches.
      (ii)   The ball is caught.

There are two ways of interpreting (17.i) and (21.i). One is to assume that they are sentences with elliptical objects, where the interpretation of the object is supplied from context, so that *John eats* is interpreted as "John eats the egg" and *Mary catches* is interpreted as "Mary catches the ball". Grimshaw (1979) discusses this phenomenon, called null complement anaphora, with respect to discourses like (22), where the complement, or 'object', of a head may be lexically unrealised, and is semantically interpreted as anaphoric to a sentence previously introduced into the discourse.

(22)   A.   John is going to be very late today.
    B.   I know (that John is going to be very late today).

Here too, the subject cannot be dropped:

(23)   A.   John is going to be very late today.
    B.   *Upsets me/*Surprises me.

If this kind of reading is what Strawson intends, then it is easy to give a syntactic explanation of why the object, but not the subject is droppable. Work on ellipsis by Lobeck (1991) shows that elliptical arguments are subject to the syntactic constraint known as the Empty Category Principle (ECP) of Chomsky (1981, 1986a,b), and Rizzi (1990). This is the principle which states that empty arguments can occur only when they stand in a close enough syntactic relation (called 'proper government') with a head or moved antecedent. In the case of ellipsis, the moved antecedent condition will not be applicable, but, Lobeck claims, elliptical elements can, and must be governed by a head. But then it is clear that a direct object, which is sister to and properly governed by the verb, is in a position where it can be ellided, while a subject, which is not a syntactic sister of a lexical head, and is therefore not properly governed, cannot be ellided. Thus, examples like (24) parallel to (17.i) and (21.i.), but with the first argument dropped, will be ungrammatical:

(24)   a.   *Eats the egg.
    b.   *Catches the ball.

Nothing special has to be said about (17.ii) and (21.ii): since in English the second argument of the passive, expressed as a complement of the preposition *by*, is optional, we don't even need to mention the rules governing ellipsis to explain why it can be dropped. And dropping the subject will be ungrammatical for exactly the same reasons as in the active case.

Another possible reading of (17.i) and (21.i) is that they use truly intransitivised predicates. On this reading *John eats* will be approximately synonymous with *John is the eater* and *Mary catches* with *Mary is the catcher*. This is a more interesting analysis for Strawson, since instead of the question of how an argument can be unexpressed (or ellided), it raises the question of how a transitive predicate can be used as an intransitive one. Strawson claims that the fact that intransitivising a predicate always leaves us with the same argument is an indication of the primacy of that argument. The grammaticality of (17) as opposed to (25) is a indication of which arguments are the pivots of which relations.

(25)   Of the pair, John and the egg, related by the *eat–be eaten* relation,
    (i)   *Eats the egg
    (ii) *Is eaten by John.

But this interpretation of (17) assumes that intransitivisation is a purely lexical operation on predicators which removes any one of the predicator's arguments, independent of syntactic constraints.

However, let us assume, as Strawson does, that a sentence needs a grammatical subject. Then the ungrammaticality of (25.i) is due to the fact that the sentence is missing a grammatical subject, and not to the fact that the pivot argument has been dropped. Filling the subject position by the second argument, as in (24) is equally impossible – without changing the meaning:

(26)   *The egg eats.

The point is that this is not necessarily because the pivot argument has been dropped. Assume, reasonably, that there is a rule of syntactic/semantic interpretation which identifies the ordered arguments of a predicator with certain positions in the sentence. Then the problem with (26) is not that the pivot argument has been dropped. It is that the second argument is syntactically realised in the position reserved for the first argument.

In other words, it is easy to explain Strawson's test for primary arguments as illustrating the grammatical necessity for a subject position; if so, it is not an argument for semantic asymmetry in the argument structure.

So what about Strawson's claim that we feel that relations have an inherent orientation and are centred around one of their arguments? Properties which look as if they are associated with the so-called pivot argument may well be associated with the position in which the argument appears, rather than being attached to the argument because of the asymmetric semantic nature of the relation. On the assumptions (i) that arguments are fed into a relational expression one at a time and (ii) that syntactic structure reflects semantic operations – which is the idea at the basis of all work in compositional semantics – the last argument to be fed into the predicator will be structurally the most prominent one. Semantic prominence will follow from this structural property, and not from any inherent semantic property. An examination of how passivisation works suggests that the latter assumption may be correct. The pivot argument changes between *admires* and *is admired by*, but it's not clear that anything else changes. The semantic difference between active and passive just is the change in orientation, and since the difference in grammatical realisation just is the matter of which argument is realised in subject position, together with the morphological marking that shows that the operation has taken place, it is much simpler to see the semantic prominence as following from structural prominence rather than trying to give some non-structural definition of what a pivot is.

There is some independent evidence that this is a good way to look at things. It has often been suggested that in pairs like (27/28) the (a) examples are 'about' three women and a storm respectively, while the (b) examples are purely presentational and present a state of affairs from no particular orientation.

(27) a. Three women entered wearing coats and hats.
      b. There entered three women wearing coats and hats.

(28) a. A storm arose suddenly.
      b. There arose suddenly a storm.

To the degree that we have intuitions about differences between the orientation of these sentences (and enough people claim that they do), it is hard to see that they can come from any difference in the meaning or orientation of the predicator. The only thing that has changed is the position in which the single argument of the predicator is realised.

Similar questions arise with verbs like *surprise* and *upset*, which are dyadic predicates, but which do not necessarily have an argument realised in subject position. Take the pair in (29):

(29) a. It surprised Mary that John won the race.
      b. That John won the race surprised Mary.

Strawson's test gives the proposition *that John won the race* as the pivot argument of *surprise*, and *Mary* as the pivot of the passive *be surprised*.

(30) Of the pair, Mary, that John won the race, related by the *surprise–be surprised* relation,
      (i) That John won the race suprised.
      (ii) Mary was surprised.

He thus predicts that the relation in both examples in (29) is presented from the orientation of the proposition (since the relation is the same in each case, although the syntactic representation is different) and that (31) is oriented toward Mary:

(31)   Mary was surprised that John won the race.

The question is, do we want to say that the relation in (29a) has a pivot? It's not clear how we could go about trying to answer this question, or even see what it means. And this just shows how vague a concept 'pivot' actually is. But, any answer that we give is going to be problematic from Strawson's point of view. If the embedded sentence is the pivot, or primary argument, how can he derive the binary structure of the proposition from the primacy of the pivot argument, since here it doesn't appear in subject position? And if it is not the primary argument, then what does it mean to say that all relations have to have a primary argument, and what is the value of the test in (30) anyway?

Notice that, despite the fact that one might assume that the unmarked case would be for the pivot to be the topic, there is some evidence from existential presuppositions that in sentences like (29a) the topic is actually the NP argument. We see that (32) appears to have no truth-value in the absence of a present King of France:

(32)   It upset the present King of France that Chirac was elected.

Again this can be changed by context. The existential presupposition disappears easily in (32) if it is the answer to (33):

(33)   Who did it upset that Chirac was elected?

So Strawson's claim that there is an inherent semantic orientation in lexical relations which can be used to derive the primacy of the subject argument and thus the structure of the proposition is not well grounded. If there is an inherent orientation involved in lexically expressed relations it is to do with whether an 'active-type' or 'passive type' of verb is lexically basic. Dowty (1982) points out that it is not accidental which order of arguments is associated with the active form and which with the passive form. He notes that despite the pair *please–like* illustrated in (18/19), it is usually the case that, given any relation R denoted by a transitive verb, although it is possible to imagine a basic lexical item which would denote the converse relation R′, "our intuitions are that any English-like language is unlikely to have such a verb". (p111) Thus we do not expect to have a verb *dnif*, meaning 'be found by', alongside the English *find*.

But Dowty makes a stronger point. It is not just that it would be redundant for the language to have both verbs; our intuitions are that it would be bizarre for any English-like language to have *dnif* **instead of** *find*. Dowty claims that this is because languages seem to follows a set of systematic principles which determine on the basis of the nature of a relation whether R or R′ is 'lexicalised'. For example: "if for any $<x,y> \in$ R, x is an entity that causes something to happen to y", R is lexicalised and not R′." (p111) Instead of lexicalising R′, there is a mechanism, passivisation, which promotes the second argument of R to the pivot position.

So where have we got to so far?

We have seen that the Aristotelian assumption that a proposition has a bipartite subject-predicate structure is widely accepted as reflecting our intuitions about syntactic and semantic sentential structure. We have seen further that, pace Geach, there is a widefelt intuition that the subject argument of the sentence is not contextually determined, but that the topic is. This means that we have to find some way of deciding why one argument of a predicator gets to be the subject, and that we cannot define the subject in terms of topic, or an aboutness relation. We have seen that there is no good basis for assuming that one thematic argument of a verb is semantically primary, and furthermore, that 'subject' can not be defined in terms of a semantic primacy or orientation defined on a set of ordered arguments of a predicator.

I have suggested that what is felt to be the semantic primacy of the subject follows not from any inherent properties that the subject thematic argument has, but from the fact that it is realised in the subject position which is, in some sense which we will make precise, a structurally prominent position. In other words, we cannot deduce the bipartite structure of the clause from the semantic prominence of one argument of a predicator, but we can explain what is felt to be the semantic and pragmatic prominence of the subject in terms of the structure of the proposition. In this way, the prominence of the subject actually becomes evidence for the bipartite structure of the proposition. It is important to stress again that being the first in a series of ordered arguments does not necessarily lead to semantic prominence. If a predicator denotes an asymmetric relation, then its arguments will have to be ordered, but this does not mean that one has to be more prominent than the others. We can hypothesise a language with a declarative sentence of the form (34), where the sentence is true just in case the height of John is greater than the height of Bill and not vice versa, but where neither argument is prominent and there is no feeling that the state of affairs is reported from the point of view of one of the participants:

(34)   is older than; John, Bill.

Tests for discourse prominence would not distinguish between either of the arguments. For example, it is claimed that out of context the more prominent subject argument in the first sentence of (35a) will be the default antecedent for the pronoun *him* in the object position of *upset*. But (35b) will be ambiguous; since neither of the arguments of *is older than* is prominent, either can be the antecedent of *him*:

(35)   a. John is older than Bill. It upsets him.
        b. is older than; John, Bill. upsets; him.

Since the more prominent, subject argument is the default sentence topic, then if there were no prominent subject, one would expect no default topic, and thus that the effects of non-referring expressions on assigning truth-values would be the same, whichever argument the non-referring expression filled. (36a) and (36b) would either both be false, or both fail to have a truth-value, unlike (37a/b) where, as we have seen, Strawson argues that the first often lacks a truth value, while the second is easily judged false.

(36) a. visited; the present King of France, the exhibition.
      b. was visited by; the exhibition, the present King of France.

(37) a. The present King of France visited the exhibition.
      b. The exhibition was visited by the present King of France.

The fact that we feel that the subject is semantically prominent, and that there is no reasonable non-structurally based account of where that prominence comes from supports the approach in which the prominence of the subject argument is derived from the position in which it appears.

This brings us back to the question of where the binary structure of the proposition comes from. We showed that it is not derived from an aboutness relation, since there are many sentences which are not 'about' an entity denoted by an argument in the sentence. We can add to the examples of sentences which do not have a sentence topic the examples in (38), whose subject is a dummy, non-thematic pleonastic. (38a) is a 'weather' construction, and (38b/c) are impersonal passives from Icelandic and Dutch respectively:

(38) a. It is snowing/It was raining when we arrived.
      b. a var synt.
         "It was swum"
      c. Er werdt gedanst.
         "It was danced"

(For (c) I follow the standard assumption for V$_2$ languages that the verb is in a position higher than the subject position, and that the pleonastic subject is moved from the subject position to first position. See, for example, den Besten 1977.) We already saw that the subject of the sentence cannot be defined in terms of an inherent semantic prominence relation among the ordered arguments of a predicator. So this leaves us with the question of whether the Aristotelian semantic definition of a proposition as an assertion that some object has a property is in fact the basic semantic notion in terms of which other notions are to be defined.

1.4. THE STRUCTURAL NATURE OF THE SUBJECT

Our discussion of the concept of semantic and pragmatic definitions of 'subject' have come back again and again to the recognition that the pragmatic and intuitive statements we have discussed all make use in a more or less explicit way of the grammatical notion of subject that we are trying to define. Our discussion has come full circle. We began with an attempt to explain the binary structure of the proposition in a Geachian way in terms of aboutness, and that was not successful. We then followed Strawson's attempt to explain it in terms of the inherent semantic primacy of one of the thematic arguments of a verbal predicator, and that was not successful either. Instead, it seems that the intuition that a particular thematic argument in a sentence is primary follows from the binary structure of the proposition and the fact that it makes one argument prominent. But this leaves us with the same set of questions that we started with, and fewer possible directions to look for an answer. We are left with the question: why do we feel that the proposition has a binary structure and what is it based on? Can we give any reasonable content to the Aristotelian notion of the proposition as a statement that something (a property) is present in something (an object)? Or is this itself derived from some other properties of the proposition? The answer to the question what makes the subject distinguished is of course dependent on the answers to the first questions. If the structure of the proposition is given in semantic or pragmatic terms, then so will the definition of subject, and if 'proposition' is defined in non-semantic terms, then the definition of 'subject' will probably change accordingly.

I am going to argue that the division of the proposition into subject and predicate does not follow from any fundamental semantic notion, and that the binary structure of the clause is not a syntactic expression of a semantic relation, but a structural property which is to be defined in purely structural terms. There are a number of different structural accounts of why the structure of the proposition is the way it is, and in the rest of this book I am going to argue for one structural theory and against several competitors.

The essence of any structural theory is as follows. The subject-predicate structure of the proposition is not inherently a relation involving topics or aboutness or focus, but follows from structural constraints on how the various parts of the sentence are combined. Structural theories differ as to the nature of these structural constraints. Categorial grammars assume that predicators apply to their arguments one by one (they are what is called 'curried functions'), and then the subject just is the last thematic argument of the verb to be fed into the sentence. In this case the structural prominence of the subject and the bipartite structure of the clause follow from the assumption that lexical heads denote curried functions and that syntactic structure reflects the order in which these operations occur (see e.g. the discussion in Dowty 1982). Although subjecthood reflects the prominence of one thematic argument, it is important to see that this is still a structural notion of 'subject', since the argument becomes prominent because of the structural properties of argument combination, and not from any inherent meaning asymmetry.

The theory of predication and subjects that I am going to present in this book differs from a categorial grammar approach. The formal properties from which the prominence of the subject follows are not defined in terms of combinatorial properties of heads and thematic arguments but in terms of a grammatical saturation relation between argument and predicate constituents which is crucially defined independently of thematic relations. I will explore what this means in detail in the next chapters, and later in the book (chapters 6 and 7) I will compare this theory with categorial theories and others. But before beginning this project, I will present in the rest of this chapter some of the prima facie evidence that the definition of 'subject' is going to have to be syntactic.

The assumptions that we seek to justify are that a sentence has a bipartite syntactic structure, one part of which is an argument constituent and the other a predicate. As a result, there is an asymmetric relation between the arguments of the verbal head, with the prominent argument being the one which is realised outside the predicate constituent. This argument realised outside the predicate constituent is the subject. Thus the burden of the syntactic theory of predication that I present is to explain what a predicate constituent is. This is what I will do in chapter 2. What I will do in the rest of this section is present the basic grammatical evidence that there is syntactic predicate constituent, and that the subject position is outside the predicate and not necessarily thematically related to it.

The very simplified syntactic structure which is assigned to a sentence S, given in (39), divides the sentence into a subject argument and a phrasal constituent headed by the verbal predicator, which contains all arguments other than the subject. In this structure, as in most of the discussion which follows, I will ignore tense and inflection. This is because I am interested in identifying the syntactic VP constituent, and showing that all arguments other than the subject form a phrasal constituent with the Verb, V, and that V does not form a constituent with the subject. In chapter 5 I will talk about the relation between tense and VP and claim that a sentence is in fact divided into subject and a possibly inflected predicate.

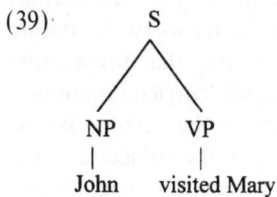

(39)·
```
            S
           / \
          /   \
        NP     VP
         |      |
       John  visited Mary
```

There are several pieces of evidence that this is the right way to look at the structure of propositions. We are interested specifically in tests which indicate that there is a VP, since this shows that the object is more closely attached to the verb than the subject and thus structurally less hierarchically prominent.

a. *VP fronting*

The examples in (40) show that a VP can be fronted to the beginning of the sentence. This indicates that the V plus its non-subject arguments form a constituent which excludes the subject. Parallel sentences in (41), where subject and verb have been fronted, stranding the direct object, are not acceptable:

(40)   a. *Visit her father* though Mary did, she still felt she should go more often.
       b. *Eat a big dinner* though we did, I confess to still being hungry.

(41) a. *Mary visit* though (she) did her father, she still felt she should go
         more often.
      b. *We eat* though we did a big dinner, I confess to still being hungry.

b. *Pseudoclefts*

Pseudoclefts show the same effects. The pseudoclefts in (42) show that
V + object form a focussable constituent, but there is no parallel sentence
focussing a constituent consisting of the subject and V:

(42) a. What Mary did then was *visit her father*.
      b. What we did next was *eat a big dinner*.

c. *VP-ellipsis*

VP ellipsis constructions like (43) show that the VP constituent can provide
an appropriate antecedent for a VP which is missing in the second sentence.
Analyses of how these constructions arise (Sag 1976, Williams 1977, Reinhart
1991) argue for an account in which the VP constituent in the second sentence
is deleted under identity with its antecedent, or in which an empty VP constituent is projected and interpreted as dependent on its antecedent. Both kinds of
analyses rely on the missing or elliptical material being the semantic content
of a VP constituent:

(43) a. Mary *read War and Peace* and Bill did too.
      b. Mary *ate an apple* and John did too.

A possible argument against using ellipsis as evidence for constituent structure
comes from constructions like (44), discussed in Reinhart (1991), and called
'bare-ellipsis' constructions, because, unlike (43), there is no material in the
second conjunct other than the NP. In particular, in contrast with (43), there
is no auxiliary verb.

(44) a. *Mary read* War and Peace, and Anna Karenina too.
      b. *The police interrogated* the education minister, but not the defence
         minister.

In (44a/b), the NPs in the second conjuncts have a natural reading in which
they are analysed as correlates of the direct object in the first conjunct; on this
reading the missing material in the second conjunct in (44a) is *Mary read*, and
in the second conjunct *the police interrogated*. An account which treats these
in the same way as (43) by simply copying in the missing material is forced to
say that what is missing does not form a constituent. Reinhart (1991) argues
against analysing bare ellipsis in this way, showing that it cannot involve simple
deletion or ellipsis under identity with an antecedent string. She shows first
that bare ellipsis occurs under different conditions from VP constituent ellipsis.
Sag (1976) and Williams (1977) show that VP constituent ellipsis is unrestricted

by grammatical constraints, in the sense that the antecedent and missing material can be as far apart as discourse coherence permits. In particular, adjacency constraints and subjacency constraints are not relevant, and both the antecedent material and the elliptical material can be deeply embedded in islands.

(45) a. I know that you think that Mary *read War and Peace*. I want to tell you that John didn't know whether Bill did or didn't (read War and Peace).
      b. What do you think about why Mary *stole the papers*? I don't know. Anyway, perhaps she didn't (steal the papers).
      c. Do you know the person who *stole the papers*? Yes, Bill did (steal the papers).

Reinhart shows that with bare ellipsis, this is different.

(46) a. Do you know the person who stole the papers?
          #Yes, Bill.
      b. #John met the man who stole the papers, but not the films/but not the woman.
      c. #The police know when Mary stole the papers, but not Bill. (but not when Bill stole the papers)
      d. *The police know when Mary stole the papers but not when Bill.

Reinhart argues that in bare ellipsis constructions the missing semantic material is a predicate derived by lambda abstracting over a sentence with a free variable in it. This sentence is derived in the antecedent clause by raising an NP and adjoining it to a sentence, resulting in a logical form of the shape [NP [.....e.....]]$_{IP}$. The evidence for this is that normal subjacency constraints govern the raising of the NP, and thus the deriving of the predicate from the antecedent. The NP cannot be raised out of wh-islands, relative clauses, etc. This means that, while VP ellipsis is possible in (45b/c), it is not possible in the parallel examples in (46) since it is not possible to raise the target NPs in the antecedent clauses out of the wh-islands in which they occur. Thus (46c) cannot have the reading "The police know when Mary stole the papers, but not when Bill stole the papers" since it is not possible to raise *Mary* out of the wh-island to derive the predicate $\lambda x.x$ *stole the papers* based on the IP [e stole the papers]. However, (46c) can have the reading "The police know when Mary stole the papers, but Bill doesn't know when Mary stole the papers". This latter reading is derived by copying in the predicate $\lambda x.x$ *knows when Mary stole the papers*, which it is possible to derive from the antecedent by raising the matrix subject *the police*. If predicates based on sentential constituents are being used in bare ellipsis, then the examples in (44) are not counterevidence to the claim that ellipsis makes use of constituents, and the examples in (43) remain evidence for a VP constituent.

d. *VP conjunction*

VP constituents can be conjoined and jointly predicated of a subject:

(47) a. John *gave a book to Mary* and *read a story to Bill.*
      b. Mary *gave the child a kiss, smiled,* and *shook John's hand.*

The constituents which are combined are headed by V and include all the arguments of V except the subject; in particular (47b) conjoins a V plus two non-subject arguments, a V with no non-subject argument and a V with one object argument. For the purposes of predicate conjunction, they all three count as being of the same constituent type.

   Sentences like (48) are a problem for the claim that verbs form constituents with their non-subject arguments but not with their subject arguments.

(48) a. *John loves* and *Mary hates* movies about space-monsters.
      b. *Mary bought* and *Bill sold* a number of old books.
      c. *John put forks* or *Mary put chopsticks* at every place.

(Example (48c) is due to Polly Jacobson p.c.) Steedman (1990) argues that *John loves* and *Mary hates* in (48a) can be treated as constituents by a categorial grammar which allows operations of type raising and function composition. These constituents can then be conjoined and applied to the NP *movies about space monsters.* Such operations allow the generalisation that only like types coordinate to be maintained, but the analysis is a problem for an account like ours which argues for the primacy of the VP constituent in the structure of the proposition. There are two points to be made in response to this. One is that *hates movies* is a more basic constituent than *Mary hates*, since only application is needed to derive it, and not type raising and function composition. In support of this is the fact that, as we have seen in the previous pages, there are a number of operations which do apply to *hates movies* and not to *Mary hates.* The second is that, as pointed out by Fred Landman (p.c.) there is some semantic evidence that the examples in (48) are better treated as sentential conjunctions with the first object deleted than as instances of constituent conjunction. Under Steedman's analysis, (48a) has the structure in (49), with the direct object in the structurally highest position in the sentence.

(49) [[[John loves] and [Mary hates]] movies about monsters]

Given this structure, we would expect the scopal properties of the direct object in (49) to be the same as those of the subject. But if we look at the examples in (50) we see that this is not the case:

(50) a. Most soldiers *got a letter from a girl* and *were visited by a boy.*
      b. *A boy visited* and *a girl wrote a letter* to most soldiers.

(50a) naturally asserts that most soldiers have the complex property expressed by the conjoined VP, namely that they each got both a letter from a girl and a visit from a boy, and this is true whether *a girl* and *a boy* have wide or narrow scope relative to *most soldiers*. But (50b) can be true under conditions which make (50a) false, namely that the set of soldiers visited by a boy and the set of soldiers written to by a girl are not same (although they can be). Again, this observation is not affected by whether or not *a girl* and *a boy* have wide or narrow scope with respect to the *most soldiers*. This means that, despite what Steedman's analysis predicts, (50) does not assert that a complex property expressed by *a boy visited and a girl wrote a letter to* holds of most soldiers. The paraphrase that captures the meaning of (50b) is given in (51):

(51)   A boy visited most soldiers and a girl wrote a letter to most soldiers.

But, this suggests that deleting *most soldiers* in the first conjunct might be a better way to derive (50b), and this means that examples of the patterns (48/49/50b) are not evidence for a subject-verb constituent after all. Note that all the examples in (48) have a reading which is derived by reduction from sentential conjunction – even, in the right context, (48c). (Imagine a context where either John or Mary is responsible for setting the table.) I assume that the reading where the quantifier has wide scope over the disjunction has a representation in which the universal quantifier has scope over a sentential disjunction and binds a variable in the position of the gap. Thus (52) will give the wide scope reading for (48c) and an analogous structure will give the reading for (50b) where *most soldiers* does have wide scope:

(52)   [every x: place setting(x) [John put a fork at x]
        ∨ [Mary put chopsticks at x]]

e. *Movement from and argument ellipsis in subject position*

We already mentioned with respect to Strawson's tests for primary arguments, that ellipsis of the object but not the subject is possible:

(53)   Of the pair, John and the egg, related by the *eating–eating* relation,
        (i)   John eats.
        (ii)   *e eats the egg.

Similar asymmetries in movements have been widely noted and discussed (e.g. Chomsky 1981, 1986a,b):

(54)   Who did you ask whether Mary saw e?
        *Who did you ask whether e saw Mary?

There is a huge amount of literature on the topic which I shan't discuss here at all (but note the reference to Lobeck (1991) above). In short, it has been argued that these movement and ellipsis operations are constrained by a grammatical recoverability condition, known as the Empty Category Principle (Chomsky 1981, 1986a, 1986b) which requires that the empty position be syntactically identified. One of the syntactic factors relevant in identification is closeness to the lexical head. When the head is verbal, it is consistently the case that an empty direct object position is 'close enough to' (=properly governed by) the verbal head for the verb to identify it. This is an indication that the syntactic dependency between verb and direct object is closer that the dependency between subject and object and is further indirect support for the VP constituent.

f. *Pleonastics*

Pleonastics are 'dummy' pronouns with no reference and no thematic content, which appear in subject position when there is no thematic NP to appear there. They provide very fundamental evidence that the structure of the proposition is given grammatically and not semantically, and that the subject position is different from other argument positions in the sentence. Here are some of the observations which we will discuss at length later in the book, in particular in chapters 3 and 7.

First, pleonastics appear in subject position but have no thematic content, as in (55):

(55)   a. It seems that John is very late today.
       b. It is unlikely that we will go to China this year.

Since the pleonastics have no obvious semantic function, the fact that they are obligatory is prima facie evidence that the subject is necessary for non-semantic/thematic reasons. Second, the examples in (55) show that there are simple assertions which do not have the semantic structure of distinguished argument + predicate. These sentences do not affirm "the presence of something in something", in Aristotelian terms; rather they affirm the existence of a certain state of affairs, and the proposition is true if the state of affairs holds, and false otherwise. They contrast with the so-called 'subject-raised' examples such as (56), which intuitively are about 'John' and 'us' respectively in a way that (55a/b) are not.

(56)   a. John seems to be very late today.
       b. We are unlikely to go to China this year.

I will be more precise about these differences later in the book. Third, pleonastics do not and cannot appear in object position, which is an indication that the constraints on objects are different from those on subjects; our preliminary hypothesis is that object position is optional from the sentential point of view, and generated only because the thematic structure of the predicator requires it.

1.5. CONCLUSIONS AND DIRECTIONS

The purpose of this chapter has been twofold; first to show that there is good evidence that propositions have a binary structure consisting of subject and predicate and that the subject of the sentence is distinguished with respect to non-subject arguments of a verb, and second to show that it is remarkably difficult to give any meaningful semantic or pragmatic explanation of these facts which does not itself rely on structural concepts.

We saw that neither the pragmatic notion of topic nor the thematic/semantic notion of primary argument of a predicate can be used to explain either the structure of the proposition or the distinguished nature of the subject. In fact it seemed that the only non-pragmatic definition of 'pivot' available was that it is the argument of the predicator which is assigned to syntactic subject position. The last section provided evidence, based on non-context dependent grammaticality judgments, that there is a syntactically recognised predicate VP constituent and that the subject position is not necessarily thematically relevant. In the light of this, an obvious direction to go is to search for a structural basis for the definition of 'proposition' and 'subject', and this is what the rest of this book is about.

I shall argue that the binary structure of the sentence is given by syntactic principles; the predicate constituent is usually verbal and it contains the main n-place predicator of the sentence and no fewer than n-1 of its arguments. There is one NP position outside the VP which contains either one of its arguments, *there* or a pleonastic *it*. (I shall not discuss *there* at all in this book, since I assume, following Williams (1984) and Landman (1998), that *there* is not a true pleonastic, but has semantic content.) The properties which are associated with the subject, which lead to its being considered a distinguished position all follow from this syntactic structure of the sentence. The subject is the most prominent argument because it is the only one which is outside the VP projection of the V, and the rest of a simple sentence is in its scope. As the most prominent argument structurally, it is also the most prominent semantic argument because of these scope relations and because the truth-value of the sentence is the result of functional application of the function denoted by the predicate to the argument denoted by the subject. The subject position is the only obligatory position, in the sense that every sentence has a subject, regardless of the argument structure of the main predicator, while the presence of objects and suchlike is dependent on the argument structure of the main predicator. Pleonastics appear only in subject position because it is the only obligatory position. 'Pragmatic aboutness' and 'semantic prominence' make use of and are dependent on syntactic prominence. The fact that applying the predicate to the subject argument give the value true or false, and that the subject is the last argument to be 'fed in', explains why the subject argument is felt to be the 'pivot' and why it is the unmarked topic. Since it is the last argument to be fed in, it is least deeply embedded and most easily available for the verification process which Strawson (1964) argues is the basis for aboutness. (Reinhart (1981) give a more formal account of pragmatic aboutness and Strawson's insight that the topic provides the entity through which the process of verifying the truth of the sentence takes place.) This dependence of pragmatics on structure reverses what is often assumed to be the dependency relation in language. It has often been suggested that structure is a 'clothing', 'form' or realisation for meaning, without autonomy or autonomous principles. The basic thesis of this book is that in the case of subjects and predicates, this is the wrong way round to look at things, and that predication is inherently structural in nature. The question that rest of this book addresses is what the correct structural definition is.

1.6. APPENDIX: SOME THEORETICAL PRELIMINARIES

In this section I will outline some of the main syntactic properties of the framework I am working in; for the most part I leave the discussion of the semantic framework till chapter 6. It should become clear which aspects of the theoretical framework are essential to the theory being developed, and which are just an 'operational language'.

A. *Syntax*

I assume a grammar of the sort presented in Chomsky (1981, 1986a,b). A syntactic string is subject to a series of constraints including the theta-criterion, binding conditions, subjacency and suchlike. I shall follow Rizzi (1986) in assuming that D-structure and S-structure are representations built on strings rather than steps in a derivational process. 'Sentence' is used in the sense of Chomsky to mean a string of words which we accept as grammatical, whether or not it can be assigned a meaningful interpretation. Chomsky's famous sentence *Colourless green ideas sleep furiously* is an example of a grammatical but uninterpretable sentence (barring non-obvious, quasi-metaphorical interpretations). This syntactic understanding of 'sentence' of course includes questions, exclamations and other strings which cannot be assigned truth-values. I will use 'proposition' for the content of a declarative sentence.

Heads are words which take complements and project phrases. Thus a verb will project several levels of verbal phrases. In the simple paradigmatic case, there will be a non-maximal V' phrase which includes the V and its object (if the V selects one) and a maximal VP phrase which has the V' and an adjunct as its daughter (if the V' is accompanied by an adjunct). Two daughters of the same node are syntactic sisters. I further assume that multiple adjunct modifiers can be added one by one, each as sister of a new X' level and the highest will be the XP. This is illustrated in (57):

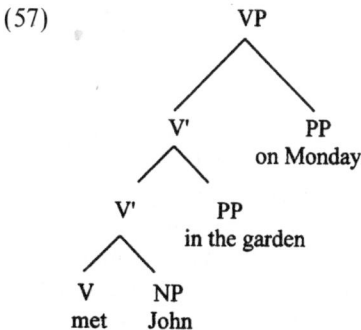

(57)

```
                        VP
                       /  \
                     V'     PP
                    /  \    on Monday
                  V'     PP
                 /  \    in the garden
               V     NP
              met    John
```

A maximal projection of a head X is the highest phrasal projection whose categorial nature is dictated by X. Maximal projections (or XPs) are entered into the tree as complements of other heads or as adjuncts/specifiers. An XP acting as complement to a head Y is added as a sister to Y under the Y' node, and an XP acting as an adjunct or specifier is added under the YP level as a sisters to Y'. The theoretical distinction between adjuncts and specifiers is not clear. I shall use 'specifier' to refer to a position in a tree which is the daughter of a maximal projection of a functional head (see below), and which can be filled by an argument. An adjunct, on the other hand, is a constituent – a non-argument constituent – whose function is modificatory.

Heads are divided into lexical heads and functional heads. Lexical heads correspond to what are traditionally known as 'content' words, and only lexical heads assign thematic roles, although not all lexical heads do so. For example, the verb *snow* is a lexical head despite the fact that it assigns no thematic roles. Nouns are also lexical heads, despite the fact that only derived nominals obviously assign thematic roles. Functional heads are those elements traditionally called 'grammatical formatives' which project phrases. I think it is possible to give a precise definition of the difference between lexical and functional heads in terms of the kinds of semantic relations that they denote, but we will not need a more precise distinction than the one I have given here. The functional heads which will chiefly interest us here are Complementiser or C, Inflection or Infl (or I) and Determiner or D. Inflection is a head which takes VP complements and whose maximal projection is a sentence. It consists of a bundle of grammatical features, including tense and agreement, and when it includes [+tense], it assigns nominative case to the subject. We talk of the subject of IP as being in [Spec,IP], i.e. the specifier of IP, where a specifier of an XP phrase is the sister of X'.

(58)

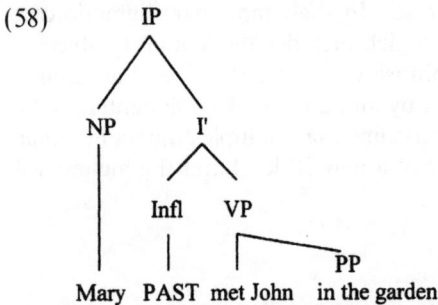

```
                    IP
                   /  \
                  /    \
                NP      I'
                 |     / \
                 |    /   \
                 | Infl    VP
                 |   |    ┌────┐
                 |   |    |    PP
              Mary PAST met John  in the garden
```

C takes IP as a complement and yields a CP e.g.*that Mary met John in the garden*, or alternatively, yields a C' which is dominated by CP. This is relevant since I follow the standard government-binding theory assumption that movement of a *wh*-word is to spec of CP, that is the position which is sister of C'. I assume a 'movement' analysis of passive and *wh*-questions; the subject of a passive sentence sits in [Spec,IP] but locally binds a trace in the object position of the V. Similarly, a *wh*-question sits in [Spec,CP] and binds a trace lower down in the sentence. An argument *wh*-word binds a trace in the position where the relevant theta-role is assigned and an adjunct *wh*-word binds a trace in the position where the corresponding adverbial could grammatically be generated. I shall further assume that D, or Determiner, is the head of nominal phrases, and from now on I'll refer to argument phrases as DPs. I'll discuss this in detail in chapter 9:9.5. A determiner will take an NP complement and yield a D' which in turn will be dominated by DP, as in (59):

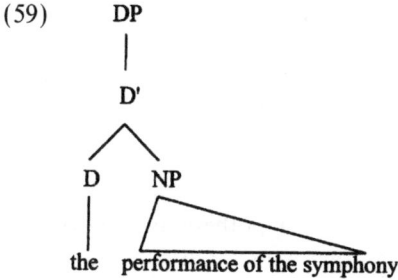

(59) DP
       |
       D'
      / \
     D   NP
     | [performance of the symphony]
    the

B. *Theta-theory*

Lexical heads (usually) express n-place relations between arguments; we talk of a head as assigning n thematic roles, or theta-roles (Chomsky 1981 and etc.), to the n syntactic constituents which denote the entities entering into the relation it denotes. I assume that a lexical head is associated with a possibly null set of thematic roles. This set indicates the number and type of thematically relevant arguments that a head must be associated with. If the set of thematic roles consists of "agent" and "theme", then in a grammatical sentence in which the head occurs there will be two arguments, one denoting the agent of the relation denoted by the verb and the other denoting the theme of the same relation. These are the thematic arguments of a head, and the head 'assigns' a theta-role to each of these constituents. Thematic roles are assigned under strict locality conditions. At least $n-1$ arguments of an n-place head must be assigned 'internally' to constituents which appear within the maximal projection of the head. The constituents which are syntactic sisters to a head are its complements; in (59a) the verb *tell* has an DP and a CP complement assigned 'theme' and (let us say) 'propositional complement' respectively, and in (59b) *give* has two DP object complements assigned 'goal' and 'theme':

(60) a. Mary told [her sister]$_{DP}$ [that she had won the prize]$_{CP}$.
      b. Mary gave [her sister]$_{DP}$ [the book]$_{DP}$.

Internal thematic roles can be assigned via a preposition. In (61), the DP object complement is the theme, and the DP object of *to* is assigned the role of 'goal' of *give*:

(61) Mary gave [the book]$_{DP}$ [to [her sister]$_{DP}$]$_{PP}$.

No more than one thematic role may be assigned to a constituent which is outside the maximal projection of the head. In (60a/b) the agent role of *tell* and *give* is assigned to *Mary*, which is situated in [Spec,IP] outside the maximal projection of the V. The single argument assigned a thematic role by a head outside its maximal projection is called its 'external argument'.

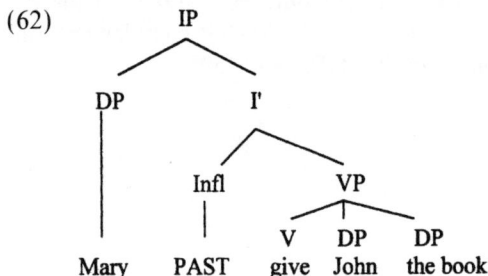

(62)

```
                    IP
          _____/  \
         DP            I'
         |          __/  \__
         |         Infl       VP
         |          |        /|\
         |          |       V  DP   DP
        Mary      PAST    give John the book
```

I am not going to assume the VP-internal subject hypothesis in this work (I will explain why at the end of chapter 4). In other words, I assume that *Mary* is base-generated in [Spec,IP] position in (60a/b), and is not base-generated in [Spec,VP] and later raised to [Spec,IP]. Note that a set of thematic roles of a lexical head can be empty: this is the case with, for example *snow*, which, as I shall show in chapter 3, assigns no theta-roles, and occurs only with a pleonastic subject.

The theta-criterion (Chomsky 1981) is a syntactic condition on theta-role assignment. The first part states that if a head has n theta-roles to assign, it must assign them to n distinct syntactic constituents. The second part of the theta-criterion states that every syntactic argument must be assigned a theta-role. This is more problematic (see Rothstein (1991) for an earlier discussion of why). The intuition behind it is that a constituent which denotes an argument must be in a structure where the argument is an argument of a relation. Higginbotham (1985) proposes a formal representation for the assignment of theta-roles. He proposes that each lexical head is associated with a theta-grid, indicating its adicity. The head *read* can be represented as in (63), indicating that it assigns two thematic roles. The italicisation of 'a_1' indicates that it is assigned externally.

(63)   read:$_V$ $<a_1, a_2>$

The head is inserted into a V node, and projects its grid, along with other properties. A DP argument saturates each position in the grid, and this is equivalent to saying that a theta-role is assigned to each saturating DP. A condition on grammaticality is that all positions in a grid projected by a head must be saturated. In *Mary read the book*, the internal argument *the book* will saturate position a2, and the external argument *Mary* will saturate a1.

I have made no reference, in this brief exposition, to the kinds of theta-roles available, such as 'agent', 'theme' and 'goal'. Dowty (1989, 1991) has suggested that thematic roles be treated as collections of characteristic properties of terms of relations; other people treat them as primitives. Rappaport and Levin (1988) have argued that the only fact relevant to syntax is the number of theta-roles that a head has to assign, and not their types; in any case the proper way to resolve this discussion isn't going to be relevant here. I assume, of course, that the theta-grid of a head correlates in a predictable way with the semantic relation it denotes, and I'll discuss the details of this in Part II. To look ahead though, I'll be assuming a neo-Davidsonian version of Davidsonian event theory (Davidson 1967), as argued for in Parsons (1990), Higginbotham (1985) and Landman (1996, 1999). For Davidson, the *butter* relation used in (64) is a 3–place relation between an event, its agent, and its theme, and the sentence asserts that there is an event of buttering with John as its agent and the bread as its theme. The event argument is bound by an existential quantifier.

(64)   John buttered the bread.

In the neo-Davidsonian version of (64), the verb *butter* denotes a predicate of events, and the thematic roles denote functions from the event to its participants. Thus (64) has the representation in (65):

(65) $\exists e$ [BUTTER(e) $\wedge$ Ag(e) = JOHN $\wedge$ Th(e) = THE BREAD $\wedge$ PAST(e)]

Higginbotham suggests that the event argument has a place in the theta-grid also, so that (63) is modified to (66):

(66) read:$_V$ $<e, a_1, a_2>$

But, if theta-grids are real syntactic entities, then it is not clear that we want this: the event argument has a clear semantic function, but it is not clear what its syntactic status is, since it is not syntactically realised. The existential quantification indicated in (65) is introduced in the semantic representation and not in syntactic structure. The neo-Davidsonian theory reflects the different syntactic status of the event argument and the other thematic arguments; the event argument is an argument of the verb, while the theta-marked arguments are the values of the functions from events to their participants introduced by the theta-roles. So, I shall assume theta-grids as in (63), and assume that these are associated with a semantic representation in which the verb is represented as a predicate of events with the appropriate thematic roles attached. The rule I will use is given in (67):

(67)   read:V $<a_1, a_2>$ $\rightarrow$ $\lambda y \lambda e$.READ(e) $\wedge$ Ag(e) = x $\wedge$ Th(e) = y

I will discuss the justification for this rule in chapter 6.

PART I

THE SYNTAX OF PREDICATION

PART

THE WAVES OF FEDERATION

CHAPTER 2

THE GRAMMATICAL THEORY OF PREDICATION

2.1. THEORETICAL ISSUES

In the previous chapter, we examined the intuition that a proposition is an instantiation of a predication relation, and established the difficulties which arise in trying to define 'subject' and 'predication' in terms of semantic/pragmatic notions of 'aboutness', 'topic', 'pivotal argument' and so on. We saw also that there is good grammatical evidence that a sentence has a binary structure, and that it is divided into two constituents of different kinds which are traditionally known as argument and predicate. The burden of the evidence thus indicates that the distinguished nature of the subject position is a grammatical fact, which follows not from the inherent structure of assertions, but from the compositional structure of sentences.

There are essentially two kinds of structural approaches which explain the binary structure of the sentence and the prominence of the subject position. The first approach, which is essentially lexical, is associated with theories of categorial grammars on the one hand, and theories of thematic roles on the other. It assumes that the structure of the sentence is projected from the thematic or subcategorisational properties of the verb (or main predicator of the sentence), and the subject is just the last argument to be fed in. I'll call this the lexical approach, and it is presented in, among other places, Dowty (1982) and Williams (1980, 1983a,b, 1987). In general in this approach, a lexical head constitutes an unsaturated function and the arguments are fed in one by one. The subject argument is the last argument to be fed in, and the principle of compositionality, together with certain assumptions about syntactic structure, guarantee that the subject will be the highest argument structurally in the sentence.

The principle of compositionality is the principle which asserts that the meaning of an expression is built up from the meaning of its parts and the operations by which they are combined, or in other words that semantic operations are paralleled by syntactic ones. The syntactic assumptions about the kind of structures that the syntactic operations result in differ from theory to theory. X-bar theory (Jackendoff 1977) assumes that hierarchical syntactic structures are built from constituents as in (1):

(1) A + B →   C

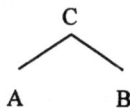

       A   B

In other words, the concatenation of two constituents A and B results in a new constituent of which A and B are the two daughters. Since any new syntactic operation will add a new argument to either the right or left of C in (1), the last argument in will have to be the highest. Bach (1979) and Dowty (1982) explicitly do not accept the general principle that syntactic structure building works as in (1); they posit rules of Right Wrap which does not simply concatenate expressions, but will insert an expression within another expression. Thus Dowty explains the Verb-Subject-Object word order in Breton by a rule which inserts the subject after the first word of the verb phrase, i.e. after the verb. But, although Right Wrap is found in English, Dowty claims, it is not found at the subject-predicate level (p86), and therefore in English, the subject is always hierarchically the highest argument.

I assume that the basic semantic operation which corresponds to the syntactic operation in (1) is function application, with either the denotation of A applying to the denotation of B or vice versa. Look how this works with a transitive verb like *see*. These principles mean that sentence *Mary saw John* will have the structure in (2):

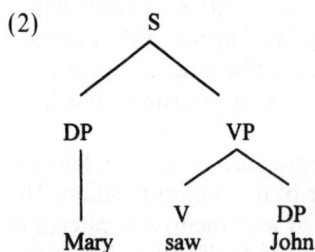

(2)

```
              S
           /    \
         /        \
       DP          VP
        |         /  \
        |        /    \
        |       V      DP
      Mary     saw    John
```

The expression *see* first combines with *John* to give the VP, and the two-place predicator SEE, denoted by *see*, first applies to the denotation of *John* to give the complex one-place expression denoted by *see John*. This in turn applies to the denotation of the argument *Mary* to give the sentence. *See John* is the predicate of the sentence because it is the function-denoting expression which is the daughter of the S node, and *Mary* is the subject because it denotes the argument which saturates that function, in other words, the last argument of SEE to be fed in.

The syntactic unsaturatedness of *see* and *see Mary* are expressed in different theories in different ways. Dowty (1982) uses Montague's type theory in which the two basic types are the type of individuals and the type of sentences, which are constituents used to make assertions. I differ from Dowty in using d to represent the type of individuals (so as to keep e for the type of events); the type of sentences remains t. (Dowty (1982) does not use representations which introduce an explicit Davidsonian event argument, and in other papers (Dowty 1991) he has argued against it.) The adicity of a predicator is represented in terms of the number of steps needed to get to the type t; *see* is an expression of type $<d, <d,t>>$, indicating that it applies, in turn, to two arguments to reach the type of sentences. Thus the type of an expression indicates the kind of semantic expression which it denotes; an expression of type $<d,t>$ will denote an expression represented as $\lambda x.V(x)$, while an expression of type $<d,<d,t>>$ will denote an expression of the form $\lambda x_1 \lambda x_2.V(x_1,x_2)$ and so on. Dowty (1991) argues that a thematic relation is a label for some set of entailments associated with a particular argument position in the argument structure of a particular verb. Thematic relations are thus kept separate from argument structure per se.

To the degree to which a predication relation is distinguished, it is distinguished as the application in which the constituent projected from the head is of type $<d,t>$, applying to a single argument to yield the sentential type t. If we have the appropriate syntactic restrictions on right and left wrap, then the subject of the sentence, as the last argument to be fed in, will be the sister of a constituent consisting of the lexical head together with all the arguments that have been fed in up to that point. Thus the prominence of the subject is hierarchical; since it is the argument which is fed in last, it is the highest up in the tree.

The information about the unsaturatedness of an expression like *see* is also expressed in Higginbotham-style theta-grids of the form *see:*$_V$ $[a_1, a_2]$ (Higginbotham 1985), although the fact that the arguments have to be fed in one at a time has to be independently stipulated or written into the grid in some way. Usually, however, theta-grids are taken to express more information than the number of arguments a verb requires. A theta-grid is often represented not as (3a), which gives the simple argument structure of *see*, but as (3b) in which the thematic restrictions are included also:

(3) a. *see:*$_V$ $[a_1, a_2]$
     b. *see:*$_V$ $[Ag_1, Th_2]$

This is important because 'argument of a head' in theta-theory is treated as equivalent to 'thematic argument of a head', and as we shall see in chapter 7, whether 'argument' is or is not restricted to thematic argument is crucial when a theory deals with the issue of pleonastics. (Rappaport and Levin (1988) argue that it is only the number and not the labels of arguments which is syntactically relevant and represented on the grid, but they too assume that 'argument' means thematic argument.) The version of the 'distinguished argument' approach which is explicitly phrased in theta-theory is that proposed in the syntactic work of Williams (1980, 1983a,b, 1987), and also Schein (1995), and I'll call this 'the thematic approach'. In the thematic approach, 'subject' is defined by its relation to a maximal projection, or predicate expression. The subject is the external thematic argument of the head of the maximal projection. However, the crucial property of the thematic theory turns out not to be the particular way in which 'distinguished argument' is defined, but the framework in which it is worked out. Williams develops his theory of predication in an essentially government-binding framework which uses NP chains to account for passive and raising constructions. In chapter 4, I will show that there is an inherent conflict between a movement analysis of passive and raising on the one hand, and a distinguished argument approach to subjecthood that Williams does not manage to resolve.

The second approach to subjects and clausal structure, which I will call the grammatical approach, is the approach of Rothstein (1983, 1984, 1992b, 1995a,b) and Chierchia (1984, 1986, 1989). These theories claim that predication is a distinguished relation which determines the most basic aspect of the structure of clauses, and that this basic structural property is independently determined, and not projected from lexical structure. A clause must have two parts, one a function (predicate) and the other an argument, and the clause is derived by applying the function to the argument. Put differently, if a clause is of type t, it is derived (ignoring the Davidsonian event argument for the moment for the sake of comparison) by applying a constituent of type $<d,t>$ to an individual d because of an independent constraint that this must be the case and not because of the lexical properties of either the main verb or any other lexical constituent. The crucial evidence for this comes from sentences where the subject argument is a pleonastic, a 'dummy' DP which adds no semantic information to the sentence, as in (4):

(4)   a. It seems that John is late.
      b. It turned out that my keys were in my pocket.
      c. It is unlikely that the child will sleep this afternoon.

If we look at sentences like those in (4) we see that the subject argument does not have any informational function. In (4a) *seem* selects for a propositional argument. Assume that *seem* is represented by (5), with the additional information that the argument of *seem* is a proposition. Taking purely thematic properties into account, type theory will assign to *seem* the type $<<s,t>, t>$, where $<s,t>$ is the type of propositions:

(5)   seem:$_V$ $<a_1>$

In other words, *seem* is an unsaturated, one-place lexical function, which denotes an unsaturated, one-place function. Then, at the VP level, *seem* has been provided with a single sentential argument, and thus it is a saturated function. However, the crucial fact is that although the verbal head has no unsaturated positions, we cannot make the assertion *seems that John is late*. It is a fact of English that this is not an acceptable utterance. In other words, although *it* adds no semantic information to the sentence, and although the information conveyed by (4a) is the same as the information conveyed by the VP, the grammar of English allows us to make an assertion using only the syntactically sentential form and not the VP form.

This means that there are structural conditions which are independent of the saturation-properties of the main predicator. For (4a), standard tests show that the sentential argument of *seem* is within the VP; thus we get VP ellipsis as in (6), from Baltin (1995):

(6)   A: It seems that Bill is crazy.
      B: It certainly does.

So, the crucial observation is that despite the fact that at the VP level all the thematic arguments of *seem* have been satisfied, the grammar forces us to go through a level where the thematically saturated VP is treated as an unsaturated expression of type $<d,t>$ in order to get to type t. Since the main predicator of the sentence *seem* has no other thematic requirements to satisfy, and since the VP must be treated as unsaturated for purely structural reasons, the argument of the VP can have no informational content, and is thus a pleonastic.

Of course, the lexical/thematic approach does not ignore the problem of pleonastics: Dowty (1982, 1985), Sag (1982), and Gazdar, Klein, Pullum and Sag (1985) all give accounts of pleonastics within some version of an argument-projection approach, and I'll discuss them in the course of the book, in particular in chapter 7. But the difference lies in how one interprets the data in (4). For the lexical/thematic approach the data in (4) are problems to be taken care of, while for the grammatical approach the examples in (4) are evidence about the fundamental nature of clausal structure which is independent of the argument structure of any of the lexical heads; namely that at the syntactic level below that of the clause there must be an operation of functional application whether or not the thematic properties of the constituent projected by V require it. This claim, which is the central claim of Rothstein (1983) and later work, and which has been independently proposed by Chierchia (1989), is what I am going to pursue and develop during this book.

There is a second cluster of theories about the structure of clauses and the distribution of pleonastics, which assumes a purely syntactic approach to the problem. These theories either take it as a stipulation that a clause must have a subject (Chomsky 1982) without providing theoretical justification for such a stipulation, or they argue that the obligatoriness of the subject position follows from syntactic properties of inflection (Borer 1986) or case/feature assignment (Fukui and Speas 1986). I'm going to argue in chapter 3 that none of these approaches work, in part because the distribution of pleonastics is not restricted to sentences; since pleonastics also appear in uninflected small clauses, their distribution cannot be dependent on inflectional properties of tensed sentences.

The four chapters that make up Part I of this book are chapters about syntax. I am going to argue that the syntactic predication relation, the saturation of a open predicate expression by an argument, is a central relation in syntax. The obligatoriness of subject position will follow from the fact that the sister of the subject is inherently an open constituent, whether or not it has still an unsaturated thematic position, and the subject argument is thus required for syntactic saturation. In the language of the type theory we have been using so far, VPs and other predicate constituents translate into logical expressions of type $<d,t>$, whether or not the lexical head of the constituent still has an unsaturated thematic role. In this chapter I will giving an outline of the grammatical theory of predication, and in chapters 3 and 4 I'll defend it against two kinds of competition. In chapter 3, we'll discuss the non-predication based approaches to subjects of Chomsky, Borer, and Fukui and Speas; and I shall argue that any adequate theory of subjecthood is going to have to be based on the predication relation. In chapter 4, we'll discuss the other competitor, the thematic based theory of predication developed by Williams. Here the argument is slightly different. I shall not be arguing against 'distinguished argument' approaches in general (that will happen later in the book), but I will be arguing that a distinguished argument approach cannot in principle be worked out in a syntactic framework which allows for movement or its equivalent.

We will be concerned here with primary predication, which includes clausal predication. Chapter 5 will discuss various forms of 'adjunct' predication, including secondary predication. Part II of the book will be concerned with the syntax-semantics interface, and at that point I will discuss 'competing' grammatical theories of predication, in particular, Chierchia (1989). Chapters 6 and 7 will also discuss explicitly the semantic interpretation of pleonastics, and we will compare the grammatical approach with the lexically oriented theories of Dowty and Sag.

I am going to restrict my discussion to English here. I am assuming, tacitly, that the kinds of principles that I am discussing, and in particular the assumption that predication is a syntactic relation, will hold for other languages as well, (we'll discuss an application to Hebrew in chapter 8), but I assume also that language particular differences may mean that these principles get realised in different ways cross linguistically. One example of this is that DPs with no informational content in English must always be realised as a pleonastic element, but this need not be the case in other languages. For example, while in English a VP headed by *seems to me* has a phonologically realised *it* subject, in standard Modern Hebrew, a VP headed by the corresponding predicate, *nire li,* has a phonologically empty element in subject position. Interestingly enough, in colloquial dialects, the subject may be filled by the pleonastic *ze.*

2.2. THE STRUCTURE OF THE THEORY

The subject position is considered by syntacticians to be a privileged syntactic position, partly because a clause, a basic syntactic unit, is often defined as consisting of a subject and a predicate (Chomsky 1981, 1982) and partly for the related reason that the subject position is the only argument position which is obligatory. It is also, as we shall see, the only position in which we find non-theta-marked lexical DPs, such as *John* in (7), which we will discuss at length later, and pleonastics, as illustrated in (4) above:

(7)   John looks as if the stock market just crashed.

In the argument movement theory of Chomsky (1981), DP arguments can be moved only to the sentential subject position, as in (8a) where the V is passive, or (8b) where the V is a typical raising verb.

(8)   a. The house$_{DPi}$ was haunted t$_i$ by ghosts.
      b. My keys$_{DPi}$ seem t$_i$ to have disappeared again.

Chomsky's account of the obligatoriness of subjects is encoded in the phrase structure rule (9a), and reformulated in Chomsky (1982) as the second clause of the Extended Projection Principle, the stipulation that clauses must have subjects. (9a) is itself a reformulation of the original phrase structure rule (9b) in a theory which analyses a sentence as a projection of a inflectional node Infl, and a nominal as a projection of D.

(9)   a. IP   →   DP   I′
       b. S   →   DP   VP

The phrase structure rules derive the obligatoriness of the subject from a stipulation on what daughter nodes IP (or S) must have. The theories of Borer (1986) and Fukui and Speas (1986) see the obligatoriness of the subject as deriving from its relation with the inflectional head which projects I′ and which takes VP as a complement. Borer argues that Infl must be coindexed with an argument and Fukui and Speas claim that case must be assigned by the nominative-assigning Infl and that the subject is obligatory so that there is an argument for case to be assigned to. Predication theories (like Williams (1980, 1987) and Rothstein (1983, 1995a,b)) claim that the crucial relation is not between Infl and the subject, but between the predicate and its subject argument. I shall argue that this is the correct approach, but that the definition of predicate and argument which make it work is different from that proposed by Williams and other theta-based theories such as Schein (1995).

In an IP generated by (9a), the main sentential predicate is the I′; in English, this I′ consists of Inflection and a predicate VP complement (but, as we see in chapter 8, there are languages where the complement of Infl need not always be VP). As I will show below, predicates are not necessarily inflected, and these non-inflected predicates require a subject as much as an I′ predicate. The obligatoriness of the subject in (9a) is thus part of a much wider issue than the 'argument of inflection' theories allow. Predicates require subjects, and clausal subjects are obligatory since a clause contains a predicate and this predicate requires a subject. But clausal predication is only one instance of a wider and more general predication relation. In fact, the predication relation in (9) is obscured by the inflectional element necessary to license the clause. For this reason, in this chapter I shall temporarily ignore the role of the inflectional element in projecting a predicate. Much of the discussion will be about non-inflected predicates, and where relevant in this chapter, I'll treat I′ as a VP with an inflectional affix. For simplicity here, I will still call the sentential node S and treat it as if it dominates DP and VP. I'll discuss the role of Inflection in English in chapter 5, and later, in chapter 8, I'll discuss how Infl can head predicates in Hebrew, a language where Infl is not necessarily affixed to a VP complement.

The structure of the discussion in Part I is as follows. In the rest of this chapter I present the grammatical theory of predication, and a series of arguments which support it. In the following chapter, I also show that an explanation of the obligatoriness of subjects has to come from a predication based theory of subjects, and not from one which presents subjects as arguments of Inflection or case. In chapter 4 I present a detailed 'case-study' of the thematic theory of predication with its technical details as developed by Williams, and compare the predictions made by the grammatical syntactic theory with those made by the thematic syntactic theory. The point will be not just that the analysis in terms of thematic roles does not work, but that it cannot work for reasons fundamental to the nature of syntax. The final section of that chapter will show how the grammatical theory can be extended to fit the 'VP-internal subject hypothesis', and in chapter 5, I'll extend my account to cover various forms of complex predication.

The importance of predication as a syntactic relation has not been disputed by generative grammarians at least since Williams' seminal paper in 1980. In that paper, he shows that there is a syntactically relevant relation of predication which holds between a subject and a predicate under a defined structural relation, and he identifies a series of instantiations of this relation. Later work, including Williams (1983a,b), Rothstein (1983, 1984), Higginbotham (1987), Browning (1987), Abney (1987) and others, has built on this. Among other things, it has been shown that predication is important as a licensing condition, in the sense of Chomsky (1986b), where it is proposed as a syntactic condition that all elements must be syntactically licensed. The intuitive idea of syntactic licensing is that the presence of each syntactic constituent in a sentence is justified by its relation with another syntactic constituent; for example, Chomsky writes, an operator is licensed "by binding a variable from which it is not 'too distant'" (1986a, p93), thus ruling out, for instance, vacuous quantification in natural language (on the assumption that quantification involves an operator). In general, a licensed syntactic element α will be syntactically dependent on another constituent, where 'α is dependent on β' means 'α is in one of a specified set of syntactic relations with β'; for the most part these syntactic relations will be asymmetric, and will include: α is *theta-marked* by β, α is *case-marked* by β, α is *properly governed* by β, and others. A relation is a *licensing relation* if it is essential for ensuring that the presence of α in a sentence S does not render S ungrammatical.

Williams' early work showed that predication, along with other relations including those mentioned above, is a licensing relation. But, our being able to use predication successfully as a licensing relation depends on there being a rigorous definition of 'predicate' which can be used to identify the constituents to be licensed by predication, and it depends on identifying the structural relation which must hold between subject and predicate. So we begin by defining 'predicate' and 'predication'.

The grammatical theory of predication assumes that a predicate is a structurally open syntactic constituent; predication is a relation between a predicate and a structurally closed constituent in which the latter closes the former by filling the open position in it. The element which closes a predicate is its subject. Predication is not just sentential: in (10a), *ate the carrots raw* is predicated of Jane, but *raw* is also predicated of *carrots*. This latter is an instance of secondary predication. And in (10b), while *consider Mary smart* is predicated of the sentential subject *Jane*, the AP *smart* is also predicated of its subject *Mary*, within what we will argue to be a small clause.

(10) a. Jane ate the carrots raw.
      b. Jane considers Mary smart.

What is crucial to this theory, and what differentiates it from theories of predication such as Williams', is that the thematic relation between the predicate and its subject is not part of the predication relation. The AP *smart* in (10b) is a predicate not because it has an external theta-role to assign, or because of any other thematic properties of the phrase or its head, but because, as an AP, it is a constituent which is inherently open or incomplete. The most immediate syntactic implication of this is that a predicate can have a subject with which it has no thematic relation, a pleonastic; the pleonastic can be the sentential subject as in (4) above, it can be the subject of small clause as in (11), but we will argue that it cannot be the subject of a secondary predicate.

(11) a. I consider it unlikely that we will arrive on time.
      b. Mary made it appear that she was very disgruntled.

The sense in which I am call a syntactic predicate 'unsaturated' is essentially Frege's in 'Function and Concept' (Frege 1891), and the relation between a predicate and its subject is the Fregean relation of 'saturation'. Frege thought of a function as an incomplete semantic entity in need of supplementation. Complete entities are objects; in the interpretation of the language of arithmetic with which he was most concerned, these are numbers and truth values, and in the interpretation of natural language, to which he saw his theory as naturally extending, these are individuals and truth values (Concept and Object, 1892). Functions are incomplete entities which cannot denote objects, and which apply to an object, the argument, to give another object, the value. The incompleteness or completeness of semantic entities is reflected in the linguistic expressions which denote them. In the expression of an arithmetic function such as $x^2 + 3$, the position which is empty is indicated by 'x', and the expression as a whole do not denote a specific number. The result of filling the empty position with a number gives an expression which is the name of a number; $3^2 + 3$ denotes the number 12.

The basic closed expressions of natural language are nominals (DPs) and sentences, those constituents which standardly saturate thematic argument positions, and I shall argue that the basic predicates are VPs and other maximal projections of lexical heads, which express properties of arguments. But, the theory of grammatical predication that I am developing here assumes that expressions are inherently open or closed as a grammatical property, and not because of the semantic entities they denote, and so we need to look for a different kind of explanation of what syntactically saturated or unsaturated means.

Since the main property that syntactic expressions have is that of combining with other expressions to make a new, grammatically acceptable string, we can look for an understanding of syntactically unsaturated and syntactically saturated in the area of the combinatorial properties of expressions. Then an unsaturated expression is one which carries in itself the information about how it combines with another expression, and saturated expressions do not. A function expression has 'slots' (to use Dummett's (1973) words), and a closed expression doesn't. If we look at the arithmetic formula, we can see that $x^2 + 3$ tells you what you have to do to get the 'next' number denoting expression, namely replace 'x' by a number expression, while '3' does not carry any information about how it can be combined other than the fact that it denotes a number and can thus fit into a number 'slot'. This same distinction can be seen in natural language. A nominal argument like *Dafna* or *my daughter* or *the croissant that I ate for breakfast* is inherently closed in that it contains no information about what syntactic constituents it can combine with. The DP *Dafna* can fit in any slot which allows a DP. It can be the subject of, and thus sister to, a VP; the direct object of and thus sister to, a transitive verb, the indirect object of a ditransitive verb (although whether it is sister to V or to V' depends on the exact syntactic analysis), or object of, and thus sister to a preposition. And there are other possibilities. In each case the categorial status and syntactic properties of the dominating node are determined not by the DP but by its syntactic sister. It is in this sense that DP does not carry information about how it can be grammatically combined, and it does not determine the properties of the structure that it enters into. In contrast, a VP like *visited John* or *tasted good* does contain information about how it is to be combined: it has to combine with a DP node and the result is a clause. Non-inflected VPs have the same property: an expression like *visit John* or *taste good* must, except in exceptional circumstances which we will discuss below, combine with a DP expression to make a small clause which can occur in positions in which small clauses are licensed, as in (12):

(12)   a. I helped [Bill visit John]
       b. She made [the meal taste good]

(I shall argue in detail below that these are in fact small clauses.) Of course, there are many kinds of unsaturated constituents which are not VPs or maximal projections; lexical heads are the most obvious example. What distinguishes predicates from other unsaturated expressions is that the unsaturatedness cannot be reduced to thematic or semantic properties, in other words, the combinatorial information that they contain does not have a semantic or thematic root, and cannot be explained by the fact that they are thematically unsaturated. This means, crucially, that VPs, APs and NPs which do not assign an external thematic role carry the same combinatorial information as other lexical XPs of the same category, and thus they combine with subjects to project a clause, small or otherwise.

   'Syntactically unsaturated/open constituent' is a primitive syntactic notion which can't be defined in terms of other syntactic properties, and, as we see in section 2.4, ultimately we will have to give a list of syntactic categories which are predicates. Categories which are predicates will indicate this by their syntactic behaviour: they will combine with DPs and dictate the syntactic nature of the node dominating them (as evidenced in particular in small clause complements), they will be ellided by predicate ellipsis, and, except in pseudoclefts and similar equative copular constructions, they will not be subjects. And this will be true of all instances of the category, irrespective of their particular thematic properties. As we will see in section 2.4, the categories which are inherently syntactically unsaturated are the maximal projections of lexical heads. Nonetheless, by describing these categories as syntactically unsaturated, instead of just listing 'categories which must have a subject', I am proposing a particular view of the grammatical interactions between syntax, the semantic representation and the semantic interpretation, as well as a general explanation of why the family of properties characterising predicates are the way they are.

'Unsaturated' has a natural meaning at the level of semantic representation. The classical tradition of formal semantics, following Montague (1970, 1973), interprets natural language expressions by translating them into the language of intensional logic (IL) and giving a semantic interpretation for the resulting logical expressions. The basic mechanism for combining expressions of IL is functional application, in which an unsaturated functional expression is applied to an expression of a designated category. Expressions of IL are assigned types indicating what their combinatorial properties are. The default type for the translation of a VP, as I said above, is $<d,t>$, indicating that it is applied to an expression of type d to give an expression of type t; $<d,t>$ is also the type of a lexical intransitive verb. The type of a transitive verb is $<d, <d,t>>$; as I discussed in section 2.1, the type is traditionally dictated by the number of thematic arguments which the verb requires. By suggesting that VPs (and other lexical XPs) are inherently syntactically unsaturated, I am making that claim that because of their syntactic category, the grammar treats the translations of these expressions as unsaturated functional expressions of type $<d,t>$, which must be applied to an argument, independent of whether or not they contain unfilled thematic argument positions. In other words, the fact that the translation of VP is an expression of type $<d,t>$, and is treated by semantic representation in IL as an unsaturated expression, follows from its grammatical category and not from any thematic features projected from the head. In chapter 6, I will present a formal theory of interpretation in which the result of applying a verb to all the arguments inside its VP is a constituent of type $<e,t>$, the type of functions from events to truth values. This is a saturated constituent, since it cannot be applied to any argument in the sentence. (I represent these constituents as expressions of the form $\lambda e.\alpha$, but there are other ways of representing the saturatedness of this type explicitly in the type theory. Landman (1999) uses sets of events instead of functions from events to truth values, and Chierchia (1989) represents the saturatedness of VPs by having them denote properties.) The result is that there is a typal mismatch: the

grammar treats all VPs as unsaturated and functional, while the expression
which results from combining the verb with its internal arguments is saturated.
I will argue that this mismatch is solved by an automatic rule of predicate
formation which takes the saturated $<e,t>$ expression into an expression of
type $<d, <e,t>>$, and that it is this operation which allows it to be applied
to the subject argument. By arguing that syntactic VP constituents – and other
lexical XPs – are inherently unsaturated syntactic constituents, I am indicating
that the unsaturatedness of the expressions they translate into is determined
by their syntactic category alone, and that the predicate formation rule is
triggered by the category of the node and not by any thematic properties of
the lexical head. Furthermore, the two crucial syntactic properties of predicate
expressions, namely that they must have subjects, and that they cannot themselves (normally) be subjects, both follow from the same property of unsaturatedness. That predicates require a syntactic subject will follow from the fact that
categorially determined unsaturatedness requires them to be applied to an
argument, and the syntax must thus provide them with one. That syntactic
predicates cannot be subjects, whether or not they are thematically saturated,
follows from the fact of their inherent syntactic unsaturatedness: a subject must
be syntactically saturated for $<d,t>$, or rather $<d, <e,t>>$, to apply to it.
The only constructions I know in which predicates can be subjects are higher
order copular constructionsm, as we will see in section 2.4. I will not talk about
these here, but I assume a specific operation on predicates which allows them
to behave as saturated constituents in this construction. Other than that,
syntactic predicates are unsaturated. There are syntactic predicates which are
not clausal, such as secondary predicates and absorbed predicates, and we will
discuss these in chapter 5. They indicate that the grammar has ways of dealing
which unsaturatedness other than direct functional application. What is
common to clausal and other syntactic forms of predication is that the unsaturatedness of the constituents involved is categorially determined.

Categorial grammars often use typal information directly in their labelling
of categories, and in such a framework, what I am calling syntactic predicates
would all be labelled X/NP (or X/DP) for some X, no matter what the thematic
properties of the category (although, as will become clear in the course of the
book, it is not straightforward to determine what X is for a particular predicate).
But specifying the information in this way does not change the basic structure
of relation between typal information and syntactic information which I am
claiming is at the heart of subjecthood.

Note by the way, that from Montague onwards, the type of argument
expressions, or, following Partee (1987), of quantified argument expressions, is
not d but $<<d,t>,t>$, the type of generalised quantifiers. On this account of
arguments, (quantified) DPs do carry combinatorial information with them.
But nonetheless, in the sense discussed above, it is still the sister of the DP
which determined whether the node dominating DP is going to be V', VP, PP,
or S(=IP), and the fact that it is more convenient to apply the DP to the VP
at sentence level rather than the other way round doesn't take away from this

basic intuition that DP does not determine the categorial status of the node dominating it. (In this way DPs will differ from NPs used as predicates). This seems to me to be a good argument for maintaining an X' notation for naming nodes rather than using a type-theoretic notion.

So, our XP predicates are unsaturated syntactic functions in the Fregean sense: just as for him a function expression dictates by its form the structure of the expression that it occurs in, so the syntactic function constituents dictate the structure of the grammatical expressions they occur in. And what makes predicates syntactic functions par excellence is that this structural property is not reducible to a thematic property. Unlike other unsaturated lexical expressions, such as lexical heads, their unsaturatedness is not projected from their thematic requirements.

The syntactic predication operation, of which the most obvious example is the relation between VP and its sister DP, is the saturation of the open position in a predicate by syntactically linking it to an argument constituent, its subject. If the head of the predicate has in its grid an external theta-role to assign, it will be assigned to the subject, and if there is no external theta role in the grid then predication will not involve theta-role assignment. A syntactic predicate will always be monadic. This is just a fact about the way language works: it prescribes one level of unsaturatedness just below the sentential level, where the function is monadic. What can be predicted is that the adicity of any syntactic predicate is the same: since its adicity is a grammatical and not a thematic fact, semantic differences between predicates cannot affect their grammatical structure. This contrasts with the adicity of lexical heads, which varies from head to head depending on the meaning of the particular lexical item.

'Predicate' is defined in (13):

(13)   A syntactic predicate is a monadic, unsaturated, syntactic function.

The licensing constraint on predicates, called the 'Predication Condition', or more properly the 'Predicate Licensing Condition' is that predicates must be syntactically saturated:

(14)   Every syntactic predicate must be syntactically saturated.

A predicate can be saturated by being linked to a non-predicate constituent, its subject, and the absence of an appropriate subject makes the sentence ungrammatical. We will frequently represent predicate linking by coindexing subject and predicate. Thus, the examples in (15) are all ungrammatical if the bracketed subjects are omitted:

(15)   a.   [The ghost]$_i$ [haunted the old house]$_i$.
       b.   [It]$_i$ [seems that [the house]$_j$ [is haunted]$_j$]$_i$.
       c.   [I]$_i$ [consider [it]$_j$ [to have rained heavily]$_j$]$_i$.

(Note that in English, a predicate appears after its subject, but this is presumably a language-specific condition of directionality.) The subject and predicate stand in a specified syntactic locality relation to each other. That the subject must c-command the predicate was argued in Williams (1980) (where α c-commands β iff the first branching node dominating α also dominated β and α does not dominate β. See Reinhart (1983) and references there). He pointed out that in (16a) the depictive predicate *drunk* can be predicated of *Mary*, but in (16b), where *Mary* is the object of a preposition, and does not c-command *drunk*, this is not so.

(16)   a.   I met [Mary]$_i$ [drunk]$_i$.
       b.   *I met [with [Mary]$_i$] [drunk]$_i$.

(I assume that *drunk* is not positioned inside the PP as a sister of *Mary* because the adjunct is interpreted as a V′ modifier. So while positioning it inside PP would be OK with respect to the c-command constraint, it would not allow it to be interpreted semantically. People for whom (16b) is not so bad, presumably do place the adjunct inside the PP, and adjust the semantic interpretation, but I am not going to discuss this reading.) Williams also argued that, with the exception of predicates contained within predicates, such as *rich* in the complex predicate *became rich*, the predicate must also c-command the subject. This is supported by Schein (1995), Simpson (1983), and others. The most obvious counterargument to the mutual c-command condition is the fact that a VP does not c-command its subject, since there is an intervening I′, as in (17):

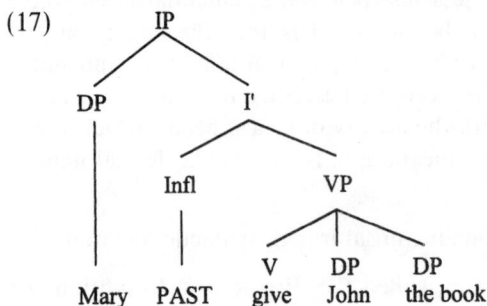

(17)

```
              IP
         ____/  \____
        DP          I'
        |         __/ \__
        |       Infl     VP
        |        |     _/ | \_
        |        |    V   DP   DP
      Mary     PAST give John the book
```

This leads to the obvious suggestion that the appropriate relation is mutual m-command, where α m-commands β if the first maximal projection dominating α also dominates β and neither α nor β dominate the other. However, despite the prima facie evidence from (17) that this is the relevant locality relation, I shall adopt the mutual c-command condition. I'll justify this in chapter 5, which discusses the question of locality relations in depth, investigating adjunct predicates, complex predicates, and the status of I′s. Until then, we will ignore all these issues, focussing on those examples where locality relations are not a problem.

We can now give a definition of predication (which we call direct predication to distinguish it from the relations involved in complex predicate formation discussed in chapter 5):

(18)   A predicate α is (directly) predicated of a non-predicate β iff α is in a local syntactic relation of mutual c-command with β and α and β are predicate-linked (= coindexed as predicate and argument).

Note that (18) makes predication a non-recursive relation: a predicate can be closed only by being linked to a closed element and not by one which needs itself to be closed by another constituent. This follows from the fact that syntactic predicates are first-order functions. A complementary property is that a predicate cannot be assigned a theta-role: theta-roles by definition identify and license closed, argument constituents. Intuitively, the theta-criterion and the predicate licensing condition thus complement each other: predication licenses the distribution of non-saturated XPs and the theta-criterion licenses the distribution of saturated XPs, though, as I argued in Rothstein (1991) there are XPs which are neither predicates nor theta-marked.

We represent predicate-linking by coindexing. The relation between (18) and (14), the Predicate Licensing Condition, is given by (19):

(19) β *saturates* α iff α is predicated of β.

The last piece of definition is given by (20):

(20) β is the *subject* of α iff α is predicated of β.

Finally, a predicate may be predicated of a DP trace. Resultative predicates, which must generally be predicated of direct objects, may be predicated of the subjects of unaccusatives and passives, but not of the subjects of intransitives, as (21a–c) show (but see Wechsler (1997), Rappaport Hovav and Levin (1998) for some counterexamples to this. However, the counterexamples don't affect the point being made here.):

(21) a. John [painted the house$_i$ red$_i$]$_{VP}$
      b. The river$_i$ [froze t$_{i/j}$ solid$_j$]$_{VP}$
      c. The house$_i$ was [painted t$_{i/j}$ red$_j$]$_{VP}$
      d. *John$_i$ [painted the house exhausted$_i$]$_{VP}$ (meaning 'until he was exhausted')

In the acceptable (21a), the predicate *red* and the direct object c-command each other. In (21b/c), the predicate and the DP-trace c-command each other. (21d) does not have a resultative reading precisely because there is no VP object argument for it to be predicated of. The only available reading is the adjunct predicate reading 'John painted the house when he was exhausted', where the AP is indirectly predicated of the subject as part of the VP, as we will discuss in chapter 5.

2.3. SMALL CLAUSES

In principle, the next task is to identify which syntactic constituents are syntactic predicates. Our analysis is going depend heavily on possible complementation patterns of ECM (Exceptional Case Marking) verbs such as *consider* and *make*. I analyse these verbs as taking single constituents as their complements:

(22) a. I consider [John/him **dangerous**$_{AP}$]
      b. The loud noise made [Bill/him **leave**$_{VP}$]

The position filled by the underlined XPs in (22) is generally agreed to be predicative independent of whether the matrix verb is supposed to take a small clause complement. If we want to use this position for the purposes of identifying predicates, it is not strictly necessary to argue that the matrix verb has this small clause complement. However, I am going to argue explicitly for the small clause analysis of these complements, and I do so for three reasons. First, the analysis will be important in chapter 3 for our discussion of pleonastics, and the claim that they appear only in subject position. Second, as I said above, the justification for calling structural predicates by that name is that they are open constituents which dictate the structure of the constituent they appear in by demanding the presence of a subject. This is shown most clearly in the small clause complements in (22) where the internal binary structure of the complement is dictated by the properties of the predicate. Thirdly, small clauses are cases of what I will be calling primary predication where inflection doesn't appear, and where the predicate clearly doesn't case-mark the subject. They thus provide examples of binary constituents where there is no relation other than predication to provide the 'glue' between the two sister nodes. These small clause complements are analysed as uninflected constituents consisting of a DP and some predicate XP, where the DP is not selected either semantically or syntactically by the matrix verb but satisfies the requirements of the predicate. However, the DP is governed by the matrix verb, which explains why it is also case-marked by it, and why it can passivise. Note that we have ample evidence that a V may govern a DP which it doesn't select. In (23), which I discuss at length in Rothstein (1992a), intransitive verbs govern and case-mark DPs which they do not select:

(23)   a. They laughed John off the stage.
       b. He$_i$ was laughed t$_i$ off the stage.

So, the fact that *consider* and *made* case-mark *John* and *Bill* respectively in (22) is not in itself evidence that they select or subcategorise for them. This point is made independently in Stowell (1991a) and Rothstein (1995a,b), both of which argue for the small clause analysis of (22). I present here some of the arguments, taking *consider, make,* and *keep/prevent* as representative of verbs which select for small clauses. (In chapter 10, I will discuss how and why different verbs select different small clauses.) I do want to make clear that the arguments apply to small clause structures in English. As work by Hoeksma (1991) and Neeleman (1994) shows, ECM predicates – and secondary predicates – in Dutch show different syntactic properties, and this may well justify treating them as forming complex predicates with the matrix verbs. But this is not the case in English. Furthermore, Dutch allows other syntactic processes, specifically verb incorporation to form serial verbs, which may well explain the differences in the way predicates are treated as well.

   The first relevant property of small clauses is that the nature of the embedded accusative-marked DP is dictated by the properties of the predicate. As (24) and (25) show, whether the embedded DP is *there*, pleonastic *it*, or theta-marked must depend on the theta-requirements of the predicate since it changes with the predicate when the matrix verb remains constant.

(24)   a. We prevented there from being an explosion.
      b. I prevented/kept it from being obvious that we were late.
      c. We consider there to be little evidence for that claim.
      d. I consider it obvious that you should have done that.
      e. We made there be no reason to suspect Mary.
      f. I made it (be) obvious that John was responsible.

(25)   a. We prevented *there/John from running the race.
      b. I prevented *it/John from arriving too early.
      c. We consider *there/Mary to have won.
      d. I consider *it/ that problem solved.
      e. We made *there/John be responsible.
      f. I made *it/Mary be suspected.

(In contrast with (24d), *I consider it obvious* is of course grammatical, with *it* having a non-pleonastic reading.)

Further evidence that the DP is not selected by the matrix verb is that the entailment relations that normally hold between verb and object don't hold here. *Consider*, *make*, and *keep* all have meanings in which they do select DP objects, but what we are arguing to be the small clause readings do not entail the direct object readings. So, while (26a), which clearly has a direct object, does entail (26b), (27a,b,c), do not entail (27a′,b′,c′) respectively:

(26)   a. John drank coffee black yesterday.
      b. John drank coffee yesterday.

(27)   a. I considered that problem uninteresting.
      a′. I considered that problem.
      b. This policy kept me from going to college.
      b′. This policy kept me.
      c. I made John (be) ready on time.
      c′. I made John.

Note also that (28a/b) are not contradictory whereas (28c) is. In (28d), which is also a small clause structure, the first conjunct actually entails the second.

(28)   a. He considers that problem difficult even though he's never seriously considered the problem itself at all.
      b. She made the dress fit, but she didn't make the dress.
      c. #Mary drank her coffee strong though she never drank her coffee.
      d. He believed the rumour false and didn't believe the rumour.

On the assumption that selected elements are sisters of the heads which select them, this means that there is no evidence that the DP following *consider*, *make*, and *prevent* is the sister of V; on the slightly more controversial assumption that V is the sister only to elements that it selects for, this DP should not be its sister. Instead, *consider* et.al. have two sets of selectional requirements: one possibility is a small clause and the second is a DP object. (Note that the account of movement which I am assuming, based on Chomsky (1981), does not allow for a Raising-to-Object analysis of these structures. Comparing Raising-to-Object with the analysis discussed here is beyond the scope of this book, although I think in general the arguments below can be used against Raising-to-Object too.)

In support of this account of these verbs, we are looking for evidence that the sister of V really is a constituent small clause, and that the DP in question is its subject. The DP object in (26) contrasts with the other examples in that it does behave like an object, and in chapter 5 I shall argue that this is because the predication relation between *coffee* and *black* is an example of secondary, adjunct predication.

Stowell (1991a) argues that the interpretation of adverbs illustrated in (29) is evidence for analysing the complements of these verbs as small clauses. Adverbs modify the constituent they occur in. Standardly, when following an object, they modify the verb which governs the object, as in (29a). However, in complements of *consider* and *make* they modify the predicate complement:

(29)   a.   They told John repeatedly to leave.
       b.   *They considered John foolishly a genius.
       c.   They consider John amazingly a genius.
       d.   They foolishly consider John a genius.
       e.   They considered John foolishly for the position of ambassador.
       f.   They made John repeatedly write his name.
       g.   They repeatedly made John write his name.

While in (29a), *repeatedly* can modify *told*, (29b) is ungrammatical, since *foolishly* is an inappropriate modifier for *a genius* and is not in a position where it can modify the matrix verb, indicating that the maximal projection immediately dominating it is not the VP headed by *consider*. (29c-e) show what adverbial modifications are possible, all of which indicate that in the predicative structures, there is a small clause. Thus, in (29c), an adverb following the DP in question does not modify the matrix verb, but can modify what we are arguing is a small clause. It is John's having the genius property which is amazing, and not their considering it. In (29d), where the adverb is higher than the matrix verb, it modifies the VP. And (29e), where the adverb follows *John* but still modifies the matrix verb, is clearly an example where, according to the entailment tests, *consider* selects for a DP argument. (29f/g) illustrate the same facts with *make*: when the adverb *repeatedly* is clearly in the matrix clause, it is the activity of making which is repeated, but in (29g) where it follows *John*, it can only be the act of writing his name which is repeated. In cases where the entailment tests indicate a direct object and secondary predication, an adverb following the direct object does modify the matrix verb.

(30) a. Mary brewed coffee repeatedly too strong.
      b. John sang the song repeatedly out of tune.
      c. They elected him repeatedly president.

Another argument is made by Kayne (1984), who points out that subjects of small clauses behave like subjects rather than objects in the type of extractions they permit.

(31) a. Who$_i$ did you tell the sister of t$_i$ stories?
      b. Who$_i$ did you tell the sister of t$_i$ to leave?
      c. *Who$_i$ do you consider [the sister of t$_i$ very smart]?
      d. *Who$_i$ did you make [the sister of t$_i$ leave]?

Rothstein (1995a,b) shows that conjunction data in (32/33) support a small clause analysis for *consider*-type complements. (32a) has a reading where the secondary predicate *iced* is predicated only of the second conjunct of the direct object, as in (32b):

(32) a. Bill drinks coffee and tea iced.
      b. Bill drinks coffee and he drinks tea iced.

However, this reading is not available for the examples in (33); (33a/b) do not have the readings in (33a′/b′), but only the irrelevant ones, where the whole DP conjunction is the subject of the predicate (this reading is of course also available for (32a)):

(33) a. *I considered the problem and the solution wrong.
      a′. I considered the problem and I considered the solution wrong.
      b. *I made the cake and the cookies burn.
      b′. I made the cake, and I made the cookies burn.

These impossible readings ought to be available if the DP subject of the predicate is a direct object of the verb, but is predicted to be impossible on the small clause analysis since (33a/b) conjoin two different constituents, a DP and a small clause, as illustrated in (34):

(34) a. *I considered [the problem]$_{DP}$ and [the solution wrong]$_{SC}$.
      b. *I made [the cake]$_{DP}$ and [the cookies burn]$_{SC}$.

There is thus strong evidence that the complements to ECM verbs are small clauses, with the accusative marked DP the subject of the small clause. The second position is the predicate position, and we will use occurrence in this position as a test for predicatehood.

Note that I am continuing to call the small clause 'SC' and that I am not treating it as a projection of a lexical head. This makes it the only (as far as I know) exocentric constituent, and creates a problem for standard X-bar theories, which assume that the categorial status of a constituent is dictated by its head. I see no way around this problem. Stowell (1981, 1983) argues that small clauses are maximal projections of the predicate, with the subject of the small clause in the specifier of XP position. He thus assigns a small clause like *John foolish* the structure in (35a) generalised to (35b):

(35)   a. [consider [John [foolish]$_{A'}$]$_{AP}$]$_{VP}$
       b. [V [DP X']$_{XP}$]$_{VP}$

However there are a number of arguments against this. First, what Stowell calls the A' behaves like a maximal projection with respect to extraction, while what he calls the AP does not:

(36)   a. [How foolish]$_i$ do you consider [John t$_i$]?
       b. *[John foolish]$_i$ was considered t$_i$
       c. *[John foolish]$_i$ is what you considered t$_i$

Second, there are nominal small clauses where the predicate nominal already has a filled specifier:

(37)   John considers [Mary [his daughter's best friend]]

Third, as (38a) shows, extraction of the small clause subject is possible even in (37), despite the fact that extraction of the specifier of a nominal is not possible, as we see in (38b/c):

(38)   a. Who does John consider [t his daughter's best friend]
       b. John likes [his daughter's best friend]]
       c. *Who does John like t's best friend

So I will continue to call these constituents simply small clauses, and I think that they are identical to the category 'A' in Jacobson (1990). We'll discuss later why these are the only constituents which don't have an X-bar categorial label.

There are a couple of other places where what seem to be small clauses turn up. One is in absolute constructions, as the complement of 'with', as discussed in Stowell (1981), Stump (1985), Beukema (1984), Beukema and Hoekstra (1983). This is illustrated in (39a). The other is in the so-called 'Mad-Magazine' constructions, discussed in Akmajian (1984), where a matrix small clause is allowed as an exclamation or query, as in (39b):

(39)   a. With John sick, we'll never get the job done on time.
       b. John sick? Then how can we get the job done on time?

I shall assume that these are indeed small clauses, and that the second constituent here too is a predicate.

2.4. A CLASSIFICATION OF SYNTACTIC CATEGORIES

The discussion of 'predicate', and 'unsaturated constituent' above showed that there can be no simple rule for dividing constituents into those which are and those which are not predicates, but that it must be a matter of observing how each categorial projection behaves. Following the discussion in the previous section, I'll take the crucial tests to be whether a category occurs as a predicate in small clause constituents, as well as whether and when it can occur as a subject. Both subject and predicate positions are filled by maximal projections, as we saw above, and we will look here only at maximal XPs. Assuming that saturatedness (or unsaturatedness) is a property that a category either does or does not have, we expect those categories which are canonical predicates and thus unsaturated, not to be subjects, which are closed – or at least we expect them only to be closed under exceptional circumstances, and we expect canonical subjects not to behave as predicates.

a.   APs and VPs are basic predicate categories. They occur in predicate position in small clause complements, and do not appear as subjects. (40e/f) show that AP can be the predicate complement in absolutive constructions and exclamative matrix small clauses, and (40g) shows that bare VP can appear in a matrix small clause. Uninflected VP does not occur in absolutives, though participle VPs do:

(40)   a.   I consider John *foolish*~AP~.
       b.   His victory made John *happy*~AP~.
       c.   Bill made John *feel very happy*~VP~
       d.   Jane saw Mary *leave the party without saying goodbye*~VP~.
       e.   With John *happy*~AP~, we can get on with business.
       f.   John *happy*~AP~? That is unlikely ...
       g.   John *take the garbage out*~VP~? I don't think so ...
       h.   With John *taking the garbage out*~VP~/*take the garbage out*~VP~ ...

Note that not all predicate positions take all categories or all instances of categories: *consider* does not take a bare VP in its complement, and its XP must in any case be stative, while the XP in the complement of *make* may be a VP and denotes a set of events. (I'll come back to this at length in chapter 10.)

   As well as the positive evidence that AP and VP occur in predicative position, we also see that they do not occur naturally as subjects, as (41) shows;

(41)   a.   *Sincere delights Eliza.
       b.   *Happy has become Peter's goal.
       c.   *Go to school late/*Be at work late annoys John.

These contrast with (42) where the corresponding nominal or gerund can appear as subjects:

(42)   a.   Sincerity/Being sincere delights Eliza.
       b.   Happiness/being happy has become Peter's goal.
       c.   Going to school late/ Being at work late annoys John.

There are two kinds of exceptions to the claim that AP and VP are not subjects; both constituents can be subjects of pseudoclefts, such as (43a/b)), and APs can be subjects of copular constructions as in (43c/d):

(43)   a. Sincere is what John tries to be.
       b. Work hard is what Mary does each day.
       c. Sincere is a good thing to be.
       d. However you look at it, dishonest is dishonest.

On the obvious assumption that pseudoclefts are a kind of copular construction, (43a/b) and (43c) turn out to be different instance of the same kind of thing: in both cases the syntactic predicate is derived via a gap in the post-copula constituent of the same kind as the subject. (43d), from Heycock and Kroch (1999), is a higher-order equative construction. The fact that AP and VP can be subjects in these constructions does not diminish the claim that they are inherently predicate constituents; the sentences in which they can be subjects are so constrained that clearly some kind of type-shifting has occurred. Thus the test for subjecthood is being the argument of a non-copula, non-equative predicate.

b.   PPs can function as predicates. This is demonstrated in (44), where they occur in predicate position in complement small clauses, absolutives, and exclamative matrix small clauses, and not in canonical subject positions.

(44)   a.   I don't consider those books *in my possession* until they have actually been delivered.
       b.   They wouldn't believe him *out of danger/out of the hospital* until they had seen him for themselves.
       c.   With Mary *out of danger*, we can relax.
       d.   Those books *in his possession*? That's a catastrophe!
       e.   *With the trumpets* pleased Mahler acoustically.

However, PPs raise three questions, aside from PP subjects of copula constructions like (45), which parallel (42/43) above:

(45)   a.   With the trumpets is how he wanted it played.
       b.   In the armchair and on the sofa are both good places to sit.

I'll mention these other issues, but I am not going to discuss them at length; they form the subject matter for serious research into the nature of prepositions. First, there are prepositions which are selected by verbs and which do not seem to head predicates. Some, but not all of these look like case-markers:

(46)   a. I spoke about the problem.
       b. The teacher gave the papers to the students.

Second, there are PPs which are adverbial and which Davidson (1967), Parsons (1990), and Landman (1999) argue are predicated of an event argument. In (47) both *to the Evening Star* and *quickly* are predicated of the event argument of *fly*:

(47)   John flew quickly to the Evening Star.

This is a problem for us, since if predication is a syntactic relation, we do not expect either the PP or the adverb to be predicated of a logical argument that is not realised as a syntactic constituent. I return to this at the end of chapter 5. Third, there are those prepositional phrases, mainly (perhaps only) locatives, which seem to denote entities, without being the subjects of specially derived predicates which force them to type-raise. Thus in (48a), in the complement of *put*, the locative PP plausibly denotes a location, the space in the cupboard, and *put* is plausibly interpreted as denoting a relation between two individuals and a location. A similar 'space' denote by a PP can be the argument of a semantically appropriate predicate, as in (48b). (48c/d) give examples of locative PPs as subjects of psych-verbs:

(48)   a.   John put the clothes in the cupboard.
      b.   I cleaned under the stairs.
      c.   ?In the shed frightened the dog.
      d.   ?On top of the cupboard delighted the child.

c.   NPs occur in English rarely except as complements of determiners. When they do occur 'alone', they are clearly predicative:

(49)   a.   They elected Clinton *president* for a second time.
      b.   They made her *chair of the department.*
      c.   Clinton (still) *president*? Who would have believed it!
      d.   With Mary *mayor*, some money may be put into education.

d.   DPs are the most typical arguments, occurring as theta-marked arguments of heads and as subjects, as well as prepositional objects. However, some DPs show predicate properties. DPs can occur in the XP position within *consider* complements, most easily with an indefinite determiner as in (50a) and some-times without any determiner at all as in (50b), and also in absolutives and matrix small clauses. They may also, on occasions, occur with definite deter-miners. DPs with strong quantifiers do not occur in this position, though Doron (1983) argues that DPs with weak quantifiers may. Proper names are also problematic, though for example Williams (1994), argues that (50i) is OK:

(50)   a.   We consider John *a genius.*
      b.   With Mary *a lawyer*, they won't need to worry about legal aid.
      c.   Mary *a lawyer*? That is good news.
      d.   ?They thought/believed him *the lawyer.*
      e.   They believed her *the lawyer they were looking for.*
      f.   They believed her *the best lawyer in town.*
      g.   *They believed John and Mary *every friend.*
      h.   ?I thought the guests *many friends of hers.*
      i.   ??I believe the Mayor *John.*

The general pattern of the data make it seem that the predicate/non-predicate status of DPs should be related to their determiners, especially as the indefinite determiner, the most common determiner to occur in a predicate nominal, has no lexical counterpart in many languages. Normally, the projection of D is an argument; I assume that D is an operator which binds the open position in NP, and allows it not to appear as a predicate in the sentence. Something like this is essentially proposed in Williams (1981), and versions of this claim appear in e.g. Abney (1987) and Longobardi (1994). However, not all determiners work this way. Indefinite and cardinal determiners can project predicative DPs, as can definites, as shown in (44c/d). I will discuss this issue at the end of chapter 9, after we have looked more closely at copular constructions, where the difficulties in distinguishing predicative from argument nominals becomes clear. For the moment, I am going to follow the simplistic position that nominal constituents headed by Ds are the canonical arguments, and that bare NPs are either complements of D or predicative.

e. The CP is inherently non-predicative. CP headed by both *that* and *for* complementisers are both internal and external arguments of lexical heads, and they do not occur in the predicate position in small clauses:

(51) a. I know *that 5 and 7 are 12*.
      b. I prefer *(for) you to do that*.
      c. *That five and seven are twelve* is known to every child.
      d. *For you to arrive late* would be unfortunate.
      e. *I consider the problem *for you to arrive late/that you arrived late*.
      f. *They consider the difficulty *that you do that*.

However, there is a syntactic operation which converts non-predicate CPs into predicates. A syntactic variable bound by a non-interrogative wh-operator or by a null operator in [Spec, CP] can be introduced, as discussed in Chomsky (1982) and Browning (1987). The resulting CP is predicative, and it contains an operator-headed chain which must meet general criteria on chain formation, as illustrated in (52).

(52) a. I consider that problem [Op$_i$ [for [you to deal with t$_i$]$_{IP}$]$_{C'}$]$_{CP}$.
      b. I bought a book [Op$_i$ [for [you to read t$_i$]$_{IP}$]$_{C'}$]$_{CP}$.
      c. The man [who$_i$ [you spoke to t$_i$]$_{IP}$]$_{CP}$.
      d. This book is [Op$_i$ [for [you to read t$_i$]$_{IP}$]$_{C'}$]$_{CP}$.
      e. With these papers still for you to read, we won't be free over the weekend.
      f. That problem for me to deal with? I don't agree!
      e. *This book is [Op$_i$ [for [you to ask who$_j$ read t$_{j/i}$]$_{IP}$]$_{C'}$]$_{CP}$.
      f. *The man [who$_i$ [you heard the rumour that John spoke to t$_i$]$_{IP}$]$_{CP}$.

Browning shows that the trace is dependent on Comp, since it must be subjacent to it, and the Comp position itself cannot be filled by another operator. These predicate CPs occur in a number of syntactic environments. (52a) is the familiar complement of *consider*. (52b) is a predicate purpose clause (see Bach (1982) and Browning (1987) for two different accounts of predicate purpose clauses). (52c) contains a relative clause which is modifying the nominal *man*, showing that predicate CPs, along with APs and predicate PPs, can also be used as modifiers. (52d) shows CP as a matrix predicate embedded under *be*. In (52e/f) the operator headed chain violates conditions on chain formation: in (52e) the trace is bound by two operators and in (52f) the chain violates the complex NP (=DP) constraint. As Browning (1987) and Rothstein (1991) both show, the operator-headed chain in the predicate is obligatory, explaining the ungrammaticality of (52e–f), where the CP does not contain a gap. Even when the CP contains a pronoun instead of gap, the constituent is not a predicate:

(53) a. *I consider that problem [for you to deal with it]$_{CP}$.
  b. *I bought a book [for you to read it]$_{CP}$.
  c. *The man [who$_i$ [you spoke to him$_i$]]$_{CP}$.

(53a/c) are ungrammatical and (53b) has only the rationale clause reading where it is not a predicate of a DP. Furthermore, an operator headed chain necessarily converts a CP into a predicate, and thus cannot occur in a CP which is in a position which is a theta-marked argument:

(54) a. *I persuaded John [for Mary to meet t].
  b. *[For John to meet t] would seem unlikely.

Our tentative conclusions at this point are as follows. AP and VP are inherently predicative. PP is predicative if P is a lexical head, but not if P is a case-marker or other grammatical formative. Bare NP is a predicate, and whether or not DP is a predicate depends on the properties of the determiner which heads it. For the most part, D will project an argument. CPs are non-predicative unless there is an operation which converts them to open predicate constituents.

I generalise these conclusions in (55) and adopt them as a working hypothesis. In the course of the book, I will address various of the obvious problems with (55).

(55) a. Inherent predicates are maximal projections of lexical heads.
  b. Derived predicates are derived from maximal projections of functional heads by syntactic operations.

We will discuss Inflection and IP in chapters 5 and 6. The problem of adverbial PPs will also be discussed in chapter 5, and chapter 9 contains a discussion of the DP/NP issue.

The central claims of the structural theory of predication can now be summed up as follows:

(56) (i) 'subject' is subject of a predicate and not 'subject of a clause'.
  (ii) 'predicate' or 'unsaturated monadic XP' is a syntactic primitive. The inherent predicates are maximal projections of lexical heads. Projections of functional heads are not predicates but may be converted into predicates by a syntactic operation.
  (iii) predication is a syntactic relation which is independent of theta-role

assignment holding between a predicate and a non-predicate (its 'subject').

(iv) predicates are not assigned theta-roles since these are assigned to syntactically closed maximal projections.

2.5. GRAMMATICAL PREDICATION

The claim of the structural theory of predication is that the syntactic predication relation is primitive, and can be autonomously defined. This does not mean that there is no mapping between semantic predicates and syntactic ones; in fact the contrary is true, as I shall show in chapter 6. But it does mean that the syntactic predication relation can be defined without reference to semantic or thematic concepts, as I did in (13/11) and (18/20). I argued in chapter 1 that a structural account of predication was necessary because there was no workable conceptual (i.e. non-structural) semantic or pragmatic account of subject as topic or subject as distinguished argument, which would explain syntactic subject-predicate relations. Williams (Williams (1980) and succeeding papers) uses theta-theory, a syntactic theory of thematic roles, to give a structural definition of distinguished argument and then of 'subject', 'predicate' and 'predication'. He proposes that the distinguished argument of a lexical head is the single thematic argument which is assigned outside the maximal projection of that head. He thus provides a syntactic account of what a 'distinguished thematic argument of a lexical head' actually is, and shows how Strawson's intuition that the subject is the distinguished argument of a predicator can be embedded in a theory of grammar. The theory of predicates and predication which I am proposing here rejects this definition. While it is clear that the subject of a predicate may be assigned a thematic role by that predicate, this is not what predication consists in. Rather, the definition of the predication relation is syntactic, and external theta-role assignment is dependent on the syntactic predication relation. I assume, following Chomsky (1981), that theta-role assignment in general only takes place when assigner and assignee stand in an appropriate syntactic relation. Internal theta-role assignment takes place either when a theta-assigner and argument are in the syntactic relation of governor and governed, or when the argument is the daughter of a PP governed by the theta-assigner. Syntactic predication is the syntactic relation under which external theta-role assignment can occur. This predicts that there will be many instances of predication where there is no external theta-marking. In chapter 4, I shall examine predictions of the thematic theory of predication in detail, but in this section I shall show that the relation between thematic role assignment and predication supports an autonomous structural theory of predication. Instances of syntactic predication are of three kinds: (a) those where external theta-role assignment does occur; (b) those where no external theta-role assignment occurs, but where a lexical DP is the subject of the predicate and intuitively there is a semantic relation between subject and predicate; (c) those where the subject of the syntactic predicate is a pleonastic DP.

Examples of (a) are the examples in (57):

(57) a. Mary ate the carrots raw.
  b. They consider John foolish.

In (57a) *raw* assigns an external theta-role to *carrots,* and the external theta-role of *eat* is assigned to the subject *Mary* via the VP *eat the carrots raw.* In (57b), *foolish* assigns an external theta-role to *John* and again the external theta-role of *consider* is assigned to the subject *they* via the entire VP *consider John foolish.*

(58/59) illustrate the second kind of situation, where the subject is a lexical DP which is not the external argument of the head of VP. There are two possibilities here. In the first case the DP is theta-marked in some other position in the sentence and moved to subject. (59a) is a passive construction, where the subject receives its theta-role via the chain terminating in the trace in [DP,VP] position (alternatively, the subject is theta-marked in the [DP,VP] position and then moved to subject position). (58b) illustrates a raising construction where the subject DP is assigned the external theta-role of the V of the embedded clause, again via the chain [Mary$_i$ ... t$_i$ ...]:

(58) a. Mary$_i$ was [haunted t$_i$ by a ghost].
  b. Mary$_i$ seems [t$_i$ to like the ghost].

The other possible situation is where the DP doesn't receive any theta-role at all. This occurs when the predicate is a CP predicate as in the examples in (52), repeated here as (59):

(59) a. I consider that problem [Op$_i$ [for [you to deal with t$_i$]$_{IP}$]$_{C'}$]$_{CP}$.
  b. I bought a book [Op$_i$ [for [you to read t$_i$]$_{IP}$]$_{C'}$]$_{CP}$.
  c. The man [who$_i$ [you spoke to t$_i$]$_{IP}$]$_{CP}$.
  d. This book is [Op$_i$ [for [you to read t$_i$]$_{IP}$]$_{C'}$]$_{CP}$.

In these examples the DP subject supplies the value for the empty DP position within the CP, indicated in each case by the trace. However, this is not a relation involving theta-assignment since CP has no external theta-role to assign. Within the CP a theta-role is assigned to a trace, but this trace is part of an operator-headed chain, and it is crucial to the theory of chain-formation (Chomsky 1981, 1986a, Browning 1987) that an operator-headed chain is sufficient to satisfy a theta-position. Williams (1987) proposes that a CP predicate assigns an external theta-role, and that it is a referential theta-role 'R'. He suggests that this position is normally bound by the complementiser in a syntactic operation which has as a semantic correlate a process of existential quantification where the domain of the quantifier is a set of facts. If an argument CP has the semantic structure $\exists f[fact(f) \land \varphi(f)]$ then we predict that the R theta-role ought to assign to an individual the property of being a particular fact. However, this is a wrong prediction. Although the CP predicates do not assign external theta-roles to their subjects, they do express properties which are semantically predicated of the denotations of their syntactic subjects. The property denoted by the CP predicate is derived by assuming that the syntactic expression denotes a sentential expression with a free variable, with the trace indicating the position of the variable, and then by lambda abstracting over the expression, treating the null operator as a lambda operator and the trace as the variable bound by it. The trace denotes an individual and the predicate CP is of the form $\lambda x.\varphi(x)$, and expresses a property of individuals, not facts. Thus the CP in (55a) denotes the property of being 'for you to deal with' (or equivalently, the set of things which are for you to deal with). A predicate CP which assigned a different external theta-role would have to denote a different predicate expression. In principle, a CP could assign an additional theta-role to the subject, or argument, of CP, but it would have to be a theta-role which could be appropriately assigned to the argument of the $\lambda x.\varphi(x)$ expressions, and not an argument which has to be assigned to an element from a different domain of entities.

Browning (1987) recognises that non-theta-assigning predicates of this type are a problem for a thematically-based definition of predication, and introduces a mechanism of agreement chains in which CP predicates must occur. Roughly, an agreement chain occurs when an operator headed chain is locally coindexed with a subject. Agreement chains license CP predicates as external theta-role assignment licenses lexical predicates. There are two problems with this mechanism. First, while it guarantees locality between predicate and subject through the formulation of the conditions on agreement chains, it is essentially stipulative. Browning claims that agreement is a crucial relation between a predicate and its subject, although in English this is not represented morphologically. But it is not clear how agreement chains represent this agreement in a nonstipulative way. Secondly, this mechanism can account only for non-thematic predicates which contain agreement chains. But as has been shown by Heycock (1991), and as I argue later in this book, there are other cases of thematic predication which do not contain agreement chains. In (60a) (modelled on examples from Heycock (1991)) the subject is in a non-theta-marked position, as we can see from the fact that a pleonastic can occur there:

(60)   a. John looks/seems as if the baby was awake all night.
        b. It seems/looks as if the baby was awake all night.

Other examples are given in (61) and (62):

(61)   a. John is Mr Smith.
        b. It is John!
        c. I believe the problem to be that you arrived late.
        d. They consider the difficulty to be that you do that.

(62)   a. I consider that John's fear of elevators.
        b. Mary made him her best friend.

(61) illustrates copular sentences where the copular does not take a predicate as a complement, so that the VP does not inherit from its complement an

external theta-role to assign. They thus exemplify a kind of non-thematic predication, since the VP predicate is headed by a copula which has an argument complement and no external theta-role to assign. (Note that (61d,e) are the grammatical forms of the unacceptable sentences in (51) where the argument CP was in predicate position.) In (61a,b) a nominal argument is embedded under a copula. In the (61c,d) the predicate in the complements of *believe* and *consider* are copulars with a CP argument. Since V projects a predicate node, the VP headed by the copula is predicate a despite the fact that its complement is non-predicative and that *be* itself doesn't assign a theta-role. I shall examine these constructions in detail in chapter 9. (62a) is an example from Moro (1997) where the subject of the predicate *John's fear of elevators* is the pronoun *that*. But since all the thematic roles which can be assigned by *fear* are assigned within the predicate, (the experiencer role to *John* and the theme role to *elevators*), the constituent cannot assign a thematic role to *that*. (62b) is an analogous example where the head of the predicate nominal is not derived from a verbal head.

All these sentences give examples of a subject argument which violates the theta-criterion since it is not theta-marked. Heycock (1991) argues that DP arguments can be licensed by theta-marking or by predication, and we will discuss the semantic justification for this principle in chapter 7.

The third type of syntactic predication relation is illustrated in (60b), and in (63):

(63) a. I believe it to have turned out that John won the race.
      b. They made it seem that John had already arrived.
      c. I consider it unlikely that we'll arrive on time.
      d. Bill found it easy to please John.
      e. I believe it possible/certain that he'll be late.

In these examples, not only does predication not involve theta-relations, but it does not reflect or parallel any semantic predication relation. Here the subject is a pleonastic inserted purely so the predicate constituent *to have turned out that John won the race* in (63a) satisfies the predicate licensing condition. (63b) is an example of another VP predicate which does not assign an external theta-role and thus needs a pleonastic subject to satisfy the predicate licensing condition, while (63d–e) illustrate AP predicates which do not assign external theta-roles and therefore take pleonastic subjects. In (61) the sentences express an identity relation, so the subject is not pleonastic, but in (63), in the absence of any semantic relation between subject and predicate, the subject of the VP has to be a pleonastic. I will follow Partee's (1987) account of how the exceptional semantic identity relation works, and I discuss this in chapter 9.

The non-thematic predicates are all instances of the XP categories listed as obligatory predicates in section 2.4. They appear in the canonical predicate position within the complement of the ECM verbs *consider, find, believe* and *make*, as (58) shows. (Remember that a constituent in this position really is licensed only by predication, and that non-predicative constituents therefore cannot occur there.) Copular constructions make the point particularly sharply. XP constituents headed by copulas can appear in these positions when the 'main constituent' of the XP is an argument. But as soon as the copula is dropped, the resulting small clause is ungrammatical, even in positions where small clauses are normally allowed. As we already noted, (64a/b), repeated from (51), contrasts with (61c/d), repeated in (65a/b), and (64c/d) contrasts with the examples in (66c/d):

(64)   a.   *I believe the problem that you arrived late.
       b.   *They consider the difficulty that you do that.
       b.   *I believe John Mr Smith.
       c.   *I believe it John.

(65)   a.   I believe the problem to be that you arrived late.
       b.   They consider the difficulty to be that you do that.
       c.   I believe John to be Mr. Smith.
       d.   I believe it to be John.

Another indication that these non-theta-assigning XPs really are syntactic predicates is that they undergo predicate ellipsis, as pointed out by Baltin (1995). He gives examples along the lines of (66a-b); (66c/d) show that the same effect occurs with weather verbs, and (66e) shows that this ellipsis occurs with AP predicates and that it is not just VP ellipsis.

(66)   a.   A: It seems that Bill is crazy.
            B: It certainly does.
       b.   A: It turned out that Mary was very smart.
            B: It sure did.
       c.   A: It rained heavily last night.
            B: It certainly did.
       d.   A: Was it is really so widely believed that the earth was flat?
            B: It sure was.
       e.   A: It is unlikely that we'll arrive on time?
            B: It sure is.

Examples like (67), pointed out by a reviewer, suggest that this is really constituent ellipsis, and not predicate ellipsis, since argument DPs can be ellided too.

(67)   a.   Is that John? It sure is.
       b.   Is Mr Smith your brother? He sure is.

However, for some people (see Williams 1994), proper names can be used more or less marginally as predicates in small clause complements of *consider* verbs, and so we would expect these constructions too. But if we take examples which are truly equative, where the ellipted constituent is undeniably an argument, as in (68), then we see that there is a real difference between predicates and arguments here:

(68) a. #The duty nurse tonight is Rina. And the duty pharmacist is too.
 b. #In this case the problem and the solution are the same. The problem
 is that the child needs to sleep. And the solution is too.

Let us sum up where we are so far. We have described a theory of grammatical predication in which maximal projections of V, A, N, and (some kinds of) P are inherently open constituents which require saturation, and we claim that the saturation of these XPs is done by linking them to a local argument, the subject. There is little doubt amongst linguists that there are predicates and that they have subjects, nor is there doubt that this relation has to be defined. What I am proposing is that the relation is a purely structural one, which is not dependent on the thematic properties of any of the heads involved. I have suggested in the final section of this chapter that there are at least three kinds of subject-predicate relations which do not reflect thematic properties of the head of the predicate. The most obviously dramatic example of subjects which are not thematically related to their predicates is pleonastic subjects. Because the behaviour and distribution of pleonastics is a central piece of evidence for the theory of syntactic predication, I devote the next chapter to it.

CHAPTER 3

THE SYNTACTIC PROPERTIES OF SUBJECTS

3.1. THE DISTRIBUTION OF PLEONASTICS

Pleonastics are syntactic arguments that do not enter into thematic relations of any kind. It has frequently been proposed in the government-binding framework that there is a generalisation that pleonastics occur only in subject position and not in object position. Postal and Pullum (1987), in a careful presentation of potential counterexamples, suggest that this generalisation is not true. However, the theory of grammatical predication that I am presenting in this chapter predicts that pleonastics should appear only in subject positions, and explains why they cannot appear anywhere else. The potential counterexamples presented by Postal and Pullum divide into two groups; some of them are genuine pleonastics which appear in what turn out to be subjects of small clause complements of ECM verbs (small clauses like those discussed in chapter 2:2.3.) The others are examples of *it* in true object position which, despite appearances, turn out not to be a pleonastic *it* but a theta-marked object of the main verb. The first set, the true pleonastics, are the topic of this section; the second set, which includes sentences like those in (1), are the topic of the second half of chapter 7 (see also Rothstein 1995a).

(1) a. I regret it every time I have dinner with him.
     b. They regretted it that he did not come.

Pleonastic *it* appears only as a subject – either a subject of an IP, or a subject of a small clause as in (2) ((=63) from the previous chapter):

(2) a. I believe it to have turned out that John won the race.
     b. They made it seem that John had already arrived.
     c. I consider it unlikely that we'll arrive on time.
     d. Bill found it easy to please John.
     e. I believe it possible/certain that he'll be late.

They can be raised like any other subject:

(3) It seems t to be unlikely that we'll arrive on time.

As Akmajian (1984) shows, we never get exclamatory matrix small clauses with pleonastic subjects, but he argues that this is for independent reasons and not

66

because of the pleonastics. Small clauses with pleonastic subjects do occur in absolutive 'with' constructions, as we'll see below.

There are four kinds of argument positions in which pleonastic *it* occurs:

i.   Pleonastic *it* can be the subject of predicates headed by verbs such as *seem*, *appear* and *turn out*, when these take tensed CP complements, either in matrix clauses as in (4a,b), in absolutives as in (4c) or in small clauses as in (2) above:

(4)   a. It seemed that John had already arrived.
      b. It turned out that he won.
      c. With it turning out that John is rich, our vacation options are expanding.

These verbs assign no external theta-role, and no lexical DP can appear in subject position (5a–b). Further, the CP complement cannot move to subject, and a pleonastic subject is the only possibility (5c–d).

(5)   a. *John seems that he has won the race.
      b. *The result turned out that he had won.
      c. *That John had already arrived seemed.
      d. *That he had won turned out/appeared.

ii.   Pleonastic *it* occurs as the subject of APs headed by predicates such as *likely*, which do not assign an external theta-role, as in the following examples:

(6)   a. I consider it unlikely that we'll arrive on time.
      b. Bill found it easy to please John.
      c. I believe it possible/certain that he'll be late.
      d. With it likely that we will be this late, I think we should scrap the visit.

Unlike with the raising verbs, the CP complement can raise to subject, and the pleonastic is only one possible subject for the construction:

(7)   a. It is likely [that John left].
      b. [That John left]$_i$ is likely t$_i$.

It has been suggested that the contrast between (5c–d) and (7b) is due to the fact that *likely* does have an external theta-role to assign to a CP, and that the CP is inherently an external argument, base generated in subject position. On this account, (7a) would be derived by extraposing the CP and inserting a pleonastic instead. However, there are (at least) three arguments that the CP is an internal argument of *likely*, and that (8) is the schema for the underlying structure in which they occur:

(8)   e is [[A [CP]]$_{A'}$]$_{AP}$.

First, it has been noted often (e.g. Williams 1983b) that only internal arguments may (though they need not) wh-move with a head. As Williams (1983b) shows, the CP argument of *likely* and *certain* does wh-move. This test shows that *possible*, which does not allow raising, but which has other properties in common with the adjectives, also takes an internal CP argument:

(9)   a. How likely that you'll be on time is it?
      b. How certain that we'll pass the course is it?
      c. How possible for me to pass the course is it?

Second, Stowell (1991b) argues that only internal arguments may ellipt in 'as is' structures. The grammaticality of (10) is further evidence that the CP arguments are internal:

(10)   a. If we are late, as is likely ...
       b. They passed with honours, as was certain from the start.
       c. If we are late, as is possible ...

Third, (11) is related to the sentences in (7), since the AP has the same lexical head. However, the complement of A is untensed, the C has been deleted, and the subject of the embedded IP has been raised to matrix subject position:

(11)   John$_i$ is likely [t$_i$ to have left].

In order for the trace in (11) to be properly governed, the CP must be the complement of the head, and thus an internal argument. If the tensed CP in (7a) were not an internal argument, then there would have to be two forms of *likely*, one with an external and one with an internal argument.

iii.   The third construction in which pleonastics appear is the passive of verbs which take CP complements like *believe* and *regret*. The external theta-role is absorbed, but the internal CP object does not necessarily move to subject position. It may remain in situ, in which case the subject position is filled by a pleonastic *it*:

(12)   a. It was regretted that they had left early.
       b. It was widely believed that the earth was flat.

(I show in chapter 7 and in Rothstein (1995a) that there is one reading of (12a) where the pronominal subject is not pleonastic. This is derived from (13a), which is the same construction as the one illustrated in (1), where I argue *it* is a theta-marked object, which in the passive moves to subject position. The reading of (12a) which we are interested in here is derived from (13b) where the CP complement stays in situ in the passive:

(13)   a. They regretted it that they had left early.
       b. They regretted that they had left early.)

iv.   The fourth instance of pleonastic *it* as subject is with weather verbs, as in (14):

(14)   It rained, it snowed, and it got colder and colder.

It has been argued (Zubizaretta 1987, Chomsky 1986a) that 'weather-*it*' is not a true pleonastic, but a quasi-argument. The evidence for this is that the pronoun apparently controls PRO in sentences such as (15a), and that PRO itself can be the subject of the weather verb *snow*. If PRO can appear in this position it must be a theta-marked position, and if *it* controls a theta-marked DP then presumably it must be theta-marked itself. However, this is not sufficient to claim even quasi-argument status for the pronoun in weather contexts, since other 'true' pleonastics behave in exactly the same way, as we see in (15b):

(15) a. It rained, before PRO snowing.
      b. At first, it seemed improbable that we would arrive at all, before PRO
         becoming more likely that we would just be very late.

The argument about the theta-marked status of 'weather *it*' rests on the assumption that in (15a) there is a PRO subject for the participial *snowing*. But, if the argument holds, and the subject of weather verbs is a quasi-argument where PRO can appear, then we might well expect arbitrary PRO to occur as the subject of infinitival weather verbs, uncontrolled by a pleonastic and licensed by the intrinsic argument properties assigned by the quasi-theta-role. But this is not the case, just as it is not the case with 'true' pleonastics: (16a–b) contrast with (16c):

(16) a. *To snow tonight (without raining first) is odd.
      b. *To be likely to arrive on time would be nice.
      c. To cook (without being required to do so) is fun.

Furthermore, 'weather PRO' cannot generally be controlled by a non-local 'weather-*it*', be it the subject of a gerund or the subject of an infinitival, though PRO can normally be controlled in such a position, (17a) below shows. Again, 'weather-*it*' patterns exactly like the pleonastic subject of *possible* and *likely*, and not like a theta-marked argument:

(17) a. To leave now would be rude, unless we have good excuses.
      b. *To snow tonight would be odd, unless it rains first.
      c. *To become less likely that we are stuck doesn't cheer me up, unless
         it is still possible that we will arrive on time.
      d. Unless we have good excuses, leaving now would be rude.
      e. *Unless it rains first, snowing tonight would be odd.
      f. *Unless it is possible that we arrive on time, becoming less likely that
         we are stuck doesn't cheer me up.

Simply adding a pleonastic to (17b/c) makes the sentences grammatical.

(18) a. For it to snow tonight would be odd, unless it rains first.
      b. For it to be less likely that we are lost doesn't cheer me up, unless it
         is still possible that we will arrive on time.

The balance of the evidence is that 'weather-it' is a pleonastic. The most reasonable explanation for the grammatical examples in (15) is that *before snowing* and *before becoming more likely that* ... are not gerunds with PRO subjects, but VP adjuncts. In (17d–f), the participle 'V-ing' is the subject of the main clause, which is prima facie evidence that it is a nominal gerund, but this is not the case in (15). There it is more plausible to treat the participle as an adjunct modifying VP, which, by a mechanism which I will propose in chapter 5, is composed with the VP and indirectly predicated of the sentential subject, giving the superficial impression of having a subject controlled by the sentential subject. Since, as we will see, there is a thematic condition on predicate composition of this kind, VP modification by verbs with no thematic subject argument will be ungrammatical. Note, by the way, that the adjunct in (15) can be truly bare, and a preposition like *before* is not obligatory:

(19)   It snowed last night, hailing and sleeting as well.

The possibility of reflexives occurring in VP modifying participles, as in (20a), cannot be taken as an indication that they have a PRO subject, since reflexives also occur in adjectival adjuncts, such as (20b) where it has been argued (Schein 1995, Williams 1983a, Rothstein 1983) that there is no PRO subject.

(20)   a. Dr Shepherd left the room, telling himself that he had taken care of everything
       b. He left the room pleased with himself.

I conclude that 'weather-*it*' also is a pleonastic which our theory of predication should account for.

   Now, in all these examples, the pleonastic occurs obligatorily as subject of a predicate which has no external theta-role to assign, but which still requires a subject. (21) demonstrates this for the four classes of pleonastic we have just examined:

(21)   a. I believe *(it) to have turned out that John won the race.
       b. I consider *(it) unlikely that we'll arrive on time.
       c. They believe *(it) to be widely believed that the earth is flat.
       d. The witch doctor made *(it) rain (where **rain** is a verb).

As we argued in chapter 2:2.3, the pleonastics in (21) are in a position which cannot be the object of the matrix verb, but must be the subject of the small clause. The reason they occur in this position is that the non-thematic predicates need a subject to satisfy the predicate licensing rule. Their thematic structure is such that they cannot license a lexical DP subject, and thus the only possible argument with which they can satisfy the predicate licensing rule is a pleonastic.

   The grammatical theory of predication claims that the entire distribution of pleonastics can be explained and predicted on the basis of the predicate licensing rule. Pleonastics can only occur where the predicate licensing rule must be satisfied, but where thematic licensing requirements do not allow a lexical DP. In most of these cases pleonastics must occur. The only instance of optionality that I can come up with is from Heycock (1991), which we discussed as (60) in chapter 2:

(22)   a. John looks/seems as if the baby was awake all night.
       b. It seems/looks as if the baby was awake all night.

I assume that this oddity is due to the properties of the 'topic' construction indicated by *as if*. I'll talk about this more in chapter 7, where I explain how non-theta-marked lexical subjects are licensed, and discuss the semantic interpretation of sentences with pleonastics.

The syntactic distributional conditions that pleonastics must meet are (i) they can occur only to satisfy the predicate licensing condition and (ii) they can occur only in non-theta-marked positions. This means that they can occur only as clausal subjects, where 'clause' covers both small and inflected clauses. It means also that they provide crucial evidence for the obligatoriness of the subject position. Let us make explicit why this is.

We defined 'subject' in chapter 2:(20), repeated here as (23), and we claimed that the purely grammatical principle given in 2:(14), which made no reference to thematic roles, governed the licensing of subjects.

(23)   β is the *subject* of α iff α is predicated of β.   (=chapter 2:(20))

(24)   Every syntactic predicate must be syntactically saturated.
                                                                (=chapter 2:(14))

The obligatoriness of the subject position in a sentence follows from (23/24) on the reasonable assumption that every sentence which doesn't have a sentence for a daughter (i.e. does not have a modifier as one of its daughters), must have a predicate for a daughter. (We'll discuss later why this is the case). In English, an inflected predicated must be a VP, while a non-inflected small clause predicate can be of any predicative category. But once there is a predicate node, there must be a subject in order for (24) to be satisfied, since linking to a subject is how a predicate gets saturated, (Aside from complex predicate formation, the only way that a predicate in a grammatical sentence can avoid satisfying (24) is if it shifts to another non-predicative type. Such type shifting occurs for example within nominals, where APs which are normally predicates have a modifying function, and in higher order copular constructions. I assume that this type shifting is structurally triggered, and that it is not available outside the particular, triggering, local structure.)

Subject position differs from internal argument positions because there is a general licensing condition on subjects which is structural and non-thematic, and independent of the particular properties of an individual predicate or its head. The subject is thus generated because of the syntactic requirement that a predicate be saturated, and this requirement is independent of lexical information about the adicity or lexical properties of the head of the predicate. The predicate licensing rule holds equally of all predicates, no matter what lexical properties the head has, and this means that the subject is equally obligatory for all predicates. Other arguments saturate positions in thematic grids, and are licensed by theta-marking, without reference to syntactic position or grammatical relation. So, whether a predicate contains non-subject arguments, and how many it contains, will vary depending on the thematic properties of the lexical head or the predicate. But the head cannot affect whether there is a subject; its theta-marking properties can affect only whether or not the subject is filled by a nominal with lexical content.

This is the answer to the first question that we posed at the beginning of chapter 2 – why subject position is the only position which is obligatory. For the object to be obligatory, there would have to be a principle comparable to the predicate-licensing rule which licensed the object position, independent of any particular properties of lexical heads.

The fact that pleonastics are restricted to clausal subject position now follows directly. Pleonastics are DPs which cannot occur in a theta-marked position. Since subject position is licensed on purely structural grounds independently of theta-restrictions, pleonastics can occur there, and since it is the only position which is licensed independently of theta-marking, it is the only position in which pleonastics may occur. Note that the same reasoning shows why non-theta-marked lexical subjects such as (22a) can occur only in subject position, since they too need to appear in a position which is licensed by purely syntactic restrictions, not thematic ones.

The restriction of pleonastics to clausal subjects, and in fact the definition of clausal subject, follows from a distinction between two kinds of predication formulated in Rothstein (1983). Forms of predication can be syntactically divided into two kinds; intuitively these are clausal predication and adjunct predication. (In Rothstein (1983) I called them 'primary' and 'secondary' predication, but as we will see in chapter 5, true secondary predication is more restricted than adjunct predication.) In adjunct predication the subject of an adjunct predicate is a theta-marked argument of another lexical head. It thus follows that the subjects of adjunct predicates cannot be pleonastics. Primary predication occurs when the subject and predicate form a constituent together, and when the subject is not thematically licensed outside the predication relation in which it occurs. Thus in (25a), *broken* is a secondary predicate of *the bike*, which is independently theta-marked as the theme of *ride*. In (25b) *win the race* is a primary predicate of *Mary*, since *Mary* is not theta-marked by anything other than the head of the VP predicated of it:

(25)   a. John rode the bike broken.
       b. Mary won the race.

Mary and *won the race* form a constituent while, as we shall see in chapter 5, *the bike* and *broken* do not form a constituent.

In (26) I propose a definition of primary predicate and primary predication, and this previews the discussion of primary and secondary predication in chapter 5:

(26)   a. α is a *primary predicate* of β, iff α is predicated of β, and α and β c-command each other and β is not theta-marked outside the predication relation with α.

b. If α is a primary predicate of β, then α and β form an instance of *primary predication.*

An instance of predication which meets the conditions in (26) will form a constituent; an inflected constituent is an IP, and a non-inflected one is a small clause. It is tempting to use the definition in (26) to define 'clause' as an instance of predication, though as we saw in chapter 2, there are instances of primary predication which are far from clausal, in any 'normal' sense of the word:

(27)   a. With John sick, we'll never get the job done on time.
       b. John sick? Then how can we get the job done on time?

The important point with respect to pleonastics is that in primary predication, the subject is not theta-marked outside the predication relation. In contrast to secondary predication, there is nothing that says that the subject has to be theta-marked. Thus the definition in (26) allows these subjects to be non-thematic.

3.2. PLEONASTICS AND CASE

There have been several suggestions that the generation of pleonastics can be accounted for in terms of case assignment. Essentially the idea is that pleonastics are realisations of case (nominative or accusative). They occur because there is a principle that if case can be assigned, it must be assigned; therefore, if no lexical argument occurs in a position to which case can be assigned, a dummy element must be inserted to realise the case features. This account is proposed in Fukui and Speas (1986), Fukui (1986), and Speas (1986), and in Authier (1991) and a variant is proposed in Borer (1986). According to Fukui and Speas, and Authier, in sentences such as (28a), a pleonastic is generated so that nominative case can be realised in [Spec,IP], while in (28b) the pleonastic is generated as an obligatory realisation of the accusative case which the matrix verb can assign:

(28)   a. It is likely that John will win.
       b. I consider it likely that John will win.

There are several serious problems with this account. It is true that there is evidence that subject position must be case-marked, even if the element filling it does not usually have to be assigned case. Thus Safir (1983) points out that while there is no evidence that small clauses have to be assigned case, a subject small clause cannot appear in a position which is not case-marked:

(29)   a. Workers angry about their pay is the situation we want to avoid.
       b. *It was believed workers angry about their pay to be unavoidable.

However, the fact that an argument has to have case does not mean that a position has to be lexically filled in order for case to be realised. There is evidence that the hypothesis that the case assigning properties of heads must be realised is simply wrong. Burzio's generalisation states that verbs which assign an external theta-role have the potential to assign accusative case, and this predicts that the ability to assign case is independent of whether the verb c-selects a direct object. If this is so, then it cannot be true that case-assigning potential must be realised since intransitives which assign an external theta-role and can supposedly assign accusative case, do not generally appear with a direct object, either lexical or pleonastic:

(30)   a. *They laughed the joke/it.
      b. *He complained the bad coffee/it.
      c. *The clock ticked the time/it.

Rothstein (1992a) argues that Burzio's prediction is correct, that the verbs in (30) do assign accusative case, and that the Fukui-Speas-Authier hypothesis about case-assignment must therefore be wrong. Intransitive verbs assign case to an DP which they do not select, and which is theta-marked by another predicate. In (31a–b) the accusative marked DPs are theta-marked by resultative predicates, while (31c) is an example of the 'X's way' construction:

(31)   a. They laughed him off the stage.
      b. He complained himself hoarse about the bad coffee.
      c. The clock ticked its way through the years.

(See the discussion in Rothstein (1992a), in part based on Carrier and Randall (1992) and Levin and Rappaport Hovav (1995), for evidence that the verbs in (31) are true intransitives and not lexically derived transitive verbs.) In the normal instance, where an intransitive verb appears without a direct object, it must simply not be realising its potential case assigning properties. Thus the hypothesis that case features must be phonetically realised cannot be maintained. While it is a necessary condition on pleonastics that they appear in a (non-theta-marked) position which is assigned case, the potential for case-assignment is not sufficient to cause them to appear. Thus the existence of pleonastic subjects in small clause complements cannot be explained by the fact that the matrix ECM verbs can assign case to that position.

Subject pleonastics also cannot be accounted for in terms of the obligatory assignment of nominative case, as Rothstein (1995a) and Heycock (1991) point out. Subject pleonastics can occur as the subjects of untensed clauses where they are assigned case by a case-assigning complementiser which has to be generated especially for this purpose. (32) illustrates this:

(32)   a. *To seem that John was late would be unadvisable.
      b. For it to seem that John was late would be unadvisable.
      c. It is important *(for it) to appear that senators are sincere. (Heycock 1991).

One cannot assume that the complementiser *for* is generated along with Inflection and that therefore there is an element which has to assign case. If that were so, then we would expect to see *for* every time there was an untensed clause, and this is not the case as (33) shows:

(33)   To leave now would be rude.

Not only does *for* not appear lexically in (33), but, since there is a PRO subject of *to leave* and PRO must be generated in an ungoverned position, we know that there cannot be a governing or case-assigning element in [Spec,CP].

The examples in (32) not only disprove the Fukui-Speas-Authier hypothesis about pleonastics, but they provide direct evidence for the theory presented here. Since the position is neither theta-marked, nor assigned case by Infl, there is no reason to generate the pleonastic in (31b,c) other than to provide a subject for the untensed VP headed by *seem* and *appear* respectively. And, if a subject is required, there is no candidate other than the pleonastic. Since a theta-role isn't assigned to the position, neither a lexical element nor PRO can be generated there, and since there is no possible antecedent, trace cannot be generated there either.

Borer's account of pleonastics differs slightly from the one just described, but the problems are essentially the same: 'for–to' clauses and ECM constructions. Borer (1986) proposes that subjects are selected by and coindexed with Infl, and are thus obligatory because the selectional properties of Infl must be satisfied whether or not it is tensed. Borer argues that the relation between Infl and its I-subject is 'privileged', and as a consequence, I-subjects cannot enter into a syntactic licensing relation with another head, and thus must be case-marked by Infl. That *for* can case-mark an I-subject is explained by the hypothesis that it is 'not really distinct from Infl' since *for* selects only a [−tense] Infl. But while *for* seems to select untensed IPs, that is a long way from saying that two distinct functional heads behave as if they are one – especially in a case where there is no head-raising of Infl to C. And, as I argued above, the relation between *for* and Infl is less close than one might originally think, since many occurrences of [−tense] Infl do not head IPs selected by *for*.

Borer's account of pleonastics in the subject position of small clause complements of ECM verbs, and in fact her account of small clause subjects in general, is at least as problematic. She assumes a null Infl node in all small clauses with which the subject is coindexed. However, the matrix V clearly assigns case to this DP, violating the privileged relation between the Infl and its subject. Borer explains this with the claim that ECM verbs select for a 'degenerate Infl' which, because of its degeneracy, allows another head to case mark its subject. The only basis for generating Infl here is the theory-internal claim that a small clause subject must be coindexed with Infl. However, the only piece of evidence for such coindexing is a privileged case-assigning relation which is violated here. The absence of any independent evidence for this Infl node and the ad hoc properties which must be ascribed to it are good reasons to reject the analysis.

3.3. THE EXTENDED PROJECTION PRINCIPLE

The other syntactic approaches to a theory of pleonastics are basically stipulative, without adequate theoretical justification. Chomsky (1982) formulates, as clause I of the Extended Projection Principle, the 'stipulation' (his own word) that 'clauses must have subjects'. Williams (1983b) offers (34) which is equally stipulative:

(34)   'It' occurs in the [NP,S] position if an external argument does not have to appear there.

The empirical problem with both these statements (aside from the inherent non-explanatoriness of stipulations) is that they rely on an independent definition of clause or S. But standard definitions of S, IP or clause (including those of Williams 1983) do not cover complements of ECM verbs, which are neither IPs or Ss. In a framework in which it is assumed that S is a projection of Inflection, or an IP, then a small clause falls under the definition of S only if we posit a null inflection as its head. But, as I mentioned as the end of the previous section, there is no indication that the small clause complements we have been discussing, like those in (35), are projections of Infl, and it is not insightful to posit a null Infl in small clauses just to be able to call these complements IPs.

(35)   a.   People consider [Mary very smart].
       b.   I consider [that Bill's fear of flying].
       c.   If you leave now, the captain will consider [you off the ship by midnight].

In any case, as we shall see in chapter 10, small clauses do not denote the same semantic objects as IPs, and positing a null Infl here would blur the distinction between inflected clauses and small clauses that we want to keep sharp. (In addition we would have to explain why null inflection, but not morphologically realised inflection, can take a non-verbal constituent as an complement.) Williams defines S as a node with NP and VP as its daughters, but as these examples show, the small clause complements of propositional attitude verbs have AP, NP, PP or, exceptionally, CP as their predicates, and not VPs, and while verbs like *make* can have small clauses with VP predicates, as we saw earlier, this need not be the case, as (36) shows:

(36)   a.   I made John be angry.
       b.   I made John angry.

So, trying to explain the presence of pleonastics in small clauses as following from the stipulation that all clauses have subjects requires an independent way of explaining how small clauses are in fact clausal. As we discussed in chapter 2:2.3, Stowell (1983, 1991) argues not that small clauses are clausal, but that all maximal projections, and not just IPs have subjects. The subject of a small clause is present because all the predicate phrases in the complements of

(35) are non-maximal and allow for a specifier. But while this explains why there can be an embedded subject in these examples, it doesn't explain why there must be, and thus does not help explaining why pleonastics can occur there.

In any case, as we showed in the discussion in chapter 2:2.3, there is a lot of evidence against the theory that small clauses are categorially maximal projections of the lexical heads of their predicates, and in favour of treating the predicate itself as a maximal projection. Heycock (1991) gives a further argument against Stowell's claim, showing that contra Stowell (1983), individual ECM verbs do not select a complement of a specific syntactic category, or small clauses headed by any particular category of predicate; she claims that the subject of a small clause is adjoined to a maximal XP to form a constituent, but it stays unclear what to call this small clause constituent. This is not surprising, because it is the only constituent (as far as I'm aware) which is not the projection of a head. But that is precisely because the structure of the constituent is given not by the properties of a head element, but by the structure of the predication relation. The predicate XP requires a subject, the matrix verb does not subcategorise for an object which can also serve as subject of the predicate, and thus the predicate selects for itself an argument, its syntactic sister, which saturates it. The only way in which the predicate can be the sister of an argument which is not the object of the verb is if the predicate and its subject form an independent constituent so that the subject is not the sister of the V:

(37)   V [DP$_{subject}$ XP$_{predicate}$]

This gives the small clause itself as the complement of the V, and, as I shall show in chapter 10, this is the right result, for although ECM verbs are not sensitive to the categorial status of the predicate of the small clause, they are sensitive to the semantic type of their complement, and thus to the kind of entity denoted by the small clause.

The only approach under which small clauses and inflected IPs are analysed as having a common structure in virtue of which they can both be classified as clauses is to analyse them as having a common predication structure, and to use the definition (26), under which a clause is an instance of primary predication. Small clauses are then uninflected instances of primary predication, while IPs are instances of primary predication in which the predicate is modified by a tense, mood or other inflectional marked. But then the claim that any clause must have a subject follows directly from the definition of predication. If a clause is an instance of primary predication, then clearly a clause must have a subject, and that is all that clause I of the Extended Projection Principle says.

For the rest of this work, I shall label small clauses 'SC'. This captures the important fact that the clausal node is generated because of formal selectional requirements of the XP itself, captured in the definitions of predicate and predication given earlier, and that it is this relation and not any feature projection from a categorial head that gives the constituent its internal structure.

Notice that this account is an argument against the view of phrase structure explored in Stowell (1981), and developed in Speas (1986). Speas proposes that phrase structure is a pure projection of the theta-grids of lexical heads (and the comparable features of functional heads). However, the obligatoriness of a subject in ECM complements which is adjoined to XP and is neither theta-marked nor functionally selected by any head shows that there is a purely syntactic general principle governing the distribution of subjects which is not reducible to selectional constraints, thematic or otherwise.

2.4. PASSIVE AND RAISING

Passive, unaccusative and raising-to-subject constructions, which are illustrated in (38a/b) (38c) and (38d/e) respectively, illustrate another phenomenon which is particularly interesting for the theory of grammatical predication, namely constructions where the thematic subject is not thematically marked as the natural external argument of the head of the predicate:

(38)   a. $Mary_i$ was haunted t_i by a ghost.
      b. [That the earth is flat]$_i$ is widely believed t_i.
      c. $They_i$ arrived t_i late.
      d. $John_i$ [seemed [t_i [to smile]$_{VP}$]$_{IP}$]$_{VP}$.
      e. $John_i$ [is likely [t_i to be late]$_{IP}$]$_{VP}$.

In a government-binding type framework, these are all constructions in which the subject of the sentence is a thematic DP which has been moved into the subject position. In (38a–c), the nominal is moved to subject from the direct object position, as the indexed trace indicates, and in the raising constructions in (38d/e), the subject is raised from a lower clause. In all cases, the raised element forms a chain with the trace left in the position from which it is raised. According to the principles of movement and theta-theory (Chomsky 1981, 1986a,b), the moved NP cannot be theta-marked in its surface position (via predication) as the external theta-argument of the predicate which is its sister, but is theta-marked in its D-structure position and moved afterwards, with the chain 'transferring' the thematic information to the subject position. This is prima facie a problem for any theory which defines 'subject' as external thematic argument of a head, since these DPs do not qualify as subjects, and I'll come back to Williams' discussion of the issue in the next chapter. Here I am interested in another question, namely, what can predication theory tell us about how NP (or DP) raising works; more specifically, why does raising occur, and why do DPs raise only to subject position? The theory of grammatical predication answers this and explains why movement in these constructions is sometimes obligatory and sometimes optional. In particular, we will want to know how raising affects sentential arguments. In these cases, raising is optional.

Thus, as shown in (39), passivising a verb like *know* can result either in the externalisation of the internal argument or the insertion of a pleonastic, and a parallel option appears with raising adjectives such as *likely*, as shown in (40):

(39)   a. That Mary had left was known.
      b. It was known that Mary had left.

(40)   a. That Mary has left already is very likely.
      b. It is very likely that Mary has left already.

Principles of government-binding theory dictate that raising occurs when two conditions are met. The XP raised must be raised from a non-case-marked position, and to a position which is not assigned a theta-role. This is guaranteed by the condition on chains: every chain must have one and only one theta-role, and one and only one case assigned to it. Previous accounts of raising, in particular Burzio (1981, 1986) have concentrated on the interaction between case and theta-marking in an explanation of raising. Burzio's generalisation is that a verb assigns accusative case (has property A) if and only if it assigns an external theta-role (has property T). This means that a verb which does not thematically license an external thematic DP in subject position will assign no accusative case to its direct object position, and thus will allow no S-structure direct object. Burzio hypothesises that nominal objects and subjects of embedded bare IP clauses raise, as in (38), in order to get case, since they are generated in a position where they cannot be case-marked by the matrix verb. The generalisation $T \leftrightarrow A$, which entails $\neg T \leftrightarrow \neg A$, means that DP will need to move to get case only when there is no thematic argument in the subject position of the VP which would prevent movement. It also prevents an accusative case-marked DP moving to subject, even if the subject position is not itself case-marked (for example if Infl is [−tense]), since case is assigned only by verbs which have an external theta-role to assign. (Locality conditions on chains prevent nominative case-marked DPs moving to a higher subject position across a CP node.) Burzio's generalisation seems well-founded; and allows us to predict why, given the constraints of the case-filter and theta-theory on chain formation, movement is possible in certain cases. However, Burzio's theory deals only with movement of DPs, and it does not explain why CP sentential complements may also be raised, since it has been widely argued (e.g. Stowell 1981) that they are not, or even may not be, assigned case. It also does not discuss whether there is any relation between raising-to-subject and the distribution of pleonastics. It seems that there should be such a relation because pleonastics and raised XPs are two kinds of subjects which share the property of not being theta-marked by the head of the VP that they are subject of, and because, as we saw in (39/40), movement and pleonastic insertion may be alternative syntactic mechanisms accompanying the lexical argument-deletion part of the passive operation.

    I hypothesise that Burzio's generalisation explains why DPs must be moved in certain cases, but that it is not a general account of why movement occurs.

The more general explanation comes from the effects of the predicate licensing condition. Since, as we argued above, the distribution of pleonastics is also governed by the predicate licensing condition, this immediately predicts a relation between the two processes.

The hypothesis is that raising to subject, like pleonastic licensing, is a mechanism for satisfying the predicate licensing condition when the head of a primary predicate does not have an external argument to assign to its subject. When an external theta-role is assigned, the subject of the predicate is a lexical argument to which that theta-role is assigned, and it is base-generated in [Spec,IP] outside the VP, or the subject of the predicate is the trace of such an argument if the argument itself is raised, as in the embedded clause in (38e). When there is no argument base-generated in that position, either a pleonastic may be inserted, or an argument may be raised to fill it, assuming the appropriate locality relations between the raised element and its trace can hold. In English, it looks as if pleonastic distribution is a 'last resort' method of providing a subject for the clause, with a pleonastic being used only when there is no DP to be raised. This explains the examples in (41):

(41) a. Mary$_i$ was haunted t$_i$ by a ghost.
      b. *It was haunted Mary by a ghost.
      c. It snowed heavily all night.

In (41c), *snow* selects neither an external argument nor an internal argument, so there is no argument base-generated in subject position, and no DP to move there. In (41a), though there is no DP base-generated as the subject of the predicate, there is an argument which can be moved there, and thus the insertion of the pleonastic is ungrammatical. More strongly, the DP in (41a) must be moved to subject position, since in its original position as object of a passive verb, it cannot receive case. This makes it seem that case-assignment and the case filter provide a subject for subject-less predicates, and that pleonastics are a last resort when this does not work. However, there is evidence against such a general explanation. Even when movement is possible, there are cases when a subject can be a pleonastic rather than a moved lexical argument. In examples like (41a–b), the case-filter rules out pleonastic insertion, because the resulting structure violates the case filter, but where this is not an issue, raising and pleonastic insertion are equally effective as methods of satisfying the predicate licensing condition. The crucial examples from English are where the argument which can be moved doesn't need to be assigned case, and this occurs where the lexical head of the predicate selects an internal CP argument. Such heads include raising adjectives such as *likely* and *certain* and passives of verbs such as *believe*. We saw examples of these in (39/40), repeated here together with some more examples:

(42) a. That Mary had left was known.
      b. It was known that Mary had left.
      c. That the earth was flat was widely believed.
      d. It was widely believed that the earth was flat.
      e. That Mary has left already is very likely.

f. It is very likely that Mary has left already.

g. That we would be late was certain.

h. It was certain that we would be late.

In these examples, the position which contains the subject of the predicate is not filled at D-structure; in (42a–d) this is because the external argument of *believe* and *know* is not assigned after passivisation, and in (42e–h) because the raising adjectives *likely* and *certain* take no external argument. The position can be filled in one of two ways. Either the CP is moved to subject position, or the CP remains in its D-structure position and a pleonastic is inserted as subject. Both are equally good solutions to the problem of how to license the predicate headed by a head which does not assign an external argument, but which needs to be linked to a subject. (According to Koster (1977), CPs never occur in subject position, but are moved through it and adjoined to IP, where they bind a trace in subject position. This gives the structure in (43) for (42a):

(43) [That we would be late [t$_i$ was certain t$_i$]]

Here, strictly speaking, the trace immediately bound by the CP is the syntactic subject of the predicate.)

The difference between the (a) and (b) examples is not semantic but pragmatic. As argued in chapter 1, the effect of raising the CP is to locate it in the position in which is it easily interpreted as the topic of the sentence. This shows in the contrast between the discourses in (44):

(44) a. That they would move to China was finally decided. It upset her mother.

b. It was finally decided that they would move to China. It upset her mother.

Thus in (44a), the unmarked topic of the first sentence is the CP *that they would move to China;* it is therefore the most obvious antecedent for the pronoun *it* in the second sentence of the discourse, giving the reading that her mother was upset by the fact that they would move to China. In (44b), the first sentence does not have a sentential topic (although it may still have a discourse topic, of course), and the most obvious antecedent for the first reading of the pronoun is the whole sentence *It was finally decided that they would move to China*, with the interpretation that her mother was upset by the decision, and not the move.

The two methods for providing a subject for the predicate are both available when the argument which is a candidate for movement does not need to be assigned case. When the relevant argument is a DP which does need to be case-marked, raising to subject must take place so that the DP can be assigned case. That this depends on the argument and not on the matrix predicate is shown by the contrast between the examples in (42) and those in (45). Here the matrix predicate takes a bare IP rather than a CP complement. The IP cannot be moved, but the subject of the embedded IP cannot be assigned case in situ, and must be moved to the empty subject position to get nominative case. Pleonastic insertion is not available as an option for providing the predicate with a subject because it would leave the embedded IP subject in a case-less position:

(45)   a.   We$_i$ were likely t$_i$ to be late.
       b.   *It was likely we/us to be late.
       c.   The earth$_i$ was widely believed t$_i$ to be flat.
       d.   *It was widely believed the earth to be flat.

We can see now why raising occurs only to subject position. DP raising, or, more correctly, argument raising, is a syntactic movement operation to a position which is licensed but empty. Since thematically licensed positions have theta-marked arguments base-generated in them, the only empty licensed position can be one which is syntactically licensed and not thematically licensed. This is the position which is licensed by the syntactic predication relation.

The discussion in this section, more than many in this book, is explicitly with the framework of government-binding theory, but the issues discussed must be raised in any theory. As far as simple passives are concerned, an approach such as Dowty (1982), which treats single argument passive (i.e. passive without a 'by' phrase) as a purely lexical operation on argument structure, would need to ask why an operation which deletes the subject argument needs to reposition the remaining nominal argument in sentential subject position, while an operation like intransitivisation, which deletes the object argument, does not need anything to be repositioned. With respect to raising, any treatment of the construction will have to ask why it is only the clausal subject position which can be filled by a thematic nominal whose thematic role is dictated non-locally. Of course, a lexicalist approach will also need to give a subcategorisational account of the pleonastics which explains their distribution. I shall discuss several such accounts of pleonastics in chapter 7. Here I shall just point out that the theory of predication together with a movement account of passive and raising allows for a very simple account of the filling of non-thematic subject positions of raising predicates. A single subcategorisational entry for *likely*, [likely$_{AP}$:—CP], plus the information that *likely* allows CP deletion gives, on the above theory, all three of the forms in (46), while a non-movement account will require three different lexical entries for *likely*. In (46) *likely* selects a CP complement and a pleonastic subject; in (46b) it selects an external CP argument; and in (46c) it selects a VP complement and a thematic subject. (See also Jacobson 1990 for a treatment of (46c) in terms of function composition.)

(46)   a.   It is likely that John will be late.
       b.   That John is late is likely.
       c.   John is likely to be late.

Similar, though I think more complicated, problems occur with the passivisation of *believe*. (47b/c) can be derived by ordinary passivisation, assuming that *believe* has the appropriate dual subcategorisation possibilities. But (47a) is really an instance of a single argument passive where the single argument is not externalised, and if argument repositioning in passive is done via a lexical rule, then this will require a separate lexical formulation.

(47) a. It was believed that John would be late.
      b. That John was late was believed.
      c. John was believed to be late.

But this is incidental to the main point of this section.

Two puzzles remain, which are beyond the scope of the discussion here, since they are not directly related to the issue of predication. One is why raising verbs such as *seem* and *appear* do not allow the complement CP to be raised to subject and require a pleonastic to be inserted (though the DP subject of the embedded clause can be raised):

(48) a. It appeared/seemed that the team would win.
      b. *That the team would win appeared/seemed.

The second point is that CPs, which do not need to be assigned case and can remain in non-case-marked object positions, cannot remain in non-case-marked subject positions nor can they be moved to non-case-marked positions:

(49) a. *It is likely that we will be late to upset her.
      b. *That John will be late to upset her would be surprising.

One possible way of explaining this is to assume Koster's (1977) analysis of the positioning of sentential subjects, namely that they move through the subject position but cannot stay there and must be adjoined to the sentence. Then the impossibility of (49) may be the result of the fact that the CP is unambiguously forced to be in subject position. Even in (49b), the CP is the subject of the predicate in an embedded clause, and cannot be interpreted as filling the position Koster proposes for sentential subjects, namely adjoined to the matrix clause. However, as a reviewer points out, the examples in (50) don't seem to be as bad as (49), and indicate that a CP in subject position may be awkward, but not ungrammatical:

(50) a. Is that John came late really unlikely?
      b. We were wondering when that John is getting married became known.
      c. For that John will be late to upset her would be surprising.

These examples, and especially the contrast between (49b) and (50), indicate that the CP must be case-marked when it is in subject position, and are support for Safir's (1983) claim, discussed in 3.2, that a phonologically realised subject must be case-marked, no matter what the category of the syntactic constituent filling it.

CHAPTER 4

PREDICATION AS A THEMATIC RELATION

4.1. THETA-ROLES AND PREDICATION

In the previous chapters I discussed several kinds of structures which are evidence for a non-lexical/thematic analysis of subjecthood, since they are cases in which the subject of a primary predicate is not assigned a thematic argument by the head of the predicate. These included constructions where the subject is a pleonastic, constructions where the DP in subject position is moved there from a lower position, and clauses where the main predicate simply doesn't assign an external theta-role. The predicates in these constructions are predicates by virtue of their syntactic structure and not by virtue of their lexical structure. A 'distinguished argument' theory which defines predicate and predication in terms of thematic arguments has to explain how XPs which do not assign external theta-roles enter into predication relations with their subjects. The way in which lexical, non-movement theories of subjects deal with these problems is very different from the way in which a movement-based theory like Williams' can deal with it (whether the movement is actual, in a 'strong' derivational theory of syntax, or 'virtual' in a representational type theory in which DP chains are built at S-structure in conformance with certain constraints, as in Rizzi (1986)). I will discuss non-movement accounts of subject hood in chapter 6 and 7; here I will consider in depth the theta-based theory developed by Williams. My argument will be that it is not possible to combine a syntactic theory which includes movement and NP (or rather, DP) chains with a distinguished argument account of subjects, predicates and predication.

The thematic account of predication developed by Williams (1980, 1983a,b, 1987) deals with pleonastic subjects and lexical, non-theta-marked subjects in different ways. The distribution of pleonastics is taken to be outside the domain of the theory of predication. Pleonastics are not seen as instances of subjects of predicates, but as filler elements whose occurrence is supposed to be governed by the stipulation in 3:(34) in the previous chapter, repeated here, which we have already shown to be problematic.

(1) 'It' occurs in the [NP,S] (=[DP,IP]) position if an external argument
    does not have to appear there.   (chapter 2:(34))

The treatment of moved DPs and other non-theta-marked DPs in Williams' work is very different. These DPs are seen as subjects of predicates, like base-generated theta-marked subjects, because they are the external arguments of the predicates, and the theory of theta-role assignment has to explain how a DP which is theta-marked as a direct object of V or as the subject of the complement of V can be the external argument of the maximal projection of V. We will examine Williams' theory in detail to show how theta-theory allows this.

The thematic account makes the predication relation dependent on theta-role assignment, and on the distinction between internal and external arguments introduced originally in Williams (1981). Williams (1983) gives the following definition of 'subject':

(2) *Subject as external argument*:
     The subject of a predicative phrase XP is the single argument of X that
     is located outside the maximal projection of X.

Both the thematic theory and the structural theory agree that 'subject' is always to be understood as 'subject of a predicate' and not as 'subject of a clause'. Both theories agree that a predicate is a maximal projection which, in virtue of its categorial properties, is not closed. But for Williams, the XP is open because it has an external theta-role to assign. The definition adopts and extends the theory of theta-role assignment of Stowell (1981) and Higginbotham (1985). As outlined in chapter 1, Higginbotham argues that a lexical head has a theta-grid which indicates the number of theta-roles that are to be assigned. No more than one theta-role may be marked as 'external', and thus no more than one theta-role can be assigned to a position outside the maximal projection of the head to which the grid is 'attached'. Williams claims that an unsaturated or unsatisfied slot in a theta-grid functions as a syntactic predicate variable; in Fregean terms, it is the presence of an unassigned theta-role which makes a constituent an unsaturated predicate. Following Higginbotham, grid features project with the head, and when a grid includes a theta-role or slot marked as external, the maximal projection will necessarily include a grid with an unsaturated slot and the whole XP will then constitute an open, monadic predicate. Its subject will be the DP saturating the external argument position, or, in Williams' terms, assigned the external argument role. In (3), the VP *sees Mary* is predicated of *John*, since the external theta-role of the head of the VP *sees* is assigned to *John*, which is outside the maximal projection of V.

(3) John sees Mary.

Thus Williams treats external argument roles as constituting predicate variables, with the monadicity of predicates following from the fact that only one theta-role can be assigned externally.

Williams (1987) gives a technical account of how this is guaranteed. He assumes that positions in the theta-grid are indexed, and that the index on the external argument position is bound by an index on the maximal projection of the head, since that argument cannot be assigned within the maximal projection. (3) has the representation in (4):

(4)   John$_i$ [see <agent$_i$ theme$_j$ > Mary$_j$]$_{VPi}$.

The grid for *see* is given in the angle brackets. The role indexed 'j' is internally assigned to *Mary*, and the index is bound by the index on the DP. The VP is then associated with a grid which contains one unassigned role indexed 'i' and this index is bound by the index on the VP. Williams calls this process of assigning the external role to the VP 'vertical binding', and he considers it as "a kind of lambda abstraction" (page 435). After this vertical binding, the VP can assign the theta-role it has acquired to a DP it governs; this is what predication consists of. A strict constraint that an XP may carry only one index, which, Williams argues, follows from the uniqueness condition of the theta-criterion, guarantees that only one position may be vertically bound; and this ensures that an XP may have only one external argument. Since the assignment of a vertically bound theta-role is predication, this also guarantees that a predicate will have only one subject. Furthermore, since a predicate is formed by vertically binding a theta-role in the grid of its head, XPs which have no external theta-role to assign are not considered predicates. For Williams, XPs like *seems that John is winning the race* or *(is) likely that he will win* are not predicates, and their relation to the pleonastic sentential subject is via the stipulation in (1) and not via predication. (Note that this means that not all sentences are instances of predication).

An important step in the account is distinguishing the 'assignment' of a theta-role, and the 'satisfaction' of a theta-position in the grid. When a theta-role is assigned internally, the argument to which it is assigned satisfies the grid position. But when a theta-role is assigned via vertical binding, the grid position isn't satisfied. Williams claims that only internal theta-role assignment and predication can satisfy grid positions and thus, while the VP is assigned the theta-role 'i', it does not satisfy that theta-role. This ensures that the process of theta-assignment does not stop at the stage of vertical binding, but continues to the predication stage.

This means that there are three operations affecting theta-role assignment:

    i. internal theta-role assignment
    ii. external theta-role assignment, or vertical binding
    iii. predication

Note that there may be more than one instance of vertical binding involved in a single predication relation. Thus (5a) has the representation (5b) (I don't include the theta-grid to make it simpler to read):

(5)   a. John seems sad.
      b. John$_i$ [seems [sad]$_{APi}$]$_{VPi}$.

Here, the AP *sad* vertically binds the external theta-role of the adjective *sad*, and the VP *seems sad* vertically binds the external theta-role of the AP and then assigns it to the subject; this is allowed since the VP has no external theta-role of its own. If the VP had its own external theta-role, then the sentence would be ungrammatical; the VP would vertically bind two theta-roles, indicating that it bore two theta-roles, and this would violate the theta-criterion. This accounts for the ungrammaticality of (6), where the VP has two indices:

(6)   *John [wants$_i$ [sad]$_j$]$_{ij}$.

(Note that for this to work, Williams (1987) needs to formulate a stronger form of the theta-criterion than the usual formulation discussed at the end of chapter 1, since in order to give the necessary restriction on vertical binding, the uniqueness criterion must apply to predicates as well as arguments.)

The difficulty occurs with passive and raising constructions, where the surface-structure subject is assigned a theta-role via the trace in the position from which it originated. Williams assumes that there is no actual movement, but that the effect of movement is derived by building chains, or their equivalents, linking a surface subject to a trace in the position which is assigned the thematic role. He assumes passive and raising structures like those in (7). In these structures, the verbs *visit* and *seem* head VPs which assign no thematic role to the subject, while the trace is assigned the theme role by *visit* in (7a) and the external theta-role by *smile* in (7b).

(7)   a. John$_i$ was [visited t$_i$ by a ghost]$_{VP}$.
      b. John$_i$ [seemed [t$_i$ [to smile]$_{VP}$]$_{IP}$]$_{VP}$.

In order to explain how the matrix subject is assigned an external theta-role by its VP sister, Williams makes use of the following stipulation:

(8)   DP trace can be assigned a theta-role, but cannot satisfy a theta-role (grid position).

Williams means by this that while NP, or rather DP, trace can be assigned a theta-role, this theta-role is still essentially considered 'unassigned', and the relevant position in the theta-grid is considered unsaturated. In order for the position to be saturated and the theta-criterion (i.e. the condition that each role must be assigned) to be satisfied, a role assigned to DP trace must be reassigned to the maximal projection via vertical binding, and then discharged via a predication relation with the subject. Thus, in (7a), the theta-role assigned to the trace of DP must be vertically bound on the VP, which then bears the same index as the trace, and this theta-role on the VP is reassigned via predication to the subject. The same operations occur in (7b), where the external theta-role of *smile* is vertically bound by VP and assigned to the trace in the embedded subject position. The index of the trace is then vertically bound by the sentence, or IP, then vertically bound again by the VP headed by *seemed*, and then finally assigned to the subject DP, which satisfies it. The appropriate representations are given in (9):

(9)   a. John$_i$ was [visited t$_i$ by a ghost]$_{VP_i}$.
      b. John$_i$ [seemed [t$_i$ [to smile]$_{VP_i}$]$_{IP_i}$]$_{VP_i}$.

The thematic part of passivisation, as in the standard government-binding approach, thus consists of preventing the external theta-role from being assigned, and the internal theme role gets externalised via vertical binding. Subject-to-subject raising consists of vertically binding a trace in an embedded [Spec,IP] by an index on the IP and then by an index on the VP which contains the IP; it is possible since the IP bears no other index. As for CP, we discussed earlier (in chapter 2:2.4) Williams' claim that CP has an external theta-role, the R role which all referential constituents have. CP thus bears an index of its own, and cannot vertically bind a DP trace within it. Since raising necessarily involves vertical binding, this correctly makes it impossible to raise out of CP.

The effect of (8) is to treat DP trace as introducing a predicate variable, on a par with unsaturated external argument roles. The reason why DP traces are necessary is apparently because of a structural constraint on grids and vertical binding, namely that only an external argument can be directly vertically bound by an index on XP. Vertical binding of internal arguments has to go via the trace, and in fact Williams (1987) makes the claim that the sole function of trace of DP movement is to license a predicate constituent in this way. Essentially, the procedure makes it possible to externalise an internal argument syntactically rather than lexically; Williams uses DP trace and vertical binding to externalise a thematic role rather than an argument, while in a 'standard' Chomskyan approach, DP movement moves a DP to subject position with the DP chain guaranteeing that it is still assigned its original thematic role. Williams claims that his treatment of trace replaces a theory of DP movement and DP chains, and shows, in support of this, that there are DP traces which cannot be derived by movement, for example in the DP in (10):

(10)   the man [believed t to have left].

The point is well-taken, but examples such as these are equally good evidence in support of a non-derivational theory of chain formation, such as that proposed in Rizzi (1986) instead of evidence for the thematic theory of predication.

Williams' theory predicts the ungrammaticality of (11), since the VP cannot vertically bind two DP traces:

(11)   *The slave$_i$/$_j$ [was given t$_i$ t$_j$]$_t$.

Finally, it is important to note that, if the theta-criterion is not to be violated, the stipulation in (8) can affect only DP trace, and not wh-trace. This is because in a VP which contains one DP trace and one wh-trace, such as (12), vertically binding both traces will result in a violation of the theta-criterion.

(12)   What$_i$ was John$_j$ [given t$_j$ t$_i$]$_{i,j}$.

Since Williams theory shares with mine the claim that predication is a syntactic relation between a maximal projection and its single argument which is defined at surface structure, it is useful to stop here and sum up exactly what his claims are and how they compare with the summary of my grammatical theory given in chapter 2:(56):

(13) i.   'subject' is subject of a predicate and not 'subject of a clause'. This claim is made by both theories. (see 2:(56.i))

ii. unsatisfied theta-roles provide predicate variables, thus every maximal projection containing an unsatisfied theta-role will be a predicate. This contrasts with the claim in (2:(56.ii) that 'syntactically open' and 'syntactic predicate' cannot be defined in terms of anything else.

iii. all predicates are monadic and this is ensured by the uniqueness clause of the theta-criterion. This contrasts with the claim in (2:56.iii) that the monadicity of syntactic predicates is not definable in terms of thematic properties.

iv. predication consists in an argument (the subject) being assigned an unsaturated theta-role by a predicate which is itself assigned that theta-role. This contrasts with the claim in (2:56.iii) that predication is a syntactic relation not reducible to any thematic relation.

v.   DP trace cannot satisfy a theta-role, and thus always constitutes a predicate variable. The grammatical theory in 2:(56) treats DP trace as no different from any other DP in terms of theta-assignment.

vi. a predicate cannot itself be theta-marked by a head; if it were, it would be assigned one index as an argument and a second index through vertically binding its own external argument and such a situation would violate the theta-criterion. The grammatical theory in 2:(56) also assumes that predicates can't be assigned a theta-role by a head.

4.2. DP TRACES AND PREDICATE VARIABLES

What Williams' thematic account of predication tries to do in a syntactic framework which allows movement is to maintain the position that the subject of a predication relation is a distinguished thematic argument of the predicate rather than being in some other relation with the head. The natural syntactic framework for a distinguished argument theory of predication is a categorial grammar kind of theory in which the subject is always base generated in its surface position and in which syntactic structure is a direct projection of the selectional requirements of head. In such a theory, it is very natural to define all grammatical relations in terms of ordered argument relations. But Williams doesn't use such a theory; he uses the syntactic aspects of theta-theory to define the notion of distinguished argument, and presents a quasi-lexical account of subject-predicate relations in a 'non-lexical' framework, using DP traces, and a movement theory of passive and raising constructions. The theory of vertical binding is developed to explain how a surface subject which has been moved to subject position can be the external argument of its predicate while being assigned a thematic role in its original position from which it was moved.

When we ask whether this theory works, we are also asking whether a distinguished argument theory can work in a syntactic framework which allows movement. I shall show that there are serious problems with Williams' theory which are inherent in any theta-based theory of predication, and that these show that the 'lexical' approach can't work in the kind of syntactic framework that Williams and I are using. This leaves open the question of whether the lexical, distinguished argument, approach works; but what we will see at this stage is that a lexical, distinguished argument theory of predication must go together with a categorial grammar type of syntactic theory.

There are three sets of problems for a movement theory which defines 'subject' in terms of external theta-role. The first is the examples in (14), where the subject is neither pleonastic, nor theta-marked by the head; nor linked to DP traces. This point is also made in Heycock (1991), from which (14a/c) are taken:

(14)   a. John is easy to please.
        b. The book is for you to read.
        c. John seems as if he is very tired.

In (14a/b), the predicate contains an operator headed chain which is assigned the object theta-role by *please* and *read* respectively. In (14c), discussed in Lappin (1983), the lexical DP is base generated in a position usually occupied by a pleonastic, implying that it is not theta-marked. These examples are a problem for any distinguished argument theory.

The second issue is the question of pleonastic subjects. As we saw in chapter 3:3.3, Williams assumes that pleonastics are outside the province of predication theory, and he has no way of accounting for where they occur. In particular, since he relies on the stipulation in (1) that sentences have subjects, and since his definition of sentence does not include the complements of *consider*-type verbs, he has no explanation for the distribution of pleonastics in what I have called small clause complements. One could try adding to the theory some notion of 'dummy theta-role' which certain heads could assign externally to pleonastic arguments. This is actually more complicated in a movement theory than in a categorial grammar approach, since it is crucial for DP movement that movement is to a non-theta-marked position. If we look at the examples in (15), then it is crucial for theta-theory that the lexical head *likely* assigns an internal theta-role to the propositional complement and does not assign an external theta-role.

(15)   a. It is likely that John will leave.
        b. [That John will leave]$_i$ is likely t$_i$.
        c. John$_i$ is likely [t$_i$ to leave].

This is because the theta-marked CP in (15b) and the theta-marked DP in (15c) can only be moved to positions which have no thematic restrictions on them, and are assigned no theta-role. In Williams' terms, if a predicate headed by *likely* assigns an external theta-role, then vertical binding of the theta-role assigned to the trace will not be possible since [likely ...]$_{AP}$ would then carry two thematic indices. For it to work, a pleonastic theta-role would have to be some kind of optional last resort theta-role which can be assigned by only certain heads and only if the assigning predicate bears no other index/assigns no other theta-role. This is ugly, but it would work.

But the real test for Williams' account is how it can get an argument which is generated in a predicate-internal position to be the external thematic argument of that predicate, appearing in surface subject position. Concretely, in (16), the subject of the sentence is theta-marked as the internal argument of the embedded verb, so in what sense is it assigned an external theta role by *seemed t$_i$ to have been forgotten t$_i$?*

(16)   John$_i$ seemed [t$_i$ to have been forgotten t$_i$]$_{IP}$.

This is what the theory of vertical binding is supposed to solve.

With respect to DP movement in passive and unaccusative constructions, it is not really possible to evaluate vertical binding as a technique nor to compare the predictions of the thematic and the grammatical theory of predication, since both theories categorise the VP immediately dominating the trace as a predicate, though on different grounds. However, the thematic and the grammatical approaches make different predictions about DP trace in raising constructions and about the predicate status of IPs. The thematic account predicts that when a DP is raised out of IP, the IP containing the DP trace will be a predicate. This is because the unsatisfied theta-role/index assigned to the trace will have to be vertically bound on the IP. The structural account claims that IP is not inherently a predicate, and cannot be converted into one via the trace. Traces convert CPs into predicates when they are part of an operator-bound chain, but since IP, unlike CP, has no position for a syntactic operator, this mechanism cannot be used. In the grammatical theory, the trace in the embedded [Spec, IP] (=[DP,S]) of (15) is a theta-marked subject, and this DP trace is the subject for its sister VP predicate, properly saturating it.

The issue rests then on the question of whether IP containing a DP trace is or is not a predicate. There are two arguments that it is not: (i) IP containing a DP trace can be a theta-marked argument; (ii) IP containing a DP trace does not occur in the same places as predicates do. The course of the discussion will also show that there are also some additional problems with the technique of vertical binding.

Firstly, Williams' theory predicts that IP containing DP trace should not be a theta-marked argument. Intuitively, we may feel there is something wrong with a constituent being a predicate and an argument, and in chapter 2:2.2 I ruled this out by making a basic structural distinction between open and closed constituents, and claiming that the constituents which saturate are not the ones which need saturating. The theory of theta-role assignment which Williams presents explicitly forbids allowing a predicate to be an argument; the uniqueness condition of the theta-criterion requires that an IP bearing the index of a vertically bound theta-role cannot itself be assigned a theta-role as an argument since then it would carry two different theta-indices. In general, since a predicate always bears the index of the role it has to assign, the theta-criterion will rule out its bearing the different index of a theta-role it is assigned. However, we find that an IP containing a DP trace can be a theta-marked argument, as (17) shows:

(17)   a. John$_i$ was believed [t$_i$ to have left]$_{IP}$.
        b. John$_i$ is likely [t$_i$ to have left]$_{IP}$.
        c. John$_i$ seems [t to have left]$_{IP}$.

Here [*t$_i$ to have left*] is the theta-marked single argument of *believed*, *likely* and *seems* respectively. The grammatical theory of predication has no problem with this, since the IP is a non-predicate argument of the matrix verb. *John* is assigned the external theta-role of *to have left* via the chain.

How could this problem be solved? One possibility is to relax the theta-criterion in such a way as to make (17) acceptable. But it is hard to see how this could be done in any perspicuous way. It could be argued that internal theta assignment and vertical binding are two different kinds of theta-relations, so that the fact that the IP has one index from vertical binding and one from internal theta-role assignment is not a problem. But, it is crucial to the unity of Williams' theory that all kinds of theta-assignment are essentially the same. More crucial is the fact that if IP in (17) both assigns and is assigned a theta-role, then the distinction between predicates and arguments which the theta-criterion embodies is blurred, and it is not possible to use it to rule out structures in which a DP is both an argument and a predicate. If theta-roles are assigned to IP predicates, it can naturally be extended to other selected predicates such as the complements of *feel* and *act*. But if we look at (18), where the DP *a fool* can be either a predicate or an argument, it seems very fundamental intuition that there is no reading where it is both.

(18)   John acted a fool.

On the theta-marked reading *act* expresses a relation between an individual and a role, and *a fool* gives the name of a part. We can tell that this is not a predicate reading, since we can get a universal quantifier there, as in (19):

(19)   John acted every male part in the play.

On the predicate reading of *a fool*, (18) has the reading that John acted as if he was a fool. But it is clear that it cannot have both readings at the same time. (18) illustrates that an internal argument cannot both be a predicate and be theta-marked; notice also that if the theory allowed an external theta-role to be assigned to a predicate, we would lose the correct prediction that predication is a non-recursive relation. To sum up, in the language of type theory, allowing an expression to assign and to be assigned a theta-role is equivalent to saying that the expression is of two different types at the same time, and phrased like that, it seems clear that this is not a move we would want to make.

The only other way that (17) can be saved is to propose that when IP is a predicate it is not assigned a theta-role. Under this account passive *believe* would have thematic properties distinct from active *believe* since it would not take a propositional complement but a predicate, and *likely* and *seem* would have different subcategorisation requirements depending on whether they also took IP or CP complements. But a central tenet of the raising analysis of these heads, and the crucial difference between a government-binding account and those like Chierchia (1984) and Jacobson (1990), is precisely that it allows these heads to have the same selectional requirements in (17) and in their counterparts in (20). The head selects thematically for a propositional complement, and the process of CP deletion triggered by the [−tense] feature on the selected complement allows raising to take place.

(17) a. John$_i$ was believed [t$_i$ to have left]$_{IP}$.
      b. John$_i$ is likely [t$_i$ to have left]$_{IP}$.
      c. John$_i$ seems [t$_i$ to have left]$_{IP}$.

(20) a. It was believed [that John had left].
      b. It was likely [that John had left].
      c. It seemed [that John had left].

If the selectional/thematic properties of raising verbs and adjectives is not kept constant across the active/passive and raised/non-raised distinction, then there is no good reason to maintain a movement account of these constructions at all.

The above discussion gave examples of so-called predicate IPs which occur in theta-marked positions. The second issue is whether IP occurs in normal, non-theta-marked, predicate positions. This is very difficult to check, since non-selected predicate positions are open to *to*-infinitivals, and in many contexts it is very difficult to distinguish between a *to*-infinitival and an IP with a trace in subject position. In principle (21a) could have the structure in either (21b) or (21c):

(21) a. I believe [John to be a fool].
      b. I believe [John$_{DP}$ [to be a fool]$_{VP}$]$_{IP}$.
      c. I believe [John$_{DP}$ [t to be a fool]$_{IP}$]$_{SC}$.

I can't see any reason to rule (21c) out, but neither is there any evidence that it is a possible structure. However, we can ask whether IP can occur in a complement position in which ordinary predicates appear where no theta-role is assigned. Assuming that the presence of an argument CP is an indication that a theta-role is assigned, we look for a head which selects predicates but not CP complements. Such a head is *act*, which can take AP, NP/DP, and PP predicates, but not IP:

(22) a. John acted [foolish]$_{AP}$.
      b. John acted [a fool]$_{DP}$.
      c. John acted [out of his depth]$_{PP}$.
      d. *John$_i$ acted [t$_i$ to be a fool]$_{IP}$.

Act does not take a CP or a bare VP complement either, but then no non-auxiliary verbal or adjectival head selects a bare VP complement, and predicate CPs appear only in the complements of adjectives like *ready* and *easy*, which select CP arguments or CP predicates, but no other category of complements. So *act* does take the full collection of predicates available to a head of this type, but as (22d) shows, IP cannot appear there. If we say that IP is not a predicate, then conditions on DP headed chains rules this out. The trace is in a chain with the matrix subject which is assigned an external theta-role by *act*, and since the trace is also assigned a theta-role, the chain is assigned two roles, which is not allowed. This is the well known consequence of raising DP to a theta-marked position. (22a–c) are acceptable because a complex predicate has been formed out of the V and its predicate complement by a process which we will discuss in the next chapter, and the VP assigns a complex external theta-role to the matrix subject. The crucial point is that if $[\dots t \dots]_{IP}$ is not a predicate, then there is no reason to expect (22d) to be licensed by the same process as the other sentences in (22), and in fact it is not. But for Williams' theory this is a problem. His theory predicts that vertical binding of an unassigned theta-role must occur in each of the examples; in (22a–c) because the head of the complement predicate has an external theta-role to assign, and in (22d) because the theta-role assigned to the trace must be vertically bound and thus counts as an external theta-role in exactly the same way as in the other cases. Williams' theory of vertical binding will have to be relaxed in any case to allow (22a–c), since it is clear that in these cases the VP will have to assign the external theta-role of both *act* and of the embedded predicate. Williams made this illegal via the theta-criterion, since in this case the VP carries two thematic indices, but in complex predication we will presumably have to allow two indices to 'merge'. (But then, something else will have to explain the ungrammaticality of (6) (repeated here):

(6)   *John [wants$_i$ [sad]$_j$]]$_{ij}$)

Since what is involved in the 'merging' of theta-indices is complex predicate formation, as I'll discuss in the next chapter, allowing it is not per se a problem. But, if such a process is allowed, and if it does not apply in (22d), then this is clear evidence that a theta-role assigned to a trace cannot be vertically bound like any other external theta-role, and is thus not an external argument. And if having an external argument is the criterion for being a predicate, then $[\dots t \dots]_{IP}$ is not a predicate.

Williams tries to protect his theory of vertical binding in these kinds of contexts by looking at examples like (23a–c), and claiming that where it looks like double vertical binding has taken place, the matrix verb is in fact a verb which assigns no external theta-role, a claim which he supports by (23d), where the matrix subject is filled by a pleonastic.

(23)   a. John feels [foolish]$_{AP}$.
        b. John feels [a fool]$_{DP}$.
        c. John feels [out of his depth]$_{PP}$.
        d. It feels that something is wrong.

This cannot be the explanation, since *acts* clearly assigns a theta-role to its external argument. All of (22a–c) entail that John acted, and there is no evidence that *act* ever assigns a pleonastic subject:

(24) *It acts that John is foolish.

In any case, if *feel* doesn't assign an external theta role, then Williams cannot explain why (25) is ungrammatical:

.(25) *John$_i$ feels [t$_i$ to be a fool]$_{IP}$

Vertical binding of more than one theta-role is going to be possible whenever a lexical head which assigns an external theta-role includes another predicate which also assigns an external theta-role, and in chapter 5 we will examine many cases of adjunct predication where this occurs, for example, in (26):

(26) a. John drove drunk.
      b. She left the room angry at herself.
      c. Mary ate the carrots raw.

What we in fact see is that the distribution of [… t …]$_{IP}$ has nothing to do with the licensing of predicates. These IPs occur in a theta-marked position, irrespective of whether this is a position which can also contain a bare predicate, as long as the head which selects them satisfies two conditions: it does not assign an external theta-role, and it allows CP deletion. Thus *unlikely*, which takes a theta-marked complement but no predicate complement, allows raising, but *possible*, with the same selectional properties does not:

(27) a. It is unlikely that John will leave.
      b. *John is unlikely happy/a fool/out of his mind.
      c. John$_i$ is unlikely [t$_i$ to leave]$_{IP}$.

(28) a. It is possible that John will leave.
      b. *John is possible happy/a fool/out of his mind.
      c. *John$_i$ is possible [t$_i$ to leave]$_{IP}$.

This shows that the possibility of getting [… t …]$_{IP}$ as a complement is not dependent on theta-assigning properties of the IP, or any other predicate properties, but on the appropriate constraints on DP movement.

In sum, the evidence does not support the claim that trace is a predicate variable, forming a predicate out of an non-predicate. Examples like (17) show that when an IP complement contains a DP trace, the IP remains the argument of a head, and the discussion of (22) shows that there is evidence against treating DP trace as a mechanism for passing a theta-role up to a containing predicate to be assigned via predication.

There is a further empirical problem with the claim that the function of DP trace is to make an internal argument available for vertical binding and external assignment via predication. Williams (1987) argues that the theory of predication can account for the distribution of DP trace entirely; its sole function is to allow an argument assigned by an embedded head, or maximal projection, to be assigned via a higher predicate which contains it. But he does not discuss the distribution of traces which are bound by pleonastics and do not enter into theta-relations at all. (29) gives examples of such traces:

(29) a. It$_i$ seems [t$_i$ to be likely that John will leave].
      b. It$_i$ happened [t$_i$ to turn out that they arrived on time].
      c. It$_i$ is certain [t$_i$ to seem that he did it on purpose].
      d. It$_i$ is likely [t$_i$ to appear that senators are sincere].

In (29a) the VP headed by *seems* assigns no external theta-role and is not, in thematic terms, a predicate. However, it must contain a DP trace as the subject of the infinitival. The position cannot be filled by PRO, which needs to be theta-marked, therefore the only possibility is a DP trace, and this must be licensed by being bound by the matrix pleonastic. Any suggestion that there is simply no subject there is rebutted by comparing these examples with (30) (=chapter 3:(32c)) from Heycock (1991), which forms a minimal contrast with (29d):

(30)   *It is important [(t) to appear that senators are sincere].

(30) is ungrammatical, as we argued already in chapter 3:3.2, because the embedded CP lacks a licensed subject. In contrast with the examples in (29), *impossible* is not a raising predicate and does not delete CP. The effect is that a DP trace inserted as the subject of *to appear* cannot be properly bound.

The traces in (29) are not theta-marked and do not free a theta-role for vertical binding. In Williams' terms the constituent in which the DP trace appears is not a predicate at all, and the thematic theory of predication, which treats DP traces as thematic predicate variables, cannot account for why these traces are necessary, nor why they must be locally bound. Chains, a purely syntactic mechanism, do the job adequately. So, a theory which does not recognise traces in passive as licensed through chains would require two separate licensing mechanisms for DP trace depending on whether or not it appeared in theta-marked positions.

Williams treatment of DP traces is connected to his concern, expressed in his 1987 paper, that there is apparent redundancy in syntactic theories which license 'displaced' DPs both by predication and by DP chains. Vertical binding is supposed to remove this redundancy by unifying both theta-assignment and predication. But, given what we know about the nature of syntax, this 'duplication' should not be a problem. A displaced, raised DP is theta-marked via its DP chain and is also the subject of its predicate. An element frequently has to meet more than one licensing condition – for example, the Case Filter is a condition on all lexical DPs whether or not they are theta-marked, and whether or not they are internal or external arguments. Precisely because syntax is not a 'pure' projection of theta-relations but is subject to syntactic constraints such as the predication condition, constituents must enter into non-theta-based syntactic relations too. Displaced arguments stand out because they perform two syntactic functions in the sentence; they saturate a predicate which is a syntactic sister, and they also satisfy a theta-role canonically assigned to a different position from the one they occupy. The two licensing relations that such a DP enters into, subject of the predicate and head of the chain, are not an indication of redundancy in the theory, but rather an indication of this double function of the constituent in the sentence.

4. CONCLUSIONS

We have seen that the thematic theory of predication doesn't deal with a number of issues which the grammatical theory of prediction explains. These include the occurrence of non-thematic predicates in small clause 'consider' complements and in predicate ellipsis constructions, the distribution of obligatory pleonastics, the relation between raising and pleonastic licensing, and the environments in which it is possible to raise out of IP. But here I want to sum up the more general differences between the theories.

The structural and thematic accounts of predication relations express fundamentally different claims about the nature of syntactic generalisations and the semantic interpretation of syntactic structures. The structural approach claims that the distinction between open and closed syntactic constituents is a syntactic primitive, and the saturation of an open constituent by a closed one, predication, is a primitive relation. As we shall see in chapter 6, syntactic predicates will be interpreted as expressions of the form (31), but, as we will argue there, the fact that an expression has this form tells us nothing about its internal structure.

(31) $\lambda x.\alpha$.

I shall argue that the abstraction operation which introduces 'λx' in (31) is an operation which happens automatically at the XP predicate level, and that it occurs independent of whether the expression a contains a free x variable. This allows for situations where the lambda abstraction is vacuous, and I will use this in chapter 7 to explain the semantic relevance of pleonastics which occur as subjects of predicate expressions where α does not contain a free variable.

Williams' theta-based theory of predication uses unassigned theta-roles as the syntactic elements which create predicates by introducing predicate variables into the semantic representation. He claims essentially that the logical structure of a predicate is (32):

(32) $\lambda x.P(x)$.

His claim is that the x variable in $P(x)$ is the translation of an unsatisfied theta-role, and that lambda abstraction is the semantic correlate of the syntactic operation of vertical binding.

The real differences between the theories are about the treatment of pleonastics, which the thematic theory ignores and which we will come back to at length in chapter 7, and in the treatment of raising constructions like (33).

(33)   John$_i$ was [likely [t$_i$ to be late]$_{IP}$]$_{AP}$.

The grammatical theory treats *be likely t to be late* as a predicate because of its categorial status, and assumes that *John* is not theta-marked via predication, but via its relation with the trace with which it forms a chain. For the thematic theory, *be likely t to be late* is a predicate because it contains an unassigned theta-role, represented by the trace, which is assigned via predication to the matrix subject. Since the unassigned theta-role is contained in an IP, IP itself must be a predicate which passes up its predicate properties and is responsible for the AP headed by *likely* and then the VP headed by *be* being predicates. But, first, (22), repeated here, showed that there is no way to treat [... t ...]$_{IP}$ as a predicate parallel to AP or any other XP, which explains its distribution in predicate complement positions:

(22)   a.   John acted [foolish]$_{AP}$.
       b.   John acted [a fool]$_{DP}$.
       c.   John acted [out of his depth]$_{PP}$.
       d.   *John$_i$ acted [t$_i$ to be a fool]$_{IP}$.

And second, our discussion of (17) showed that [... t ...]$_{IP}$ must be able to satisfy argument slots in a theta-grid.

(17)   a.   John$_i$ was believed [t$_i$ to have left]$_{IP}$.
       b.   John$_i$ is likely [t$_i$ to have left]$_{IP}$.
       c.   John$_i$ seems [t$_i$ to have left]$_{IP}$.

So, all in all, there is no evidence for treating these IPs as predicates.

But (17) has implications beyond Williams' thematic theory of subjects and predication. The problem raised by (17) is inherent in any theory which treats [... t ...]$_{IP}$ as a constituent which can be a propositional complement of a head. The thematic approach is really the best worked out account of 'subject' as a distinguished thematic argument of a predicate. Since any 'movement' theory of raising is going to treat IP complements as arguments, the problem raised by (17) is going to arise in any 'distinguished argument' theory worked out in a movement framework. Thus the conclusion is that an 'abstract' theory of syntax, which allows movement, either actual or virtual, is forced to reject a distinguished argument theory of subjects.

A preference for abstract syntax or non-movement syntax is not a good reason for adopting one or another theory of predication; as I said at the beginning of chapter 2, the grammatical theory and the distinguished argument, or lexical theory have very different ideas about what the predication relation is, and we will come back to that in detail in later chapters. But it is a far from trivial point that the distinguished argument theory cannot be worked out together with a movement theory of syntax.

5. APPENDIX: VP INTERNAL-SUBJECTS

As mentioned before, I have not explored data or formulated my account in a framework which postulates VP-internal subjects. Whether or not there is generally a VP-internal syntactic subject position in English seems to me still to be a very open question. I assume that *make* and *let* do have 'bare VP complements', as in (34), with a subject adjoined to a VP:

(34)   I made/let [John [leave]$_{VP}$]$_{VP'}$].

But that is a long way from assuming that any such VP' level is a complement of Infl in standard inflected sentence, as in (35):

(35)   [John$_i$ [Infl [t$_i$ [saw Mary]$_{VP}$]$_{VP'}$]$_{I'}$]$_{IP}$.

In this appendix, I'm not going to argue the case either way, but I do want to make two points. First, although I have made my claims while assuming that the subject is base generated in [Spec,IP], the arguments transfer straightforwardly to an account where the external argument of head of VP is base-generated inside the VP. It is no easier to justify the distribution of pleonastics, the occurrence of non-thematic XP predicates, or the occurrence of raising of and from IP in a VP-internal subject theory than it is in the framework used here. Heycock (1991) argues this carefully, showing that in these structures, as our theory would predict, the predication condition applies within both VP and IP. Diesing, Santorini and Heycock, have each in a number of papers, argued for a VP internal subject position in Germanic languages, and here too Heycock has argued that the predicate saturation condition must be met at both levels. In particular, what Heycock shows is that pleonastics occur in what are assumed to be VP-subject positions in these analyses.

The second point is a caveat about the type of evidence brought in favour of VP-internal subjects in English. It has been argued that it is conceptually pleasing to base generate the external argument of a lexical head within the maximal projection of the head, and that raising the argument outside the XP leaves a trace which functions as a predicate variable. Thus, in (35), the trace in [Spec,VP] indicates a predicate variable which allows the VP to be translated as a predicate. But exactly what we have seen in section 4:3 of this chapter is that DP traces do not constitute predicate variables, and what the earlier sections of the chapter show is that a DP trace, or even an unassigned theta-role, is not necessary for an XP to be a predicate. The argument that DP trace in [Spec,VP] indicates a predicate variable postulates a transparency in the relation between syntactic structure and semantic structure which the facts about the language do not allow us to maintain.

CHAPTER 5

THE SYNTACTIC FORMS OF PREDICATION

5.1. INTRODUCTION

In chapter 2 I argued for a syntactic predication relation which cannot be reduced to a thematic relation. I argued that this syntactic relation is a saturation relation between a predicate and an argument, its subject, and I claimed that there was a locality relation between subject and predicate, namely that subject and predicate have to c-command each other. The discussion in chapter 2 concentrated on primary, or clausal, predication relations, and in particular on the predication relation within small clause complements of *consider* and other ECM verbs, where the predication relation is realised in its simplest form. By this I mean that small clause predication has two basic characteristics, and the predication relation is more complicated if either of these properties is changed. Small clause predication is **direct** predication, by which I mean that the subject and predicate c-command each other, and it is **primary** predication, which means that the subject and predicate form a constituent. If either of these properties does not hold of a predication relation, then we need to say something more than what was said in chapter 2.

This chapter examines a variety of forms of the predication relation, and focuses on a number of cases where the predication relation is in some sense less straightforward. The first set of examples are cases where the predicate does not c-command its subject, and is **indirectly** predicated of its subject by becoming part of a complex predicate. I discuss the process by which complex predicate formation takes place, a process which I call **predicate absorption**, and examine how it works in three different contexts. In section 2, I will discuss the first two instances: selected predicate complements such as *foolish* in (1a) and the CP complement in (1b), and adjunct predicates such as *drunk* in (1c). Section 3 will discuss the complex predicate formation involved in the relation between Inflection and VP, as illustrated in standard matrix clauses in (1d), which has the underlying structure (1d'). (Note that (1b) is an example of recursive embedding: the CP is the complement of *available* and the predicate *available for you to read* is the complement of *be*, and the VP headed by *be* is the complement of I'):

(1) a. John [acted **foolish**].
     b. The books [are [available **for you to read t**]]
     c. Bill [drove the car **drunk**].
     d. John ran.
     d'. [John [PAST [run]$_{VP}$]$_{I'}$]$_{IP}$.

100

I shall show that given the appropriate definition of predicate absorption, the mutual c-command condition on predication can be maintained. Mutual c-command constraints hold between the complex predicate and its subject, though not between the absorbed predicate and the subject. I show that there are structural conditions on when absorption can occur, and that the absorption process is not restricted to theta-assigning predicates. It must thus be a syntactic process, and distinct from a thematic process such as the mechanism of theta-identification proposed in Higginbotham (1985), or the process of complex predicate formation on argument structure of Butt (1995). Section 4 contains a discussion of primary predication and the Extended Projection Principle in the light of the analysis of Inflection and I', and section 5 discusses direct instances of **secondary predication**. These are structures where the mutual c-command condition is straightforwardly satisfied, but where the subject and predicate do not form a constituent. We call these **secondary predication** structures, and they are represented by the examples in (2), which are familiar from chapter 2:

(2)   a. Mary drinks her coffee$_i$ **black$_i$**.
       b. They ate the carrots$_i$ **raw$_i$**.

In these cases, there will be no syntactic complex predicate formation, or absorption, and secondary predicates such as *black* and *raw* in (2) will be directly predicated of their subjects. I shall not treat these cases as instances of complex predication: predicate absorption will be possible – and required – only when the resulting complex predicate forms a syntactic constituent, as in the examples in (1). I will thus disagree with theories such as Neeleman (1994), in which the V + secondary predicates in examples such as (2), as well as the V + small clause predicates discussed in chapter 2, are treated as complex predicates. Neeleman (1994) shows that there is good syntactic reason to treat these as complex predicates in Dutch, but in English this is not the case. In English, these V + predicates do not form constituents, and do not behave syntactically as constituents. In chapter 2:2.3, I already argued that complements of ECM verbs are best treated as small clauses, and here I shall show that while secondary predicates are unlike small clause predicates in that they do not form constituents with their subjects, they also differ from the subject adjuncts that I treat as indirect predicates. Finally we briefly mention adverbs as a syntactic category which does not fall under the scope of predication theory at all.

The general claim of this chapter will be to develop the point made in chapter 2, that predication is a syntactic and not a thematic or theta-based relation. We begin with a discussion of predicate absorption and the process of complex predicate formation.

5.2. Predicate absorption and complex predicate formation

5.2.1. *The process of absorption*

There are many occurrences of XP predicates which are not in positions where they can be saturated by DP subjects which they c-command. We'll leave aside for the moment the question of predicates embedded under Inflection, and look at the examples given in (1a/b), which are repeated here with structures assigned.

(3)   a. John [acted [**foolish**]$_{AP}$]$_{VP}$.
      b. The books [are [available [**for you to read** t]$_{CP}$]$_{AP}$]$_{VP}$.
      c. Bill [[drove the car]$_{V'}$ **drunk**]$_{AP}$]$_{VP}$.

In each example the predicate in bold is contained within a maximal projection which does not include a possible subject for it. (3a) and (3b) are cases where the embedded predicate is selected by the head which is its sister. In (3a) *foolish* is selected by *act*, and contained within the VP *acted foolish*, which is predicated of *John*. The DP *John* is intuitively the subject of the AP, since it was he who seemed in some way foolish, though (4a) does not entail that John was foolish. (He may have acted foolish out of some very intelligent motive, as for example in (4):

(4)   Wisely, David acted foolish before Avimelech.)

However, [DP,IP] cannot be the local subject of the AP, since it is outside the VP and the AP does not c-command it. Nor do we want it to be the local subject of the AP; if it were, then *foolish* would be directly predicated of *John* and that would imply that we should get direct semantic predication too. But then (3a) and (4) should entail that John (or David) had the foolish property, which they don't. Note that (4a) is not synonymous with 'John acted foolishly', and the AP cannot be treated as if it were an adverb. Also, as we noted in chapter 4, *act* shows no signs of being a raising or unaccusative verb, so it cannot be argued that *foolish* is predicated of a trace in object position of the VP. *Act* never occurs with a pleonastic subject, and its French and Italian counterparts, *agir* and *agire*, appear with *avoir* and *avere* respectively, unlike unaccusative verbs which take *être* or *essere*. (Choice of auxiliary is argued to be a foolproof test of accusativity/unaccusativity in Italian, and a good indication of it in French. See Rosen (1984), Burzio (1986), Levin and Rappaport Hovav (1995), and references there.) (3b) gives another example of a predicate selected as a complement, which does not c-command it subject. We have what has been analysed (Chomsky 1982, Browning 1987) as a null operator construction, with the S-structure in (5); *available* selects a CP predicate complement, and the embedded sentential predicate contains an empty object bound by a null operator in Spec of CP.

(5)   The books are [available [Op$_i$ [for you to read t$_i$]]$_{CP}$]$_{AP}$.

Again, there is no subject which the embedded predicate c-commands. However, the implied subject of the sentential predicate is the matrix subject *the books*, since it gives the value of the empty object. The structural issue arises again with respect to the whole AP *available for you to read*, which is itself a complement of *be*, and thus does not c-command *the books* either. (3c) is an instance of an adjunct predicate which does not c-command its subject. Here, *Bill* is clearly the subject of *drunk*, since the sentence entails that he had the 'drunk' property at the relevant time. Andrews (1982) shows that adjunct predicates like these must be part of the VP since they are moved and deleted in operations applying to VP.

(6) a. Drive the car drunk though John did, ...
     b. Bill drove the car drunk and so did Bill (drive the car drunk/*drive the car).
     c. What Bill did was drive the car drunk.

What occurs in these examples is that the predicate is absorbed into the predicate expression which immediately dominates it, forming a complex syntactic predicate. The complex predicate is constrained by the predicate-licensing condition in (14) from chapter 2, repeated here:

(7) Every syntactic predicate must be syntactically saturated.

The larger predicate must thus be properly saturated by a subject which it c-commands. If it is, then the embedded predicate will satisfy the licensing condition in (7) by being absorbed into a properly saturated predicate. We say that embedded, absorbed predicates are 'indirectly saturated'. Thus in (4a), the predicate *foolish* is absorbed into the VP which immediately dominates it, and because this VP is properly saturated by the matrix subject *John* (we are still, for the moment, ignoring Inflection), the AP is indirectly saturated and indirectly satisfies (7). A similar process occurs in (3b–c).

We can represent this indirect saturation relation in the syntax by indexing in the following way. Assume that a predicate is indexed, and that the relation of saturation, or linking, is represented by coindexing a predicate with its subject. Absorption can be represented by the passing up of the index of the embedded predicate to the dominating predicate, as in (8):

(8) John_i [acted [foolish]$_{\text{AP}i}$]$_{\text{VP}i}$.

Notice that while this passing up of an index looks superficially like vertical binding, its purpose and effect is different. The point of vertical binding was to ensure that the external argument of an embedded predicate got passed up to a XP that dominated it on the condition that the dominating XP did not have an external argument to assign. The point of absorption is to identify the unsaturated position of an embedded predicate (as we will see, whether or not the predicate assigns an external theta-role) with the unsaturated position of a dominating predicate, independent of whether either of them is a thematic position. The mechanism of complex predicate formation is thus syntactically parallel to Higginbotham's (1985) account of theta-identification, though, as we will see below, theta-identification identifies only unassigned theta-roles, while we are concerned here with unsaturated syntactic positions, regardless of their thematic properties. Both have in common that the goal is to enable embedded predicates which do not c-command their subjects to satisfy a relation with that subject. They are thus very different in goal from theories such as Neeleman's (Neeleman 1994) which argues that secondary predicates and ECM predicates in Dutch are best treated as forming complex predicates with the matrix heads.

The percolation of indices that we are discussing here is a syntactic mechanism which guarantees that an unsaturated argument position is saturated by a syntactic argument. As I said in chapter 2, I assume that a denotation of a syntactic predicate will have a semantic relation with the denotation of the argument which saturates it, but what exactly that semantic relation is will depend on a variety of syntactic and semantic factors. Where the absorbed predicate is selected by a lexical head, the semantic relation between predicate and subject will be dictated by the meaning of the selecting head. Thus, in (8), the indexing indicates that the denotation of *John* will be the argument which saturates the variable position in the denotation of *foolish*, but the syntactic configuration indicates that the foolish property is not being directly predicated of the individual John, but only indirectly via the complex predicate. Because *foolish* is selected by the head *act*, the nature of the predication will be determined by the meaning of *act*. I shall argue in chapter 6 that verbs of this type are modal, and that (8) means something like 'in all worlds in which the way in which John acted reflects reality, John has the foolish property'.

A more complex syntactic example in which this syntactic percolation ensures that the right DP is identified as the value for an unsaturated predicate position is (1b), which is indexed as in (9):

(9)   The books$_i$ [are [available [Op$_i$ [for$_i$ you to read t$_i$]]$_{CPi}$]$_{APi}$]$_{VPi}$

Assume, following Chomsky (1986a,b), that a head and its maximal projection bear the same index and that there is also Spec-head agreement. We want the subject of the complex predicate to give the value for the empty object in the VP of the absorbed predicate. Indexing proceeds in the following steps: (i) a trace is coindexed with the head of the chain that it is in. This coindexes the operator with the trace; (ii) a specifier is coindexed with its head. This coindexes the Operator with the Comp *for*; (iii) a head passes its index to its maximal projection, thus the CP predicate and its head bear the same index; (iv) absorption results in the embedded predicate and the dominating predicate sharing the same index; thus the index of the original gap is passed up to the predicate headed by *available*; (v) absorption occurs again with the same index passed up to the predicate headed by *be*; (vi) predication assigns *the books*, the subject of the dominating predicate, the same index as the predicate bears. As a result we get the indexed structure in (9), where the subject and the trace in the embedded predicate carry the same index. Since the value of the empty object is dependent on the subject, this is the result we want. Again, the syntactic indexing indicates which DP will contribute the value for the empty position, but the semantic relation between predicate and subject is dictated by the selecting head. *Available* is one of the adjectives that selects a CP predicate complement, where the predicate has a 'purposive' function, which limits the availability. Thus we get discourses like (10):

(10) The books are available for you to read. They are not available for you to take out of the library.

The first sentence in (10) does not entail that the books are (generally) available; the CP limits the degree of availability. (Note that I am differing here from Bach (1982), which treats the complement of *available* like any other purpose clause. But in adjunct purpose clauses, the addition of the adjunct does not affect the entailment relations. (11a) and (11b) both entail that I brought the books, and (11c) entails that I have the books:

(11) a. I brought the books.
      b. I brought the books for you to read (not for you to draw pictures on).
      c. I have the books for you to read (not for you to take home).)

I assume for the moment that absorption into a predicate headed by *be* does not affect the semantic interpretation, though we shall see in chapter 10 that this is not the case.

An absorbed predicate is thus indirectly saturated by the subject of the complex predicate. We define indirect saturation formally as follows:

(12) *Indirect saturation*
      A predicate α is *indirectly saturated* by β iff there is a predicate γ such that γ directly dominates α, and γ is predicated of, or directly saturated by β, or γ is indirectly saturated by β.

This definition allows for predicate absorption to be recursive: a predicate can be absorbed into a complex predicate which is itself absorbed into a dominating predicate. There are many instances of recursive absorption in addition to the recursive embedding in (3b), where the predicate headed by *available* is itself a complement of the copula. (13) shows that recursive embedding can occur with multiple embeddings of lexical predicates too:

(13) The children sound ready for you to put t to bed.

I analyse *sound* as selecting a predicate complement and not as a verb which allows raising to subject from a non-tensed propositional complement. This is because despite the parallel between (14a) and (15a), *sound* does not display paradigmatic raising properties, as the contrast with *seem* in examples (14b–c)/(15b–c) show:

(14) a. John sounded sad.
      b. *John sounded to be sad.
      c. *It sounded that John was sad.

(15)   a.   John seemed sad.
     b.   John$_i$ seemed t$_i$ to be sad.
     c.   It seemed that John was sad.

In (13), the CP predicate *for you to put t to bed* is absorbed into the complex predicate *ready for you to put t to bed*, which itself is the absorbed into the VP predicate headed by *sounds*.

Exactly the same process is involved in (3c), repeated here with the appropriate indices, where the predicate is an adjunct.

(16)   Bill$_i$ [[drove the car]$_V$ **drunk**]$_{AP_i}$]$_{VP_i}$.

The difference between this example and the cases where the absorbed predicate is selected is that here the interpretation will have to be by some general rule, and the semantic relation between absorbed predicate and subject is not determined by the lexical meaning of the selecting head. Thus we see that in the examples discussed above, the sentences did not necessarily entail that the subject had the property denoted by the absorbed predicate. In (3a), *John acted foolish* clearly didn't entail that John was foolish. But (16) does entail that Bill was drunk, and this will turn out to be a general property of adjunct predicates, as we will see in the next chapter.

The obvious question to ask is: why introduce a mechanism of predicate absorption, instead of relaxing the locality condition so that the predicate need not c-command the subject, though the subject would still have to c-command the predicate. (Williams (1980) suggests in a footnote that weakening the locality conditions is the appropriate way to take care of such clearly complex predicates as *became rich*, although his discussion of vertical binding in Williams (1987) implies that this is only possible if the head of the higher predicate does not assign a theta-role, as we discussed in the previous chapter.) Under the weaker locality conditions, the embedded predicate would be directly saturated by the c-commanding subject.

The answer is that two facts are correctly predicted by the absorption account, but do not get an explanation under the weaker locality conditions. The first fact is that the embedded predicate and the dominating predicate must have the same subject. Thus the absorption account rules out the impossible reading of (17), where *ready* and the CP have different subjects, although the complex predicate as a whole can be predicated of either the subject or the object:

(17)   The children left their friends [ready [for Mary to put t to bed]$_{CP}$]$_{AP}$.

The complex predicate *ready for Mary to put to bed* can be directly predicated of *their friends*, which it c-commands, with the reading that their friends are ready for Mary to put them (the friends) to bed, or it can be absorbed into the V headed by *left* and be indirectly saturated by the subject in which case (17) means that when the children left they were ready for Mary to put them (the children) to bed. The readings which are impossible are where the CP predicate is predicated of a DP which is not the subject of the AP headed by *ready*. The sentence cannot mean that the children were ready for Mary to put their friends to bed, or that their friends were ready for Mary to put the children to bed. If the predicate AP headed by *ready* and the CP *for Mary to put t to bed* were directly saturated independently by a c-commanding subject, these readings should be possible.

The second prediction of the definition of absorption is that an embedded predicate can be predicated of a subject which it does not c-command only if it is directly embedded within another predicate that can be directly saturated. If a non-predicate XP immediately dominates the embedded predicate and intervenes between it and a higher predicate, absorption into the higher predicate cannot take place. If a predicate could be directly saturated by a c-commanding DP, then this constraint should not apply.

It is hard to evaluate this prediction because the relevant plausible constructions occur rarely. A construction which does seem to bear out the prediction is nominal degree phrases. We turn to an analysis of these in the next section.

5.2.2. *Degree phrases*

Degree phrases are maximal projections headed by degree words such as *too*, *enough*, and *so*. Detailed analyses of these phrases have been given in Bresnan (1973), Jackendoff (1977), Abney (1987), Rothstein (1991). I assume here that degree heads are functional heads that select two complements; an XP and a CP or 'extent clause'. The XP is most frequently an AP, but may also be a DP or a PP. Thus in (18), the degree phrase in bold is headed by *too*, which selects an AP *stubborn*, and an extent CP *for you to do anything to help him*.

(18)   John is **too stubborn for you to do anything to help him**.

The sentence predicates of the individual denoted by *John* the property of having the stubbornness property to the extent that it is not possible for you to do anything to help him.

What is particularly interesting to us here is that, as argued in Rothstein (1991), the extent CP has the rare characteristic that it can be either a predicate or a non-predicate. Thus both (19a) and (19b), with the structures in (19a'/19b'), contain grammatical degree phrases:

(19)   a.   John is too stubborn for you to help him.
       a'.   John is [too [stubborn]$_{AP}$ [for you to help him]$_{CP}$]$_{DegP}$.
       b.   John is too stubborn for you to help t.
       b'.   John is [too [stubborn]$_{AP}$ [for you to help t]$_{CP}$]$_{DegP}$.

In (19a) the extent clause is propositional, and is licensed solely by being one of the selected complements of *too*, but in (19b) the selected CP is a predicate and needs to be licensed as a predicate by saturation as well. The subject of the predicate will give the value of the empty object, and intuitions about the meaning thus tell us that the subject of the predicate is *John*. The CP predicate is licensed because it is absorbed into the degree phrase and indirectly saturated by the subject that the degree phrase is predicated of. (I am treating both predicate and non-predicate CP in (19a/b) as selected by the degree head *too*, and thus they are sisters of the head and the AP. Chomsky (1986b) suggests that the that the two CP extent clauses are not generated in the same position within the degree phrase: he analyses the predicate CP as a complement of A, and thus its sister, while the non-predicate CP is adjoined to either A′ or AP. Neither of these positions correlate with the semantic function of the CP, which is that it measures the extent of the degree, and I have argued against the structures that Chomsky proposes in Rothstein (1991). However, for the purposes of the discussion here, it does not matter where the CP is generated, as long as it is inside the degree phrase. It is not important whether the CP is adjoined to the sister of the AP *stubborn* and both are absorbed into the predicate headed by *too*, or whether the CP is absorbed first into the AP headed by *stubborn*, which is then itself absorbed into the degree phrase.)

Degree phrases, then, have an important characteristic; they select two complements: an XP (usually an AP, DP or PP) and an extent phrase, and the status of the degree phrase as a predicate or an argument is dependent on the status of the first, XP, complement. So far we have looked at a degree phrase where the head is an AP: since the AP headed by *stubborn* in (19) is a predicate, the whole degree phrase is a predicate, and this is independent of the predicate/non-predicate status of the extent CP. But in (20), the degree phrase is nominal, and is in a theta-marked position, theta-marked as the internal argument of *bought*, and the XP complement of *too* is a nominal argument expression:

(20)   We bought **too many apples for us to finish them before they got rotten**.

We can therefore use these phrases to test the prediction made above about the indirect saturation of predicates. I claimed that indirect saturation occurred where the predicate could be absorbed into an immediately dominating predicate node which was directly saturated (or was itself absorbed into an appropriate predicate), but that crucially a predicate could not be absorbed into a non-predicative constituent. The extent phrases in degree expressions are instances of a licensed CP which, if it is predicative, must be absorbed. The prediction is that in (19b), where the whole degree phrase is a predicate, absorption of the predicative CP is possible, but in nominal degree phrases which are theta-marked and thus non-predicative, absorption will be impossible.

The prediction turns out to be true. The contrasts in (21) were noted independently, though without explanation, in Browning (1987):

(21)   a.   Too many people to dance with them all come to the party.
       b.   *Too many people to dance with came to the party.
       c.   I brought home too many books to read them all in one night.
       d.   *I brought home too many books to read in one night.

Browning notes that for some people the (b) and (d) examples are marginal. She suggests that this is because the embedded CP is being interpreted as an infinitival relative, and she shows that, since these relatives do not stack, inserting an explicit infinitival relative makes the marginal sentences bad, as the following examples show:

(22) a. Too many [people to interview t] to talk to them all before noon arrived at nine.
   b. *Too many [people to interview t] to talk to t before noon arrived at nine.
   c. I brought home too many [papers to grade t] to write comments on them.
   d. *I brought home too many [papers to grade t] to write comments on t.

(Another possible explanation of the marginality, in some dialects, of the b/d examples is that the determiner and N, for example, *many books* in (21d), are identified as a constituent, albeit a non-maximal one, and that this constituent is then the subject of the predicative CP. But, since it is the whole degree phrase, and not det + N which is the theta-marked object of the main verb, and the preference is for maximal theta-marked subjects, this results only in marginality. Furthermore, on the analysis we developed in chapter 2, and will return to below, a predicate and its non-theta-marked subject form a constituent. Thus analysing the predicate CP as predicated of the nominal complement of *too* will give the degree head a proposition as a complement and not two distinct constituents.)

Since a CP extent clause is selected by the degree head in all degree phrases and licensed by its relation with this head, it will always be possible in a non-predicative form, as (21a,c) and (22a,c) showed. This allows us to isolate the cause of ungrammaticality in the b/d examples as the predicativeness of the CP. The constraints proposed on absorption explain why these, and not the parallel example in (19b), are ungrammatical. We also correctly predict that when a nominal degree phrase is predicative, the embedded CP may contain a gap, as it can be absorbed into the dominating predicate and indirectly saturated. This is shown in (23):

(23) The books$_i$ were too many for us to carry t$_i$ home.

Adverbial degree phrases also confirm the first prediction that we made about predicate absorption, namely that the embedded predicate and the dominating predicate must share the same subject. Adverbial phrases in general are predicated of the event argument of the verb (Davidson 1967, Parsons 1990), as I shall discuss below. CPs contained in adverbial degree phrases characteristically cannot be predicative:

(24) John runs too quickly for us to catch *(him).

If the subject of the adverbial degree phrase is the event argument of the verb and predicate absorption results in the variable in the embedded CP having the value of this subject, then this event argument must give the value for the empty object. The event, however, is not an appropriate semantic value for the object of *catch* and the sentence is not acceptable. This predicts correctly that (25a) will be grammatical. (This was originally noted by an anonymous reviewer of a paper that never made it into print):

(25)   a. They danced [too beautifully [for the audience to ignore t]].
        b. He knocked [too gently [for us to hear t]].

Here, an event can be an appropriate object for the verb in the embedded predicate, and thus a gap may occur, since the predicate can be absorbed into the degree phrase and predicated indirectly of its subject. (25b), suggested by Anita Mittwoch, illustrates the same point: the crucial point is that the understood object of *hear* has to be the knock and not the person knocking.

    Another issue that we are now able to explain is the distribution of pleonastic subjects with 'tough' adjectives in degree phrases. The relevant contrasts are given in (26–27):

(26)   a.   It is [too [easy to solve that problem] [for me to set it on the exam]].
        b.   That problem is [too [easy to solve t] [for me to set it on the exam]].

(27)   a.   *It is [too [easy to solve that problem] [for me to set t on the exam]].
        b.   That problem is [too [easy to solve t] [for me to set t on the exam]].

When the 'tough' degree phrase has a propositional (i.e. non-predicative) extent clause, the subject can be either a pleonastic or a lexical DP, and the complement of the adjective can be either propositional or predicative. This is shown in (26). However, if the extent clause is predicative, as in (27), then the complement of the adjective must also be predicative and the subject cannot be pleonastic, as the contrast between (27a/b) shows.

    The point is that if the extent clause is predicative, it must be absorbed into a predicate which has a subject which can provide an appropriate value for the gap in the CP. A pleonastic subject cannot provide a value for the object gap in the predicative extent CP in (27a). Although the predicative CP doesn't assign an external thematic role, it requires a lexical DP as its subject to provide content for the empty position bound by the null operator. In (27b), the extent predicate is absorbed into an AP headed by *easy* which is predicated of the DP *the problem*, which gives an appropriate value for the empty position in *for me to set t on the exam*, and the sentence is acceptable. In (26), where the extent clause is not a predicate, the issue doesn't arise, and either a pleonastic or lexical DP is acceptable as subject of the degree clause.

5.2.3. *Predicate absorption is a syntactic relation*

In chapter 2 I argued that predication is a syntactic and not a thematic relation; I will make the same move here and argue explicitly that predicate absorption is a syntactic relation and is not reducible to a thematic relation. In particular, it is to be distinguished from Higginbotham's (1985) account of theta-identification, which looks much like predicate absorption or complex predicate formation, except that it affects only thematic arguments.

Addressing the problem of theta-assignment in examples like (28), Higginbotham proposes that the theta-roles of the nominal *birds* and the AP *green* are merged through a process of theta-identification, producing a combined theta-position in the grid of the NP. This position is then discharged by the determiner through theta-binding. (For details see Higginbotham (1985)).

(28)   I bought [the [[green]$_{AP}$ birds]]$_{NP}$]$_{DP}$.

Obviously, this process could also account for the discharge of the theta-role assigned by *foolish* or *drunk* in (1a/c), repeated here:

(29)   a. John [acted [foolish]$_{AP}$]$_{VP}$.
         b. Bill [drove the car [drunk]$_{AP}$]$_{VP}$.

Indeed, some such process must occur as a correlate of predicate absorption, since the embedded predicates do have a theta-role to assign and the matrix subject is assigned a complex theta-role, rather than two separate theta-roles. But the fact that there is a process of (or similar to) theta-identification does not obviate the necessity for recognising the operation of predicate absorption, which is distinct from theta-identification in the same way that predication and external theta-role assignment are distinct. External theta-role assignment can take place when the syntactic relation of predication holds. Theta-identification can take place when the syntactic operation of predicate absorption occurs. As in chapter 2, the evidence for this twofold: first, the syntactic operation occurs when there is no theta-relation, and second, the thematic relation is dependent on the syntactic conditions being met. The second follows from the definition of theta-identification. The first can be shown by looking at a number of examples starting with (30):

(30)   It sounds unlikely that we will arrive on time.

Here the AP headed by *unlikely*, which, as we saw in chapter 2, requires saturation, has been absorbed into the VP headed by *sounds*, though, neither AP nor VP assign an external theta-role.   In addition, as we saw in chapter 2, predicate CPs, or null operator CPs, have no external theta-role to assign, since all theta-grids have been saturated within the CP with the operator-headed chain satisfying the theta-role assigned to the position filled by the trace. The fact that these CPs need a subject is thus syntactic, and is not dictated by the presence of an undischarged theta-role. But, as the discussion of (13), repeated here as (31) shows, the embedded CP predicate is absorbed, though no theta-identification can take place.

(31)   The children$_i$ sound ready for you to put t$_i$ to bed.

A fact which indicates the syntactic reality of predicate absorption is that predicate ellipsis can elide only the main clause predicate of a sentence, and cannot target an embedded absorbed predicate. We know from examples like (32a) that ellipsis does not apply only to VPs. Despite the fact that the embedded predicate is available as an antecedent for the anaphoric *so*, as in (32b), attempts to elide the same predicate result in ungrammaticality:

(32)   a.   John is unlikely to win, as is Bill/and Bill is too.
       b.   John feels sad and Bill seems so.

(33)   a.   *John feels sad and Bill seems too.
       b.   *Mary looks cheerful and Jane sounds.

If absorption converts a predicate from an autonomous constituent into part of a complex predicate, then we have an explanation for why the absorbed predicates *sad* and *cheerful* cannot be targeted by the ellipsis process. Note also that this is true whether or not the predicates assign an external theta-role: (35) is based on Baltin's (1993) examples, cited in chapter 2, and repeated here as (34):

(34)   A: It seems that Bill is crazy.
       B: It certainly does.

(35)   A: It seems likely that Bill is crazy.
       B: *It certainly does seem/It certainly seems.
            c.f. 'It certainly does'.

It is true that in (32) the ellided predicate *unlikely to win* is embedded under *be* and yet it can be ellided. I take this to be due to the special status of *be* as the 'stative' parallel of *do* in ellipsis contexts. Note that the same fact is true of predicates embedded under *do* in (36):

(36)   a. John did want to leave and so did Bill.
       b. John didn't want to leave and neither did Bill.

If we assume that a verb like *feel* syntactically selects a predicate and denotes a constituent which requires a predicate complement, then we predict that it should be able to take as a complement a syntactic predicate which does not assign an external theta-role. An example of such a sentence is given in (37):

(37)   John feels unlikely that he will go.

We assume that (37) satisfies the theta-criterion since *John* is assigned a theta-role by *feel*. Although the sentence is syntactically OK, it sounds very bad. Its syntactic status is shown by the fact that it compares well with (38), where *feel* selects something which is neither a predicate nor a CP, as we argued in chapter 4:

(38)   John feels [t to be a fool].

The unacceptability of (37) follows from the fact that it cannot be interpreted semantically, as I will show at the end of chapter 6.

Finally, in this section we compare how the operation of absorption deals with locality conditions on adjunct predication with Roberts' (1988) proposal that the VP-internal subject hypothesis can explain these locality conditions. Given Andrews' (1982) arguments that adjectival predicates such as *happy* in (39a) are VP-internal, hanging from the highest node of the VP, and assuming that subjects and predicate should c-command each other, Roberts (1988) proposes the structure in (39b), with the subject base generated empty:

(39) a. John$_i$ left the room happy$_i$.
       b. [e [John [leave the room]$_{V'}$ happy]$_{VP}$].
       c. John$_i$ met Mary$_j$ drunk$_j$ drunk$_i$.
       d. [e [John$_i$ [met Mary$_j$ drunk$_j$]$_{V'}$ drunk$_j$]$_{VP}$].

Predicates of objects are inside the V′ where they c-command and are c-commanded by the object, and predicates of the subject are adjoined to V′, directly under the VP. Since the VP-internal subject is also directly under the VP, the predicate and the VP-internal subject can c-command each other.

In the theory presented here, predicating the AP of the VP-internal subject is not necessary, since the AP adjoined to V′ will be absorbed into the VP and predicated indirectly of the subject via the VP. The absorption explanation is to be preferred since it accounts not only for subject-oriented adjuncts, but also for predicate complements such as *foolish* in the examples repeated here:

(40) John$_i$ [acted [foolish]$_i$]$_i$.

Roberts' analysis cannot account for such examples since it is crucial for him that both subject and predicate are outside the V′ in order for a mutual c-command condition to be maintained. While this is possible in (39), predicate complements must be within V′.

5.3. INFLECTION, IP AND PREDICATION

Up till now, I have avoided discussing Inflection and its projections, and instead concentrated the discussion on maximal projections of lexical heads, and on projections of C. The former, as we saw, are inherently predicative, and the latter are inherently non-predicative, but can be converted into predicates by the syntactic device of operator headed chains. IP, a projection of another functional category, Infl, does not pattern either like a lexical projection or like the functional projection CP, and its behaviour raises several questions. The first question about projections of Infl centres on I′ and the status of the locality conditions. An IP in English has the structure (41):

(41) [DP [Infl VP]$_{I'}$]$_{IP}$.

I have claimed that predication holds under a relation of mutual c-command, but it is clear that given the structure in (41), VP cannot c-command [DP,IP]. There are three possible solutions. I'll give all three, and then show why there is some evidence for the third.

The first way to go is to argue that the relevant relation for calculating locality relations for predication is m-command, and that since the VP m-commands the subject, locality conditions are met. This predicts that other X′ nodes should not be relevant for calculating locality conditions either. I shall argue later that this is the wrong prediction, since secondary predicates of direct objects, such as those illustrated in (2), are generated only under V′ where they c-command the direct object, and not under VP, where they would still m-command the direct object.

The second possibility is to stipulate that predication is simply blind to I′ and that I′ is not relevant for locality relations. This raises the question of why I′ is not relevant.

Third, it could be that the I′ node is itself a predicate, and predicated of the subject under the relation of mutual c-command. In this latter case, the VP in (41) is absorbed into I′ by the process of predicate absorption and indirectly saturated by the subject. It turns out that it is difficult to distinguish between these latter two explanations, but I shall show that there is reason to argue for the second.

The idea that I′ is a syntactic predicate is a little startling, coming as it does in the middle of a discussion about predicate maximal projections. I am proposing a structure in which I′ projects a predicate node, and the I′ is predicated of the DP in Spec of IP, resulting in a closed argument IP, which can stand either as an argument in the complement of ECM verbs, or as a complete, independent assertion. So the structure of I-projections differs from other projections in that the I′ node is the predicate and the saturation comes within the maximal projection, as opposed to other projections where the maximal projection is a predicate and saturation is by an argument outside the maximal projection.

The direct evidence that I′ is a predicate comes from an analysis of Hebrew copular constructions which I will present in detail in chapter 8. To give a preview, Hebrew Infl differs from English Infl since it does not necessarily take a VP complement. Furthermore, Hebrew allows 'small', or inflectionless, 'present tense' copular sentences, and thus in a large number of sentences Infl looks like it is optional. I show in chapter 8 that Infl is optional only if the Infl-less sentence forms an instance of primary predication. If it would not consist of a subject and a syntactic predicate, Infl is obligatory. (There are other semantic conditions under which Pron is also obligatory, which we will discuss in chapter 8, but these need not concern us here.) The examples in (42) contrast:

(42)   a.   dani (hu)   nexmad$_{AP}$/more$_{NP}$.
              dani COP nice/   teacher
              "Dani is nice/Dani is a teacher."

        b.   dani *(hu)   mar cohen.
              dani   COP mr cohen
              intended reading: "Dani is Mr Cohen."

In (42a), where the constituent following the copula is a predicate, the Infl-less sentence is an instance of predication. In (42b), the sentence without Infl is a string of two referential DPs, neither of which can be predicated of the other. I argue that Infl is obligatory in sentences like (42b) because it projects an I′ predicate, containing the Infl and its DP complement, and that the I′ can be directly predicated of the subject while the argument DP cannot be. Infl is likewise obligatory when the post-copula constituent is an argument CP:

(43) Haba'aya   *(hi)   Se ani roca la'azov
      The problem   Pron that I   want to leave
      "The problem is that I want to leave."

(Hebrew in general does not allow sentential predicates with operator chains other than as nominal modifiers in relative clause constructions, so minimal contrasts with (43) aren't possible.)

If I′ is a predicate, then it is predicated directly of [DP,IP], and its VP complement is absorbed into I′ and indirectly saturated by the subject. (Note that we must modify the claim of the previous section that ellipsis doesn't apply to absorbed predicates: it clearly applies to VP predicate complements of Infl, and we are now hypothesising that they are absorbed. But we have already seen in the previous section (examples (32)) that ellipsis does, and must, apply to the complement of a copula and presumably these two exceptions are related.)

What follows from the assumption that I′ is a predicate? If I′ is a predicate and IP is a saturated constituent, then one obvious question is whether saturation within IP is obligatory. Does it follow from the nature of IP itself that it is saturated, or does it merely turn out to be the case that general conditions on saturation require the I′ predicate to be saturated within the IP. The evidence is that it is the latter. If we look at all the possible environments in which I′ can occur we see that it is in almost every case impossible to get a grammatical structure in which the I′ is not saturated by Spec of IP. But there is one construction in which a predicative IP does occur. I will look briefly at the environments in which IP occurs, and show on a case by case basis why saturation must almost always be IP internal; we'll then identify the single possible environment where a predicate IP is possible.

(i) IP can be a matrix clause. In this case, I′ must be saturated within IP. IP cannot be a predicate since there is nothing outside the IP to predicate it of.

(ii) IP can be a 'bare IP' complement of an ECM verb as in (44):

(44)   They considered [John [to have succeeded]$_{I'}$]$_{IP}$.

Here I′ must be saturated within IP because IP is a theta-marked complement of the verb *consider*, which takes two arguments, and IP cannot saturate a place in the matrix verb's thematic argument structure unless it is closed.

(iii) IP can be a complement of C, where CP is the complement of a matrix head, as in (45a/b) or a subject argument, as in (45c/d).

(45) a. I prefer/want [(for) [you to leave]$_{IP}$]$_{CP}$.
      b. Bill murmured [that [you must leave]$_{IP}$]$_{CP}$.
      c. [[For you to leave]$_{IP}$]$_{CP}$ would upset them.
      d. [[That you left]$_{IP}$]$_{CP}$ upset them.

If IP were a predicate, it would have to be either predicated of its sister argument, which is clearly not possible here, or be absorbed into an immediately dominating predicate constituent. Here the dominating constituent is a non-predicate projection of C, and absorption is not possible. The CPs in (45) are not predicates, since (a) they do not contain an operator chain terminating in a trace and (b) they are thematic arguments of the matrix verb, and so must be saturated.

  (iv) IP is a complement of C where C heads a predicate CP. Here we might expect to find a predicate IP, since we might expect absorption of a predicate IP into a predicate CP to be possible. In fact this cannot occur. The head C, which syntactically selects an IP complement, selects a syntactically closed constituent. Semantically, it selects a proposition and not a predicate. The complement of C, even in a predicate CP, is a non-predicate constituent since the trace in the IP is free within the IP, and bound only outside the C', as we see in (46):

(46) I invited John [Op$_i$ [for [Mary to entertain t$_i$]$_{IP}$]$_{C'}$]$_{CP}$.

In other words, the complement of C is the non-predicate IP [Mary to entertain t], containing the trace which is free within IP.

  (v) The fifth possibility is that IP can be a bare IP adjunct. Here we may indeed have the kind of predicate we are looking for. The relevant example are 'subject control' purpose clauses, with the subject gap in (47a), which is often analysed as (47b):

(47) a. I brought John to entertain Mary.
      b. I brought John [Op$_i$ [C [t$_i$ [to entertain Mary]$_{I'}$]$_{IP}$]$_{C'}$]$_{CP}$.

Suppose that we analyse (47a) not as (47b), but as a constituent which is lacking a subject, along the lines proposed in Jones (1991); however, instead of analysing the infinitival as a VP, we will assume that *to* projects an I' node, but that the I' does not have a DP argument as its sister. The resulting structure is in (48), in which the IP is an unsaturated predicate, predicated as a secondary predicate of the DP *John*:

(48) I brought John$_i$ [[to entertain Mary]$_{I'i}$]$_{IPi}$.

  The subject of the IP, *John* would then saturate the IP and, indirectly, the VP absorbed into it. There are two reasons to prefer (48) to (47b), one theoretical, and one empirical. The theoretical problem is that (47b) contains an A' chain, the null operator chain, which is not case-marked, and this violates conditions on operator chains (see the discussion in Browning (1987)). The empirical argument in favour of the bare IP adjunct analysis is that extraction of adjuncts from within an IP that can be analysed in this way is much better than one would expect extraction of an adjunct to be. (49a) is much better than (49b):

(49) a. How$_i$ did you bring John [to entertain the children t$_i$].
      b. *How$_i$ did you bring the kids$_j$ [Op$_j$ for John to entertain t$_j$ t$_i$].

In (49a) where we have 'subject control' of the purpose clause, and thus, I have suggested, a bare IP predicate, *how* can be construed as binding an adjunct trace within the IP. An appropriate answer can be 'with conjuring tricks'. In (49b), where the purpose clause must contain a null operator to bind the object gap within the IP, and thus must be a CP, adjunct extraction from within the purpose clause is not possible. If (49a) is extraction out of an IP, and (49b) extraction out of a CP, then the difference in structures will explain the difference in grammaticality. In (49a) movement crosses only two IP nodes, which we know from ECM constructions is not a problem, whereas in (49b) we have extraction out of an adjunct CP. If the two were to have the same structure then there should be no such difference.

Bare IP predicates such as these will be possible only with subject control predicates, since it is only here that the predicate is projected syntactically. If a purpose clause has an object gap, as in the examples in (49b) and (50a/b), then I' is saturated by the element in Spec of IP.

(50) a. I brought the book [Op$_i$ [for [Mary to read t$_i$]$_{IP}$]$_{C'}$]$_{CP}$.
      b. I brought the book [Op$_i$ [e [PRO to read t$_i$]$_{IP}$]$_{C'}$]$_{CP}$.
      c. *How did you bring the book [Op$_i$ [e [PRO to read t$_i$]$_{IP}$]$_{C'}$]$_{CP}$.

In (49b) and (50a) the I' is saturated by a lexical subject, *John* and *Mary*, respectively. In (50b), the trace in the object position of the embedded VP must be bound by a null operator, which means that there must be a full CP with a PRO subject which saturates the I'. Note that, as we would predict, (50c) shows that the extraction of adjuncts out of the purpose clause is impossible also here.

I assume that infinitival relative modifiers such as (51) can be given a syntactic analysis similar to the one I have just given for subject control purpose clauses, with the IP *to fix the sink* treated as an IP without a subject, although these IP expressions are modifiers and not predicates:

(51) The man [[to fix the sink]$_{I'}$]$_{IPi}$.

(Williams 1980 suggests a very different analysis for the subject-oriented purpose clause in (48). He treats the purpose clause as a bare IP with a PRO subject, where PRO functions as a syntactic predicate variable. This conflicts with standard assumptions that PRO is syntactically an argument, and also that it is non-governed, since as a VP adjunct in (48), IP and thus PRO will be governed by V. It also requires giving a non-uniform analysis of PRO, where it functions syntactically as a bound predicate variable in cases of control, and a free variable when it is arbitrary.)

(vi) The sixth possibility is that IP is part of a 'with' adjunct:

(52)   With Mary to show us the way, we'll have no problem finding their house.

Here, it is reasonable to assume that P takes an argument as a complement, and that the I' *to show us the way* must be saturated by a sister node so as to provide the saturated complement for *with*.

Let's sum up where we are so far. Based largely on the Hebrew data, we analyse I' as a predicate. We see no contradiction between the fact that I' is a predicate and IP isn't, since it turns out not to be the case that IP must be saturated. Rather, the grammatical environments in which IP occurs are such that IP cannot normally be a predicate, and thus saturation of the I' must be internal. If IP occurs in a position in which it can be a predicate, then IP can contain nothing except a bare unsaturated I'. Note that this predicts that in principle ECM infinitival complements such as (53a) will be ambiguous between the structure as normally assigned, in (53b), and the 'IP predicate' structure in (53c). At the moment I can't see any problem with this:

(53)   a. I believe John to be a genius.
        b. I believe [John [to be a genius]$_{I'}$]$_{IP}$.
        c. I believe [John [to be a genius]$_{IP}$]$_{SC}$.

What this discussion shows is that the obligatoriness of [DP,IP] in an IP is not absolute; [DP,IP] will be obligatory to saturate the I' predicate only if the IP predicate which would otherwise dominate it could not be syntactically saturated as a predicate. In such a case, direct saturation of the I' by a sentential subject will be the only way of satisfying the predicate linking rule.

This raises a number of questions, the most obvious of which are the following: (i) why is I' a predicate, whereas up to now we have been discussing only XP predicates? (ii) why can IP be internally saturated when no other XP that we have looked at can be? (iii) if IP need not be internally saturated then what of the extended projection principle? We turn to these in the next section.

5.4. IPs, SUBJECTS AND PRIMARY PREDICATION

5.4.1. *The syntactic position of subjects*

Let us begin with the first question, namely why I' is crucially a predicate, when other inherent predicates are all maximal projections. There are two possible answers. One is that the X' constituents of other inherent predicates are also predicate expressions, but since there is no possibility of saturating them within the XP, they are automatically absorbed into the XP expression. On this account, the V' constituent expression in (54) is also a predicate, but there is no possibility of directly predicating it of an argument since an argument cannot occur between V' and AP for reasons of case-assignment, so it must be absorbed into a predicate VP.

(54) a. John PAST [[eat the carrots]$_{V'}$]$_{VP}$.
      b. John PAST [[eat the carrots]$_{V'}$ in the kitchen]$_{VP}$.

In (54a), the V′ is in any case identical to the VP, while in (54b) the VP contains extra adjunct material. Syntactically, this is a fairly straightforward move, although it would complicate the semantics. The other possible answer is to look not at how X′ (where X is lexical) and I′ are similar, but at how they are different. From this point of view the crucial thing is that where heads of maximal projection predicates denote relations, the Infl head denotes a predicate modifier, and is of type $<<d,t>,<d,t>>$, (or, assuming that VPs denote sets of events, of type $<<d,<e,t>>,<d,<e,t>>>$). I′ is therefore a predicate because of the modification function of Infl: if it selects a predicate and denotes a classical modification function which yields as output the same type that it applies to, then I′ will have to denote a predicate too. (In chapter 8, I will argue for a type shifting account of the identity sentences which preserves the type of Infl in (42b).) Thus maximal XP predicates and I′ are predicates for different syntactic reasons: maximal lexical XPs are predicates because they inherently require saturation, while I′s are predicates because they are modifiers which apply to their argument without changing its type. We will see in chapter 6 that this difference is reflected in the semantics: maximal lexical XP predicates translate as constituents over which lambda abstraction automatically takes place (i.e. the translation of a lexical XP is automatically prefixed by 'λx', while no such operation applies to I′, which is of the form λx.α by virtue of the form of its complement.

What does it mean for an XP to be internally saturated, and why is IP the only maximal projection which can be internally saturated? A predicate is internally saturated if the predicate and its subject argument form a maximal projection which is a projection of the head of the predicate. So when we say that IP is internally saturated, we mean that I′ is a predicate, and I′ and its subject argument form a maximal constituent whose properties are dictated by the I. I′ is then not maximal. When we say that VP is not internally saturated, we are asserting that while VP and its argument form a constituent, the constituent they form is not a projection of V, and the predicate itself still has the properties of a maximal projection. Stowell (1983) has argued for 'subjects across categories', which is equivalent to the claim that XPs are internally saturated, while Fukui and Speas (1986) claim that only functional heads have specifier positions, which is tantamount to claiming that subjects across lexical categories is impossible. The evidence shows that the latter claim is correct, as we argued already in chapter 2:2.3. Heycock (1991) independently argues that complement of ECM verbs in constructions like (55) consist of XP predicates with adjoined subjects. While she labels the adjunction constructions 'VP', 'AP', and 'DP' respectively instead of 'SC', she too argues that it is the predicate which is the maximal projection of the lexical head, and not the small clause.

(55) a. Sarah made [the boys [repair the damage]$_{VP}$]$_{SC}$.
      b. I believe [John [very foolish]$_{AP}$]$_{SC}$.
      c. I consider[her [my best friend]$_{DP}$]$_{SC}$.

We already pointed out in chapter 2:2.3 that it is the predicate and not the small clause which is the maximal projection with respect to movement, and that nominal predicates with DP heads have a filled Spec of DP which indicates that the subject of the predicate is not a specifier, as in (56) and (57):

(56) a. [How foolish]$_i$ do you consider [John t$_i$].
      b. *[John foolish]$_i$ was considered t$_i$.
      c. *[John foolish]$_i$ is what you considered t$_i$.

(57) John considers [Mary [his daughter's best friend]].

Heycock (1991) points out that in VP small clauses it is the predicate VP which can be questioned using *do*, and not the verbal small clause:

(58) a. What did Sarah make the boys do? Repair the damage.
      b. *What did Sarah make do? The boys repair the damage.

Of course in general, small clause complements cannot be questioned, and this is presumably because although they form constituents these constituents are not projections of heads, and do not form categories that can be filled by traces.

(59) a. What does John believe? *Mary a genius and Bill an idiot.
      b. *What did Sarah make? The boys repair the damage.

Heycock proposes that not only should these small clauses be analysed as adjoined structures, but that, in a parallel fashion, the subject of IP should be analysed as an adjoined position. This would mean that I′ should in essence be treated as a maximal projection, and no predicate would be internally saturated. But there is evidence against this. Thus, while (60a) is not perfect, it is much better than (59a), indicating that IP is a constituent which can be questioned. (60b) shows that while AP predicates can be questioned out of small clauses, I′ predicates cannot:

(60) a. What does John believe? Mary to be a genius and Bill to be an idiot.
      b. What do you consider John? Foolish/*To be foolish.

So we will continue to treat IP as the only constituent projected from a head which can have a predicate and its subject for its daughters, and maintain the claim that I′ is peculiar in being a non-maximal predicate. This peculiarity follows from the modificatory role of Infl, and it reflects a difference in the way in which the semantic correlates of these constituents behave.

5.4.2. *The Extended Projection Principle revisited*

In chapter 3:3.3, I discussed clause I of the 'Extended Projection Principle', namely the claim that all sentences or clauses had subjects, and various explanations for this which have been proposed. The discussion there centered largely on the necessity of explaining the obligatoriness of pleonastics in small clauses. I argued that on the assumption that 'clause' is an instance of primary predication where the subject and predicate form a constituent, then nothing need be said explicitly about the need for clausal subjects, since it followed from general constraints about predicate saturation. Primary predicates need subjects, thus clauses, small or otherwise, need subjects. In the light of the above discussion, this needs to be revised somewhat. First note that while we have argued that all clauses are primary predication structures, there is no simple syntactic definition of 'sentence' or 'clause' in terms of categories, since IPs, argument small clauses, absolutives, and Akmajian's 'Mad Magazine' clauses discussed in the chapter 2 are all instances of primary predication. This means that the intuition embodied in the Extended Projection Principle that clauses have subjects is part of the more general principle that predicates have subjects. And we need the wider definition, as we saw in chapter 3, to explain why pleonastics turn up in such non-clause-like entities as 'with' absolutives, as in (61):

(61)   a. With it raining so hard, we should probably take a cab.
       b. With it turning out that John is rich, I think our vacation options are expanding.
       c. With it likely that we will be this late, I think we should scrap the visit.

Second, we now have a second reason to express the Extended Projection Principle in terms of predication. We saw in the previous section that not all IPs have IP internal subjects. The predicate IP discussed in section 3, illustrated in (48) and repeated here as (62), is an example of an IP predicate which does not have an internal subject and which is a secondary predicate of the direct object of the matrix verb:

(62)   I brought John$_i$ [[to entertain Mary]$_{I'i}$]$_{IPi}$.

The fact that there are IPs in which subjects do not occur (IP-internally) is an indication of the fact that the need to satisfy constraints on predication is indeed what makes the subject obligatory. IP subjects appear to be obligatory because the predicate within the IP requires saturation and the context in which the IP occurs requires IP to be a saturated constituent and thus the predicate to be saturated within IP. But, if it is possible for the IP to be an unsaturated constituent, then the Spec of IP subject position is not obligatory; the IP can be a secondary predicate and the predicate within IP can be saturated indirectly via the IP predication. This means that we must revise the claim that we took for granted in chapter 3, namely that subject position is obligatory; its apparent obligatoriness follows from constraints on predicate saturation which mean that it is almost impossible for an IP to be a predicate, and that the predicate which is the daughter of IP thus almost always has to be saturated within IP.

5.5. PRIMARY AND SECONDARY PREDICATION

5.5.1. *Some history*

I made the original formal distinction between primary and secondary predication in Rothstein (1983), where I identified primary predication as essentially clausal predication, and secondary predication as essentially the predication of adjuncts. The basic saturation relation worked the same way for both primary and secondary predication, but the constraints on each were different, so that they looked like different kinds of predication. The distinction between primary and secondary predication needs to be refined in the light of the analysis in this chapter and chapter 2, but the original insight that they are different kinds of occurrences of the syntactic predication relation still holds good.

So far we have identified direct primary predication as predication where the predicate and the subject c-command each other, and where the subject doesn't have a thematic relation with anything other than its predicate. The basic intuition of Rothstein (1983), that instances of primary predication form either sentences (IPs) or small clauses, is maintained, and captured in the definition of primary predication, given in chapter 3:(26) and repeated here:

(63) a. α is a primary predicate of β, iff α is predicated of β, and α and β c-command each other, and β is not theta-marked outside the predication relation with α.

     b. If α is a primary predicate of β, then α and β form an instance of primary predication.

An instance of predication which meets the conditions in (63) will form a constituent, and in the last chapter I called this kind of predication 'constituent predication'. Both IP and small clause predications will form constituents, and they have syntactic properties in common, but despite this they have different semantic denotations, as we will discuss in chapter 10.

What I called secondary predication in 1983, by which I meant adjunct predication, is now divided into two kinds. One kind is subsumed under indirect predication, where a predicate is absorbed into another predicate and the highest predicate enters into a primary predication relation with the subject. This is what occurs in sentences like (64), where, as we have seen, *drunk* is absorbed into *drive the car*, and *drive the car drunk* is absorbed into the I', and the whole I' is directly predicated of the subject:

(64)   John [[drove the car [**drunk**]$_{AP}$]$_{VP}$]$_{I'}$.

The other kind of adjunct predication, which I will continue to call 'secondary predication' is the adjunct predication illustrated in (65):

(65) a. Mary ate the carrots **raw**.
     b. They elected Jane **president**.
     c. She drinks her coffee **black and bitter**.
     d. I believe John **sober**.

Here the adjunct predicate is directly predicated of the direct object without being absorbed at all, but unlike with primary predication, the subject and predicate do not form a constituent. The original observation was that while the subject in an instance of primary predication is licensed by the predication relation, the subject of a secondary predicate is also governed by the condition that it is theta-marked in a relation outside the predication relation. Note the secondary predicate reading of (65d), which contrasts with the primary, small clause reading we have discussed up to now. Here *John* is the theta-marked object of *believe*, and *sober* is a secondary predicate, and the sentence means 'I believe John when he is sober' (example from Napoli 1998).

5.5.2. *Secondary predication is direct non-constituent predication*

Secondary predication is defined as follows:

(66) a. α is a *secondary predicate* of β iff α is predicated of β, and α and β c-command each other and β is theta-marked by a head not contained in α.

  b. If α is a secondary predicate of β, then α and β form an instance of *secondary predication*.

The most obvious correlate and consequence of the difference between primary and secondary predication is that an instance of primary predication forms a constituent, while an instance of secondary predication doesn't. Let us review briefly the evidence for this which we already discussed in the presentation of small clauses in chapter 2:3. By hypothesis, in ECM small clause complements, which we argued were instances of primary predication, the subject of the embedded predicate is not theta-marked by the matrix verb, while in secondary predication it is. Thus in (67a), the subject of the predicate *difficult*, is licensed because it is the subject of that predicate, while in (67b) *her coffee* is licensed because it is assigned the internal theta-argument of the verb *drink*. The predicate *very strong* is thus predicated of an argument of another lexical head.

(67) a. I thought [that problem difficult]$_{SC}$.
  b. Mary [drank [her coffee] [very strong]$_{AP}$]$_{VP}$.

As a consequence, *very strong* is an adjunct and it is not necessary to license its subject DP: if it were dropped, the resulting sentence would still be grammatical. In (67a), the predicate licenses *that problem* through predication, and if it is dropped the sentence becomes ungrammatical since the DP is not licensed.

(68) a. *I thought that problem.
  b. Mary drank her coffee.

In (69/70) it looks as if dropping the primary predicate does not make the sentence ungrammatical, but this is because *consider* and *believe* can select either a small clause or a DP, and in the (b) examples, the DP option is being exploited:

The syntactic forms of predication

(69)   a. John considered the problem difficult.
        b. John considered the problem.

(70)   a. Mary believes John foolish.
        b. Mary believes John.

The difference shows up in the entailments: (67b) entails (68b) since if Mary drank her coffee strong, she drank her coffee, but the (a) examples in (69/70) do not entail (69b/70b), since if Mary believes John foolish she does not necessarily believe John and if John considers the problem difficult he does not necessarily consider the problem. This is shown in (71):

(71)   a. #Mary drank her coffee strong though she never drank her coffee.
        b. He considers that problem difficult, even though he's never considered the problem (itself) at all.
        c. John believes Bill a liar, and he doesn't believe Bill.

We also, in chapter 2:2.3, cited Stowell's (1991a) evidence from the syntactic distribution of adverbial modifiers that secondary predicates are part of the VP. He argued that adverbs modify within the constituent they occur in, and that in sentences with secondary adjunct predicates, adverbs following the accusative marked object behave as if the secondary predicate isn't there and modify the governing verb. This is not the case in *consider* complements. In (72a), the adverb modifies the matrix verb, but not in (72b):

(72)   a. Mary eats carrots repeatedly raw.
        b. They considered him sincerely upset.

Kayne (1984) shows that subjects of secondary predicates behave like objects with regard to the extractions they permit, while subjects of small clauses behave like subjects:

(73)   a. Who$_i$ did you meet the sister of t$_i$ drunk.
        b. *Who$_i$ do you consider the sister of t$_i$ very smart?

Finally, unlike small clause complements, a DP with secondary predicate can be conjoined with a bare DP complement as a complement of a verb. As I showed in chapter 2, (74a/b) are truth-conditionally equivalent, but (74a/b) are not:

(74)   a. Bill drinks coffee and tea iced.
        b. Bill drinks coffee and he drinks tea iced.

(75)   a. *I considered the problem and the solution wrong.
        b. I considered the problem, and I considered the solution wrong.

As I argued in Rothstein (1983, 1984), predication and theta-marking have in common that they are saturation relations. A theta-marked constituent, DP or CP, saturates a position in theta-grid, while a subject saturates the position in a syntactic predicate. We can see then that constituent structure indicates

that the difference between primary and secondary predication is as hypothesised: in a primary predication, all saturation relations are between the subject
and the predicate. In a secondary predication, where the subject of the predicate
is also theta-marked outside the predication relation, this subject is part of two
different saturation relations: it saturates a position in a theta-grid of the matrix
verb and saturates the predicate predicated of it.

The analysis that I am assuming for these constructions predicates the
adjunct directly of its subject without the intervention of a PRO. I am thus
assuming a structure like (76a) rather than (76b):

(76) a. John [[eats carrots raw]$_{V'}$]$_{VP}$.
      b. John [eats carrots]$_{V'}$ [PRO raw]]$_{VP}$.

I follow in this the analyses of Schein (1995), Williams (1983a), McNulty
(1988), Rapoport (1991) and others, and I will not repeat their arguments here.
McNulty in particular reviews the possible structural configurations for (76b)
and argues that none can answer the fundamental problem with the 'PRO
subject' hypothesis, namely that a PRO subject of a secondary predicate cannot
fail to be in a governed position. The structure in (76a) makes AP a sister of
the DP object and thus they c-command each other. This makes secondary
predication direct. I'll turn now to the evidence that the AP is indeed the
daughter of V'.

5.5.3. *Secondary predication is within V'*

Following the strict mutual c-command constraint on subjects and predicates,
I have assumed that secondary predicates are generated under V'. There are
several pieces of evidence that this is indeed the case.

First, although secondary predicates can occur after an instrumental PP or
an adverb, it is preferable to place them before:

(77) a. John eats carrots raw with his fingers.
      b. ?John eats carrots with his fingers raw.

Bresnan (1982) argues that instrumental modifiers such as *with his fingers*,
though they are not subcategorised by the verb, are arguments introduced by
a lexical rule of 'instrumentalisation'. Thus, if (77a) is preferred over (77b), this
is evidence that the predicate is generated at the argument level and preferably
adjacent to the argument it is predicated of. (77b) can be analysed with the
secondary predicate scrambled to the end of this sentence, which is why it is
less preferred and not ungrammatical, but there is a difference in acceptability
which the diacritics show.

The rest of the discussion involves contrasting these secondary predicates of
direct objects with adjuncts predicate of subjects, such as *drunk* in (78), discussed earlier in this chapter.

(78) John drove the car drunk.

As Andrews (1982) shows, and as we saw in (6) above, these predicates are within the VP. As such, they cannot c-command their subjects and cannot be direct predicates of the subjects. I argued above that they are indirect predicates, absorbed into the VP and thus the I'. According to the definition we gave in (66), they are not secondary predicates. *John*, the indirect subject of *drunk*, is indeed theta-marked by another head, the verb *drive*, but since *drive drunk* is a complex predicate, *John* is not theta-marked outside the predication relation in which it occurs. *Drunk* is also not a primary predicate, since part of the definition of primary predicate is that it must c-command its subject. Primary and secondary predication is a distinction which applies to direct and not to indirect predication.

Comparison between the syntactic behaviour of subject oriented adjuncts and secondary predicates shows us that as we would expect they are generated in different places in the VP. As (79a/b) shows, a secondary predicate of an object preferably precedes a VP internal adverb, while (79c/d) shows that an adjunct indirectly predicated of the subject need not precede the adverb. (79e) is ambiguous between a reading where the adjunct is predicated of the direct object and one where it is predicated of the subject, but in (79f) the adjunct is unambiguously subject-oriented:

(79) a. John eats carrots raw happily.
      b. ?John eats carrots happily raw.
      c. Mary ran the Marathon last week sick.
      d. Mary ran the Marathon sick last week.
      e. John met Mary drunk last week.
      f. John met Mary last week drunk.

VP movement and pseudo-clefting show the same differences. It is well-known that some operations which apply to VP apply to V' as well. '*Though*-movement' preferably applies to the largest constituent, although it is marginally possible to apply it to V', while pseudoclefting can apply to any constituent which is a V' or larger:

(80) a. Sing nude though John does, ...
      b. ?Sing though John does nude, ...
      c. Eat dinner happily though the baby did, she was glad to see her mother.
      d. ?Eat dinner though the baby did happily, ...

(81) a. What John does is sing nude.
      b. What John does nude is sing.
      c. What the baby did all afternoon was eat chocolate pudding happily.
      d. What the baby did happily was eat chocolate pudding.

Though the (b/d) examples are not as good as the (a/c) examples, they are much better that when the same operations 'strand' secondary predicates of direct objects. (82b/d) are ungrammatical:

(82)   a.   Eat carrots raw though John does ...
     b.   *Eat carrots though John does raw ...
     c.   What John does is eat carrots raw.
     d.   *What John does raw is eat carrots.

This is clear evidence that these secondary adjunct predicates are obligatorily within the V′ constituent, in a position where they c-command their subjects, and where their subjects c-command them. The ambiguity of (79e) is thus structural, with *drunk* in a different syntactic position depending on what argument it is predicated of. (83a) represents the secondary predicate directly predicated of the object, while (83b) is the structure in which the adjunct is absorbed into the VP and indirectly predicated of the subject.

(83)   a.   John [[met Mary drunk]$_{V'}$]$_{VP}$.
     b.   John [[met Mary]$_{V'}$ drunk]$_{VP}$.

The combination of the mutual c-command constraint and what we may call the theta-constraint – the constraint that the subject of a secondary predicate is theta-marked by another lexical head – constrains the possible environments in which adjuncts of this kind occur. The constraint that a verb assigns an internal theta-role to a syntactic sister and the mutual c-command constraint on predication together guarantee that a secondary predicate and its subject cannot form a constituent.

A possible problem for this account which I shall present, but which I am not going to try and answer here are the so-called intransitive resultative constructions. The secondary predicates we have been discussing so far are termed 'depictives' in Halliday (1967) and they express the state that their subject is in when the assertion of the main predicate holds. 'John ate the carrots raw' can be paraphrased roughly as 'John ate the carrots and the carrots were raw when he ate them.' (See also discussion in Halliday 1967, Williams 1980, Simpson 1983, Rothstein 1983, McNulty 1988, Rapoport 1991, McNally 1997. I discuss the interpretation further in chapter 6.) Depictives are to be distinguished from resultative predicates, such as (84), which can only be predicated of the direct object, where the predicate gives the state of its subject at the end of the event given by the main predicate (Simpson 1983, Carrier and Randall 1992, Levin and Rappaport Hovav 1995):

(84)   a.   They watered the tulips flat.
     b.   They painted the house red.
     c.   They hammered the metal flat.

The occurrence of resultatives is constrained by the nature of the matrix verb, as well as the general mutual c-command condition on predication. A major distinction between these and the adjunct predicates we describe above is that resultatives can be predicated of arguments which are not theta-marked by any lexical head:

(85)   a. They laughed John off the stage.
        b. He cried himself sick.
        c. She ran the soles off her shoes.

There are different opinions about the structure of these. In the examples in (84) both predicate and subject are argued to be daughters of V', but while Carrier and Randall argue the same for (85), Levin and Rappaport Hovav suggest that another possible structure is for the subject and predicate to form a small clause complement to the V. The two structures are given in (86):

(86)   a. They [laughed John off the stage]$_{VP}$.
        b. They [laughed [John off the stage]$_{SC}$]$_{VP}$.

These kinds of intransitive resultatives pose a question for our account. If the structure is as in (86a), then intransitive resultatives do not behave like secondary predicates according to our definition in (66) since the subject of the resultative is not a theta-marked argument of a lexical head. If the structure is an in (86b) then we have an example of uninflected primary predication which is not in an argument position, and the question is how the small clause itself is licensed. In chapter 6, section 5.1, I'll discuss the semantic interpretation of these structures, and I'll show that the theory of interpretation that I develop easily provides an interpretation for the structure in (86b). I'll show there that the rule for assigning a resultative interpretation to these constructions establishes a semantic relation between the V and the small clause which is sufficiently analogous to the relation between a head and its theta-marked object that it serves to license the small clause.

6. ADVERBS

The category which is absent from our discussion here is that of adverbs. I am not going to discuss them, and I want only to point out that they appear not to be predicates at all. In the spirit of Davidson (1967), and following Parsons' (1990) neo-Davidsonian analysis of events, I assume that verbs denote predicates of events and that adverbs and adverbial PPs are interpreted in the semantic representation of the sentence as predicates of the event argument of the verb. Assuming that the event argument is bound by an existential quantifier, a neo-Davidsonian representation for the famous sentence in (87a) will be something like (87b):

(87)   a. Jones buttered the toast slowly in the bathroom with a knife.
        b. $\exists e$ [BUTTER (e) $\wedge$ Agent(e) = JOHN $\wedge$ Theme(e) = THE TOAST
           $\wedge$ SLOWLY(e) $\wedge$ IN THE BATHROOM(e)
           $\wedge$ WITH A KNIFE(e)].

Now, it is a reasonable assumption that the syntactic predication relation is interpreted semantically with syntactic predicates denoting predicates which are predicated of the denotation of the relevant syntactic subject. Yet here we have expressions which look like predicates of events, expressed by the syntactic expressions *slowly, in the bathroom* and *with a knife*, and these syntactic expressions are not syntactically saturated.

In Rothstein (1983), I noted this problem, and I tried arguing that AGR in Inflection was a nominal element, and that the adverbs could then be syntactically predicated of Inflection. But this cannot work, since adverbs appear in bare infinitive complements where there is no Inflection:

(88) I saw John run quickly.

I assume that the absence of a predication relation is because adverbs are just not syntactic predicates. They never appear in a position in which they can be predicated of a syntactic argument; this is not because they must be predicated of events, since even if the argument denotes an event, it cannot have an adverb predicated of it. The examples in (89) are all unacceptable with adverbial predicates, though the corresponding adjectives are all OK.

(89) a. The destruction of the city was *brutally/brutal.
      b. The reading of the verdict was *slowly/slow.
      c. John considered [the running *slowly/slow].

Treating adverbs as non-predicates complies with the generalisation (55) in chapter 2 that inherent predicates are maximal projections of lexical heads. Adverbs are usually not considered projections of lexical heads, especially since adverbs derived from adjectives lose the most characteristic property of lexical heads, that of assigning theta-roles. I assume that adverbs are not predicates because they are inherently modificatory in character. They differ from APs and predicate CPs, which have primarily a predicative use, and a derived modificatory use within NPs. I assume that modifying APs and CPs are syntactically licensed by absorption, and are semantically interpreted as modifying expressions derived from predicates. I'll return to this in chapter 9. But adverbs have no such basic predicative use, and are inherently a different kind of constituent. The only problem for the syntactic theory that I have been developing is how the CP is licensed in (91), repeated from (25b) above:

(91) He knocked [too gently [for us to hear e]].

Here the predicate CP is absorbed into the adverbial degree expression *too gently for us to hear* which is not a syntactic predicate. But then the CP predicate will not strictly be licensed by absorption, since the constituent it is absorbed into will not be predicated of a subject, but will ultimately modify the event argument of the verb. (This is indicated by the fact that it is the event argument of the VP which provides the value for the object of *hear*). But I am not going to try and solve this problem without a discussion of the semantic interpretation of degree phrases and degree adverbials, which will have to be left for another time.

PART II

THE SEMANTICS OF PREDICATION

CHAPTER 6

INTERPRETATION

6.1. Assumptions

In this chapter, we discuss how the structures that I have been arguing for up to now are interpreted. The crucial syntactic point that I have been making is that certain syntactic constituents, namely maximal projections of lexical heads, are syntactically one-place predicates, no matter where they occur in the sentence, and no matter what their thematic structure is. I make some basic assumptions about the relation between the syntactic structure and the semantic interpretation: that syntactic predicates translate as semantic predicates, and that if α is the semantic translation of XP, then α needs to be applied to the denotation of the syntactic argument of which XP is syntactically predicated. Put together, this means that in the semantic representation, the denotations of syntactic predicates must all be of the form $\lambda x.\alpha$, independently of the structural configuration in which they appear, and independently of the thematic adicity of α. I shall propose that this is effected by means of a rule of predicate formation which operates automatically at the predicate XP node in the tree, and which prefixes the semantic interpretation of a predicate XP by a λx operator. (Note that the theory uses x as a distinguished variable by means of which the grammar keeps track which argument ends up in subject position, and I'll talk more of this in the course of the chapter.) I'll assume that a verbal or adjectival expression which has assigned all its internal arguments denotes a set of events, and that the effect of predicate formation is to take a verbal/adjectival expression of type $<e,t>$ into $<d,<e,t>>$, whether it is a main predicate or an adjunct predicate, and independent of whether it has an external argument to assign. In this chapter, I'll be concerned with the interpretation of clausal and adjunct predicates which do assign an external argument, and the structures that we will be giving an interpretation for are those that we have argued for in the previous chapters. I'll concentrate on VP and AP predicates, and I'll leave predicative NPs and AP modifiers to chapter 9. I'll turn to an extensive discussion of pleonastic subjects in the next chapter.

First, some syntactic assumptions. I am assuming indexed S-structures in the sense of Chomsky (1981, 1986a); in other words I am assuming that in passive and raising constructions the subject DP of the verb is coindexed, either directly or indirectly (via a chain with more than one link), with a trace which is theta-marked but not case-marked, and that a wh-word is similarly coindexed with a trace which is theta-marked and case-marked. I also assume that predicates are coindexed with their subjects and that embedded predicates share an index with the predicates into which they are absorbed, as discussed in chapter 5.

There are certain desiderata that the procedure of interpretation has to meet. It has to be compositional. It has to guarantee that a constituent syntactically licensed as a predicate is interpreted as a predicate. The syntactic predicate is saturated syntactically (directly or indirectly) by a syntactic subject, and the interpretation procedure must guarantee that the denotation of the syntactic predicate is itself applied to the element denoted by the saturating syntactic subject. Also, it must ensure that when the head of the syntactic predicate has an external theta-role to assign to the subject, the argument denoted by the subject fills the corresponding thematic role.

There are a few other general syntactic issues to clarify. A syntactic tree consists of a series of nodes arranged in precedence and dominance relations such that each node is either a head, or a projection of a head where X^n immediately dominates X^{n-1}. In any set of nodes which stand in the sister relation, only one node can be non-maximal; the non-maximal node determines the category of the immediately dominating node. All the other nodes are therefore maximal projections. In most cases, in any set of sister nodes, one node is non-maximal. The exception is the small clause; we saw examples of embedded small clauses in chapters 2 and 3 and we discuss matrix small clauses in chapter 8. In a small clause, which is the basic instance of primary predication, the clausal node dominates two maximal projections, the predicate constituent and the subject. As I have argued in part I, the syntactic component recognises maximal projections of certain categories as syntactic predicates and requires that they satisfy the predicate linking rule, in other words that they be syntactically saturated, in order for the structure in which they occur to be grammatical.

Second, heads select complements. Functional heads of a particular category predictably select a single syntactic complement of a particular category. For example Infl, in English, selects a VP, and C selects IP. (We discuss Det and NP in chapter 9.) In contrast, various lexical heads of the same category may select complements which differ in the number of elements and their syntactic type, depending on the particular selectional properties of the head. In addition to the head-complement relation, there is a relation of thematic (theta-) role assignment. A head may assign a number of thematic roles to non-predicative (argument) DPs and CPs, of which no more than one may be assigned to an argument outside the maximal projection of the head (the external argument) and the others are assigned to complements. Elements theta-marked by a head denote participants in the event introduced by the head. As I argued in Rothstein (1991), selectional restrictions cannot be expressed in terms of theta-marking. Theta-marking is the syntactic correlate of the relation between first order predicates and their arguments. Since there are lexical heads which select non-argument complements, not all selectional relations can be expressed in thematic terms. The major syntactic relevance of the theta-relation seems to be to guarantee that a syntactic head has as many syntactic arguments as the corresponding semantic predicate has individual arguments, and to make clear, via syntactic constraints on theta-assignment, that there must be a syntactically local relation between an head and its arguments. Theta-assignment relations are represented in a theta-grid (Higginbotham 1985). I assume, following Davidson (1967), Parsons (1990), and many others, that verbs denote expressions which have an event argument. However, I differ from Higginbotham (1985), in that I assume that the event argument is not represented in the theta-grid; the theta-grid represents the syntactic elements with which the head has a thematic relation, and the event argument, unlike the other thematic arguments of the head, is not represented in the tree by a syntactic constituent.

A theta-grid is part of the lexical representation of the head, and a head + theta-grid is a syntactic object, partially determining the syntactic structure of the tree in which it occurs, and more particularly, the structure of the syntactic subtree which is projected by the head: for V the VP, for A the AP. It represents the thematic arguments of a head and marks no more than one of them as external. Here are two possible representations for the theta-grid for *read*:

(1)   a. read:$_V$ $<a_1, a_2>$
      b. read$_V$: $<\Theta_{Ag}, \Theta_{Th}>$ (equivalently $<Ag, Th>$)

(1a), the format given in chapter 1:(63), encodes the fact that *read* is a verbal head which assigns two theta roles, and that the first argument is realised external to the maximal projection of the verb. (This is represented by italicising a_1 in the grid). The second format encodes also the additional information that the two theta-roles which *read* assigns are 'agent' and 'theme', and that it is the agent argument which is is realised externally. The syntactic assumption of Higginbotham (1985) is that the verb is inserted into the tree with its theta-grid and that the syntactic process of theta-role assignment involves saturating, or cancelling, positions in the theta-grid. Assuming this, *read* will appear at the V node with the theta-grid in (1); the VP will be associated with a theta-grid in which the theme theta-role has been cancelled but in which the agent role is still open. Only at the IP level, after the external theta-role has been assigned, will the theta-grid be fully saturated. This procedure represents the claim that information about the external theta-role of a head is available within the local projection of the head.

It has been suggested (Marantz 1984, Kratzer 1994) that an external argument should not be represented as part of the theta-grid of the verb, precisely because it is outside the maximal VP projection and thus not lexically present in the subtree whose structure the V most directly determines. While I agree with Marantz and Kratzer that the relation between the head and its external argument is fundamentally different from the relation between the head and its internal arguments, I do not think that the best way to represent this is by lexically detaching the external argument from the head. There are two independent pieces of data which argue against the Marantz/Kratzer approach. Both indicate that information about the external argument is available for procedures inside the maximal projection, even though the argument is not syntactically realised there. First, operations like passive result in the former external argument being optionally realised within the VP as a *by*-phrase, either directly, as a PP headed by *by* or, in some theories, with the *by* phrase interpreted as an adjunct of an existentially bound former-external argument. The connection between the *by*-phrase and the external argument is shown by the fact that, as is well known, the *by*-phrase complement PP in non-lexical passives bears the same thematic role as the external subject in the non-passive case; an agentive subject leads to an agentive *by*-phrase complement, an experiencer subject leads to an experiencer *by*-phrase complement and etc. (Levin and Rappaport 1986). That the *by*-phrase is within the VP can be seen from the fact that in a passive sentence it can be ellided by VP ellipsis together with the rest of the VP:

(2)   The poster was read by every boy, and the news headline was too (read by every boy).

    Second, in nominalisations of verbs, an unexpressed 'external' argument can be the subject of an adjunct predicate within the nominalisation as in (3):

(3)   The performance of the national anthem drunk upset everyone tremendously.

I take these both as indications that the external argument is 'attached' to the verb and represented in the theta-grid. We'll see below that this is important for the interpretation procedure that I'll propose.

6.2. INTERPRETATION

Syntactic structures are interpreted in a standard functional type-theoretic language with lambda abstraction, but with a domain sorted into individuals and events. I use d for the type of individuals, and e for the type of events. I assume that these domains have the structure of a Boolean semilattice, with the sum operation, $\sqcup$, and the part of relation, $\sqsubseteq$, defined in the usual way: $x \sqsubseteq y$ iff $x \sqcup y = y$. (See Link 1983, 1987, and others). The domain of individuals will be divided into an atomic structure which gives the denotation of count nouns, and a non-atomic structure which is used in the interpretation of mass nouns. For the moment, I will leave open the question of whether event domain is atomic or mixed; this will be the subject of chapter 10.

    Lexical heads express relations between entities from both domains. *Read* denotes a relation between individuals and an event; and *snow*, which assigns no theta-roles but has an event argument, denotes a property of events. I will assume, for the moment, following Chierchia (1993), Greenberg (1994), Condoravi (1992), that all adjectives have an event argument. (This will be modified in chapter 10.) I assume a standard type theory: type $<a,b>$ is, as usual, the type of function from a entities into b entities. Among others, the following instantiations are important:

$<e,t>$: the function from events into truth values. I will assume that this is the type of sentences at IP, and of small clauses. So IPs and small clauses will denote sets of events. I assume that at the IP level existential closure over the event argument takes place, bringing us to type t (and from there to propositions). I assume that Inflection is crucial in inducing event existential closure, and further that 'uninflected' small clauses denote sets of events (but see chapter 10 for some modification).

$<d,t>$ and $<d,<d,t>>$: the type of one and two place functions from individuals into truth-values. The first is the type of simple common nouns and the second the type of relational nouns like *mother of*. (In these cases, *of* is inserted before the object as a case-assigner in the syntax).

$<d,<e,t>>$ and $<d,<d,<e,t>>>$: these are traditionally the types of intransitive verbs (and VPs) and transitive verbs, respectively. The intransitive verbs are interpreted as functions from individuals to sets of events, while transitive verbs are interpreted as (curried) functions from pairs of individuals into sets of events. Similarly, intransitive adjectives and transitive adjectives are usually assumed to have these types, and I assume that it must also be available for predicate nominals. But, it this correlation between lexical heads denoting n-place relations and logical expressions of type $<d_1 ... d_n,t>$ which we will be revising.

I essentially assume a neo-Davidsonian semantic theory in which verbs denote one-place predicates of events and thematic roles denote functions from events into their participants (Link 1987, Parsons 1990, Landman 1996, 1999), but we will be revising somewhat the theory's approach to the interpretation of thematic roles. In the standard neo-Davidsonian approach, the lexical item *read* denotes the set of reading events. The two thematic roles that it assigns denote two functions from events into individuals, which map the event onto a participant in the event, where the 'label' on the thematic role (agent, patient, theme etc.) indicates the nature of the participation. The semantic function of the theta-grid is thus to introduce these thematic roles. According to the standard neo-Davidsonian theory, the lexical item in (4a) (=1) denotes the expression in (4b):

(4) a. read$_V$: $<\Theta_{Ag}, \Theta_{Th}>$ (=(1))
    b. $\lambda y \lambda x \lambda e.\text{READ}(e) \wedge Ag(e) = x \wedge Th(e) = y$

The V is interpreted as denoting a set of events, and the information in the grid indicates which participant-introducing functions the verb is obligatorily associated with. The denotations of theta-marked constituents are fed into the interpretation by functional application. Adjectives will also denote sets of events and the thematic roles which adjectives assign will also denote functions from the relevant events into participants. (I'll avoid the question of whether adjectives assign the same set of thematic roles as verbs do, and I'll assume that the theta-grid of an adjective contains a list of ordered arguments, where 'arg' (or 'a') is short for 'value of a thematic role'. As with verbs, no more than one 'arg' may be marked as external. An illustration is given in (5):

(5) **proud$_A$**: $< Arg_1, Arg_2 >$)

The crucial modification that I make in standard neo-Davidsonian theory concerns (4b). I propose that the difference between internal and external theta-roles concerns what provokes functional application. Functional application involving internal arguments is lexically triggered, while functional application involving the external argument is not. What this means is that there is a difference between how the internal and external argument show up in the logical expression denoted by a head. The internal arguments introduce conjuncts where the value of the function is a variable bound by a lambda operator, while the external argument introduces a conjunct where the value of the function expressed is a free variable. Instead of (4b), the interpretation of (4a) is (6), making use of the rule that I gave in chapter 1, example (67):

(6) read$_V$: $<\Theta_{Ag}, \Theta_{Th} > \rightarrow \lambda y \lambda e.\text{READ}(e) \wedge \text{Ag}(e) = x \wedge \text{Th}(e) = y$

The structure $[read, \text{DP}]_{V'}$ is interpreted as APPLY[READ, DP$'$] where APPLY is functional application if the types fit, and functional application with standard type shifting if they don't. This means that the type of the VP is going to be $<e,t>$, the type of sets of events. The feeding in of the external argument does not come from the functional properties of the expression which the head denotes. Instead, at the maximal projection level, where the syntax identifies a syntactic predicate which must be syntactically saturated, there is an operation of predicate formation in which a semantic expression is prefixed by 'λx', and gives us an expression of type $<d, <e,t>>$, and this expression then applies to the denotation of the subject.

(7) *Predicate Formation*:
     If α is the translation of a syntactic predicate then $\alpha \rightarrow \lambda x.\alpha$

Predicate Formation occurs automatically when the grammar identifies the syntactic predicate. Suppose we have derived a VP *read War and Peace* with the following interpretation:

(8) $\lambda e.\text{READ}(e) \wedge \text{Ag}(e) = x \wedge \text{Th}(e) = \text{W\&P}$

At the VP level, Predicate Formation will apply automatically to the interpretation (8) to give (9):

(9) $\lambda x \lambda e.\text{READ}(e) \wedge \text{Ag}(e) = x \wedge \text{Th}(e) = \text{W\&P}$

After predicate formation, this predicate applies to the subject argument.

One of the implications of this theory of predicate formation is that the traditional mapping between syntactic types and semantic functions must be revised. A transitive verb like *read* has the same type in its active and passive form, namely $<d, <e,t>>$; and an intransitive verb (and also a verb such as *snow*, as we will see below) is of type $<e,t>$. The fact that VPs after predicate abstraction are uniformly of type $<d, <e,t>>$ results not from the semantic properties of the head of V, but from the properties of the VP node. The same will hold for adjectives, as we will see in section 4.

The theory also makes explicit the relation between the notions 'subject of a predicate' and 'theta-marked argument of a head' and gives semantic content to the notion 'external argument'. *Read*, which has an event argument and two thematic roles to assign, translates as in (6) above, where the event argument and only one of the variables introduced by theta-roles are bound by lambda operators. This represents the fact that there is a distinction between putting lexical or thematic constraints on an argument and licensing functional application of an expression to an argument. Thematic roles introduce constraints on participants in an event: in (6) the conjunct $Th(e) = y$ tells us that the event denoted by *read* is constrained to have a theme participant, and, if we assume a general rule assigning theme arguments to direct object position, we will have the information that the argument in direct object position is constrained to be the theme participant of READ. But this per se is not sufficient to trigger functional application of the verb to the direct object position. What allows application of the verb to the direct object of *read* is the λy operator prefixing the expression in (6). The fact that the x argument is not bound by a lambda in (6) indicates that the verb itself does not trigger functional application to the external agent argument. This is only possible after predicate formation, as in (9). So, this theory gives semantic content to the notions of internal and external argument: a verb may exert thematic constraints on all of the arguments associated with it, but it triggers application only to its internal arguments. It is the VP node, where predicate formation takes place, which licenses application to the 'external' argument.

We can formulate this in the Fregean terms of 'saturated' and 'unsaturated' in the following way. Semantically, expressions of type $<d, <e,t>>$ or $<d, <d, <e,t>>>$, interpreted as functions from individuals into sets of events, are *explicitly unsaturated* expressions. Expressions of type $<e,t>$ are saturated predicates, but they are of two two kinds. IPs and small clauses are of type $<e,t>$ and denote saturated expressions where the thematic functions from the event argument into participants have all been assigned values. VPs, before predicate formation, are also of type $<e,t>$. But while the expressions they denote are formally saturated, they are *implicitly unsaturated*, in that they encode the information that the verb is still lacking an argument. Thus (8) is an implicitly unsaturated expression, since it encodes the information that the interpretation varies depending on the value assigned to a distinguished variable 'x' (more about the distinguished variable below). Predicate formation turns an implicitly unsaturated expression into an explicitly unsaturated expression of the form in (9) above, which expresses the need for another argument in the typed structure. (We will discuss predicate XPs which are not implicitly unsaturated in the next chapter, on pleonastics.)

Note that this proposal captures what we might call the 'non-lexical' aspects of Marantz and Kratzer's proposals. I argued above that the thematic information about the 'external' argument is present in cases where there is no lexical external argument, and that this means we cannot detach the external theta-role from the verb entirely. What I have done here is give expression to the fact that while the thematic constraints on the external argument are dictated by the verbal head, the grammatical operation of 'taking an argument' which is represented by functional application, is not licensed by the V, but by the VP which it heads.

In the following sections I will show how this system works on a number of examples which include simple sentences, passives, raising constructions and small clauses, and adjunct predicates. Then I will compare this approach to a very similar idea in Chierchia (1989) and also to a different approach to subjects in Dowty (1982).

6.3. HOW THIS WORKS

6.3.1. *Simple clauses*

(10) a. $read_V$: $<\Theta_{Ag}, \Theta_{Th}>$
      b. $\lambda y \lambda e.READ(e) \wedge Ag(e) = x \wedge Th(e) = y$
      c. Mary read War and Peace.

(11) $\exists e\ [READ(e) \wedge Ag(e) = M \wedge Th(e) = W\&P]$
      See the derivation tree in figure 1.

The lexical entry that we had in (4), repeated in (10a), is translated in the logical language as the expression (10b). If it is used in a sentence such as (10c), the derivation tree will be as in figure 1. The expression in (10b) allows

$\exists e\ [READ(e) \wedge Ag(e) = M \wedge Th(e) = W\&P]$

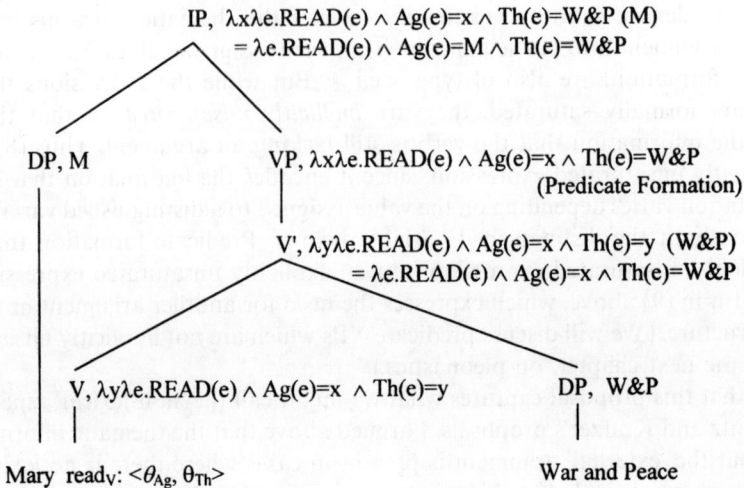

Figure 1.

for the feeding in of the event argument and also of the internal argument, but not the external argument. The verb applies to the internal argument at the V′ level, to yield an expression of type <e,t>, and then at the maximal projection level, predicate formation takes place, to give an expression of type <d, <e,t>> and it is only as a result of this that the external argument can be fed in. (Note that I have completely ignored Infl and I′; I will discuss these nodes separately in section 6.5.3.)

A ditransitive verb such as *give*, assigning agent, theme and goal theta-roles, will denote the expression in (12a) and (12b) will have be interpreted as (12c), with the derivation tree in figure 2.

(12) a. $\lambda z \lambda y \lambda e.\text{GIVE}(e) \wedge \text{Ag}(e) = x \wedge \text{Th}(e) = y \wedge \text{Gl}(e) = z$
      b. Mary gave Bill War and Peace
      c. $\exists e.[\text{GIVE}(e) \wedge \text{Ag}(e) = M \wedge \text{Th}(e) = W\&P \wedge \text{Gl}(e) = B]$
          See derivation tree in figure 2.

$\exists e[\text{GIVE}(e) \wedge \text{Ag}(e) = M \wedge \text{Th}(e) = W\&P \wedge \text{Gl}(e) = B]$

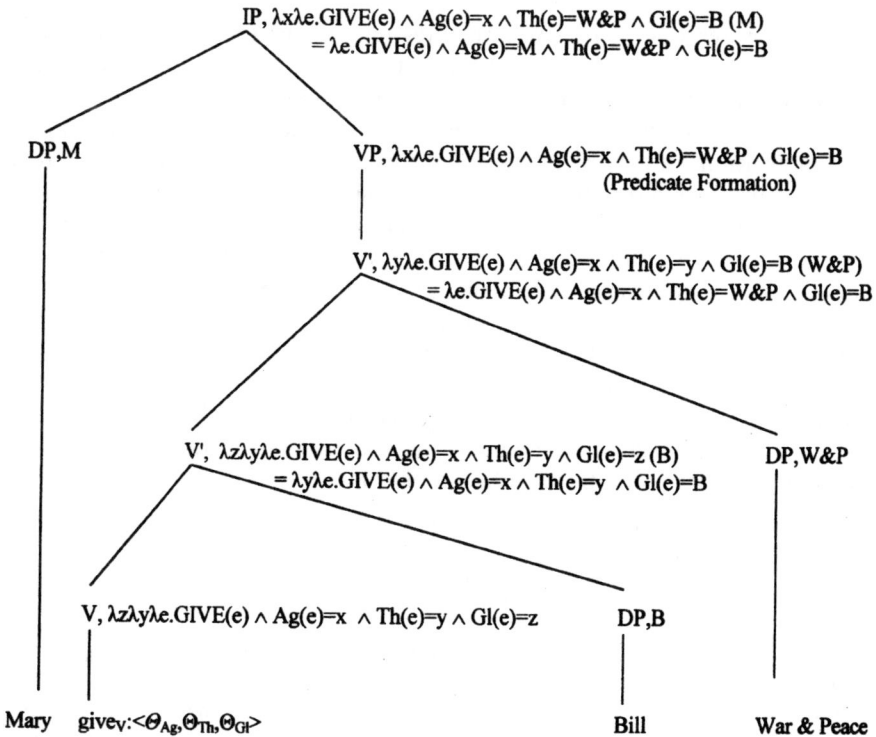

Figure 2.

6.3.2. *Passive*

I assume that passive is a lexical operation on lexical items which existentially binds the external theta-role (thus making it unavailable for assignment), and removes the verb's capacity to assign accusative case. The rules governing the assignment of the other theta-roles don't change, and therefore the theme argument is still assigned to object position, as in the structures we discussed in chapter 2. Since case is not assigned to that position, the object moves to subject position, leaving a DP trace behind. Equivalently, since the object position, while governed, is not assigned case, the only DP which can fill it is trace, which must then be locally bound by an argument which is part of a case-marked and theta-marked chain. Such an argument can only be found in the subject position. The lexical operation of passive is given in (13a). I follow Chierchia (1989), in assuming that the passive verb denotes almost the same function as the active, with the difference that the implicit first argument is bound by an existential quantifier instead of being free, as in (13b).

(13)   passivization:
  a: $read_V$: $<\Theta_{Ag}, \Theta_{Th}> \rightarrow read\text{-}EN_V$: $<\Theta_{Th}>$
  b: $\lambda y \lambda e.READ(e) \wedge Ag(e) = x \wedge Th(e) = y$
     $\rightarrow \lambda y \lambda e.\exists z[READ(e) \wedge Ag(e) = z \wedge Th(e) = y]$

The interpretation of passive structures requires us to make explicit some assumptions about variables. I assume that a variable x is distinguished in the grammatical derivation in that it can be introduced only in certain specific places; this allows us to keep track of which argument ultimately ends up in subject position. (It may be the case that this is not strictly necessary, and that failure to use such a distinguished variable will result in generating along with the structures that we want, ungrammatical ones which will be ruled out by the binding theory and constraints on the formulation of wh-chains.) The x variable so far has been used in two places: it is the value of the thematic function introduced by the external argument, and it is the variable introduced with the lambda in predicate formation, and this of course means that the lambda will bind the external argument and that predicate application at the VP level will saturate this argument. Another place in which the x variable is used is as the translation of non-case-marked traces, and thus figure 3 gives the derivation for (14b), the translation of (14a):

(14)   a.   War and Peace was read.
       b. $\exists e \exists z[READ(e) \wedge Ag(e) = z \wedge Th(e) = W\&P]$
            See derivation tree in figure 3.

We see that there are only internal arguments, and (ignoring the event argument) there are exactly as many unsaturated positions as there are internal arguments to fill them. It looks as if at the VP level there will be nothing for the predicate abstraction to abstract over. However, the internal argument is syntactically saturated by a trace; the function denoted by passive READ

∃e∃z[READ(e) ∧ Ag(e)=z ∧ Th(e)=W&P]

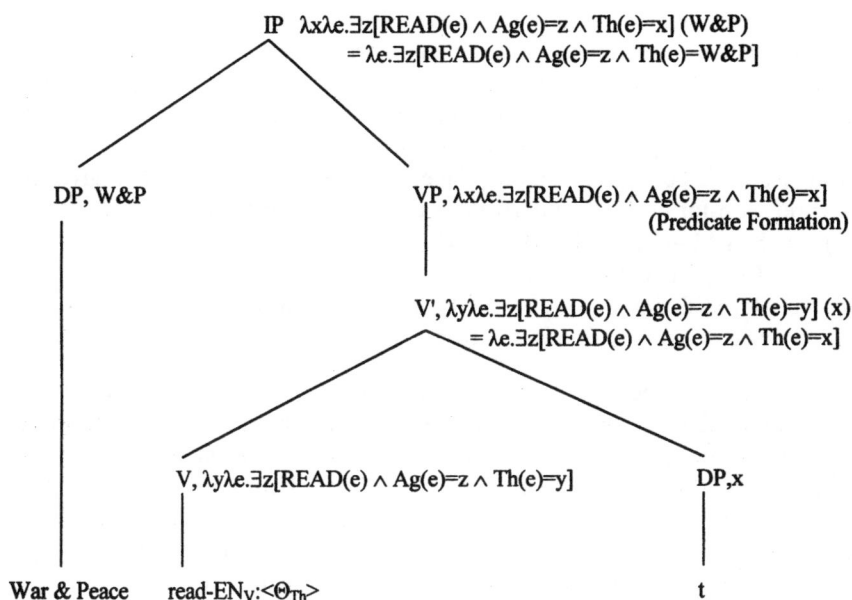

IP λxλe.∃z[READ(e) ∧ Ag(e)=z ∧ Th(e)=x] (W&P)
= λe.∃z[READ(e) ∧ Ag(e)=z ∧ Th(e)=W&P]

DP, W&P

VP, λxλe.∃z[READ(e) ∧ Ag(e)=z ∧ Th(e)=x]
(Predicate Formation)

V', λyλe.∃z[READ(e) ∧ Ag(e)=z ∧ Th(e)=y] (x)
= λe.∃z[READ(e) ∧ Ag(e)=z ∧ Th(e)=x]

V, λyλe.∃z[READ(e) ∧ Ag(e)=z ∧ Th(e)=y]   DP,x

War & Peace   read-EN$_V$:<Θ$_{Th}$>   t

Figure 3.

(READ-EN) is applied to the trace, which yields an expression with a free variable. Predicate formation binds this variable, and the resulting VP predicate then applies to the subject, ensuring that the subject argument will have the thematic value of the internal theta-role. Assuming a movement analysis of unaccusatives, the interpretation of uaccusatives will work in exactly the same way.

The assumption that both the external argument of the verb and the DP (non-case-marked) trace are represented in the semantic representation by the same distinguished variable represents the direct role that DP trace has in 'externalising' an internal argument. DP trace is a mechanism which allows the syntax to treat passive and active forms of the verb as if they had the same subcategorisation frame; further, if we consider both passive and unaccusative verbs, DP trace allows us to maintain the claim that the theme role is always assigned to direct object position. Case factors are responsible for the fact that a phonologically realised lexical argument cannot be realised as the direct object of passive and unaccusative verbs, and that the theta-role must be assigned to a trace, or place holder. This trace is translated as an x variable; after the passive verb has applied to the trace to give the value of the theme argument, there are no lexical factors which will trigger further function application to this position and, like the lexical external argument, it is dependent on the predicational configuration in which it occurs to get an interpretation.

6.3.3. *DP-raising*

DP raising works in essentially the same way, since all non-case marked traces are interpreted as x. I assume that type of *seem* is $<p, <e,t>>$; i.e it takes propositions into functions from events into truth values. Both 'It seemed that John cried' and 'John seemed to cry' will be true if there is an eventuality in which the proposition that John cried seemed to be true. We'll discuss the example with the pleonastic subject in the next chapter, and deal with the raising example here. *Seem* denotes the expression in (15a), and (15c) gives the interpretation for (15b). The derivation tree is given in figure 4:

(15)   a. $SEEM \rightarrow \lambda p \lambda e.SEEM(e) \wedge Th(e) = p$

      b.   John$_i$ seemed t$_i$ to cry

      c. $\exists e[SEEM(e) \wedge Th(e) = {}^{\wedge}\exists e'[CRY(e') \wedge Ag(e') = J]]$

         See derivation tree in figure 4.

The trace denotes the variable x, and the result of predicate abstraction at the matrix VP level is that this variable is bound by the lambda operator introduced at that level; the resulting expression is applied to the subject, and the variable is replaced by the denotation of the matrix subject. This means that the matrix subject denotation saturates the position originally filled by the trace denotation, and, as the indexing indicates, this is the result we want. (A more complicated account will be needed to deal with the de dicto reading of 'A unicorn seemed to be in the garden last night', but I am not going to discuss that here.)

6.3.4. *Small clause complements*

As said above, I take the small clause to be of type $<e,t>$, and to denote a sets of events. Small clauses, as we saw in chapter 2, are arguments of thematic roles, and are thus to be interpreted as values of functions from the event argument of the matrix predicate into its participants; Vlach (1983) proposes the truth conditions in (16) for sentences with perception verbs and small clause complements.

(16)   V(x,E) is true if x stands in the V relation with a member of the set of events E.

So *Mary saw John leave* is true if Mary stands in the **see** relation with a member of the set of events denoted by *John leave*. I assume that Vlach's analysis of perception-verb complements can be extended to other verbs with small clause complements too. (See chapter 10 for discussion). In particular, we can take *consider* to denote a relation between an individual, an event and a set of events; (17) will be true just in case there is an event of Mary standing in the 'consider' relation with a set of events of Bill being sick, and this will be the case if she considers there to be such an event.

(17)   Mary considers Bill drunk.

$\exists e[\text{SEEM}(e) \wedge \text{Th}(e) = {}^{\wedge}\exists e'[\text{CRY}(e') \wedge \text{Ag}(e') = J]$

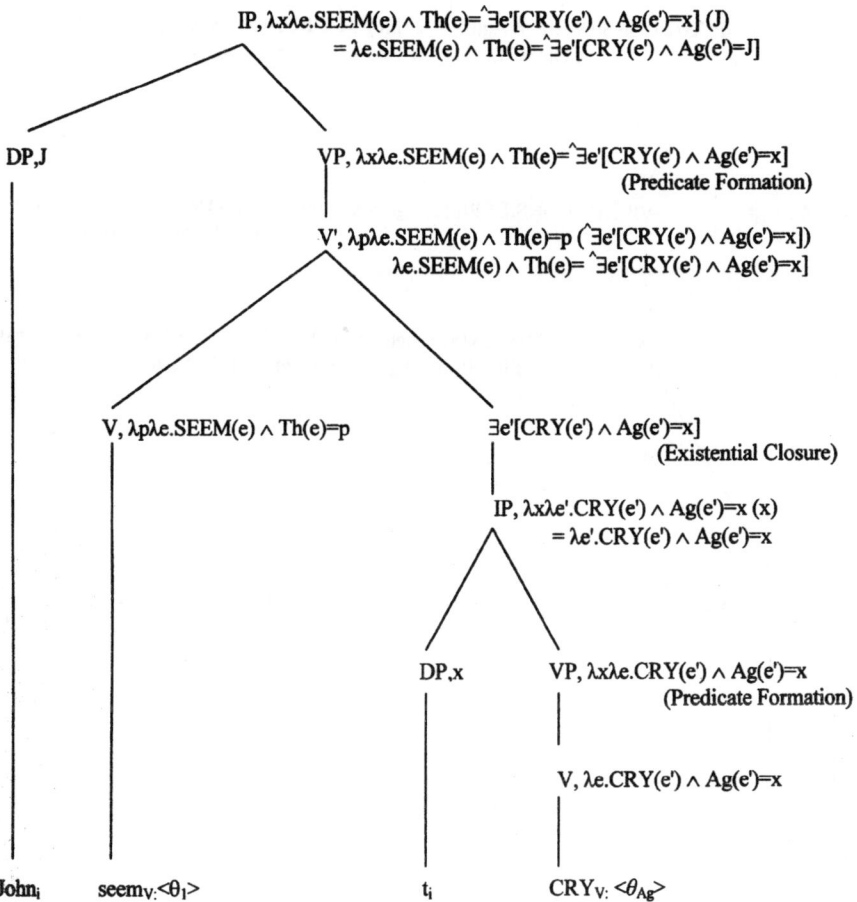

IP, $\lambda x \lambda e.\text{SEEM}(e) \wedge \text{Th}(e) = {}^{\wedge}\exists e'[\text{CRY}(e') \wedge \text{Ag}(e') = x]$ (J)
$= \lambda e.\text{SEEM}(e) \wedge \text{Th}(e) = {}^{\wedge}\exists e'[\text{CRY}(e') \wedge \text{Ag}(e') = J]$

DP,J

VP, $\lambda x \lambda e.\text{SEEM}(e) \wedge \text{Th}(e) = {}^{\wedge}\exists e'[\text{CRY}(e') \wedge \text{Ag}(e') = x]$
(Predicate Formation)

V', $\lambda p \lambda e.\text{SEEM}(e) \wedge \text{Th}(e) = p$ $({}^{\wedge}\exists e'[\text{CRY}(e') \wedge \text{Ag}(e') = x])$
$\lambda e.\text{SEEM}(e) \wedge \text{Th}(e) = {}^{\wedge}\exists e'[\text{CRY}(e') \wedge \text{Ag}(e') = x]$

V, $\lambda p \lambda e.\text{SEEM}(e) \wedge \text{Th}(e) = p$

$\exists e'[\text{CRY}(e') \wedge \text{Ag}(e') = x]$
(Existential Closure)

IP, $\lambda x \lambda e'.\text{CRY}(e') \wedge \text{Ag}(e') = x$ (x)
$= \lambda e'.\text{CRY}(e') \wedge \text{Ag}(e') = x$

DP,x

VP, $\lambda x \lambda e.\text{CRY}(e') \wedge \text{Ag}(e') = x$
(Predicate Formation)

V, $\lambda e.\text{CRY}(e') \wedge \text{Ag}(e') = x$

John$_i$ seem$_{V:<\theta_1>}$ t$_i$ CRY$_{V: <\theta_{Ag}>}$

Figure 4.

(18) is the derivation for (17). The derivation tree is given in figure 5.

(18) $\exists e[\text{CONSIDER}(e) \wedge \text{Ag}(e) = M \wedge \text{Th}(e) = \lambda e'.\text{DRUNK}(e')$
$\wedge \text{Arg}_1(e') = B]$
See derivation tree in figure 5.

6.3.5. *CP predicates*

I argued in chapter 2 that CP predicates are derived predicates rather than inherent predicates. Unlike the VP and AP predicates we have been considering up to now, CPs are inherently arguments and function as predicates only if they contain an operator in spec of CP heading a chain whose lowest node is

$\exists e[CONSIDER(e) \land Ag(e)=M \land Th(e)=\lambda e'.DRUNK(e') \land Arg_1(e')=B]$

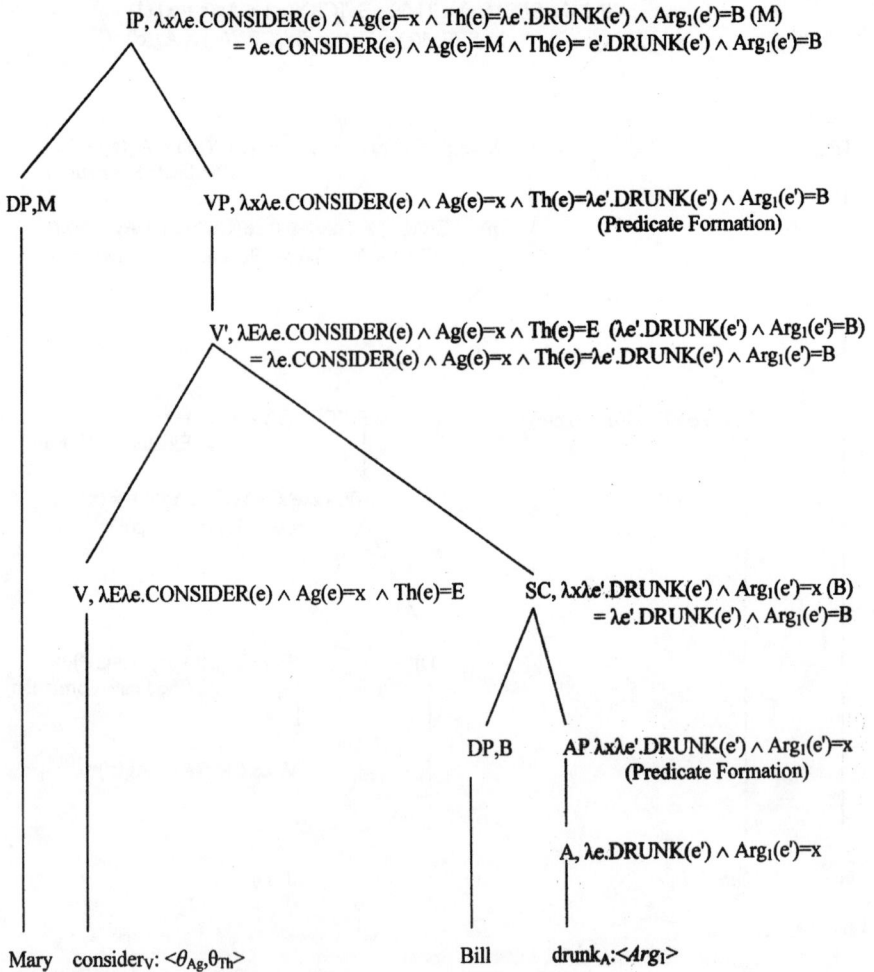

Figure 5.

a case-marked trace. In English relative clauses, the operator may, but need not always, be lexically realised, as in 'the book (which) John gave me', while in other 'null operator constructions, such as purpose clauses, the operator is phonologically null. The uncontroversial assumption to make is that the wh-operator is translated by a lambda operator, converting the sentence into a predicate, and that it binds the variable which is the translation of the wh-trace. This means that wh-predicates are not, and should not, be introduced by the rule of predicate formation in (8). The rule in (8) applies only to those XPs which the grammar recognises as inherently predicative; constituents which are converted into syntactic predicates by 'local' predicate-formation operations contain a syntactic operator which is translated into semantic λ-operator.

In order to make sure that the lambda operator which translates the wh-operator binds the case-marked variable, we may want to make an additional assumption, namely that there is a second distinguished variable, x', which is reserved for the denotation of case-marked, or wh-trace, and which is introduced in the $\lambda x'$ prefix as the translation of the wh-operator. However, this is a matter for the interpretation of wh-chains. What we are interested in here is ensuring that the lambda operator introduced by predicate formation doesn't bind a wh-trace, and this is guaranteed by the assumption that the ways of introducing the distinguished x variable into the grammar do not include wh-trace.

Here is an example of a nominal including a relative clause, with the derivation tree in figure 6:

(19) a. the [book [which$_i$ Mary$_j$ was given t$_j$ t$_i$]]]
     b. $\sigma y[[\text{book}(y) \wedge [\exists e \exists z[\text{GIVE}(e) \wedge \text{Ag}(e) = z \wedge \text{Th}(e) = y \wedge \text{Gl}(e) = \text{M}]]$
       See derivation tree in figure 6.

The conjunction rule used at the NP level is standard generalised conjunction at type $<d,t>$, where $\wedge_{<d,t>} = \lambda Q \lambda P \lambda x.P(x) \wedge Q(x)$. 'THE' is Link's '$\sigma$' function (Link 1983).

6.4. ADJUNCT AND ABSORBED PREDICATES

6.4.1. *Secondary predicates*

In this section I extend the account to deal with the adjunct syntactic predicates discussed in chapter 5, and exemplified in (20):

(20) a. The police arrested Bill drunk.
     b. He drinks his coffee sweetened.
     c. John acted foolish.
     d. Bill drove the car drunk.

In chapter 5 I distinguished between the predicates in (20a/b), and those in (20c/d). This first I called 'secondary predicates', and these are licensed syntactically since they are syntactic sisters of their subjects, the direct objects of the verbs. The second are 'absorbed' predicates, since they absorbed into the XP which dominates them and are thus indirectly predicated of the subject of the sentence which they do not c-command. A further instance of an absorbed predicate is the complement of copular *be*, as in (21); I will discuss the interpretation of these structures in chapter 10.

(21) John is tall.

σy[[book(y) ∧ [∃e∃z[GIVE(e) ∧ Ag(e)=z ∧ Th(e)=y ∧ Gl(e)=M]]

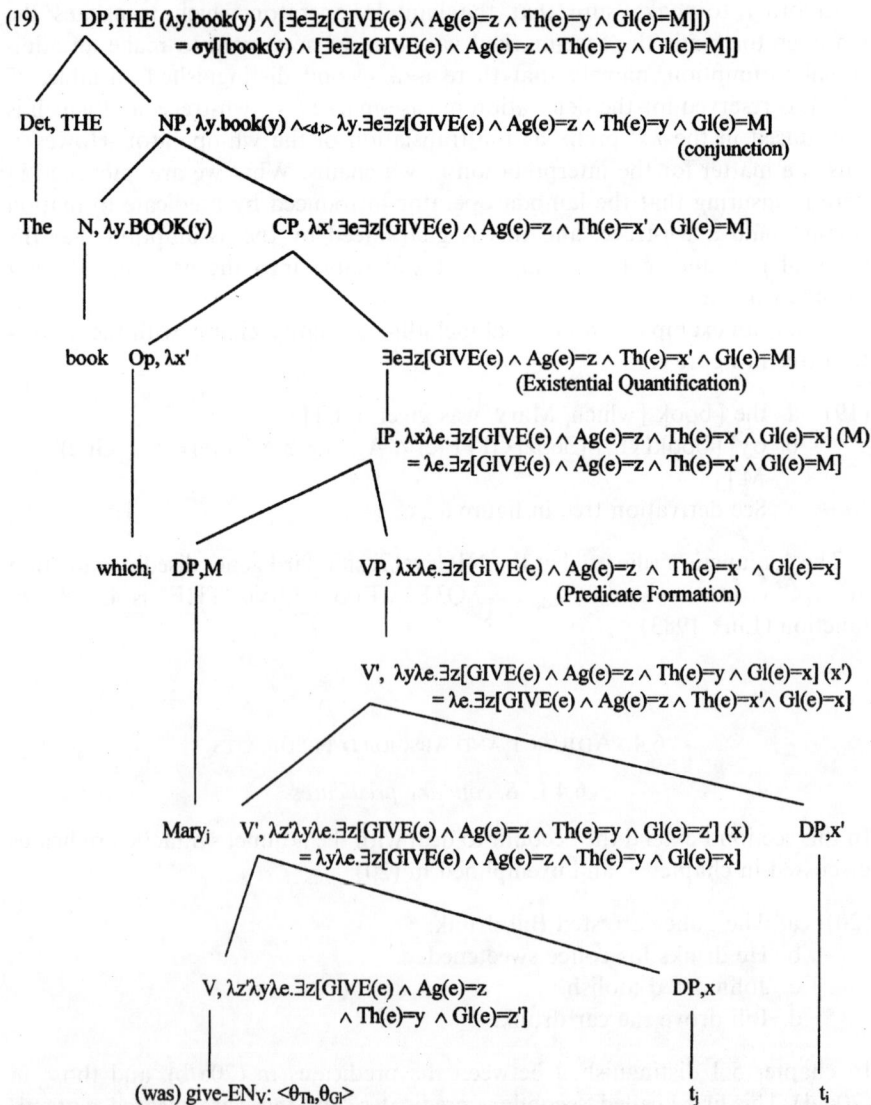

(19)   DP,THE (λy.book(y) ∧ [∃e∃z[GIVE(e) ∧ Ag(e)=z ∧ Th(e)=y ∧ Gl(e)=M]])
         = σy[[book(y) ∧ [∃e∃z[GIVE(e) ∧ Ag(e)=z ∧ Th(e)=y ∧ Gl(e)=M]]

Det, THE   NP, λy.book(y) ∧<d,t> λy.∃e∃z[GIVE(e) ∧ Ag(e)=z ∧ Th(e)=y ∧ Gl(e)=M]
                                                                          (conjunction)

The   N, λy.BOOK(y)   CP, λx'.∃e∃z[GIVE(e) ∧ Ag(e)=z ∧ Th(e)=x' ∧ Gl(e)=M]

book   Op, λx'   ∃e∃z[GIVE(e) ∧ Ag(e)=z ∧ Th(e)=x' ∧ Gl(e)=M]
                                                  (Existential Quantification)

                         IP, λxλe.∃z[GIVE(e) ∧ Ag(e)=z ∧ Th(e)=x' ∧ Gl(e)=x] (M)
                         = λe.∃z[GIVE(e) ∧ Ag(e)=z ∧ Th(e)=x' ∧ Gl(e)=M]

whichᵢ DP,M   VP, λxλe.∃z[GIVE(e) ∧ Ag(e)=z ∧ Th(e)=x' ∧ Gl(e)=x]
                                                  (Predicate Formation)

                         V', λyλe.∃z[GIVE(e) ∧ Ag(e)=z ∧ Th(e)=y ∧ Gl(e)=x] (x')
                         = λe.∃z[GIVE(e) ∧ Ag(e)=z ∧ Th(e)=x'∧ Gl(e)=x]

Maryⱼ V', λz'λyλe.∃z[GIVE(e) ∧ Ag(e)=z ∧ Th(e)=y ∧ Gl(e)=z'] (x)   DP,x'
       = λyλe.∃z[GIVE(e) ∧ Ag(e)=z ∧ Th(e)=y ∧ Gl(e)=x]

V, λz'λyλe.∃z[GIVE(e) ∧ Ag(e)=z   DP,x
   ∧ Th(e)=y ∧ Gl(e)=z']

(was) give-ENᵥ: <θ_Th,θ_Gl>   tⱼ   tᵢ

Figure 6.

We will look first at the interpretation of secondary predicates. Following the
conclusions of the discussion of chapter 5, (20a) is assigned the syntactic
structure in (22). (I include Infl and I′ in the syntactic tree here, but I will
continue to ignore them in the interpretation until section 6.5.3)

(22)

```
                        IP
              ┌─────────┴──────────┐
            DP                     I'
            │              ┌───────┴───────┐
            │            Infl             VP
            │              │               │
            │              │              V'
            │              │        ┌──────┼──────┐
            │              │        V     DP     AP
      The police      PAST arrested      Bill   drunk
```

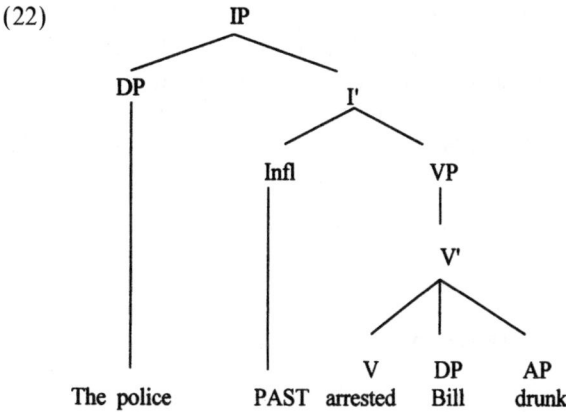

I have argued that the external argument of a head corresponds to a variable in the representation of the lexical meaning of the head which is not bound by a lambda operator. When its internal arguments are satisfied, the expression will be of type $<e,t>$, denoting a predicate of events. Predicate formation converts it to an expression of type $<d, <e,t>>$. We want to maintain the same core account of secondary predication as we did for primary predication; first because it is a central premise of the theory that 'predicate' and 'syntactic predication' are defined independent of where an XP constituent appears in a sentence, and second because our claim about the representation of lexical heads is also general and independent of the idiosyncratic properties of a head. A predicate such as *drunk* can appear as both a primary and a secondary predicate, as (23) shows;

(23)   a. Mary considers Bill drunk. (= 18)
       b. The police arrested Bill drunk.

Drunk must have the same lexical interpretation in each case – the logical expression $\lambda e.\text{DRUNK}(e) \wedge \text{Arg}_1(e) = x$. Predicate formation takes place at the XP level independent of whether the ultimate destiny of the XP expression is to be a primary predicate, a secondary predicate, or an absorbed predicate of the kind we will discuss below.

However, despite the fact that the AP is a predicate of the DP object and that a lambda operator should be introduced at the AP level, we cannot, in (23b), apply the function denoted by the AP directly to the denotation of the direct object. We saw in (18), the derivation for (23a), that where the denotation of *drunk* applies directly to its sister DP it 'uses up' the DP and gives a small clause. Although I argued in chapter 5 that *drunk* in (23b) is also a sister of its subject, I also showed that there is no small clause in a secondary predication structure, and that the direct object must be the argument both of the secondary predicate and the matrix verb. We therefore do not want the secondary predicate to apply directly and independently to its subject, in the way that the small clause predicate does in (18). Instead, we want the direct object to be an argument of both the matrix verb and the secondary predicate, reflecting the fact that it saturates positions in the theta-grids of both lexical heads. We do this by conjoining the AP predicate drunk with the denotation of the verbal predicate, and applying the result to the direct object. In (23b), *arrest* and *drunk* have the interpretations in (24a,b); predicate formation applies to the AP predicate, as in (24c) and the V' level of the tree looks like (25):

(24)   a.   V, $\lambda y \lambda e.\text{ARREST}(e) \wedge \text{Ag}(e) = x \wedge \text{Th}(e) = y$

   $\text{arrest}_V: <\theta_{Ag}, \theta_{Th}>$

   b.   A, $\lambda e.\text{DRUNK}(e) \wedge \text{Arg}_1(e) = x$

   $\text{drunk}_A: <Arg_1>$

   c.   AP, $\lambda x \lambda e.\text{DRUNK}(e) \wedge \text{Arg}_1(e) = x$

(25)

```
                              V'
            _____/ |  _____
           /                   |                  \
 V, λyλe.ARREST(e) ∧ Ag(e)=x ∧ Th(e)=y   DP,B     AP, λxλe.DRUNK(e) ∧ Arg₁(e)=x
           |                   |                  (Predicate Formation)
           |                   |                   |
           |                   |                   |
  arrestᵥ: <θAg, θTh>         Bill         drunkA: <Arg₁>
```

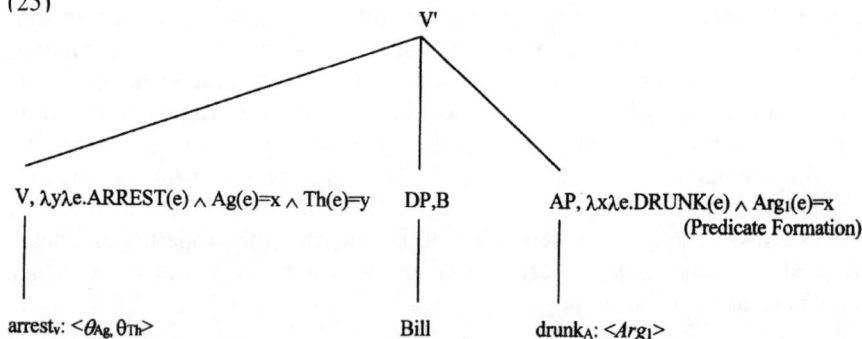

The V and the AP can be conjoined using generalised conjunction at the type of $<d, <e,t>>$. As has been discussed in Lasersohn (1992, 1995), conjunctions at types involving events must result in a plurality of events, which can be captured using the summing operation (see also Landman 1996). The effect of conjoining the predicates in (24a,c) is to give a relation between individuals and events which contain as parts the event of an individual being arrested by x and an event of that individual being drunk. The conjunction rule for event-based types in (26) gives (27) as the meaning of the V' in (25), where '⊔' is interpreted as the sum operation:

(26)   general event-based conjunction
   $\alpha_{<d, <e,t>>} + \beta_{<d, <e,t>>} := \lambda y \lambda e. \exists e_1 \exists e_2 [e = e_1 \sqcup e_2 \wedge \alpha(e_1, y) \wedge \beta(e_2, y)]$

(27) $\lambda y \lambda e. \exists e_1 \exists e_2 [e = e_1 \sqcup e_2 \wedge \text{ARREST}(e_1) \wedge \text{Ag}(e_1) = x \wedge \text{Th}(e_1) = y$
   $\wedge \text{DRUNK}(e_2) \wedge \text{Arg}_1(e_2) = y]$

The conjunction rule existentially binds the event variable in each predicate and gives a new, complex predicate which denotes a set of events which are the sum of an event of the kind denoted by V and an event of the kind denoted by the adjective. The rest of the derivation is unproblematic and the derivation tree is given in figure 7.

(28) $\exists e \exists e_1 \exists e_2 [e = e_1 \sqcup e_2 \wedge \text{ARREST}(e_1) \wedge \text{Ag}(e_1) = P \wedge \text{Th}(e_1) = B$
$\wedge \text{Arg}_1(e_2) = B]$

See derivation tree in figure 7.

The sentence is true if there was an event which has a part which is an event of the police arresting Bill and a part which is an event of Bill being drunk. The two parts must be temporally connected – the event of Bill being drunk must last at least as long as the event of arresting – and this temporal dependence follows from the fact that tense, and other temporal modifiers, introduced above the V′ level, will modify the highest e which is the summed event.

We see that secondary predication differs from primary predication despite the fact that in both cases predicate formation applies at the XP level in the same way. In primary predication the predicate is applied directly to the subject, while in secondary predication the predicate is predicated of its subject via conjunction with the verb.

6.4.2. *Predicate absorption*

In chapter 5, it looked as if secondary predicates, such as (16a,b) had more in common with primary, clausal predicates, since both c-commanded their subjects, than they had in common with other so-called adjunct predicates licensed by predicate absorption, and this seemed counter-intuitive. If we look at the semantic interpretations, we can see that while both kinds of adjunct predications involve conjunction, secondary predication is indeed a more straightforward operation than absorption.

Intuitively, absorbed predicates work the same way as the secondary predicates discussed in 6.4.1. Both the examples in (29) seem to involve conjunction in the same way that (28) does:

(29) a. John [ran [drunk]$_{AP}$]$_{VP}$
      b. John [[[met Mary]$_{V'}$ [drunk]$_{AP}$]$_{VP}$

(29a) means that there was an event which had an event of John running as a part and an event of John being drunk as a (co-temporaneous) part. On the subject-adjunct reading of (29b), where *drunk* is predicated of John, we get an analogous reading: there was an event which had John meeting Mary as a part and John being drunk as a co-temporaneous part.

The problem is that while (28) involved conjoining two predicates of the same type, and was thus a simple instance of generalised conjunction involving events, here the conjunction involves expressions of different types.

We showed in chapter 5 that the subject-adjunct predicates in (29) must be within the VP, but, in the case of (29b), it cannot be within V′. If the AP is the daughter of VP, as the partial derivation in (30) shows, then we need to conjoin the AP predicate with its sister after predicate formation has applied to the AP but before it applies to the VP.

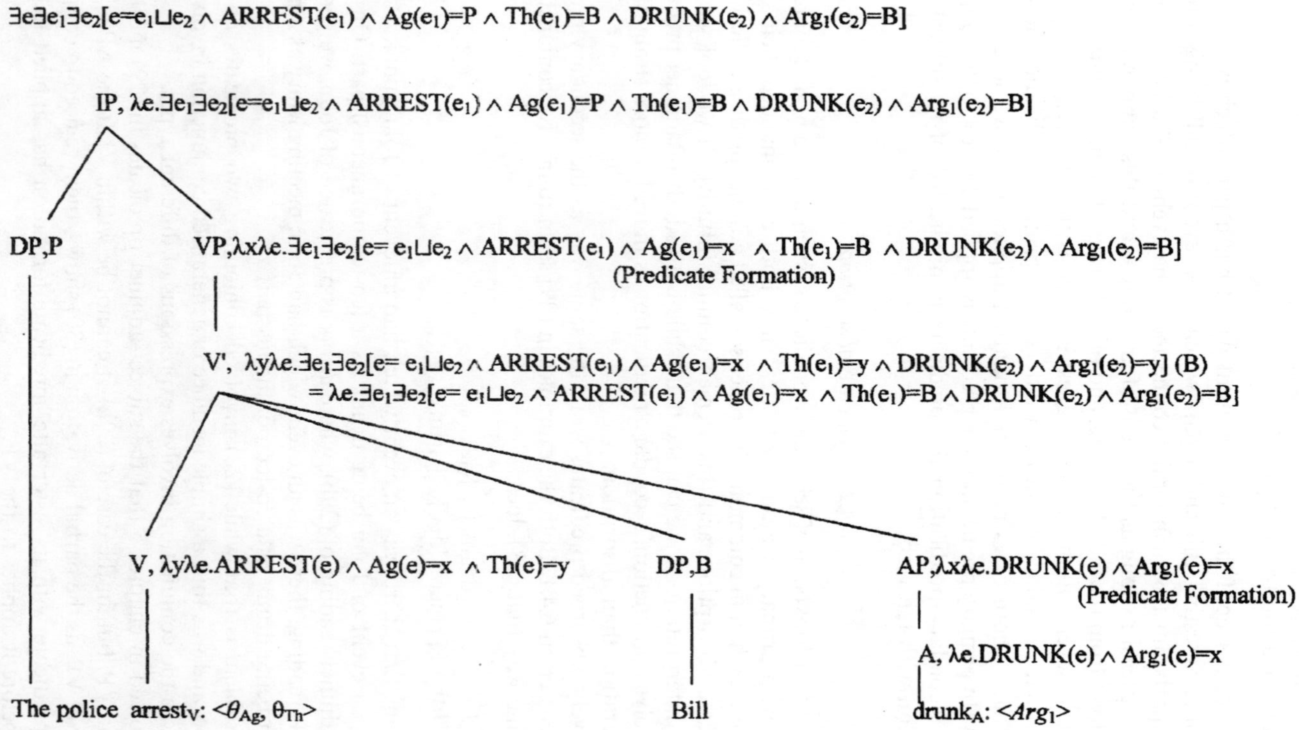

∃e∃e₁∃e₂[e=e₁⊔e₂ ∧ ARREST(e₁) ∧ Ag(e₁)=P ∧ Th(e₁)=B ∧ DRUNK(e₂) ∧ Arg₁(e₂)=B]

IP, λe.∃e₁∃e₂[e=e₁⊔e₂ ∧ ARREST(e₁) ∧ Ag(e₁)=P ∧ Th(e₁)=B ∧ DRUNK(e₂) ∧ Arg₁(e₂)=B]

DP,P

VP,λxλe.∃e₁∃e₂[e= e₁⊔e₂ ∧ ARREST(e₁) ∧ Ag(e₁)=x   ∧ Th(e₁)=B ∧ DRUNK(e₂) ∧ Arg₁(e₂)=B]
(Predicate Formation)

V', λyλe.∃e₁∃e₂[e= e₁⊔e₂ ∧ ARREST(e₁) ∧ Ag(e₁)=x ∧ Th(e₁)=y ∧ DRUNK(e₂) ∧ Arg₁(e₂)=y] (B)
= λe.∃e₁∃e₂[e= e₁⊔e₂ ∧ ARREST(e₁) ∧ Ag(e₁)=x ∧ Th(e₁)=B ∧ DRUNK(e₂) ∧ Arg₁(e₂)=B]

V, λyλe.ARREST(e) ∧ Ag(e)=x ∧ Th(e)=y

DP,B

AP,λxλe.DRUNK(e) ∧ Arg₁(e)=x
(Predicate Formation)

Bill

A, λe.DRUNK(e) ∧ Arg₁(e)=x

drunk_A: <*Arg₁*>

The police   arrest_V: <θ_Ag, θ_Th>

Figure 7.

(30)

```
                              VP
              _____/_____
             /                        \
   V,λe.RUN(e) ∧ Ag(e)=x       AP, λxλe.DRUNK(e) ∧ Arg₁(e)=x
             |                     (Predicate Formation)
             |                            |
             |                 A, λxλe.DRUNK(e) ∧ Arg₁(e)=x
             |                            |
     runᵥ:<θ_Ag>              drunk_A:<Arg₁>
```

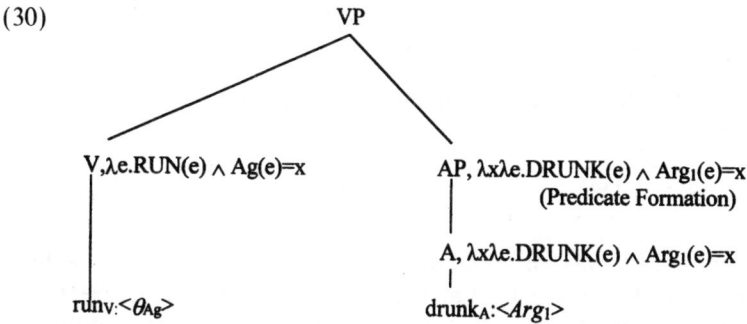

At this stage, the two expressions we are interested in are of different types; the V is $<e,t>$ and the AP is $<d,<e,t>>$. In (29b) we will have the same problem. *Drunk* will be the sister of the V′ *meet Mary*, which is also of type $<e,t>$ since it denotes $\lambda e.\text{MEET}(e) \wedge \text{Ag}(e) = x \wedge \text{Th}(e) = \text{MARY}$. A suggestion that Predicate Formation should not apply to the AP would solve the problem here, but at the expense of secondary predication as in (28), where it is crucial that the predicate AP and the V are both of type $<d,<e,t>>$. And it is appropriate that it is the subject-adjuncts which are the more complex construction. Secondary predication with object-oriented adjuncts essentially involves predicating two predicates of the same argument simultaneously, and this is represented in the tree by the fact that both V and AP in (28) are syntactic sisters of their shared argument. But subject-oriented adjunct predication, as I argued in chapter 5, involves 'postponing' the application of the AP predicate, and forming a complex predicate by absorbing the AP into the VP. In other words, instead of two separate predicates sharing an argument, as in (28), we have two separate predicates combining to form a single complex predicate which applies to a single argument.

The 'absorption' operation we require to form this complex predicate is in two stages and involves first bringing the AP to type $<e,t>$ by applying it to the distinguished variable x, and then applying the generalised event-based conjunction at type $<e,t>$. The rule is given in (31), and included both stages:

(31) $+^*$: predicate absorption (semantic)

$$\alpha_{<e,t>} +^* \beta_{<d,<e,t>>}(x) := \lambda e.\exists e_1 \exists e_2 [e = e_1 \sqcup e_2 \wedge \alpha(e_1) \wedge (\beta(x))(e_2)]$$

Assume that α is the denotation of *run* and β is the denotation of *drunk*. The result of applying (31) to α and β is (32):

(32) $\lambda e.\text{RUN}(e) \wedge \text{Ag}(e) = x +^* \lambda x \lambda e'.\text{DRUNK}(e') \wedge \text{Arg}_1(e') = x(x)$
$\quad = \lambda e.\text{RUN}(e) \wedge \text{Ag}(e) = x + \lambda e'.\text{DRUNK}(e') \wedge \text{Arg}_1(e') = x$
$\quad = \lambda e.\exists e_1 \exists e_2 [e = e_1 \sqcup e_2 \wedge \text{RUN}(e_1) \wedge \text{Ag}(e_1) = x \wedge \text{DRUNK}(e_2)$
$\quad \quad \wedge \text{Arg}_1(e_2) = x]$

Predicate formation then applies to the VP in the last line of (32) to give the predicate in (33):

(33) $\lambda x \lambda e. \exists e_1 \exists e_2 [e = e_1 \sqcup e_2 \wedge \text{RUN}(e_1) \wedge \text{Ag}(e_1) = x$
$\wedge \text{DRUNK}(e_2) \wedge \text{Arg}_1(e_2) = x]$

This is then applied to the subject *John* and the result after existential quantification is (34):

(34) $\exists e \exists e_1 \exists e_2 [e = e_1 \sqcup e_2 \wedge \text{RUN}(e_1) \wedge \text{Ag}(e_1) = x$
$\wedge \text{DRUNK}(e_2) \wedge \text{Arg}_1(e_2) = x]$

In other words, there was an event which is the sum of the events of John running and John being drunk. Again, the constraint that these events are cotemporaneous follows from the fact that temporal constraints are introduced by the Inflection node above the VP level, as modifiers of the highest e variable, after the scope of the two lower existential quantifiers over e_1 and e_2 respectively have been closed.

Note that the rule in (31) makes use of the distinguished variable x in an additional way, as the variable to which the predicate AP must be applied. We can sum up the ways in which the distinguished variable is introduced:

i.   lexical: 'x' is the value of the external theta-role of a head
ii.   predicate formation: prefixes an expression with 'λx'
iii. DP-trace: denotes 'x'
iv.   predicate absorption:
      $\text{CONJOIN}[\alpha_{<e,t>}, \beta_{<d,<e,t>>}] = \alpha_{<e,t>} \sqcup \beta_{<d,<e,t>>}(x)$
      These are the only ways I assume of introducing x into the derivation, (with one caveat: we will see in chapter 9 that the operation involved in the interpretation of identity, or equative, constructions also introduces an x variable).

Thus in (32), the distinguished variable is introduced as the value of the Agent role of RUN and of Arg_1 of DRUNK by (i), in the λ-prefix of DRUNK by (ii) and as the variable to which the denotation of *drunk* is applied to by (iv), allowing us to keep track of the position which is to be bound by the highest λ-operator. Note that x must be an unsorted variable, ranging over individuals and events because of verbs such as *prove* and *remember*, which select either an individual or an event as their external argument and argument in direct object position respectively. There are various technical ways of dealing with this which I will not go into since we won't be dealing explicitly with derivations which raise this problem, although the issue is relevant for the discussion in the next chapter.

6.4.3. *The syntax-semantics interface*

Let us sum up where we have got to so far.

We have introduced a rule of predicate formation that translates inherent syntactic predicates as expressions of type $<d, <e,t>>$, independent of the structural configuration in which these predicates appear. We have isolated four kinds of constructions in which these predicates appear. One is as a main clause predicate as in (35a), the others are all within the VP:

(35)   a. $[DP (I + VP)]_{IP}$ (example (11))
       b. $[V [DP XP]_{SC}]$ (example (18))
       c. $[[V NP XP]_{V'}]_{VP}$ (example (28))
       d. $[[V]_{V'} XP]_{VP}$ (example (32))

The syntactic predicate-linking rule relates a predicate α and an argument which is its syntactic sister; the semantic corollary is application of $\lambda x.\alpha$ to the denotation of the argument. In (35a/b) the predicate is saturated (i.e. reduced from type $<d, <e,t>>$ to type $<e,t>$) by being applied directly to the denotation of its syntactic sister; the result is a constituent of type $<e,t>$. In (35a) this is an IP, which is then existentially quantified over to give a expression of type t, while in (35b), the result is a small clause denoting a set of events. We can give explicit rules for interpreting these syntactic structures, as in (36) where '+' on the left is the syntactic concatenation operator. (I continue to ignore Infl till section 6.5.3):

(36)   a. $<DP + VP \to IP,   IP = APPLY[VP,DP]>$
       b. $<DP + XP \to SC,   SC = APPLY[XP,DP]>$

(35c/d) are instances of adjunct predication, where the predicate and argument do not form a constituent. The explicit rules for interpreting these syntactic structures are given in (37a/b), which are the instances of secondary predication and subject-oriented adjunct predication respectively; the first is the structure in which the generalised event based conjunction rule in (26) is used, and the second the structure which uses the predicate absorption rule in (31):

(37)   a. $<V + NP + XP \to V',   V' = APPLY[V + XP, NP]>$
       b. $<V' + XP \to V'',   V'' = V' + *XP>$

However, although (36/37) give the rules for interpreting the various tree structures in (35), we do not, in fact, need these rules since it does not need to be stated explicitly whether in a certain configuration a particular predicate is saturated by direct functional application, generalised event-based conjunction or predicate absorption. We can assume that the various operations are freely available, and that the grammar filters out the results of using an operation inappropriately. I have been arguing that when a predicate applies directly to an argument, the result of the application is a constituent. Then direct predicate application will be allowed only if the resulting $<e,t>$ constituent is licenced. Such a constituent can be licensed by existential closure, if the predicate has been modified by inflection, as in (35a), or by being assigned a theta-role, if it is a small clause, as in (35b). But, suppose that direct application occurs when the configuration is as in (35c), then we will get a structure in which the matrix verb cannot discharge its internal argument, as in (38):

(38)   The police arrested $[John drunk]_{SC}$

Since the set of events denoted by *John drunk* cannot be the theme of the verb *arrest*, the verb cannot find an internal argument and the derivation blocks. This means that interpretation is possible only if the secondary predicate is conjoined with the verb and they are applied jointly to the argument, so that both predicates can 'share' it. Similarly, a predicate which is sister to a V′ constituent cannot be saturated by direct application or application in conjunction, since it does not have a nominal sister argument. The only available procedure that can apply is predicate absorption, as in the +* conjunction rule (31), which will result in indirect application of the predicate to a higher subject. Thus the choice of semantic operation essentially type driven.

Note, by the way, that the theory as it stands predicts that adjunct predicates cannot be oriented to indirect objects. Assume that (39a) gives the expression denoted by *give* as it is used in both (39b) and (39c):

(39)   a. $\lambda z \lambda y \lambda e.\text{GIVE}(e) \wedge \text{Ag}(e) = x \wedge \text{Th}(e) = y \wedge \text{Goal}(e) = z$
       b.   John gave the book to Mary
       c.   John gave Mary the book.

We see in (40) that indirect objects cannot host adjunct predicates; Mary cannot be drunk in (40a), and (40b) is infelicitous. (Thanks to Fred Landman for example (40b).):

(40)   a.   John gave Mary the book drunk.
       b.   #The computer sold John the encyclopedia drunk.

On the assumption that secondary predication involves conjunction of like types at type $<d, <e,t>>$, predicating the adjunct of the indirect object will be impossible since it would involve conjoining the verb, at type $<d, <d, <e,t>>>$, with the adjunct predicate at type $<d, <e,t>>$. It could be argued that predicate absorption involves precisely conjunction of non-like types, so the question is why does the grammar not allow a parallel rule here? But, it would be a very different rule. The absorption rule in (31) conjoined a predicate of the form $\lambda x \lambda e.\alpha$ with a verb at type $<e,t>$ by applying the predicate to a variable and then conjoining the resulting expressions at $<e,t>$. But conjoining a verb at type $<d, <d, <e,t>>>$ with a predicate at type $<d, <e,t>>$ would require applying the verb to two variables and the predicate to one variable, conjunction at type $<e,t>$ and then abstraction over the appropriate variables to get back a three place verb again. It is plausible that the grammar might allow a rule of the form (31), but not the rule we would need here.

6.5. Some other issues

6.5.1. *Resultatives*

The adjunct predicates that we have looked at so far have all been what are known as 'depictive' predicates; they hold of their subject at the time that the event given by the matrix verb is going on. As we have seen, they can be predicated of the subject or object of the main verb. Resultative predicates such as those in (41) differ from depictives in that they can only be predicated of the direct object. (Wechsler (1997) and Rappaport Hovav and Levin (1999) argue that there are some subject-oriented resultatives. I am not going to discuss this here, though I argue elsewhere that these are not true resultatives):

(41) a. Mary painted the house red.
      b. Jane sang the baby asleep.
      c. He shouted himself hoarse.
      d. The house$_i$ was painted t$_i$ red.
      e. *John ran the race tired. (on the reading: until he was tired)
      f. *Bill sung the song hoarse. (on the reading: until he was hoarse)

'Direct object' here is a structural concept, defined as 'DP governed by V' and not a semantic or thematic concept defined in terms of selection, since in (41b/c) the subject of the resultative is governed by a matrix verb which is intransitive and which assigns it no theta-role. Syntactic constituency tests such as those discussed in chapter 5:5 show that the resultative predicates can be generated only under V', which is what the mutual c-command condition on predication predicts for direct object predicates. (See Levin and Rappaport Hovav (1995) for more discussion of these issues.) This is illustrated in (42).

(42) a. *Mary painted the house happily red.
      b. *What Mary did red was paint the house.
      c. *Paint the house though Mary did red ...

The examples in (41c) indicate another major difference between resultatives and depictives. While resultatives may not be predicated of a subject, they do not have to be predicated of a thematic argument of the verbal head. In (41c) what Simpson (1983) called a 'fake reflexive' is used; this is an anaphor in direct object position which is assigned the external theta-role of the predicate, and bound by the subject. The fake reflexive is often seen as a 'trick' to get around the direct object restriction and predicate a resultative of the subject. But (41b) shows that a resultative can be predicated of a non-anaphoric, non-thematic argument; the non-thematicity of the direct object is thus independent of any anaphoric relation it may have with the matrix subject.

This property of resultatives distinguishes them from depictives, which must be predicated of a thematic argument. Thus (43a) is in principle ambiguous between a depictive reading (I cooked the carrots when they were dry) and a resultative reading (I cooked the carrots until they were dry), and the same for (43b):

(43) a. I cooked the carrots dry.
      b. John rode the horse exhausted.

However, (44a) with a 'fake' reflexive, can only have the resultative reading, 'John cried until he was sick', and not 'John cried when he was sick'. Similarly, (44b) can mean only that Jane sang and as a result the baby was asleep, and not that she sang when the baby was asleep.

(44)   a. John cried himself sick.
        b. Jane sang the baby asleep.

This means that depictives must be truly 'secondary' predicates, while this is not the case for resultatives. By the criteria given in chapter 5, these 'intransitive resultatives', as they have been called, are not secondary predicates, since secondary predicates are predicated of the thematic argument of a different head. On the other hand, for them to be primary predicates, they should form a constituent with their subjects, and that constituent needs to be licensed. Up till now, instances of non-matrix primary predication are all theta-marked constituents, which are thus thematic arguments of a verbal expression, or adjuncts introduced by the relation-denoting preposition *with*. So these examples look like neither primary nor secondary predication, and the question is what are they? Furthermore, given that we have been adding adjunct predicates via conjunction of like types, it is very strange to see a resultative in (41a) added within V′ to a verbal predicate of type $<d, <e,t>>$ and in (41b/c) to verbal constituents of type $<e,t>$. It turns out that under minimal assumptions about the syntax, the structures can be interpreted straightforwardly.

There are two possible syntactic structures that one can assign to intransitive resultatives. I assume, non-controversially, that transitive resultatives such as (41a) have the structure in (45a), reflecting the fact that the subject of the resultative is the theta-marked direct object of the verb. This structure is the same as that of secondary depictive adjunct predicates predicated of direct objects. There are two possibilities for intransitive resultatives such as (41b); either they can be assigned the same structure as the transitives, illustrated in (45b), or they can be analysed as in (45c), where the resultative and its subject form a constituent:

(45)   a. Mary [[painted [the house]$_{DP}$ [red]$_{AP}$]$_{V'}$]$_{VP}$
        b. Jane [[sang [the baby]$_{DP}$ [asleep]$_{AP}$]$_{V'}$]$_{VP}$
        c. Jane [[sang [[the baby]$_{DP}$ [asleep]$_{AP}$]$_{SC}$]$_{V'}$]$_{VP}$

In (45b), we have what looks like a secondary predicate construction which does not meet the thematic constraints on secondary predication, since the subject of *asleep* is not theta-marked by *sang*. On the other hand it is not a primary predication either, since the subject and predicate do not form a constituent. In (45c), we represent subject plus predicate as a constituent, but, following our discussion in chapter 5:5, this constituent will not be a licensed instance of primary predication since the constituent itself is not theta-marked. Levin and Rappaport Hovav (1995) discuss both possibilities and say that there is no real syntactic or thematic evidence to pick one over the other, while Carrier and Randall (1992) choose (45b). The account of interpretation which we have proposed here clearly predicts that the structure should be (45c).

Let's assume, following Levin and Rappaport Hovav (1995), Wechsler (1997), Rappaport Hovav and Levin (1999), that what resultatives do is give information about the state initiated by the culminating point of an event. We can then formulate a resultative conjunction rule for transitive resultatives as in (46):

(46) Resultative conjunction:

$\alpha +^R_{<d, <et>>} \beta$:

$= \lambda y \lambda e. \exists e_1 \exists e_2 [e = e_1 \sqcup e_2 \wedge \alpha(e_1,y) \wedge \beta(e_2,y) \wedge cul(e_1) \sqsubseteq e_2]$

Cul is the based on the culmination function introduced in Parsons (1990) which maps an accomplishment onto the time of its telic point; Parsons thus formulates in a neo-Davidsonian framework the insight in Dowty (1979) that accomplishment events are lexically constrained to give information about their telic point. (46) tells us that resultative predicates are added to transitive verbs exactly as depictive predicates are, but it specifies an additional relation between the event of the matrix verb and the denotation of the predicate, namely that the culmination of the verbally introduced event is part of the event of the eventuality introduced by the AP. (47) shows how this rule is used in the interpretation of (41a), where α = PAINT and β = RED:

(41) a. Mary painted the house red.

(47) $\alpha := \lambda y \lambda e. PAINT(e) \wedge Ag(e) = x \wedge Th(e) = y$

$\beta := \lambda x \lambda e. RED(e) \wedge Arg_1(e) = x$

$\alpha +^R_{<d, <et>>} \beta =$

$\lambda y \lambda e. \exists e_1 \exists e_2 [e = e_1 \sqcup e_2 \wedge PAINT(e_1) \wedge Ag(e_1) = x \wedge Th(e_1) = y$
$\wedge RED(e_2) \wedge Arg_1(e_2) = y \wedge cul(e_1) \sqsubseteq e_2]$

This complex predicate will then apply to the object NP *the house* (h) to give (48) as the denotation of the VP *paint the house red*.

(48) $\lambda y \lambda e. \exists e_1 \exists e_2 [e = e_1 \sqcup e_2 \wedge PAINT(e_1) \wedge Ag(e_1) = x \wedge Th(e_1) = y$
$\wedge RED(e_2) \wedge Arg_1(e_2) = y \wedge cul(e_1) \sqsubseteq e_2](h)$

$= \lambda e. \exists e_1 \exists e_2 [e = e_1 \sqcup e_2 \wedge PAINT(e_1) \wedge Ag(e_1) = x \wedge Th(e_1) = h$
$\wedge RED(e_2) \wedge Arg_1(e_2) = h \wedge cul(e_1) \sqsubseteq e_2]$

Predicate formation followed by application to the subject and existential quantification will give (49) as the interpretation of (41a):

(49) $\exists e \exists e_1 \exists e_2 [e = e_1 \sqcup e_2 \wedge PAINT(e_1) \wedge Ag(e_1) = MARY \wedge Th(e_1) = h$
$\wedge RED(e_2) \wedge Arg_1(e_2) = h \wedge cul(e_1) \sqsubseteq e_2]$

Now assume that both transitive and intransitive resultatives are interpreted by essentially the same rule. We do this by generalising (46) to apply to pairs of constituents which are not only of type $<d, <e,t>>$. An intransitive verb is of type $<e,t>$ at the V' level, so an obvious move is to suggest that resultative conjunction applies also at type $<e,t>$. Our rule will look like (50):

(50) Generalised Resultative conjunction:

$\alpha +^R_{<d1,...dn <e,t>>} \beta$:

$= \lambda y_n ... \lambda y_1 \lambda e. \exists e_1 \exists e_2 [e = e_1 \sqcup e_2 \wedge \alpha(y_1, ... y_n,e_1)$
$\wedge \beta(y_1, ... y_n,e_2)(y) \wedge cul(e_1) \sqsubseteq e_2]$

This is the simplest way of making explicit the fact that intransitive and transitive resultatives are instances of the same phenomenon.

But in order for this to work, we need to assume the structure (45c) for intransitive resultatives. If we assume (45b) then while the verb is of type $<e,t>$, the AP will be of type $<d, <e,t>>$. We solved this mismatch in depictive predicates in rule (31) by first lowering the predicate AP to $<e,t>$ and then conjoining it with the intransitive verb, and applying the resulting complex predicate to the subject. But this is not an appropriate solution here, since the whole point is that the resultative applies to an argument which is not an argument of the verb. Given the structure in (45c) the derivation goes simply and the apparent mismatches solve themselves:

(41b)   Jane sang the baby asleep.

(51)   a. $[asleep]_A \rightarrow \lambda e'.\text{ASLEEP}(e') \wedge \text{Arg}_1(e') = x$

   b. $[asleep]_{AP} \rightarrow \lambda x \lambda e'.\text{ASLEEP}(e') \wedge \text{Arg}_1(e') = x$

   (Predicate Formation)

   c. $[\text{the baby asleep}]_{SC} \rightarrow \lambda x \lambda e'.\text{ASLEEP}(e') \wedge \text{Arg}_1(e') = x\,(\text{B})$
      $= \lambda e'.\text{ASLEEP}(e') \wedge \text{Arg}_1(e') = \text{B}$ (APPLY)

   d. $[\text{sing } [\text{the baby asleep}]_{V'}] \rightarrow$
      $\lambda e.\text{SING}(e) \wedge \text{Ag}(e) = x +^R_{<d1,...dn<e,t>>} \lambda e'.\text{ASLEEP}(e') \wedge \text{Arg}_1(e') = \text{B}$
      $= \lambda e.\exists e_1 \exists e_2 [e = e_1 \sqcup e_2 \wedge \text{SING}(e_1) \wedge \text{Ag}(e_1) = x \wedge \text{ASLEEP}(e_2)$
      $\wedge \text{Arg}_1(e_2) = \text{B} \wedge \text{cul}(e_1) \sqsubseteq e_2]$ (Generalised Resultative Conj.)

   e. $[\text{sing the baby asleep}]_{VP}$
      $\rightarrow \lambda x \lambda e.\exists e_1 \exists e_2 [e = e_1 \sqcup e_2 \wedge \text{SING}(e_1) \wedge \text{Ag}(e_1) = x$
      $\wedge \text{ASLEEP}(e_2) \wedge \text{Arg}_1(e_2) = \text{B} \wedge \text{cul}(e_1) \sqsubseteq e_2]$

   (Predicate Formation)

   f. $[\text{Jane sang the baby asleep}]_{IP} \rightarrow$
      $\lambda x \lambda e.\exists e_1 \exists e_2 [e = e_1 \sqcup e_2 \wedge \text{SING}(e_1) \wedge \text{Ag}(e_1) = x \wedge \text{ASLEEP}(e_2)$
      $\wedge \text{Arg}_1(e_2) = \text{B} \wedge \text{cul}(e_1) \sqsubseteq e_2]\,(\text{J})$
      $= \exists e \exists e_1 \exists e_2 [e = e_1 \sqcup e_2 \wedge \text{SING}(e_1) \wedge \text{Ag}(e_1) = \text{J} \wedge \text{ASLEEP}(e_2)$
      $\wedge \text{Arg}_1(e_2) = \text{B} \wedge \text{cul}(e_1) \sqsubseteq e_2]$ (APPLY + $\exists$-closure)

Now that we have seen how to interpret these structures, we can see why they are grammatical while they fit neither into the category of primary nor secondary predicates. The thematic constraints on primary and secondary predicates are necessary to guarantee that the event denoted by the predicate is related to the event of the main verb. Depictive predicates are related to the event of the main verb since the predicate and the V 'share' a participant; this is represented by the fact that the subject of the depictive predicate is theta-marked by the matrix verb and must thus be a participant in the event denoted by the V. In (20a), repeated here as (52), the event of John being drunk is related to the event of the police arresting John because John is simultaneously a participant in both.

(52)   The police arrested John drunk.

Primary predicates (unless they are IPs, in which case they are licensed independently via the IP level existential quantification) are related to the event denoted by V more directly, since the constituent consisting of the primary predicate and its subject is either theta-marked by V, either as a subject or as the object of an ECM verbs, or is the complement of the relation-denoting preposition *with* as in examples (61) in chapter 5. The predicates in resultative constructions do not necessarily share a participant with the event denoted by V, nor are they theta-marked by V, but they are related to the main V by the relation $\mathbf{cul(e_1)} \sqsubseteq \mathbf{e_2}$. It is this semantic relation, introduced by the interpretation rule, which licenses this structure. This is a further indication of the fact, noted in many discussions of resultatives, that compared to the depictive constructions, the resultative behaves more like a lexical complement.

The fact that resultatives cannot be predicated of the subject is captured in the theory by the fact that the predicate absorption rule in (31) does not have a resultative counterpart. Why this is has presumably to do with why the culminations of events are not usually defined by their relation to subject arguments. And why that is the case is too big a question to go into here, but see Rothstein (2000) for some discussion.

6.5.2. *Subcategorised predicates*

In the discussion on predicate absorption in chapter 5, I argued that subcategorised predicates such as those in (53) are also coindexed indirectly with a structural subject through predicate absorption.

(53) a. Mary felt tired.
      b. John acted foolish.

Clearly, these predicates are not to be interpreted via conjunction: (53b) does not mean that Mary felt and was tired, nor (53b) that John acted and was foolish. Rather, these are sentences headed by modal verbs which assert that Mary had the tired property and John had the foolish property in the set of worlds picked out by *feel* and *act* respectively, namely those worlds where the facts reflects how the individual acts and what the individual feels. Basic tests of substitutivity show that *feel* and *act* are indeed modal. Thus if John acted the president of the club, and the president of the club is Ms. Smith, it doesn't follow that John acted Ms. Smith. And if all the happy people in the world are rich, it still does not follow that if Mary felt happy, she felt rich. Zimmerman (1992) argues that the best way to treat intensional verbs such as *seek*, is as selecting for a property. We can treat *feel* and *act* in the same way. And following Chierchia's (1984) account of control, where he treats *try* as a modal, and the control relation as a modal relation, we can give the relation between the subject of the matrix verb and the subject of the predicate through a meaning postulate. On this basis, meanings for the two verbs will be something like (54). 'Ex' is the role 'experiencer', P is a variable over properties, REALISE (e,w) means that e is actual in w, and $\text{FEEL}_{x,w}$ and $\text{ACT}_{x,w}$ are the sets of worlds where how x feels and how x acts are realised respectively:

(54)   a. feel$_V$: $\lambda P\lambda e.\text{FEEL}(e) \wedge \text{Th}(e) = P \wedge \text{Ex}(e) = x$
      condition:
      $\forall e \forall P \forall x \forall w [\text{FEEL}(e) \wedge \text{Th}(e) = P \wedge \text{Ex}(e) = x \wedge \text{REALISE}(e,w)$
        $\rightarrow \forall v \in \text{FEEL}_{x,w}: \exists e'[\,^{\vee}P(e') \wedge \text{Arg}_1(e') = x \wedge \text{REALISE}(e',v)]]$
    b. act$_V$: $\lambda P\lambda e.\text{ACT}(e) \wedge \text{Th}(e) = P \wedge \text{Ex}(e) = x$
      condition:
      $\forall e \forall P \forall x \forall w [\text{ACT}(e) \wedge \text{Th}(e) = P \wedge \text{Ex}(e) = x \wedge \text{REALISE}(e,w)$
        $\rightarrow \forall v \in \text{ACT}_{x,w}: \exists e'[\,^{\vee}P(e') \wedge \text{Arg}_1(e') = x \wedge \text{REALISE}(e',v)]]$

(54a) treats *feel* as denoting a function from properties to sets of events with an individual and a property as participants; the meaning postulate says that if e is an actual event of x's feeling P in w, then in all those worlds in which what x feels in w is actually the case, x will have the $^{\vee}P$ property. (54b) works in exactly the same way.

I argued in chapter 5 that the syntactic predicate linking rule applies to subcategorised predicates as well as to non-subcategorised ones. And I argued at the beginning of this chapter that syntactic linking is directly reflected in the interpretation of the sentence, since if a syntactic predicate α is linked to a syntactic argument β, the denotation of α will be applied to the denotation of β. We see that this is not the case here, since the subcategorised predicates are not applied to the arguments with which they are linked at S-structure; instead the link between the embedded predicate and its subject is expressed only as a control relation captured in the meaning postulate. If we want the syntactic linking to be directly reflected in the meaning of the sentence, then we could reformulate (54) with a propositional complement as in (55). In this way the syntactic linking will correlate with the sharing of variables, just as in the adjunct cases:

(55)
a. feel$_V$: $\lambda P\lambda e.\text{FEEL}(e) \wedge \text{Th}(e) = \,^{\wedge}(\exists e'[\,^{\vee}P(e') \wedge \text{Arg}(e') = x]) \wedge \text{Ex}(e) = x$
    condition:
    $\forall P \forall x \forall w \forall e [\text{FEEL}(e) \wedge \text{Th}(e) = \,^{\wedge}(\exists e'[\,^{\vee}P(e') \wedge \text{Arg}(e') = x]) \wedge \text{Ex}(e) = x$
      $\rightarrow \text{FEEL}_{x,w} \in \,^{\wedge}(\exists e'[\,^{\vee}P(e') \wedge \text{Arg}(e') = x])]$
b. act$_V$: $\lambda P\lambda e.\text{ACT}(e) \wedge \text{Th}(e) = \,^{\wedge}(\exists e'[\,^{\vee}P(e') \wedge \text{Arg}(e') = x])$
    condition:
    $\forall P \forall x \forall w \forall e [\text{ACT}(e) \wedge \text{Th}(e) = \,^{\wedge}(\exists e'[\,^{\vee}P(e') \wedge \text{Arg}(e') = x]) \wedge \text{Ex}(e) = x$
      $\rightarrow \text{ACT}_{x,w} \in \,^{\wedge}(\exists e'[\,^{\vee}P(e') \wedge \text{Arg}(e') = x])]$

Here, the theme of *feel* is the proposition that there is an event in which x has the $^{\vee}P$ property. The meaning postulate says that if there is an event of an individual having the FEEL relation to the proposition that x has the $^{\vee}P$ property, then the worlds where what x feels is actual are members of the set of worlds denoted by the proposition that x has the $^{\vee}P$ property. And similarly for *act*. Applying (55) to the predicate *tired* and doing predicate formation on the denotation of *feels tired* at the VP level gives (56a), and application to the subject argument and existential closure give (56b) as the meaning of (53a). The meaning postulate is as in (56c):

(56)

a. $\lambda x \lambda e . \text{FEEL}(e) \wedge \text{Th}(e) = {}^{\wedge}(\exists e'[{}^{\vee}\text{TIRED}(e') \wedge \text{Arg}(e) = x]) \wedge \text{Ex}(e) = x$

b. $\exists e[\text{FEEL}(e) \wedge \text{Th}(e) = {}^{\wedge}(\exists e'[{}^{\vee}\text{TIRED}(e') \wedge \text{Arg}(e) = \text{MARY}])$
$\qquad \wedge \text{Ex}(e) = \text{MARY}]$

c. condition:

$\forall P \forall x \forall w \forall e[\text{FEEL}(e) \wedge \text{Th}(e) = {}^{\wedge}(\exists e'[{}^{\vee}\text{TIRED}(e') \wedge \text{Arg}(e') = \text{MARY}])$
$\qquad \wedge \text{Ex}(e) = \text{MARY}$
$\qquad \rightarrow \text{FEEL}_{\text{MARY},w} \in {}^{\wedge}(\exists e'[{}^{\vee}\text{TIRED}(e') \wedge \text{Arg}(e') = \text{MARY}])]$

In words: there was an event of feeling which had Mary as experiencer and the proposition that Mary was tired as theme; and the condition is that in every case in which there is such an event in w, then in worlds in which what Mary feels in w is actual, the proposition that she is tired is true.

Note that this will explain the oddness of sentences such as (37) from chapter 5, repeated here, as (57a). It will have the representation in (57b):

(57) a. John feels unlikely that he will go.

b. $\exists e[\text{FEEL}(e) \wedge \text{Th}(e) =$
$\qquad {}^{\wedge}(\exists e'[{}^{\vee}\text{UNLIKELY THAT HE WILL GO}(e')])$
$\qquad \wedge \text{Ex}(e) = \text{JOHN}]$

The embedded predicate *unlikely that he will go* is syntactically absorbed into the VP. But it assigns no thematic argument role, and therefore the expression denoted by the predicate is not semantically predicated of the denotation of the syntactic subject.

6.5.3. *Inflection in English*

The inflection node in English causes a problem for predication theories because it interferes with the strict c-command relation between VP predicates and their subjects in IPs, as (58) shows.

(58) a. John met Mary

b. [John [Infl [meet Mary]]$_{I'}$]$_{IP}$

As we saw at the end of chapter 5, there is evidence from the differences between subject- and object-oriented adjunct predicates that the relation between predicates should be stated in terms of strict c-command. Object-oriented adjunct predicates must be generated lower than subject-oriented adjuncts; the former occur under V', adjacent to the object, while the subject-oriented adjuncts occur directly under the VP node. The only apparent violation of this strict c-command relation is the relation between subject and predicate indicated in (58b). One might hypothesise that while lexical non-maximal nodes do block predication relations, functional non-maximal nodes do not. Since C does not take predicate complements, but only argument complements which are converted into predicates at the CP level, this hypothesis cannot be checked without a study of Ds and DPs, which we are not entering into here. In chapter 5, I made the simpler

assumption that predicate absorption takes place between I' and its VP complement, so that the complex predicate I' and the subject in [Spec, IP] are syntactic
sisters. The semantic correlate of this is to assume that Infl is semantically a
modifier, and thus it is of type $<\alpha,\alpha>$, even though it is a head; this is compatible
with analyses of Infl as introducing tense as a modifier of the event argument of
V, and essentially treats Infl as an ordinary auxiliary verb.

I therefore assume that the semantic type of Infl is $<<d,<e,t>>, <d,<e,t>>>$;
it takes as complement a predicate – in English always a VP – and yields a
predicate of the same type. I assume that tense features are added by Infl; what
features they are depends on the particular content of the Infl, but they are
added as modifiers of e. In (58) Infl takes as its complement the expression
denoted by *met Mary*, given in (59a) and yields something like (59b) as its value:

(59) a. $\lambda x\lambda e.\text{MEET}(e) \wedge \text{Th}(e) = \text{MARY} \wedge \text{Ag}(e) = x$
      b. $\lambda x\lambda e.\text{MEET}(e) \wedge \text{Th}(e) = \text{MARY} \wedge \text{Ag}(e) = \wedge \text{Past}(e)$

6.6. COMPARISONS

6.6.1. *Dowty's (1982) theory of grammatical relations*

In the next chapter, I shall discuss how the theory deals with the pleonastic
DP *it*, and I shall compare how different approaches to subject deal with the
issue of pleonastics. Here, without reference to pleonastics, I want to contrast
my theory of subjects with two other semantically oriented approaches, the
categorial grammar based theory of Dowty (1982), and Chierchia's property
based theory (Chierchia 1989).

Dowty (1982) takes as its goal the formulation of a theory of grammatical
relations within the framework of Montague grammar. Dowty proposes a set of
universal syntactic rules which are used in operations which differ from language
to language, and he defines grammatical relations as rules of this kind. The general
principle of grammatical relations that he uses is given in (60) (his (6)):

(60) A verb that ultimately takes n arguments is always treated as combining
      by a syntactic rule with exactly one argument to produce a phrase of
      the same category as a verb of $n - 1$ arguments.

The subject-predicate rule and the verb-object rule, formulated in accordance
with this principle in Montague's format for syntactic rules, are given in (61a/b):

(61) S1: $<F_1, <IV,T>,t>$ (Subject-Predicate Rule)
      S2: $<F_2, <TV,T>,IV>$ (Verb-Direct Object Rule)

In these ordered triples, the first member, 'F', names a syntactic operation (in
English concatenation plus number agreement and case-marking), the second
member is the sequence of categories that are the input to the rule, and the
third member is the category of the output of the rule (Dowty (p85)). The
subject-predicate rule applies to an intransitive verb and a term and yields a

sentence, and the direct object rule applies to a transitive verb and a term and yields an intransitive verb. The rules in (61) minus the language specific definitions of 'F' are the universal definitions of subject and predicate.

What this theory has in common with the one developed here is that it defines subject, predicate and predication as syntactic concepts; however, it differs in that it treats 'subject' as the last syntactic argument to be entered into the tree, and other than that as no different in kind from any other grammatical relation.

The difference between Dowty's theory of subjects and predication and the one I am developing here is twofold. First, because the subject is just 'the last argument to be fed in', it makes no distinction between the 'highest' or external argument and the others. In (61) the difference between the subject-predicate rule and the verb-direct object rule is only in the categorial specifications of the members of the triple and not in the nature of the rule. In contrast, I have been arguing that application of the VP to the external argument is because of the properties of the VP, and not because of the lexical, thematic or categorial properties of the head of the V. Thus, subject and direct object are different in nature; direct object is there because of the lexical properties of the head, while the subject is there because of the categorial properties of the VP. The major effects of this difference show up in the treatment of pleonastics, which we will look at in the next chapter.

A second difference is that the rule in (61a) is construction specific. By that I mean that it applies to an intransitive verb, or VP and an NP (or DP), and yields a sentence. Since 'subject' is defined as the argument which takes an expression into type t, it is part of the definition that it is dominated by an IP. Leaving aside the role of Inflection in generating a sentence, and its effect on these rules, Dowty's definition of 'subject' in (61a) takes into account only subject-predication relations between a subject and a predicate in sentences with VP predicates. We can widen the definition by translating the rules into a neo-Davidsonian framework, and define the subject-predicate rule as the rule which applies a maximal XP expression of type $<d, <e,t>>$ to a term to yield an expression of type $<e,t>$, and this would then give a definition which would apply to subject of IP and subject of small clauses, in other words to subjects of primary predicates. But I do not see how a Dowty-style rule could apply both to primary and secondary predicates. The advantage of defining 'predicate' and 'subject' independently of the configuration within which they occur is that we have a definition which applies not only to all categories, but also to the different syntactic forms of predication.

6.6.2. *Chierchia's property theory*

The syntactic theory of predication which is in many ways closest to the one I have presented here is that of Chierchia (1984, 1986, 1989) and Chierchia and Turner (1988). Chierchia develops a theory of predication within the semantic framework of property theory, which aims among other things at answering the question of how properties can be predicated of themselves, as in examples like (62):

(62)   a. Being wise is wise.
      b. Cheerfulness is cheerful.
      c. The property of being autoidentical has the property of being autoidentical.

The basic premise of the theory is that properties have two modes of presentation. They are unsaturated one place properties of the kind we are most familiar with, which can be saturated by being predicated of individuals, and in addition, each property has an individual correlate which is saturated and which acts as an argument. The basic sorts of Chierchia's language include not only individuals and truth values (or information units in Chierchia and Turner 1988) but also individual properties (or nominalised functions) which are saturated constituents of type π. Thus in (62b), the first order predicate 'cheerful' can be predicated of the individual property or nominalised predicate 'cheerfulness'. I have been working within an event-based semantic framework (and it will be clear especially in part III and IV why this is crucial) and since I am not going to deal at all with issues of nominalisation, I shall not try and compare or criticise the semantic arguments which Chierchia gives. However, his syntactic theory, especially the one he sets out in Chierchia (1989) is similar in some crucial respects to what I am doing here, and it is instructive to compare them. I shall restrict myself to as discussion of Chierchia (1989), which gives the fullest discussion of the syntactic and interpretive issues I have treated here.

I have proposed treating standard n-place relations (i.e. excluding passive and unaccusative functions) as (curried) $n-1$ place functions from $n-1$ arguments into sets of events, and with the nth argument fed in after an operation of predicate abstraction. Chierchia (1986, 1989) assumes that properties are included among the basic individuals and represents an n-place relation as a (curried) function from $n-1$ individuals into saturated properties; VP thus denotes an individual property of type π. For example a two place relation such as *MEET* will be represented as a function from entities into properties of type $<d,\pi>$. The predication relation $\cup$ is introduced by Inflection (more properly, tense in Inflection), and is a function from properties into propositional functions. $<d,p>$ is the type of propositional functions from entities into propositions) and $\cup$ is an operation from π into $<d,p>$. The derivation of *John met Mary* looks like (63). *Meet* denotes the expression in (63b). The expression in (63b) applies to MARY to give the VP denotation of type π in (63c). Inflection then introduces the predication operator which takes the VP into a propositional function as in (63d) and the interpretation of the IP is as in (63e):

(63)   a.   John met Mary.
      b.   meet$_{<d,p>}$ →   MEET
      c.   meet Mary$_p$ →   MEET(m)
      d.   Infl + meet$_{<d,p>}$ → $\cup$MEET(m)
      e.   John met Mary$_p$ → $\cup$(MEET(m))(j)

Thus in Chierchia's analysis also, predication is a syntactic operation introduced by a non-lexical node in the syntax and not dependent on a lexical or thematic property of the head. So what are the differences? Again they are twofold. We will see in the next chapter that the syntactic abstraction analysis I present here will allow a much simpler account of expletives; for Chierchia the predication operator applies to properties, and it cannot apply to the denotations of VPs which take expletive subjects since these denote propositions. Second, Chierchia relies on Inflection to introduce the predication operator. He thus restricts predicate-denoting expressions to inflected XPs, and in English this means inflected VPs. As it stands, his analysis rules out bare VP predicates such as the one in the complement clause in (64a), non-verbal small clause predicates, such as (64b) and secondary and absorbed predicates and resultatives such as those discussed in sections 4 and 5 of this chapter, illustrated in (64c–f).

(64) a. John saw Mary **leave**.
     b. Mary considered Jane **very clever**.
     c. They ate carrots **raw**.
     d. John drove the car **drunk**.
     e. Mary painted the house **red**.
     f. He laughed himself **sick**.

In Chierchia's theory, the bold-marked constituents are all of the type π, and denote individual properties. Since they are interpreted as predicates, some syntactically null predication operator will have to be introduced to map them from π into $<d,p>$. Chierchia can not rely on Inflection to do this. One might try positing null inflection to do the job; aside from the problematic aspects of introducing such a node purely to denote the predication operator, there is another unconvincing factor. It is not Inflection per se for Chierchia which denotes the predication operator, but the [+tense] feature within Inflection. This is crucial for Chierchia since he argues that infinitival VPs headed by *to*, such as *to run* and *to meet Mary*, denote individual properties and not predicates. Even if we wanted to introduce a null Inflection, it would not naturally denote the predication operator unless it contained a [+tense] feature, which we would expect to be semantically interpreted. There does not seem to be semantic evidence for such an independent tense feature on the predicates in (64) – in fact the contrary is true of depictives, which, as we saw, have to hold at the time specified by the matrix predicate. So it looks as if what is needed is a rule mapping from π into predicates which is not introduced by a syntactic constituent but which applies automatically to certain syntactic XPs, those which are to denote predicates. If we substitute 'set of events' for π and 'predicate abstraction' for predication operator, then we will see that what is needed is essentially what I have been proposing here. Precisely because Chierchia's definition of 'predication' makes it a syntactic saturation operation which is not dependent on the lexical properties of the head, an operation introduced automatically at the XP level is needed, and this will require a syntactic definition of predicate which looks like the one argued for in part I.

As far as expletives are concerned, I shall show in the next chapter that the two theories differ in the way they account for them, and that the event based treatment is simpler.

CHAPTER 7

THE SEMANTICS OF PLEONASTICS

7.1. FORMAL INTERPRETATION

7.1.1. *Pleonastics and a theory of subjects*

As has been clear from chapter 1, pleonastics are a major issue for any theory of subjects, predication or clausal structure. The obligatory presence of non-thematic DPs in subject position with no apparent role in the interpretation of the clause is a challenge for any theory which wants to try and explain what the nature of clausal structure is. And for a compositional theory of interpretation, which assumes that syntactic operations are correlated with semantic operations, the question is what semantic operation could be paired with inserting an obligatory, but meaningless DP in subject position. Depending on the kind of theory, the problem takes a slightly different shape, and suggests a different kind of solution. Recent theories which seriously discuss the issue, in particular Sag (1982), Dowty (1985), Gazdar, Klein, Pullum and Sag (1985) and Chierchia (1989) assume that pleonastic *it* denotes a dummy or null element ⊥, which Dowty (1985), following Lauri Kartunnen, calls the 'ugly object'; the semantic correlate of inserting a pleonastic in the subject position is functional application to ⊥. The question is how to motivate such an operation. I am only going to discuss the *it* pleonastic here: as McCloskey (1991) shows, *there* has very different properties from *it*, and needs to be discussed separately.

For a categorial grammar, which takes as a premise that syntactic structure (and in particular, the array of syntactic arguments) is a projection of the subcategorisational properties of verbs, an obvious solution is to propose that some heads subcategorise for pleonastics, and in their semantic representation require application to an argument which is constrained to be ⊥. This is essentially the solution offered in Sag (1982). Dowty (1985) and also Chierchia (1989) propose solutions which essentially involve stipulating vacuous lambda abstraction at the VP level where there is no thematic external argument, resulting in a predicate of the form $\lambda x.\alpha$. (Dowty argues that his version of this operation is essentially equivalent to the subcategorisation option.) In each case, the solution needs to be supported by an explanation of how it is motivated; why should a lexical head select a pleonastic, and why should some VPs require vacuous lambda abstraction to occur.

I am going to argue here that the theory I have been presenting up till now predicts without any further stipulation that application to the dummy ⊥ should occur exactly where it does occur. Automatic predicate formation at the syntactic XP level has resulted up till now in lambda binding a free variable which is the value of the so-called 'external' theta-role; pleonastics occur precisely when there is no free variable for the automatically introduced λx-expression to bind. I shall argue below that this shows that pleonastics are not a 'problem', or an 'exception' for a theory to take care of, but rather a mechanism which reveals a fundamental fact about the language: a clausal structure must, at the pre-clausal level, consist of an open constituent and an argument. Application of an open constituent to an argument is what the creation of clausal structure consists in, whether or not there is a thematic relation to be encoded at that level. This section then presents a semantic argument predicting the distribution of pleonastics which parallels the syntactic arguments presented in chapter 3.

Before going into this in detail, I want to mention two other ways of dealing with pleonastics in a theory of interpretation. One is essentially to ignore them. We could do this by giving up on strict compositionality and assuming that non-thematically relevant DPs are just ignored by the interpretative component. The explanation for the distribution of pleonastics would then be purely syntactic, in terms of feature matching, case assignment or some similar mechanism, which would not have a semantic correlate, and which would be a syntactic operation which would not be interpreted. The problem with that, aside from the fact that I assume we don't want to give up on compositionality, is that as we saw in chapter 3, explanations for the distribution of pleonastics in terms of syntactic features, case assignment, or stipulative syntactic rules just don't work. Instead, as I argued in chapter 3, the best syntactic explanation for the distribution of pleonastic *it* is in terms of the constraint that syntactic predicates must be linked to a subject, and the syntactic predication relation is crucially the kind of syntactic relation which must be interpreted.

I have argued (in chapter 6) that a crucial factor in the interpretation of syntactic structures is that there is a strict correlation between syntactic predicates and logical expressions of form $<d,\alpha>$. (I say $<d,\alpha>$, since inherent XP predicates where X is a lexical head are of type $<d, <e,t>>$ and CP predicates are of type $<d,t>$.) But this raises a different question for interpretation: what does it mean for a syntactic expression to be mapped onto a logical expression of type $<d,\alpha>$, i.e. of the form λx.α, if the expression does not contain a variable for the λx to bind. And presumably the interpretation of pleonastics will be explained as part of this issue.

Another account of how to deal with the interpretation of pleonastic *it* is known as the 'expletive replacement account', and is associated with Chomsky (1986a), although the basic idea dates back to much earlier familiar discussions of *there*-insertion contexts. The idea is that the pleonastic is essentially a syntactic place-holder associated with a lexically realised argument, and that the latter is semantically interpreted as if it were in the position of the expletive.

We could no doubt develop a mechanism which would do this for us, but there are a number of reasons not to do so. One is that I have argued, contra Chomsky (1981), that weather verbs in English are associated with genuine pleonastics. That means that an expletive replacement account of pleonastics could not work for expletives like the subjects in (1) which are not associated with any other argument:

(1)   It was raining.

Second, as Baltin (1995) mentions, VP predicates with pleonastic subjects can be antecedents for VP ellipsis, as in (2):

(2)   A: It seems that John is crazy.
      B: It certain does.

In (2B) the antecedent for the deleted VP is the semantic interpretation of the expression *seems that John is crazy*. And, as we saw in chapter 1, interpretation of VP ellipsis is a discourse phenomenon, done after the semantic representation is built up. But that means that at the level at which (2B) is interpreted, the CP argument of *seem* must be within the VP, and not interpreted in the position of the pleonastic subject.

7.1.2. *Interpreting pleonastics*

The framework I have been developing offers a straightforward way of interpreting pleonastic *it*. (Note again that I am not going to discuss *there*, for which there is evidence that it is not empty of meaning. Most recently, even, Landman (1998) argues that *there* is not nominal.)   Pleonastic *it* is the most minimal of the pronouns, the realisation of the least marked, most neutral features. A pleonastic occurrence of *it* is a use of *it* in a non-theta-marked position, where it makes no contribution to the statement of the truth-conditions of the sentence; in other words it has no real reference.

I argued in chapter 3 that pleonastics are elements which are used by the syntax of a language to provide syntactic subjects for IP and small clause predicates which need to be saturated in the syntax but which semantically do not take an external argument. Examples are given in (3):

(3)   a. It **seems that John is tired**.
      b. It was **obvious that Mary had won**.
      c. It **rained**. (see chapter 3 for arguments that weather *it* really is pleonastic).
      d. John saw it **rain**.
      e. Bill considered it **certain that Mary would win**.
      f. They made it **turn out that the child won the game**.

The question is how to interpret the XPs in (3), and the semantic relation between the denotations of the XPs and the subject. In each example in (3), we would say intuitively that the XP in bold differs from 'standard' XPs since it does not denote a function from individuals to sets of events, but simply a set of events. Existential quantification over the event argument would result in a proposition with a truth value irregardless of whether or not there is a subject. Nonetheless, the theory we have been developing argues that the XPs in (3) are all syntactic predicates, and that predicate formation will take place at the XP level in the semantic representation. Since it is an integral part of the theory that XPs are interpreted as predicates because of their syntactic form and independently of their thematic properties, this theoretical consequence is not one we can make light of or ignore. Furthermore, since I have been assuming a principle of strong compositionality, which requires that each syntactic operation is paired with a semantic operation, we are doubly committed to there being a semantic operation which correlates with the syntactic predication relation in all of these examples. This means that there must be a functional application operation in which the denotation of the XP is applied to the denotation of the pleonastic subjects.

I shall assume, following Sag (1982), Dowty (1985), Gazdar, Klein, Pullum and Sag (1985) and Chierchia (1989) that the pleonastic *it* denotes $\perp$, the dummy or null element, or 'ugly object', as Kartunnen called it. In the subcategorisation approach to pleonastics, an XP meaning applies to $\perp$ if and only if the head of the XP subcategorises for a pleonastic subject. In the approach of Dowty (1985) and Gazdar, Klein, Pullum and Sag (1985), vacuous lambda abstraction, over XP predicates of type t results in an expression which can apply only to $\perp$. Dowty (1985) points out in a footnote in order to 'forestall suspicion that there might be something illegitimate about the appeal to vacuous lambda abstraction here' that the subcategorisation approach is an alternative which will work equally well. (note 19). I am going to argue for the vacuous lambda abstraction approach, but in such a way that it cannot be equally well expressed in terms of subcategorisation.

The dummy element $\perp$ is of type d, but it has no real properties. It is the denotation of the minimal pronoun in its pleonastic use. To make use of this element, we need a type logical language (and interpretation) in which the principle of λ-conversion is valid, and in which an expression $\perp$, of type d, denotes an object, $\perp$, which is *as much as is logically possible* an object without 'real' properties. Minimally, this will mean that any thematic statement of the form $R(e) = \perp$ is going to be undefined (where 'R' ranges over thematic and argument roles). (This means, by the way, that $\perp$ must be distinguished from the undefined object '#'. If role R is not defined for a particular event, we express this by setting $R(e) = \#$, if we have # in the language. In such a case $R(e) = \#$ is going to be true, while $R(e) = \perp$ will be undefined. For example, # is the value of the agent role for events in the denotations of unaccusative verbs.) The idea is that a statement $(\lambda x. \exists e [E(e) \wedge R(e) = x])\,(\perp)$ is undefined, since conversion gives $\exists e [E(e) \wedge R(e) = \perp]$, where $\perp$ fills a thematic position. But $(\lambda x. \exists e [E(e) \wedge R(e) = \alpha])\,(\perp) = \exists e [E(e) \wedge R(e) = \alpha]$. For this to work, we need a logical language in which λ-conversion holds (because we need to be allowed to convert $\perp$ in). Working out the logical details of a language with the minimal information object $\perp$ is far from trivial, and is far beyond the scope of this chapter, though I assume that the idea can be given a coherent form.

The minimal information object is used in the interpretation of predicates such as the XPs in (3), which are syntactically saturated by the pleonastic, do not assign an external theta-role, and do not contain a DP trace. Like all predicate XPs, before predicate formation they denote sets of events and are of type $<e,t>$, but unlike the XPs we have looked at so far, they contain no free x variable, and there is nothing for the operator introduce by predicate formation to bind. After predicate formation they will be prefixed by a vacuous lambda operator. For example, the verbal projection *rain* in (3c) denotes the set of events $\lambda e.RAIN(e)$, as in (4a). Predicate formation applies automatically to this expression to give the VP which is of type $<d, <e,t>>$ and denotes a function from individuals to sets of events; however, the lambda operator introduced by predicate formation binds no variable, as we see in (4b):

(4) a. $[\text{rain}]_{V'}$ → $\lambda e.RAIN(e)$
     b. $[\text{rain}]_{VP}$ → $\lambda x \lambda e.RAIN(e)$ (Predicate Formation)
     c. $[\text{rained}]_{I'}$ → $\lambda x \lambda e.RAIN(e) \wedge PAST(e)$
     d. $[\text{it rained}]_{IP}$ → $\lambda x \lambda e.RAIN(e) \wedge PAST(e) (\perp)$
                                 $= \lambda e.RAIN(e) \wedge PAST(e)$

     e. $\exists e[RAIN(e) \wedge PAST(e)]$

As (4d) shows, the denotation of VP (more precisely, of I′) is applied to $\perp$, to give a predicate of events (type $<e,t>$); of course the same predicate of events given in (4a), plus a temporal modifier. Existential closure over the event argument results in (4e) as the interpretation of the sentence 'it rained'.

The VP meaning in (4b) must be predicated of the null object $\perp$ and of nothing else. It is clear that it must be predicated of something, and $\perp$ is the only option, precisely because the lambda operator binds no x variable. The reasoning behind this is as follows. The contribution of a subject DP to the meaning of a clause is to take a function from individuals to events into a set of events. Existential closure over the event argument gives an expression which denotes a truth value; a sentence is true if there is an event which has certain properties, including the properties of having particular participants. Let us take a sentence like (5a). Before predicate formation the verbal projection denotes a set of events given in (5b). The set of events contains events which share a number of properties, specified by the sentential conjuncts, including $MEET(e)$, $Th(e) = MARY$ and $IN(e) = THE\ GARDEN$. The agent denoting property is only partially specified, since at the VP level, the sentential conjunct $Ag(e) = x$ contains a free variable.

(5) a. John met Mary in the garden.
     b. $\lambda e.MEET(e) \wedge Ag(e) = x \wedge Th(e) = MARY \wedge IN(e) = THE$
         GARDEN
     c. $\lambda e.MEET(e) \wedge Ag(e) = JOHN \wedge Th(e) = MARY \wedge IN(e)$
         $= THE\ GARDEN$

The IP in (5a) denotes before existential closure a subset of the set of events named in (5b), namely the subset of events of meeting Mary in the garden which have John as agent. This set, denoted by (5c) is derived from (5b) by filling in JOHN as the value of the x variable. Without such a value, no truth value can be assigned after existential closure since the sentence will contain a free variable. The subject thus has a crucial role to play in determining the membership of the set denoted by the IP. However, with predicates like those in (3) where the XP does not contain a free variable, the set of events denoted by IP is fully determined by the content of the predicate VP, and there is no semantic role for the meaning of the subject to play. If the subject DP is lexical, then its meaning is going to play no part in the interpretation of the sentence, and its informational content will 'get lost', violating what we can call a principle of Strong Compositionality. The Principle of Strong Compositionality intuitively says that lexical information should not get lost in the course of the semantic composition (and it thus has an approximate equivalent in the principle of full interpretation (=PFI) of Chomsky (1986a)). This will make sentences like (6) ungrammatical:

(6) a. *The boy seems that John is tired.
     b. *The fact was obvious that Mary had won.
     c. *Jove rained.

The Principle of Strong Compositionality/PFI permit these predicates to be applied only to the null element which has no informational content, and thus nothing to lose in the application. In other words, the only way in which a predicate structure of the above sort can get an interpretation compatible with Full Interpretation is if it is applied to the null element, and the only syntactic DP which can denote the null element is a pleonastic pronoun.

The strength of this account, as I said above, is that nothing special needs to be said about why the expression denoted by the XP is an expression which needs to be applied to an individual argument. That is just the type of syntactic predicate XPs. In chapter 3 I argued that nothing needs to be said about the syntax of expletives: the distribution of *it* follows from the claim that all non-saturating XPs are syntactic predicates. Since VP and AP are non-saturating, they are predicates and must be saturated, and if they do not assign an external theta-role, they must be saturated by a pleonastic. In an analogous way, the semantic interpretation of pleonastics follows from the claim that predicate formation occurs automatically at the XP level, where XP is a syntactic predicate. When the lambda operator introduced by predicate formation does not bind a variable, then the only semantically appropriate argument for the expression to apply to is the one where no information is lost in the application. Thus we predict, without stipulating it, where a vacuous lambda operator will occur, and why a pleonastic must denote the dummy object $\perp$.

As far as I know, all other accounts of the interpretation of pleonastic subjects require at least one of two stipulative mechanisms. Either it must be stipulated where vacuous lambda abstraction must occur in order to explain why VPs such as those in (3) must be treated as predicates, or there must be a lexical rule specifying that the heads of the predicates in (3) select a pleonastic subject. Sag (1982) explicitly uses the second approach, proposing that the null element is thematically selected for by certain lexical heads, and entered into the selectional restrictions and subcategorisation frame of those heads. (In Sag's theory, in which *it* and *there* are both treated as pleonastics, subcategorisation also takes care of guaranteeing that the right pleonastic occurs, but crucially, the fact of a pleonastic, as well as the choice of a particular pleonastic, is dictated by the subcategorisation mechanism.) Some heads, like *certain*, will have two different subcategorisation frames, one where they select a thematic subject and one where they select the null element as subject, as illustrated in (7).

(7)   a. John is certain that Mary will leave.
       b. It is certain that Mary will leave.

Dowty (1985) proposes that there is vacuous lambda abstraction over XPs which are headed by pleonastic-selecting items, though he points out in a footnote that he considers selection to be an equally good mechanism. Since it has to be specified lexically which XPs induce vacuous lambda abstraction, the two mechanisms have to be equivalent. Gazdar, Klein, Pullum and Sag (1985) give a precise expression to Dowty's idea, by proposing that lexical rules introduce the vacuous lambda operator in the relevant expressions, thus essentially merging the two approaches. They analyse *bother* as used in (8a) as being categorially of type $<NP, <S, <NP,S>>>$, (where NP denotes a generalised quantifier and S denotes a proposition of type $<s,t>$ (page 222). Since it is lexically specified that the subject of *bother* is constrained to be *it*, the verb must denote the expression in (8b), where p is a variable over propositions of type $<s,t>$ and T is a variable of the type of generalised quantifiers, i.e. $<d, <d,t>>$.

(8)   a. It bothers Kim that Sandy is short.
       b. $\lambda T_1 \lambda p \lambda T_2.BOTHER(T_1)(p)$
       c. $\lambda T_2.BOTHER(KIM)(THAT\ SANDY\ IS\ SHORT)\ (\bot)$

λT_2 in (8b) does not bind any variable, and after the expression in (8b) has applied first to the denotation of *Kim* and second to the denotation of the sentential complement, we will get the expression in (8c), which is constrained to be applied to $\bot$.

The crucial difference between this theory and what I am proposing is that in (8b) the vacuous lambda operator is part of the meaning of the verb; this is equivalent to saying that it is introduced because it is lexically stipulated that this use of *bother* has a pleonastic *it* for subject. (Gazdar et al. (1985) propose that this stipulation is introduced via a rule permitting *bother* to undergo '*it* extraposition', but there will be other cases such as weather verbs and *seem* where the pleonastic subject will not be a result of extraposition.)

In our theory, the presence of a vacuous lambda operator and pleonastic subject in the translation of (8a) follows from the fact that predicate formation introduces a lambda operator at the VP level independent of the meaning of the VP, and that in this particular case, the arguments of *bother* are all satisfied internally, leaving no variable for the operator to bind. The derivation is given in (9), with predicate formation occurring at (9d), application to ⊥ in (9e) and existential closure at (9f).

(9)   a. $[bother]_V \rightarrow \lambda y \lambda p \lambda e.BOTHER(e) \wedge Th(e) = p \wedge Ex(e) = y$

  b. $[bother \; Kim]_{V'} \rightarrow \lambda y \lambda p \lambda e.BOTHER(e) \wedge Th(e) = p \wedge Ex(e) = y$ (K)
       $= \lambda p \lambda e.BOTHER(e) \wedge Th(e) = p \wedge Ex(e) = K$

  c. $[bother \; Kim \; that \; Sandy \; was \; short]_{V'} \rightarrow$
       $\lambda p \lambda e.BOTHER(e) \wedge Th(e) = p$
       $\wedge \; Ex(e) = K$ (THAT SANDY WAS SHORT)
       $= \lambda e.BOTHER(e) \wedge Th(e) = THAT \; SANDY \; WAS \; SHORT \wedge Ex(e) = K$

  d. $[bother \; Kim \; that \; Sandy \; was \; short]_{VP} \rightarrow$
       $\lambda x \lambda e.BOTHER(e) \wedge Th(e) = THAT \; SANDY \; WAS \; SHORT \wedge Ex(e) = K$

  e. $[It \; bother \; Kim \; that \; Sandy \; was \; short]_{IP} \rightarrow$
       $\lambda x \lambda e.BOTHER(e) \wedge Th(e) =$
       THAT SANDY WAS SHORT $\wedge \; Ex(e) = K$ (⊥)
       $= \lambda e.BOTHER(e) \wedge Th(e) = THAT \; SANDY \; WAS \; SHORT \wedge Ex(e) = K$

  f. $\exists e[BOTHER(e) \wedge Th(e) = THAT \; SANDY \; WAS \; SHORT \wedge Ex(e) = K]$

A reviewer has suggested that using a general operation of automatic lambda prefixation at the XP level instead of lexically specified vacuous lambda abstraction if the predicate is marked as selecting a pleonastic could be seen as 'generalisation to the worst case'. But this is to miss the point about what predicate formation tells us about the nature of the grammar.

In the Dowty–Sag–Gazdar et al. approaches to pleonastics, the need for a pleonastic subject is seen as a requirement exercised by a lexical head on its highest argument position. This is no surprise, since all these approaches adopt some version of a categorial grammar approach to syntax, in which syntactic structure is a projection of the subcategorisational properties of heads, and syntactic arguments are realised in order to saturate positions in the argument structure of a verb. If there is no independent rule of grammar, unconnected with the thematic properties of heads, which can require, or licence, arguments, then even non-thematic arguments will have to be related somehow to the thematic structure of heads. It seems to me that there is some internal contradiction in arguing that the distribution of non-thematic arguments is governed by lexical selection, since it is, at least in some sense, lexical selection which makes an argument thematic. But more serious is the fact that treating pleonastics as subcategorised means that the central questions about these elements remain unanswered. I take the central questions to be (i) why should a non-thematic argument be required by a head at all? And (ii) if we can require non-thematic arguments, why are they only subjects? To expand on (i), if thematic roles express constraints on the arguments of the relation expressed by a head, and reflect constraints on the participants in the event denoted by the head, then we would not expect a head to dictate that a syntactic argument has no semantic content. This means that we would not expect a head to specify that an argument is pleonastic. For a head to to exert a thematic constraint that an argument is pleonastic is essentially a constraint by a head that the argument filling a particular syntactic position is semantically empty. But this makes sense only if there is a syntactic definition of the position in terms independent of the head's selectional properties, and a syntactic requirement that the position is filled. This means that there would have to be a non-lexical definition of 'subject position', and a non-lexical requirement that subjects occur. But this is what a theory denies if it assumes that syntactic argument structure is projected directly from heads.

If there is such an independent requirement on subject position, then, I would argue, it is conceptually simpler to assume that a pleonastic occurs if the head has nothing to say about the grammatically required position, rather than to assume that a head specifically requires it to be empty.

The question in (ii) is equally unanswered by a subcategorisational/lexical theory of pleonastics: if heads can select pleonastics, then there is no way of explaining why such non-thematic arguments occur only in subject position and not in object position or indirect object position too. The subcategorisation approach, in whichever form it comes, has no answer to this, other than that it is a lexical property of some heads that they have these subjects, and that the absence of non-subject pleonastics is just a lexical gap. Restricting pleonastics to subject position is descriptively adequate, but has no explanatory force, since there is no a independent definition of subject other than 'highest argument of a head'.

In the approach I am arguing for here, the demand for a pleonastic is not a requirement of a lexical head, but a general requirement of the grammar which states that syntactic categories of certain kinds, namely VP, AP, NP and lexically headed PPs, are of type $<d, <e,t>>$ and need saturation by a subject, independently of the lexical properties or argument-taking properties of the lexical head of the predicate. The theory differs sharply from categorial approaches precisely because I claim that not all aspects of syntactic structure are projected by heads, and the need for pleonastic subjects in particular is an indication that this is so. Put differently, the theory of automatic predicate formation makes it a central fact about the grammar that, while the basic type of clauses and small clauses is $<e,t>$, the operation which takes you into the $<e,t>$ must be an operation of predicate application. Thus $<e,t>$ must have $<d, <e,t>>$ and d as daughters, whatever the thematic properties or content of these expressions is. Pleonastics are elements which allow this general grammatical requirement to be met.

So, both *snow* and *eat the apple* are type $<e,t>$ at the V' level and type $<d, <e,t>>$ at the VP level. Strong compositionality (or Full Interpretation), which guarantees that no information gets lost in the interpretation, will require *snow* to take a pleonastic, while the thematic requirements of *eat the apple* will require that the subject of the predicate must be the value of the agent role. Thus the subjects each have a different status in relation to their predicates, which if pleonastics are lexically selected gets lost. (Note that whole issue is independent of the question of why some heads assign all their arguments internally. I am in fact assuming that there are canonical position for realising particular thematic arguments: 'agent' is canonically associated with subject position, and 'theme' is canonically associated with direct object position, independently of whether there is an argument realised outside the VP. However, the existence of 'weather' verbs, which assign no arguments at all and which require a pleonastic subject, show that pleonastics are not just mechanisms for guaranteeing that certain thematic arguments of a head are realised internally.)

Another matter which this approach to pleonastics makes clear is the status of the subject 'argument' and the role of theta-marking. I proposed in chapter 6 that an n-place thematic expression is usually translated as a (curried) $n-1$ place logical expression. Thus *eat*, which has an event argument and two thematic roles to assign, translates as (10), where the event argument and only one of the variables introduced by theta-roles are bound by lambda operators:

(10) $\lambda y \lambda e . \text{EAT}(e) \wedge \text{Ag}(e) = x \wedge \text{Th}(e) = y$

I argued there that this represents the fact that what allows application of an expression headed by *eat* to an external argument is not dictated by the V but by the VP in which it occurs. There is thus a distinction between lexically constraining an argument and licensing functional application of an expression to an argument, and in this situation pleonastics are the kind of element we would expect to find. Thematic roles introduce constraints on participants in an event: in (10) the conjunction *Th(e)* = *y* tells us that the event denoted by *eat* is constrained to have a theme participant, and, if we assume a general rule assigning theme arguments to direct object position, we will have the information that the argument in direct object position is constrained to be the theme participant of EAT. But this per se is not sufficient to trigger functional application of the verb to the direct object position. This is a grammatical relation, triggered by the λy operator prefixing the expression in (10). So, then the fact that the x argument is not bound by a lambda in (10) indicates that the verb itself does not trigger functional application to the agent argument. But if functional application is triggered independently of the lexical properties of the head, then we would expect to get pleonastic elements which can be the arguments of the functional application in the absence of lexical constraints on the position.

7.1.3. *Pleonastics in property theory*

Chierchia (1989) gives a different account of expletives and dummy objects in the framework of property theory. As we saw in chapter 6:6.7.2, he treats properties as having two modes of presentation; there is the unsaturated predicate and its individual property correlate π. The individual π is the denotation of the VP; predication is an operation which takes π into a propositional function from entities into truth values, where the value is true if the entity denoted by the subject has the property π and false otherwise. This is illustrated in (11):

(11) a. Predication ($\cup$)
     $\cup$: $\pi \rightarrow$ <d,p>;
   b. type(RUN) = π,
      type($\cup$RUN) = <d,p>
      $\cup$RUN(JOHN) = John runs

The predication operator is introduced by Inflection. As Chierchia points out, this process cannot be applied to the VPs in (3) since *seems that John is tired*, *obvious that Mary had won* and *snow* do not denote properties but propositions (in his framework) and sets of events (in ours). He introduces a semantic rule of expletivisation which applies to a VP translation which does not contain an individual variable, mapping it on to a property which can then be predicated only of $\perp$. His rule looks like this:

(12)   Expletivisation (E)
   i. logical type:
       $p \rightarrow \pi$
   ii. semantic content:
       $\cup$[E(seem(p))] ($\perp$) = seem(p)
       $\cup$[E(seem(p))] (x) = undefined for any x $\neq \perp$

I have argued that the inappropriateness of predicating a predicate of the form (seem(p)) of anything other that $\perp$ follows from the Strong Compositionality/Full Interpretation, and that it does not need to be stipulated independently. Chierchia could easily argue the same thing. The difference between the two accounts is not in the choice of $\perp$ as subject, but in how application of the $\perp$ element is triggered. For Chierchia, expletivisation is an independent two-stage rule, which, before it introduces the predication operator, maps a proposition onto an entity of type π which can be the input to predication. The effect is to add, as he puts it, a truth conditionally inert subject to a proposition. It is most properly seen as a type-shifting operation, triggered by the predication operator, which Inflection introduces, which raises expletive taking VPs to the type at which the predication operator can apply to them.

The two-stage process is needed because predication, for Chierchia, is not merely a lambda abstraction operation, which can apply to an expression of any type, but an operation which is defined as being of logical type $\pi \rightarrow$ <d,p>, and thus cannot operate on propositions. This means that while predication is an automatic operation in Chierchia's theory, which does not need to be explicitly stated for expletive taking VPs, he has transferred to an earlier stage the problem of getting these VPs to the type at which the automatic operation can apply to them. Expletivisation is in this sense Chierchia's equivalent of the process of vacuous lambda abstraction which Dowty, Sag and Gazdar et al. use to get to the right type to apply to a subject. Again, this contrasts with our account in which the lambda operator required for application to the subject argument is introduced at the interpretation of a specified syntactic level, the XP, without reference to the semantic content of XP, and in which nothing special has to be said about pleonastics.

Note that Chierchia will have to guarantee that expletivisation is triggered by any operator which applies to properties, and not just the predication operator. Chierchia analyses *for* in (13a) as an operator which applies to an individual, denoted by *John*, and a property, denoted by *to run*, and yields a proposition, which is then the subject argument of *dangerous*. Presumably Chierchia would want the same operator to apply to the denotation of *it* and *to rain while we are in the wadi* in (13b):

(13)   a. For John to run would be dangerous.
       b. For it to rain while we are in the wadi would be dangerous.

But then the rule in (12.i) will need to apply to *rain*, raising it from p into π, so that together with ⊥, it can be the input to the *for* operation.

7.2.   MORE ABOUT FULL INTERPRETATION

7.2.1. *Pleonastics are just ordinary pronouns*

This way of treating the interpretation of pleonastics has implications for how exactly we understand the phenomenon. We have seen that we do not have a special Pleonastic Rule, but rather that the interpretation of pleonastics uses a minimal information object ⊥ of type d, with no real properties. This implies that a pleonastic is not a peculiar kind of DP, but rather an ordinary pronoun with a minimal information interpretation. I assume that pronouns denote variables which range over the domain of individuals, and which are either bound, or remain free and get their value fixed contextually. *It* denotes an unsorted variable, ranging over the domain of individuals and events. (This will become clear in section 7.3). A pleonastic use of *it* will be one in which the linguistic context in which it occurs forces its denotation to be ⊥. Let us see how this occurs.

Normally, the interpretation of a DP is determined by its internal lexical structure; I assume that proper names and definites denote individuals and that quantificational DPs denote sets of sets of a kind determined by the meaning of the quantifier. Conditions on the meaning of a DP are given by the theta-role of the head which directly, or indirectly for an external argument, governs it. Thus if the position is marked agentive, the denotation of the DP has to be something which has a will and so forth. With pronouns, the features on the pronoun dictate what kind of entity or entities can be denotation of that position; whether they are male, female or neuter, and how many of them there are.

If we compare sentences like (14a,b), the only difference between the two matrix subjects is that in (14b) the matrix subject position is not assigned a theta-role.

(14)   a. It runs.
       b. It seems that John is tired.

It in (14a), denotes some neuter object which has the property of running. The DP is assigned a thematic role, agent, by the verb *run*; the fact that it is assigned a theta-role indicates that the denotation fills an argument slot in the predicate denoted by VP, and the kind of theta-role assigned to it indicates what role the denotation of the VP plays in the event which the sentence picks out. In (14b), the DP *it* is not assigned any theta-role at all. This indicates that if it is interpreted as denoting anything, there is no relation for its denotation to be an argument of. The meaning of the DP will contribute nothing to the meaning of the sentence, and the Principle of Full Interpretation/Strong Compositionality will be violated. However, since the DP contains no syntactic structure or grammatical features which need to be interpreted, it can be taken as pleonastic, denoting the null, dummy, minimal information element. It is licensed syntactically, since it is the subject saturating the VP, the non-theta-assigning predicate headed by *seems*, and it denotes ⊥, which has no properties, so its meaning does not get lost in the interpretation of the sentence. Thus, nothing special has to be said about the interpretation of pleonastics.

Minimal contrasts are found with lexical heads which take a single argument which can be moved to subject position, such as *obvious*, argued by Cinque (1989) to be ergative. *Obvious* assigns one internal theta-role, which in (15a) is assigned to the CP complement. The CP, since it need not be case-marked, remains as the complement to A. The subject of the predicate is then the non-theta-marked pleonastic *it*. In (15b) the theta-marked CP argument has been moved to subject position. In (15c), the theta-marked complement is a DP, but this moves to subject position to avoid violating the Case Filter. Being theta-marked, it must be interpreted thematically.

(15)   a. It was obvious that we'd be late.
       b. That we'd be late was obvious.
       c. It was obvious.

The difference between the pleonastic and thematic *it* can be tested in conjunction constructions: when the APs (or more properly the I′ containing the APs) in (15) are conjoined with constituents headed by a lexical item assigning an external Θ-role, the difference between the pleonastic *it* in (15a) and the referential *it* in (15c) shows up. (16) demonstrates this:

(16)   a.   That the concert was a success was obvious and pleased her very
            much.

b. *It was obvious that the concert was a success, and pleased her very much.

c. It was obvious and convinced the audience completely.

In (16a) the constituent *pleased her very much* is conjoined with *was obvious*. Both VPs assign a 'propositional' theta-role, which they assign to the shared CP subject. In (16b), where the subject is also shared, *obvious* assigns its single theta-role to the internal CP, and takes a pleonastic subject. *Pleased* on the other hand, does not assign an internal propositional theta-role, and thus needs to assign an external theta-role to the subject. The conflict between interpreting *it* as pleonastic with respect to *obvious* and theta-marked with respect to *pleased* means that the sentence is ungrammatical. (16c), where both conjuncts theta-mark *it*, is grammatical, and *it* is given a contextually appropriate reference, e.g. 'the argument'.

(17) shows how minimal the difference is between the two uses of *it*, since the sentence is ambiguous depending on whether the pronoun *it* is genuinely referential or is being used pleonastically. The sentence is ambiguous between the reading which asserts the certainty of our being late for dinner, and the reading which asserts that some individual which can be denoted by *it* – the dog, for example – was certain that we'd be late for dinner.

(17)   It was certain that we'd be late for dinner.

This ambiguity stems from the fact that *certain* may assign either a single theta-role to its complement, or two theta-roles, one to the complement CP and another to the 'bearer', as shown in (18), where in (18a) the parenthetical forces a pleonastic subject:

(18)   a. It was certain, if unfortunate, that we'd be late.
       b. John was certain that we'd be late.

Since the ambiguity is due to the optionality of the external theta-role of *certain*, there is only one possible tree structure for (18). If *certain* assigns an external theta-role, it is interpreted as thematic. When no theta-role is assigned to the subject position, which is independently licensed by predication, it is interpreted pleonastically. Its denotation cannot be incorporated into the semantic representation, and it can denote only the null element. Instead of positing two homophonous forms of *certain*, or associating with it two different lexical translation rules, we posit one form with an optional external argument. The meaning of dyadic *certain* is predictably related to the meaning of the adjective when the external argument isn't assigned. Without an external argument, it predicates a high degree of probability to the proposition denoted by its complement, but since no 'bearer' or experiencer argument gives a participant in the eventuality, the certainty is general. When *certain* assigns an external argument too, it predicates the same high degree of probability to the proposition, but adds a 'bearer' or experiencer participant to the eventuality and the certainty is relativised to this individual, or asserted to be 'in her/his mind'. (19) gives interpretations for (18) (without the parenthetical):

(19) a. ∃e[CERTAIN(e) ∧ Th(e) = (THAT WE'D BE LATE)]
      b. ∃e[CERTAIN(e) ∧ Th(e) = (THAT WE'D BE LATE)
            ∧ Ex(e) = JOHN]

Sure works the same way, and Cinque (1989) provides evidence that this is the correct analysis of the Italian analogues. *Seems* never assigns an external argument, but as was pointed out by a reviewer of Rothstein (1995a), the optional indirect object has the same relativising effect. (20a,b) are semantically related in the same way as (18a,b), since (20a) makes an unqualified assertion that there is an eventuality of their being good evidence that John is tired, while in (20b) Mary is a participant in the 'seeming' eventuality, and the sentence asserts that there is evidence which indicates to Mary that John is tired.

(20)   a. It seems that John is tired.
       b. It seems to Mary that John is tired.

7.2.2. Non-theta-marked lexical subjects are possible

The discussion in 2.1 has shown that pleonastic *it* is really an ordinary pronoun with a minimal informational use. One of the implications of this is that a pleonastic pronoun violates clause (i) of the theta-criterion, by which I mean a principle of the form (21):

(21) **Theta-Criterion**
      i.   Every DP must be assigned one and only one theta-role.
      ii. Every theta-role must be assigned to one and only one DP.

This is not surprising; many accounts of the theta-criterion relativise (21.i) to exclude pleonastics, by restricting 'every DP' to 'every argument DP' or 'every non-pleonastic' DP. (McCloskey 1991 shows that we cannot argue that *it* and the CP complement of an expletive-taking head form a chain; it is therefore not possible to argue that the pronoun shares the theta-role of the CP.) However, suppose we argue, as we have done, that there is no such thing as a 'pleonastic DP' but rather a pleonastic use of the minimal referential pronoun, and that the pronoun in this use is syntactically and semantically an argument of a predicate with a denotation, ⊥. Then there is no natural syntactic way to exclude (21.i) from applying to pleonastics. One reaction might be to define 'pleonastic pronoun' as one to which (21.i) does not apply. Another is to ask whether non-theta-marked pronouns are an instance of a more widespread phenomenon. Pleonastics are syntactically licensed only by being subjects of syntactic predicates, and without reference to (21); are there other DPs which are licensed in the same way? Indeed there are a number of constructions in which non-theta-marked, case-marked DPs occur as subjects of predicates. (22a) is one such example, and Heycock (1991) gives (22c) and (22e) as others:

(22)   a. The book is for you to read.
     b. The book is [Op$_i$ for [you to read t$_i$]]
     c. The book is easy to read.
     d. The book is [easy [Op$_i$ [to read t$_i$]]
     e. That man seems as if his daughter kept him up all night.

In (22a,c), the CP predicate assigns no external theta-role, since its verb internally theta-marks the trace bound by the null operator. This operator-headed chain satisfies the theta-requirements of the verb, and though the subject DP *the book* supplies the value of the object of the verb *read*, it is not theta-marked by it. (I argued this explicitly in chapter 3.) Since *easy* in (22c) assigns no external theta-role, it cannot theta-mark the subject DP and *that man* in (22e) is not theta-marked by *seems* either. Nonetheless, these non-theta-marked expressions are interpreted as fully referential, and DPs in this position can denote individuals, generalised quantifiers or any other standard lexical DP interpretation. (Rothstein (1991) also discusses CP complements of degree phrases which are selected, but not theta-marked.)

How do these expressions get interpreted if they are not theta-marked? We saw above that whether or not a pronoun receives a pleonastic interpretation depends of the structure of the logical predicate predicated of it. In the same way, we would expect the interpretation of the subjects in (22) to be determined by the structure of the predicate. The pleonastically interpreted pronoun has to be pleonastic because there is no way to use the informational content of an expression in that position in assigning a truth-value to a sentence. The examples in (22) must thus be OK because there is some way of using their informational content in interpreting the sentence. In (22a,c) this is possible, because the predicates contain a predicate CP; as I showed in the previous chapter, this CP has an operator at the [Spec,CP] level which is interpreted as a lambda operator binding the free variable denoted by the wh-trace, which we can represent very crudely as λy.FOR YOU TO READ(y). The CP denotes a one-place semantic predicate requiring a lexical argument, although it does not assign an external theta-role.

(22e) is a more complicated; the subject is not theta-marked and, in addition, the syntactic predicate does not denote an open expression, such as a CP predicate. (22e) contrasts with examples like (23) where a lexical subject is not permitted:

(23)   a. *That man snows.
     b. *That man seems that he is tired.
     c. *The book is easy for you to read the journal.

I assume that it is *as if* which makes this sentence OK, and that it is interpreted as a having a topic-comment structure, with the denotation of the subject being interpreted as the topic of the expression denoted by *seems as if CP*. *As if* makes it possible to interpret the syntactic predicate as a comment, related semantically to the topic, and thus the DP denoted by the subject can be incorporated into the semantic representation of the sentence at the topic-comment level. *As* has a related function in (24); while *as if* in (22e) identifies the comment element, *as* in (24) identifies the left-dislocated topic:

(24)   a. As for John, his daughter seems to have been up all night.
       b. As for John, the baby kept him up all night.

Two points support this explanation of (22e). First, unlike (22a,d) there is no predictable interpretive relation between the matrix subject and the rest of the sentence. The sentence is acceptable to the extent that a context can be constructed to make the VP an appropriate 'comment' on the topic. (25a) is as interpretable as (25b):

(25)   a. John seems as if the sun is shining today.
       b. As for John, the sun is shining today.

Also, Lappin (1983) showed that the *seems as if* construction is most acceptable when the lower CP contains a pronoun coreferential with the matrix subject. The examples in (24) show that standard topic-comment structures show parallel properties. However, this topic-comment reading of *seems as if* constructions like (22e) is not obligatory: topicless sentences are pragmatically acceptable (see e.g. Strawson 1964). The kind of ambiguity caused by optional theta-marking, which was illustrated in (17), thus shows up again here. (26) has two readings:

(26)   It seems as if it wants to go out.

Since *it* in the embedded clause is in a position theta-marked by *want*, it is always thematic, and referential. But, in the matrix clause *it* can either be interpreted as the topic of the sentence, in which case it is most plausibly interpreted as denoting the individual denoted by the embedded it, or it can be pleonastic, denoting $\perp$, and the sentence is topicless.

We can see then that DPs don't have to be theta-marked, or in a theta-chain in order to be referential. Rather, there is a condition, which we have put down to Strong Compositionality/Full Interpretation that no informational content can be lost in the interpretation of a sentence. A DP, theta-marked or not, is allowed if its meaning is incorporated into the interpretation of the sentence. If it is not, as in examples like (23), the sentence is ungrammatical. It follows that the only kind of DP which can be used in constructions like (23) are DPs with no informational content, and which denote the null element $\perp$.

What does this mean for the question of syntactic licensing? Heycock (1991) proposes on the basis of these data that argument DPs can be licensed by theta-marking or by predication. In the light of our discussion, we can sharpen this. If licensing is the syntactic relation indicating that a DP is a syntactic argument of a head, it must be the syntactic correlation of functional application. Then theta-assignment will license internal arguments of heads because a verb which internally theta-marks a position always triggers functional application to that argument in that position. But we have seen that external theta-marking is neither necessary nor sufficient to license a DP, and this follows from the fact that while a head theta-marks an external position it does not trigger functional application to that position. What makes the subject a syntactic argument of the predicate, and thus of the lexical head of the predicate, is the fact that it enters into a predication relation with the predicate, whether or not it is theta-marked. The head of the predicate may theta-mark the position, and thus constrain it thematically, but this is a separate issue.

So, setting aside DP complements of P, which we will not discuss here, (27) sums up DP licensing constraints (note that DPs in both object and subject position will still have to be case-marked.)

(27) **DP licensing**
Non-predicational DPs are licensed as syntactic arguments by internal theta-marking or as subjects of predicates.

In the light of (27), the status of the theta-criterion is very much weakened. (21.i) stated that all DPs had to receive one and only one theta-role. We saw in chapter 5, the 'only one' condition doesn't hold since adjunct depictive predicates must have two theta-roles, though assigned by different predicates. This means that (21.i) cannot be stronger than the statement that no DP may be assigned more than one theta-role by a single head.

But now we see that the 'at least one' condition doesn't hold either, and that some DPs are not assigned any theta-roles. What we are left with is clause (21.ii), stating that each theta-role must be assigned to a unique DP. The intuition which this seems to be capturing concerns the relation between the semantic and syntactic expressions. If we ignore the event argument introduced by the verb, which does not count since it does not ever have a syntactic constituent as a correlate, the number of syntactic arguments that a head has is the same as the number of variable positions in the logical expression which it denotes. The theta-grid mediates between the logical expressions associated with a head and the syntactic environment in which it occurs. While the verb *read* strictly denotes a set of reading events, it is associated with the logical expression in (28a). The lexical expression in (28b), which is also associated with *read*, represents a mapping between the logical and the syntactic representation by indicating which variable positions in (28a) must have a syntactic representation.

(28) a. $\lambda y \lambda e.\text{READ}(e) \wedge \text{Ag}(e) = x \wedge \text{Th}(e) = y$
   b. read_V: $< \Theta_{Ag}, \Theta_{Th} >$

It does not follow that the mapping is necessarily from the logical representation to the lexical or syntactic representation. Given that we know that a verb denotes a set of events, we can see (28b) as the expression which not only dictates the number of syntactic arguments that a verb must have, but as indicating what information must be included in the logical expression in addition to the given $\lambda e.\text{V}(e)$. Either way, the theta-grid is a representation of the correlation between the logical expression and the syntactic expression, and clause II of the theta-criterion is a statement about how to use the theta-grid: the grid represents the variable positions which have syntactic correlates (with the marking of the external argument, if there is one, indicating which variable, if any, is free in the logical expression). (21.ii) states that each of these syntactically expressed positions in the grid must be filled by a different syntactic expression. The theta-grid thus associates with a lexical item a lexical relation which is derived from a logical expression of the kind in (28a). The theta-criterion then ensure that the number of syntactic arguments associated with the head in the sentence is the same as the adicity of the lexical relation represented in the grid. This can be summed up as in (29):

(29)   **Revised theta-criterion**
        An n-place lexical relation, represented in an n-place theta-grid, is lexically realised by a head that has n syntactic arguments.

The joint effect of (29) and the statement in (27) will guarantee that a non-predicative DP is either theta-marked, or the subject of a predicate.

A final question that we can ask in this section is why the Principle of Full Interpretation allows *it* to be a pleonastic, a DP with no informational content. I assume that pronouns, unlike lexical DPs, have no internal lexical structure, but are realisations of grammatical features. It has been argued (for example, in Abney 1987) that they are intransitive determiners heading DPs. Since they lack the internal lexical structure of a full nominal, there is no structural or lexical information to be lost if they are not interpreted, and the possibility of their not having a semantic interpretation arises. However, most pronouns cannot be pleonastic. Features other than the minimal, unmarked array must also be interpreted, and which these features are is a syntactic property of a particular language. In English, person and plurality must be interpreted, as must be masculine or feminine features, while in French, person, plurality and [+feminine] must be interpreted. Thus (30) is unacceptable with *he* as subject for the same reason that (23c) is, though *it* is fine in that position:

(23c)   *The book/It is easy for you to read the journal.
(30)   It/*He is easy for you to read the journal.

This implies that the 'minimal syntactic features' are an unmarked, default, grammatical form. This further implies that pleonastics will always be realisations of sets of minimal syntactic features. I hope that cross-linguistic accounts of agreement will support this. Data on agreement that seems to do so is Icelandic verb agreement. When the matrix subject is non-nominative, the matrix verb does not agree with the subject. If there is a nominative object, the verb agrees with that, but if there is no such object, the verb is in the third person singular form, whatever the person and plurality of either subject or object, implying that these minimal features are the unmarked form when there are no agreement relations to override it (see Zaenen, Maling and Thrainsson 1985). As predicted, the Icelandic pleonastic is also a third person, singular, neuter pronoun.

7.3. OBJECT PLEONASTICS

7.3.1. *Theoretical predictions*

The theory presented so far predicts that there should be no object pleonastics. Pleonastics occur as subjects of predicates because the position is syntactically licensed non-thematically via predication. If there were to be pleonastic objects, there would have to be a non-thematic basis for licensing object position also, which is exactly what is denied by the discussion culminating in the generalisation in (27). If non-subjects can only be thematically licensed, then an object will have to have a thematic interpretation. Despite claims to the contrary, most notably Postal and Pullum (1988) (henceforth P&P) and Authier (1991), this prediction is correct. I show in this section that apparent objects which are not subjects of embedded predicates, such as those in (31), are theta-marked pronouns with a semantic interpretation.

(31)   a. I regretted (it) that he was late.
       b. They never mentioned (it) to the candidate that the job was poorly paid.
       c. I resent it every time you say that.
       d. I hate it when you are late.

It has been assumed (see, for example the discussion in P&P) that these are extraposition structures in which the lexical CP or DP is base-generated in [DP,VP] position and then moved out of it, leaving a pleonastic to fill the empty position. The extraposed element is interpreted as if it is the direct object, and the pronoun has no semantic significance. As far as I know, there are no explanations for why extraposition should occur at least in (31a–c), nor of how the pleonastic or the extraposed element are licensed. (One might suggest that in (31d) the *when* phrase has been extraposed since it is not syntactically of the form to appear in direct object position, but see the discussion below.) In fact, Stowell (1981) claims that CP complements of verbs are always extraposed from direct object position in order not to violate the Case Resistance Principle, and that they leave behind a trace and not a full DP. If this is so, an extraposition account of (31a,b) would have to posit a different form of the process, explaining why a full DP replaces a trace, and why this occurs as an alternate in a limited subset of the cases where extraposition is standardly possible. There is thus no prima facie evidence that the sentences in (31) are extraposition structures, nor are there non-thematic principles which license the object position, and I shall show later that there is evidence against an extraposition account. Authier (1991) offers a non-extraposition account of (31). Claiming that the pronoun is base-generated under the V′ as a realisation of accusative case, he suggests that the lexical XP is base-generated in a caseless position, adjoined to V′, where it can still be theta-marked by V. He maintains an extraposition account of (31a,b) when the *it* is not present, arguing that here the CP has moved to be adjoined to VP, leaving a case-marked variable

behind. Aside from the fundamental problem that case-assignment is not obligatory, as we discussed in chapter 3, there are several internal problems with
Authier's account. The analysis of extraposition and base-generation that he
gives does not allow us to explain why it is sometimes obligatory and sometimes
optional, as the contrast between (31a,b) and (32) shows:

(32)   I like *(it) that she has good manners.

Furthermore, he cannot account for (31c). On his theory *every time you say
that*, as a Θ-marked DP, must be assigned case, and cannot be base-generated
in a caseless V'-adjoined position.

   In the theory presented here, the pronouns in (31) must be theta-marked
and semantically interpreted, and the so-called 'extraposed' XP must be independently licensed. We expect *it* to behave like a pronoun and like a theta-
marked argument. This means that (i) it either denotes an individual meeting
its feature specifications, or is interpreted as a variable when bound by an
operator, and that (ii) it will be internally theta-marked by the matrix verb.
As I shall show, these predictions are born out. I shall also show that there
are three different types of constructions illustrated in (31), and thus three
different ways in which the so-called 'extraposed' or 'adjoined' element is
licensed.

7.3.2. The constructions

7.3.2.1. 'it' + an adverbial quantifier

We begin with the construction illustrated in (31c,d), where *it* is followed by a
DP. (33) gives more examples:

(33)   a. I regret it every time I have dinner with John.
       b. The children enjoy it every time you tell them a story.
       c. They announced it publicly every time they decided to move house.
       d. They remembered it every time you were late.
       e. He used to (dis)like it when it thundered loudly.

In these examples *it* displays classic pronoun behaviour, being ambiguous
between a variable bound by the adverbial quantifier and a free pronominal.
On the bound reading (33a) means 'for every event of having dinner with John,
I regret that event,' and (33b,e) have analogous interpretations. On the free
reading, (33a) has the interpretation 'on every occasion of having dinner with
John, I regret a specific thing, or fact or event' – for example that he never
brings enough money to pay his share of the bill. Note that in (33c), *it* ranges
over events of deciding to move house and not the moving itself, as will be
predicted by our formal structure below. In (33a,d) the adverbial is a bare DP,
and is licensed in whatever way other bare DP adverbials are licensed (see, for
example, Larson 1985). In (33e) the bare DP is replaced by an adverbial *when*
clause. We shall concentrate on the structure of (33a–d) here, but a parallel

account of (33e) should be possible. (33e) is closely related to the 'irrealis if' construction, discussed in Pullum (1987) and P&P, and illustrated in (34). I shall not discuss these, but I claim that here too the pronoun is not pleonastic but refers to the unrealised event denoted by the sentential complement of *if*:

(34) I'd hate it if it rained.

Returning to (33a,d), we can identify the semantic role of *it* by noting the change of meaning in the sentence if it is omitted:

(35) a. I regretted every time I had dinner with John.
      b. The children enjoy every time you tell them a story.
      c. They announced publicly every time they (had) decided to move house.
      d. They remembered every time you were late.

Here the *every* phrase (which I will call 'QP') is the object of the verb. In the examples in (33), where the QP is an operator binding the pronoun, there is a 'matching' relation between events named by the QP and events named by the matrix verb. (33a) asserts that every event of my having dinner with John is matched with an event of my regretting having dinner with him. (35a), by contrast, asserts that I regretted all the occasions of having dinner with him, but makes no claims about how many regretting events there were. Thus it, but not (33a), is appropriate if after ten years of happy dinner occasions, something occurs which makes me regret that I ever had dinner with John in the past. The contrast holds in the other examples too: (33c) for example requires an announcement at the time of each decision to move, while (35c) can be properly used in a situation in which they stood up one day and announced a list of all the decisions to move that they had ever made. This explains another contrast: in examples like (33), where the main clause event and the event of the adverbial are matched, the tenses of the matrix verb and the verb embedded in the QP must match, while there is no such restriction on the examples in (35). (36) illustrates this with *regret*, and the same contrast holds for other examples.

(36) a. I regret it every time you do/*did/*will do that.
      b. I regretted it every time you did/*do/*will do that.
      c. I (already) regret every time you did/do/?will do that.
      d. I will regret every time you did/do that.

Note that the contrast between (33) and (35) is not a distributive – collective dichotomy: (35a) allows a distributive reading, but it does not force it. It also allows a cumulative reading, where, for example, I have fits of regrets every few years, so that all in all every dinner was regretted, though not one by one. Another difference is that when the QP is an adverbial, another temporal adverbial is not possible, but when it is an object, the temporal adverbial position is available. This explains the contrast between (37a) and (37b), on the reading where the pronoun is bound:

(37)   a.   Sooner or later, he regretted every time he went there.
        b.   *Sooner or later, he regretted it every time he went there.

Note that the *it* in (33) is a variable bound by a quantifier over events, and not an anaphor coindexed with a DP within the adverbial. Thus in (38a), *it* is bound by the QP and is not coindexed with *a story*. Only if the adverbial is preposed, as in (38b), may *it* be dependent on *a story*, rather than bound by the quantifier, but this, dependent on linear order, is a matter of pragmatic coreference, as discussed in Kadmon (1987).

(38)   a.   I enjoyed it every time he told a story.
        b.   Every time he told a story, I enjoyed it.

A detailed analysis of the semantics of this construction is presented in Rothstein (1995c). The sentence *I regret it* has the semantic representation in (37):

(39) $\exists e\ [REGRET(e) \wedge Ag(e) = I \wedge Th(e) = e']$

Regret has an event argument e, and assigns two theta-roles, Agent and Theme. It is a property of *regret* that it can take an entity from either the domain of individuals or the domain of events as its internal argument. In (39), an event is chosen, and the event e′ is the value of *Th*. The matrix clause is closed by default existential closure, and it reads 'there is an regretting event, e, of which I am the agent and the event e′ is the theme'. The QP *every time I had dinner with John* is translated as in (40):

(40) $\forall e'[HAD\ DINNER(e') \wedge Ag(e') = I \wedge WITH(e') = JOHN]$

The Q *every* is a quantifier over events (this restriction is given by the nominal head time) and the restriction within the domain of events is given by the clause, *I had dinner with John*. HAD DINNER takes an event argument, e′, the agent of which is I, and the *with* argument of which is John. As I argue in detail in Rothstein (1995c), the QP is related to the matrix verb by a (partial) function, which I call M (for 'matching'), and which is not lexically realised. We can think of it as a expressed by a null preposition, analogous to the null locative prepositions which may occur in (41a) and which must be used in (41b):

(41)   a.   I visit him (on) Mondays
        b.   I visit him (*on) every Monday

M, like a theta-role, is a function, and maps events denoted by the matrix verb onto the denotation of the adverbial quantifier. Using M to combine (39) and (40), we have (42b) as the interpretation for (33a), repeated here as (42a):

(42)   a.   I regretted it every time I had dinner with John
        b. $\forall e'[HAD\ DINNER(e') \wedge Ag(e') = I \wedge WITH(e') = JOHN$
               $\rightarrow \exists e[REGRET(e) \wedge Ag(e) = I \wedge Th(e) = e' \wedge M(e) = e']]$

(42b) says that for every event e′ of my having dinner with John, there is an event e of my regretting e′ and e is mapped onto e′ by M. The functional nature of M guarantees that there will be at least as many events of regretting as there are of having dinner, giving the matching effect discussed above. If *it* is interpreted as free rather than as a bound variable, then the representation of (33a) will be almost identical to (42), except that the value of *Th* will not be a variable bound by the quantifier, but will be a free variable either in the domain of individuals or events.

The semantic contrast between (33a) and (35a) where the QP is the direct object, can now be made precise.

(33)   a. I regret it every time I have dinner with John.
(35)   a. I regretted every time I had dinner with John.

In (33a), the QP is an adverbial operator binding the variable in object position, while in (35a) it is itself the object of the verb. In such a position it is interpreted as any other quantificational DP. It can be assigned scope, as in (43a) or it can be interpreted in situ as in (43b), it which case it gets a sum interpretation (see Landman 1996, and references cited there.) (43b) uses Link's operation of sum formation, which we already introduced in chapter 6, which maps a set of individuals or events onto the plural individual or event which is in that set (Link 1987).

(43)   a. $\forall e'[\text{HAD DINNER}(e') \wedge \text{Ag}(e') = \text{I} \wedge \text{WITH}(e') = \text{JOHN}$
$\rightarrow \exists e[\text{REGRET}(e) \wedge \text{Ag}(e) = \text{I} \wedge \text{Th}(e) = e']]$
b. $\exists e\ [\text{REGRET}(e) \wedge \text{Ag}(e) = \text{I} \wedge \text{Th}(e) =$
$\sqcup (\lambda e'.\text{HAD DINNER}(e') \wedge \text{Ag}(e') = \text{I} \wedge \text{WITH}(e') = \text{John})]$

The fact that two readings are available for (35a) is due to the different conditions on argument and adverbial quantifiers: adverbial QPs must be assigned scope and argument QPs need not be.

We can see that with respect to binding, *it* in these constructions behaves like any other pronoun, and we turn now to the issue of theta-marking. Although it is rather unclear what semantic restrictions on arguments strictly come under theta-theory, evidence for theta-marking would be that the semantic properties of the object position are dependent on the choice of the verb. In this case the semantic property we are interested in is what kind of entity the V allows the pronoun to denote. *Regret* allows its theme argument to range over events or individuals while *claim* does not allow events, as we see with the gerund and derived nominal complements in (44), and this is evidence that *regret* and *claim* theta-mark the object position.

(44)   a.   Alexander regretted *that he had destroyed the city.*
          Alexander regretted *the city.*
          Alexander regretted *destroying the city.*
          Alexander regretted *the destruction of the city.*
      b.   Alexander claimed *that he had destroyed the city.*
          Alexander claimed *the city.*
          *Alexander claimed *destroying the city.*
          *Alexander claimed *the destruction of the city.*

The pronominal object of *regret* can be bound by the event quantifier because it can range over events. If a verb does not allow its theme to be in the domain of events, then we predict, correctly, that it won't occur in bound constructions like (33). While nothing prevents *claim* from taking a pronominal DP object, this cannot be bound by an event quantifier. (45b) contrasts minimally with the examples in (33), since it does not have a reading where *it* is bound by *every time he saw you*:

(45)   a.   He claimed it, but it wasn't true.
        b.   *He claimed it$_i$ [every time he saw you]$_i$.

This is quite general. Hegarty (1992), citing Cattell (1978), distinguishes verbs whose CP complements denote events 'either actual or at issue in the discourse' and those whose CP complements are propositional. Those in the first class pattern like (33), and the others like (45b), as (46a/b) shows:

(46)   a.   They verify/deny/announce/forget/notice it$_i$ [every time he does that]$_i$.
        b.   *They believe/think/assume/maintain/say/suppose/assert it$_i$ [every time he does that]$_i$.

(46b) does have a reading where *it* is not bound by the QP, but denotes a free variable, as is predicted by the claims that the pronoun has independent thematic status and that its theta-properties are given by the verb and not by its relation to the QP.

A further piece of evidence showing that the pronouns bound by these quantifiers are theta-marked is provided by the examples discussed in section 7.2.1, where a pronoun may or may not be interpreted pleonastically depending on other constituents in the sentence. We saw that the subject of *obvious* was interpreted pleonastically only if the adjective had a complement; it is a pleonastic in (47a) but not (47b) (assuming that (47b) is not used in a null complement anaphora context), and the same is true for the 'psych' predicate in (48):

(47)   a.   It was obvious that we'd be late.
        b.   It was obvious.

(48)   a.   It upset her that we went there.
        b.   It upset her.

As the theory predicts, *it* can be bound by an event quantifier only when it is theta-marked, i.e. in (47b) and (48b). In (49b/d) where the pronoun is theta-marked, it can be bound by the quantifier, but in (49a/c) where it is a pleonastic, there is no bound reading available.

(49)   a.   *It$_i$ was obvious that we'd be late [every time he got angry]$_i$.
        b.   It$_i$ was obvious [every time he got angry]$_i$.
        c.   *It$_i$ upset her that we went there [every time he got angry]$_i$.
        d.   It$_i$ upset her [every time he got angry]$_i$.

Note that all the properties of the theta-marked object should be preserved under passivisation, in particular it should still be possible for the QP to bind it. There are pragmatic reasons why these sentences sometimes sound clumsy, but (50) shows that the prediction is correct:

(50) a. It$_i$ was deeply resented [every time the government put up its own salaries]$_i$.
      b. It$_i$ was announced in advance [every time a guest lecturer visited the department]$_i$.

7.3.2.2. 'it' + CP

Though the contrasts are less dramatic, we can show that the pronoun in the *it* + CP construction illustrated in (31a) and the other examples in (51) is also not pleonastic.

(51) a. Mary regretted it that he was late. (=31a)
      b. They confirmed it that you had passed the entrance exam.
      c. He resented it that his friends worked so hard.
      d. They announced it that she had passed her exams.

Again, theta-theory and the theory of pronouns predict how the pronominal object behaves. *It* must have essentially the same semantic function as the *it* objects in (33), except that in the absence of a quantifier, the bound interpretation will never be available. The pronoun is free, and will denote a specific entity recoverable from the discourse. Theta-marking by the matrix verb dictates the thematic relation which is asserted to hold between the referent of *it* and the event denoted by the verb, and thus restricts this referent to something capable of entering into such a relation.

In the examples in (51), *it* is optional, and including or dropping it does not seem to make an appreciable difference in meaning. Notice, however, that there are cases where the two versions are not equivalent, and this is because where the direct object is *it*, the CP is not within the VP. Thus, in the ellipsis constructions in (52), the version with *it* has only a strict identity reading, while (52b) has a both a sloppy and a strict reading. (Thanks to Fred Landman for pointing this out.)

(52) a. Mary regretted it that she was late, and so did Jane.
      b. Mary regretted that she was late and so did Jane.

The fact that the sentences in (51) are truth-conditionally equivalent to the *it*-less versions is not evidence that *it* contributes nothing to the interpretation. *It* objects do affect meaning in a predictable way, though these sentences don't show it. Since a pronoun denotes a specific entity, identifiable through syntactic coindexing or through pragmatic factors, the *it* in (51) will be appropriate when the object of the matrix verb is a specific event. Bolinger (1977) claims that *it* in these circumstances "must refer to some fact already broached", and that the pronoun is anaphoric to the CP. As I shall show, I don't think that the relationship between *it* and the CP is one of anaphoric dependence, but the idea that *it* refers to something already broached, an event already mentioned or for other reasons contextually prominent, seems right, since this is the kind of pragmatic feature which generally makes an entity available as the reference of a deictic pronoun. (53), adapted from Bolinger, is a good example of how *it* contributes to meaning:

(53) a. John and Mary have announced that they got married.
      b. John and Mary have announced it that they got married.

(53a), without *it*, is appropriate as a report of the fact that John and Mary made an announcement of information which is new to the speaker. (53b) is more appropriate if the speaker is reporting that John and Mary have made a public announcement of an event that she already knew to have occurred. The pronoun denotes a specific event prominent in the discourse and the CP identifies that event explicitly. The same account explains the differences in (54), (from Bolinger, 4:39/40):

(54) a. If he asks you to help just say that you regret (*it) that you can't.
      b. You shouldn't regret it that you were helpful.

(54a), where *it* is inappropriate, involves a hypothetical regret with a non-specific object, whereas in (54b) the object of *regret* is an actual event.

On the assumption that *it* is thematic, these verbs then appear to have two sets of selectional properties. *Announce* and *regret* select either a DP complement, which has its denotation in the domain of events, or a CP complement, which denotes a proposition.

Note that this explains immediately why in examples like (32), repeated here, the *it* is obligatory: *like* selects a DP complement, but not a CP complement.

(32) I like *(it) that she has good manners.

When the verb selects for a DP *it* complement, the question is how the CP in the construction is licensed. The evidence is that the examples in (51) are a form of right dislocation construction; certainly, as the data from VP ellipsis in (52) shows, the CP is not part of the VP, since if it were it should be possible to get a sloppy reading for the pronoun. This means that the structure for (51a) should be something like (55):

(55)

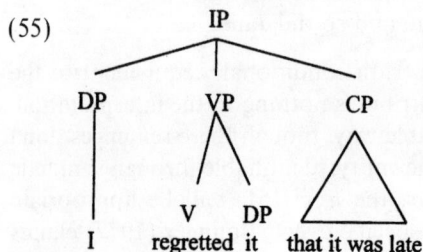

The relation between pronoun and CP is that the event denoted by the pronoun supports or provides evidence for the truth of the proposition. Assume that the domain of events varies across worlds. We can define an SUPPORT relation between an event and a proposition as in (56), using the REALISE relation from chapter 6:(54) that holds between an event and a world if the event is actual in that world:

(56) $\forall e \forall p \forall w [SUPPORT(e,p) \rightarrow [REALISE(e,w) \rightarrow w \in p]]$

In words, an event e supports p if whenever e is an event which is realised in w, p is true in w. This gives (57) as the interpretation of (51a):

(57) $\exists e \exists e'[REGRET(e) \land Ag(e) = MARY \land Th(e) = e'$
      $\land SUPPORT(e, {}^{\wedge}THAT\ HE\ WAS\ LATE)]$

'There was an event of regretting which had Mary as agent and e' as a theme and e' supports the proposition 'that he was late'.

Various questions can be raised about this construction. Sylvain Bromberger noted (p.c.) that we must ask why a plural pronoun can never be used to refer to a multiplicity of events:

(58) *I regretted them that she left and he arrived.

But this seems to be related not to plurality restrictions on the pronoun, but to the fact that conjunctions of CPs never function as pluralities. (I gather that this judgement is stronger in British English than in American English):

(59) That John left and that Mary arrived is/*are much regretted/believed.

We can use plural pronouns to denote pluralities of events in appositive structures like (60), as the reviewer of Rothstein (1995a) pointed out:

(60) a. I regret them, all those times I listened to you.
      b. I enjoyed them, those strange events that we got involved in.

But here, the pronoun is modified by a DP and not a CP, which is further evidence that the problem with (58) lies in trying to treat a conjunction of CPs as denoting a plurality (rather than a simplex singleton or group) and not in using the pronoun to denote a plurality of events.

We can now explain subtle meaning differences between minimal pairs such as (61), which differ only in whether there is a pronominal object. (61b) is taken from actual discourse:

(61) a. I regret that I am falling asleep.
      b. I regret it that I am falling asleep.

In (61a), the object of regret is a proposition, while in (61b) is it a pronoun, which is definite. (61a) would be appropriate if the speaker simply regrets falling asleep. (61b) was uttered in a situation where the speaker did not regret falling asleep itself (she was far too jet-lagged to regret that), but rather regretted the particular event of her falling asleep during the dinner party going on around her. This difference in meaning is explained by the fact that in (61b), the object of regret is a definite event, which supports the truth of proposition that the speaker is falling asleep. The event which is the object of *regret* need not be identical to an event of falling asleep, but can be a bigger event that has an event of falling asleep as a proper part. This was the case here: the speaker regrets the bigger event of which 'I am falling asleep' is a (relevant) part.

Another effect of the pronoun on meaning shows up because it can be bound by a QP. The pronouns in (51) should, as well as being the subject of the CP, also be available for binding by an event quantifier. Judgments are subtle, but they seem to confirm the prediction. Contrast (62a) and (62b):

(62)   a. Every time we meet, I regret it that there's a fight.
       b. Every time we meet, I regret that there's a fight.

(62a) asserts that for every time we meet, there is an event of my regretting about that meeting that there is a fight. (62b) asserts that every time we meet there is an event of regretting a fight, but no assertion that a (different) fight is related to each meeting and that this fight is regretted. This difference in meaning follows from the fact that in (62a), *it* as well as being the subject of the predicate CP, is bound by the QP *every time we meet*. Semantic representations for (62) are given in (63), where **CP** is the proposition denoted by CP. M is again the function relating the event argument of the main clause and the adverbial:

(63)   a. $\forall e[\text{MEET}(e) \wedge \text{Ag}(e) = \text{WE} \rightarrow \exists e'[\text{REGRET}(e') \wedge \text{Ag}(e') = I$
          $\wedge \text{Th}(e') = e \wedge \text{M}(e) = e' \wedge \text{SUPPORT}(e, \textbf{CP})]]$
       b. $\forall e[\text{MEET}(e) \wedge \text{Ag}(e) = \text{WE} \rightarrow \exists e'[\text{REGRET}(e') \wedge \text{Ag}(e') = I$
          $\wedge \text{Th}(e') = \textbf{CP} \wedge \text{M}(e') = e]]$

(63a) reads 'for every event e of our meeting, there is an event e' of my regretting e, and e is an event which supports the proposition "that there was a fight"'. (63b), where there is no bound pronominal, asserts that 'for every event e of our meeting, there is an event e' of my regretting that there was a fight', but there is no assertion about the number of fights or their distribution over meetings.

Finally, if these pronouns are not pleonastic, then we expect them to passivise, in structures analogous to (50). The passive of (51a) is given in (64a). The pronominal object of the active verb has been passivised, and the subject *it* is referential. However, (64a) is phonologically identical to (64b):

(64)   a. It$_i$ was regretted t$_i$ that he was late.
       b. It was regretted that he was late.

(64b) is one of the passive forms of *They regretted that he was late*, where the CP object remains in situ and *it* is pleonastic. Both examples in (64) are truth-conditionally equivalent, and it is difficult to distinguish them. One way of doing so is through coordination constructions, as we saw with (16). VP coordination is not possible with a pleonastic subject if the second coordinate assigns a theta-role to its external argument. If both structures in (64) are available, then the S-structure should coordinate with VPs which require a theta-marked subject as well as with VPs whose subjects is interpreted pleonastically. In this it should contrast with (65a), where the verb does not take an *it* + CP complement in the active form, so that the source of the pronoun can only be pleonastic:

(65) a. It was believed/suspected that John was a crook.
      b. *They believed/suspected (*it) that John was a crook.

For pragmatic reasons, including the possibility of ellipsis, this prediction is difficult to test, but at least some informants find a contrast in (66):

(66) a. It was regretted that Nixon had lied and considered
          [t a disgrace to the nation].
      b. ?It was believed that Nixon had lied and considered
          [t a disgrace to the nation].

In each case, the second coordinate needs a non-pleonastic subject as an antecedent for the theta-marked trace which is the subject of the predicate *a disgrace to the nation*. In (62a), where *it* has a theta-marked source, *it* is a possible antecedent for the trace, and the sentence is unambiguously interpreted as asserting that Nixon's having lied was considered a disgrace to the nation. In (66b), the matrix subject can only be a pleonastic and is the only antecedent for the trace in the complement of *consider*. This means that there is no argument for the predicate NP to be predicated of. The reason that (66b) is not impossible is that we can analyse the complement of *consider* as having a pleonastic subject, the theta-marked argument of *a disgrace to the nation* being elliptical. The content of the argument is then supplied contextually, and not syntactically. In support of this, my informants point out that in (66a) it is clear what is a disgrace, whereas in (66b) it can be Nixon's having lied, or Nixon himself, or some other factor, depending on the context.

7.3.2.3. *Dislocation structures*

The discussion so far has focussed on verbs which select an event as an thematic argument. Quantifiers over events can only bind pronominals if the verb allows their denotation to be in the domain of events. However, there is no clear evidence that the *it* + CP construction is possible only when the pronoun denotes an event. In fact there is some evidence that *it* + CP is possible even when the pronoun does not denote an event:

(67) a. They suspected it that he was a spy.
      b. You just assumed/believed it that he would help.
      c. I never supposed it that they would help.
      d. I expected it that the baby would be up all night.

The matrix verbs in (67) cannot take gerund complements, nor can they occur with the pronoun bound by an event quantifier:

(68)   a. *They suspected/assumed/expected/supposed John's stealing the dia-
monds.
b. *They suspected/assumed/expected/supposed it every time he told
a lie.

Some verbs, of course, can take either an event or a non-event complement, as
Vendler (1967) points out, citing *mention* as an example. In (69a) the CP does
not denote an event, while in (69b) *it* is bound by an event quantifier, and in
(69c) *mention* takes a gerund complement:

(69)   a. They never mentioned it to the candidate that the job was poorly
paid.
b. They upset him by mentioning it every time he made a mistake.
c. They mentioned John's making so many mistakes to the supervisor.

Notice that the semantic effect of adding the pronoun is the same in (51) and
in (67). The verbs in (67) are factive when *it* is present, and are not when *it* is
omitted. (70a,b) strongly imply the truth of their complements, while the
corresponding examples without *it* do not. (71) and (72) illustrate this:

(70)   a.   They had suspected it that she would be arrested.
b.   They suspected it that he was a spy.

(71)   a.   They had expected that she'd be arrested, and were relieved when
she wasn't.
b. ???They had expected it that she'd be arrested, and were relieved when
she wasn't.
c. ???They had been expecting it that she might be arrested.

(72)   a.   They suspected that he was a spy before his undivided loyalty was
proven.
b. ???They suspected it that he was a spy before his undivided loyalty
was proven.

Verbs like *expect* and *suspect* are more or less factive on a scale, and the degree
of definiteness of the complement increases the likelihood of *it* being given a
factive interpretation. Since the pronoun is definite, it can only occur with the
factive reading. (71b,c) and (72b) are odd precisely because the factivity implied
by the pronominal object conflicts with semantic content of the CP, producing
the same semantic effect as in (54).
Note also (73), a variant of the dislocation structures in (70):

(73)   a. I expect it of you that you will help.
b. I'd never have believed it of him that he would do that.

I assume that this means that the *it* + CP construction is not restricted to event
complements; in the examples in (67), the value of the pronoun ranges over
facts, and the relation between the denotation of the pronoun and the denotation of CP is analogous to the relation we proposed in (56). In other words,

(67a) is true if there is an event of my standing in the 'suspect' relation with a fact which supports or provides evidence for the proposition 'that he was a spy' being true.

7.4. REMAINING QUESTIONS

P&P organise their examples of so-called pleonastic objects into six groups. I'll sum up by reviewing their groupings and show that all their example types are either not objects or not pleonastics.

. First, some pronominals within verbal complements are genuinely pleonastic. These are the kinds of sentences we discussed at length in part I, and they are not evidence for pleonastic objects, since they are licensed as subjects of non-theta-assigning predicates within the (possibly small) clausal complements of ECM verbs. Examples of these are repeated here:

(74)   a. I consider it(to be)obvious that you should have done that.
      b. I prevented/kept it from being obvious that you were late.

The examples in (75), (P&P's (31)), are the same type as (74):

(75)   a. I figured it out to be more than 300 miles to Tulsa.
      b. I figured it out to be impossible to get there by noon.
      c. She made it out to be only 49% probable that we would get there
         on time.
      d. She reasoned it out to be incorrect to make that assumption.

The matrix verbs in (75) are ECM verbs taking a clausal complement, and the predicate of that complement does not assign a thematic role. The tensed forms of (75) are (76):

(76)   a. I figured out that it was more than 300 miles to Tulsa.
      b. I figured out that it was impossible to get there by noon.
      c. She made out that it was only 49% probable that we would get there
         on time.
      d. She reasoned out that it was incorrect to make that assumption.

In (75–76), the matrix verb is part of a verb + particle combination. In (76), the particle is adjacent to its verb, but in (75) it moves exactly as it does in (77) when the object is a pronoun:

(77)   a. I looked up the number/I looked the number up.
      b. I looked it up/*I looked up it.

When DP in the complement of *make out/reason out/figure out* is not a pronoun, the alternation in (77a) is available:

(78)   a. I made out/figured out/reasoned out the answer to be 42.
      b. I made/reasoned/figured the answer out to be 42.

The relative positions of the particle and small clause subject results from particle movement, whatever the correct account of this movement is, and properties of ECM constructions. Authier (1991) suggests that the DP subject of a small clause can be raised to the position adjacent to the matrix verb, interacting with adverbs as shown in (79). A similar movement could explain how the small clause subject is adjacent to the verb in (75):

(79)   I believe him$_i$ irrefutably [t$_i$ to be a liar].

(Note, though, that Stowell (1991a) claims the adverb in (80a) (his (17a)), can be construed only with the lower clause, while (80b) (his (17b)) is ungrammatical, casting doubt on Authier's account:

(80)   a.   John believed Mary repeatedly to have left.
             (Mary left repeatedly)
         b.   *John believed Mary sincerely to have left.)

Particle movement may even be a PF phenomenon, in which case the relation between (75) and (78) would not be constrained by syntactic conditions on movement.

The pronouns reviewed so far, which are obligatory and non-thematic, are truly pleonastic. They are distinguished from the second major group of constructions, the examples in (31), repeated here as (81):

(81)   a. I regretted (it) that he was late.
         b. They never mentioned (it) to the candidate that the job was poorly paid.
         c. I resent it every time you say that.
         d. I hate it when you are late.

We saw that here the pronoun is a theta-marked argument, and that three different constructions are represented. (81a) and (81b) are dislocation structures, where the CP is related to the pronoun via the SUPPORT relation. In (81c) and (81d), the pronoun is bound by an adverbial – a bare DP in the former case and a temporal clause in the latter. I assume 'extraposed irrealis clauses' such as (82) to be similar.

(82)   I would prefer it if Kim were not informed.

If the constructions in (81a) are interpreted as we have suggested, then if they are extraposition structures, we have shown that extraposition from object does not involve a pleonastic pronoun. It is probably less misleading to think of them as right dislocation structures. Several other issues raised by P&P reduce to general properties of dislocation structures. A parenthetical may occur between the *it* and the CP as it may occur between any DP pronoun and its dislocated relatum:

(83)   a. I resent it, I may tell you, that you say these things.
         b. I know him, let me tell you, that brother of yours.

The fact that *it* may be an object of a preposition, as in (84a–c) is unsurprising;

since the *it* is an ordinary object, it can be the object of a verb + P combination just like any other DP. Since the right-dislocated DP to which the pronoun is related is outside the VP, and is not c-commanded by the direct object anyway, it will not make a difference in (84a–c) that the pronoun is embedded within a PP. It makes no difference in (84d) either:

(84) a. I depend upon it that their paper will expose crooked politicians.
      b. I was counting on it that you would be there.
      c. What do you make of it that he is late.
      d. You can't count on/depend on him, your brother.

The final set of examples which P&P discuss have not been treated so far in this paper. These are cases where a neuter pronoun turns up as the object to a verb without a CP predicated of it or an adverbial binding it, as in (85). Some of the verbs that are brought as examples seem idiomatic, but in most cases, although reference of the pronominal is unspecified, it is not non-specific. The less idiomatic the use of the verb, the easier it is to understand what the pronoun is referring to, and to replace it with a non-pronominal object.

(85) a. have it out with – have the matter out with
      b. fight it out with – fight the matter out with
      c. keep it up – keep up the work/the appearance
      d. rush it – rush the matter/things
      e. buy it (be deceived by) – buy the story
      f. walk it – walk the distance
      g. get it together – get your act together

These examples show that the unspecified nature of referent of the pronoun does not mean that it has no reference, or no semantic input into the interpretation of the sentence. The pronoun here is restricted to the neuter form because it refers almost always to something abstract. This abstract entity is usually specific: there is a particular issue to be fought out in (85b), and a specific appearance/effort to be kept up in (85c). The pronouns can be often be passivised, as (86) shows:

(86) a. It was rushed, but we finally got the job done.
      b. It was kept up for a long time.
      c. It's being fought out with the management right now.

If these examples seem unnatural, it is because passivisation raises to subject a contextually prominent element, since in the unmarked case the matrix subject is the topic of the sentence. Out of context, passives with unspecified pronominal subjects are odd. If the expressions in (85) are used in questions, the specific nature of the referent of *it* becomes prominent. As Bolinger (1977) notes, it is used when the speaker assumes that "his hearer shares knowledge of an identity". This is made clear by the responses in (87) (after Bolinger's examples):

(87) a. Did you have it out with him yet? – Have what out with him?
      b. I was disappointed by how easily they bought it. – Bought what?

There are examples analogous to (85) which are idiomatic, and there it is not possible to find a referent for the pronoun. Candidates for idiomaticity are *I take it that S* and *beat it*. Some expletives are borderline – thus *damn it* may be equivalent to *damn* but may also mean 'damn some specific thing' as in 'damn him' or 'damn this place'. In other cases, the it is a 'polite usage', as in *move it* for *move your ass*. These idiomatic and non-productive examples alone, however, are not sufficient to support the claim that there is a general phenomenon of object pleonastics. Generally in these cases, as (85)–(87) show, the contribution of the pronoun to the sentence is exactly what our analysis of pronominal objects predicts. It denotes a specific entity which is specified contextually, and the range of its denotation is determined by the thematic and semantic properties of the verb.

PART III

THE SYNTAX AND SEMANTICS OF COPULAR CONSTRUCTIONS

CHAPTER 8

PREDICATION STRUCTURES IN MODERN HEBREW
IDENTITY CONSTRUCTIONS

8.1. INTRODUCTION

This chapter presents an analysis of simple Hebrew identity sentences which I offer as a case study in the syntax of predication. Briefly, the facts are that Modern Hebrew (henceforth just 'Hebrew') allows assertions to be made with matrix small clauses; consisting of just a subject and a non-verbal predicate. It also allows 'inflected small clauses', where a pronominal copula, either personal (PronH) or impersonal (PronZ), realises Infl, and takes a non-verbal maximal projection as a complement. As far as the personal pronominal copula is concerned, it looks as if it is optional, since both inflected and non-inflected forms of the small clauses occur. However, in identity sentences, only the inflected form is possible. The point of this chapter is to argue that the absence of uninflected identity small clauses follows from the requirement that every clause is an instance of a syntactic predication structure. I shall argue that where the post-copula XP is inherently a predicate, a predicate structure is formed whether or not Inflection is present, but that when the post-copula element is an argument and referential, Inflection is necessary to create a syntactic predication structure; furthermore, Infl is necessary to trigger the type shift which allows the identity sentence to be interpreted as a semantic predication structure.

One important bibliographical point. Since the first version of this chapter was written, there has been much interesting work done on the syntax and the semantics of the pronominal copula. Greenberg (1998, 1999) analyses the pronominal copula in simple present predicational sentences as the marker of a generic operator, and Sichel (1997) and Heller (1999) offer analyses of the differences between personal PronH and impersonal PronZ. None of these analyses discusses the problem of the contrast between predicational and identity sentences with regard to the optionality of the personal pronominal copula (except for Sichel, who essentially updates the account in Rapoport (1987)), and in fact, as we will see later in the chapter, Greenberg (1998) explicitly argues that her analysis cannot be extended to cover the identity sentences. So the analysis presented here should be seen as complementing these more recent studies, and my failure to discuss them in depth should not be taken as ignoring them but as a restriction of the discussion to issues directly related to the topic of the book. As I am going to be discussing data about the personal pronominal copula only, I won't specify 'personal' each time, and I will call it simply 'Pron'.

I begin this chapter by reviewing the data mentioned in chapter 5:5.3, which shows that the pronominal copula is obligatory in identity sentences. I will present in depth Doron's (1983) arguments that the pronominal copula is in Infl, since it is important for the argument that the pronominal copula is indeed in Infl, and I will discuss explanations previously offered by Doron and by Rapoport (1987) for why this copula is obligatory in identity sentences. I then present my own account of the distribution of the pronominal copula, based on the syntactic analysis of I′ given in chapter 5, and the semantic account in chapter 6. Assuming that the pronominal copula is analysed as a realisation of Infl, the facts about when it is obligatory in a sentence follow from the claim made in chapter 2 that every clause is an instance of a predication relation. The Infl node is generally optional in clauses which are not marked for tense, since these form small clauses, where a predicate is syntactically predicated of a subject. Where the sentence is a statement of identity, with both major lexical categories referential and no predicate expressions, no predication relation can hold between them without the intervention of another element. Since Infl projects I′, which is a syntactically open node, or a formal predicate, as discussed in chapter 5, it creates the predication structure necessary to license the clause. I'll show in section 8.5 what the semantics of these structures are, and I conclude this chapter by comparing this account with the analysis of Pron in Greenberg (1998, 1999), showing that rather than the latter subsuming the former, the two explanations are complementary.

8.2. THE DATA

The contrast that interests us in this chapter is shown in (1) and (2), and follows from two crucial differences between Hebrew and English; Hebrew, unlike English, does not require every matrix indicative clause to be inflected, and Hebrew, unlike English, does not require Inflection (Infl) to take a verbal complement:

(1) a. dani (hu)   nexmad$_{AP}$.
     dani m.sg. nice
     "Dani is nice."
  b. dani (hu)   rofe$_{NP}$.
     dani m.sg. doctor
     "Dani is a doctor."
  c. dani (hu)   be-tel aviv$_{PP}$.
     dani m.sg. in-tel aviv
     "Dani is in Tel Aviv."

(2) a. dani *(hu)   mar yosef_{DP}.
        dani m.sg. mr   yosef
        "Dani is Mr Yosef."
     b. ha- mora   Selanu *(hi) Rina_{DP}.
        the teacher our   f.sg. rina
        "Our teacher is Rina."

(m: masculine, f: feminine; sg.: singular, pl.: plural).

Thus, Hebrew allows predicational sentences to be truly small or bare of inflection, and, when Infl need not be affixed onto a verbal projection, inflected non-verbal matrix clauses are possible, as indicated in (1). However, sentences expressing identity must obligatorily include Infl. Thus Hebrew shows in matrix sentences the pattern which English allows only in small clause complements of ECM verbs like *consider*, as we saw in chapter 2. The relevant data are repeated here:

(3) a. The winner *(is) a good runner.
     b. The winner *(is) Mary.

(4) a. I consider the winner (to be) a good runner.
     b. I consider the winner *(to be) Mary.

The big difference between the Hebrew pattern in (1/2) and the English pattern in (4) is that in the latter case a verbal projection is required to licence the identity structures. I shall argue in chapter 9 that *be* in English is required to create a predication structure in the complement in (4b), and in chapter 10 I shall argue that *be* is not semantically empty.

What enables Hebrew to allow matrix small clauses is the fact that in the present tense, Infl is apparently not obligatory. But what allows inflected small clauses is the fact that the Hebrew 'present tense' Infl does not need to be affixed onto a verbal projection, but can be realised directly in Infl. When talking about the Hebrew data, we tend to say that the present tense copula is not a form of the verbal copula *h.y.y.*, but is pronominal and realised in Infl. But if we think of a copula as a kind of verb, then it is more accurate to say that Hebrew does not use a verbal copula in the present tense, relying on a non-verbal Infl instead. Still, the term pronominal copula is too deeply embedded in the literature to change it at this stage.

There are four forms of this pronominal copula and, since Doron (1983), it is called Pron, because the forms are phonologically identical to the four third person pronouns.

(5) m.sg.: hu   f.sg.: hi   m.pl.: hem   f.pl.: hen

When it is necessary to distinguish Pron from the impersonal, or demonstrative, pronoun *ze*, Pron is called 'PronH', and the impersonal pronominal copula is called 'PronZ' (see Heller 1999).

The generalisation which concerns us at the moment is that the pronominal copula is optional in sentences where the constituent following it is an AP or a PP, as in (1a–b), but obligatory where the parallel constituent is a name, as in (2). If the second constituent is a nominal which can be interpreted as a predicate, then Pron is optional, as we see in (6):

(6) dani (hu) more ba- universita.
      dani m.sg. teacher in the university
      "Dani is a teacher at the university"

However, Doron (1983) argues that where the post-copula element is a definite noun phrase which at a stretch can be interpreted as predicative, the interpretation is affected by whether or not Pron appears. In a sentence like (7a), where there is no Pron, the sentence must be interpreted as predicative (although for some people the sentence is marginal). When Pron appears, as in (7b), the sentence is ambiguous between this interpretation (marginally for those for whom (7a) is marginal) and the more easily obtainable statement of identity.

(7) a. dani ha- more.
         dani the-teacher
         "Dani is the teacher."
      b. dani hu   ha- more.
         dani m.sg. the-teacher
         "Dani is the teacher."

As both Doron and Greenberg (1994) show, the second nominal expression has the syntactic properties of a non-predicate when it is preceded by Pron. Thus, Doron (p113) shows that non-restrictive relatives, which occur only after referring expressions, can appear only in sentences where Pron is present:

(8) a. *dani more/ ha-more, Se ani makira oto Sanim.
         dani teacher/the-teacher, that I   know him years
      b. dani hu   ha- more, Se ani makira oto Sanim.
         dani m.sg. the-teacher, that I   know him years
         "Dani is the teacher, whom I have known for years."

Doron shows that there is a restricted set of circumstances in which nominals which look like names may occur in a copular sentence without Pron. This is when the name is interpreted not as referring to an individual, but as expressing a role. Thus if parts are being assigned in a play, the following would be appropriate:

(9) (Doron p116)
      ha- yom dani (hu)   ben gurion ve roni (hu)   moSe Saret.
      the day dani (m.sg.) ben-gurion & roni (m.sg.) moshe sharet
      "Today, Dani is Ben-Gurion and Roni is Moshe Sharet."

Doron (1983) argues convincingly that the pronominal copula is a realisation of agreement (Agr) features in Inflection, and is not verbal. Modern Hebrew has two fully inflected tenses, past and future, in which the forms are marked for person, number and gender, and a 'defective' present tense, in which verbal stems are marked only for number and gender, and which patterns according to the adjectival paradigm. (It has often been suggested that this so-called present tense is really a participal.) The copula stem *h.y.y.* is fully inflected in the past and future, but in Modern Hebrew it has no present forms. (Although these are available in grammar books, for all practical purposes they are now obsolete.) Instead, the pronominal copula in (5) is used. Doron (1983) presents the evidence that this Pron is not an alternative present form of the verb *h.y.y.*, but is realised in Inflection. Although Pron cannot cooccur with a verb, as (10) shows, its behaviour differs from that of verbs in crucial ways.

(10) *dani hu   holex
      dani m.sg. goes

First, the negation particle *lo* precedes verbals and cannot follow them, as we see in (11).

(11) (Doron p100)
      dani lo roce banana.   c.f. *dani roce lo banana
      dani not wants banana
      "Dani does not want a banana."

While *h.y.y.* behaves like any other verb with respect to the location of negation, Pron must be followed by negation:

(12) a. dani lo   haya   student./dani lo   yihye   student.
          dani NEG be-PAST student/ dani NEG be-FUT student
          "Dani was not a student."/"Dani will not be a student."
      b. *dani haya lo student/dani yihye lo student

(13) a. dani hu   lo   student./*dani lo   hu   student
          dani m.sg. NEG student/ dani NEG m.sg. student

The same pattern shows up with the emphatic *ken*. Adverbials such a *be-emet*, 'really', also usually precede the verb, but always follow Pron (see also Berman and Grosu 1976):

(14) (Doron p102)
      a. dani (hu)   be-emet/ulay   ha-baxur Se- raiti.
          dani (m.sg.) really/ perhaps the   guy that saw-I
          "Dani is really/maybe the guy that I saw."
      b. *dani be-emet/ulay   hu   ha- baxur Se- raiti.
          dani really/ maybe (m.sg.) the guy   that saw-I

(15) a. dani haya   ?be-emet/*ulay   ha- baxur Se- raiti.
          dani be-PAST really/   perhaps the guy   that saw-I
          "Dani was really/*maybe the guy that I saw."
      b. dani be-emet/ulay   haya   ha- baxur Se- raiti.
          dani really/ perhaps be-PAST the guy   that saw-I
          "Dani really/maybe was the guy that I saw."

((15a) is marginal with *be-emet*, to the degree that it is possible to take the modifier as directly modifying *nexmad*. Such a reading is impossible for *ulay*.) Doron cites Berman and Grosu (1976) as making two other distinctions between *h.y.y.* and Pron: *h.y.y.*, but not Pron, may carry contrastive stress:

(16)   moSe háya   xaxam./*moSe hú   xaxam. (Doron 4.(82))
       moshe be-PAST clever/ moshe m.sg. clever
       "Moshe **was** clever"/"Moshe **is** clever."

Second, *h.y.y.*, but not Pron may occur sentence-finally. This may be connected to the clitic status of Pron, since (18c), where Pron is followed by *lo* is fine:

(17)   (Doron p104)
       a. ma   ata xoSev Se   dani haya?
          what you think that dani was
       b. ma   ata xoSev Se   haya dani?
          what you think that was dani
          both: "What do you think that Dani was?"

(18)   a. *ma   ata xoSev Se   dani hu?
          what you think that dani m.sg.
       b. ?ma   ata xoSev Se   hu   dani?
          what you think that m.sg. dani
          "What do you think Dani is"?
       c. ma   ata xoSev Se   dani hu   lo?
          what you think that dani m.sg. NEG
          "What do you think Dani is not?"

Pron is not a verb; despite its pronominal form, it also is not a subject, and sentences which contain Pron cannot be analysed as left-dislocation structures. Berman and Grosu (1976) show that the sentences in (19)–(20) lack the intonational pause which follows the dislocated element and precedes the subject, marked orthographically by a comma in (19), which characterises left dislocation structures:

(19)   dani ve- rina, hem nexmadim.
       dani and rina they nice-m.pl.
       "As for Dani and Rina, they are nice"

Also, a nonspecific indefinite nominal may be the subject of a copular sentence with Pron, whereas it may not be the dislocated constituent in a left-dislocation structure (examples from Doron p106):

(20)   a. paxot anaSim hem nexmadim.
          few   people m.pl. nice
          "Fewer people are nice lately"
       b. *paxot anaSim, hem metaylim ba-rexov.
          few   people, they walk in   the street

Doron brings two additional arguments of her own. The subject pronoun in left-dislocated sentences must agree in person, number and gender with the dislocated element, as (21a) shows. In copular identity sentences such as (21b), there is no such constraint:

(21) a. *ani, hu hamore.
          I,   he teacher
      b. ani hu   ha- more.
          I   m.sg. the teacher
          "I am the teacher."

In addition, Doron points out that resumptive pronouns are not allowed in the highest subject position of a relative clause. (22a) thus contrasts with (22b):

(22) a. ha- iS   Se t ohev   bananot   (Doron p107)
          the-man that love-PRES bananas
          "The man that loves bananas"
      b. *ha- iS   Se hu ohev   bananot
          the-man that m.sg love-PRES bananas
          "The man that he loves bananas."

If Pron were a subject pronoun, we would expect it not to be allowed in that position. However, not only does it occur there, but it is obligatory:

(23) a. ha- iS   Se hu   more   (Doron p107)
          the man that m.sg. teacher
          "The man that is a teacher"
      b. *ha- iS   Se   more
          the man that teacher

Doron concludes that the pronominal copula is neither a subject pronoun, nor a verbal element, and thus, if it belongs neither to the subject nor to the verbal predicate, it must be realised in Infl. Doron analyses Pron as a clitic which realises Agr features in Infl, and she remains agnostic as to whether sentences with no Pron have an empty Infl, or are bare small clauses. I shall follow Doron in assuming that Pron is realised in Infl, but I shall assume that the Pron-less sentences are bare small clauses for the same reasons that I have not assumed any empty Infl node in English up till now (see the discussion at the end of chapter 6). The S-structures that I assign are those in (24). (From now on, I'll write simply 'Pron' instead of giving the features in Pron.):

(24) a. [[dani]$_{DP}$ [nexmad ad meod]$_{AP}$]$_{SC}$
              dani   nice   very
      b. [[dani]$_{DP}$ [[hu]$_{Infl}$ [nexmad ad meod]$_{AP}$]$_{I'}$]$_{IP}$
              dani   Pron   nice   very
          both "Dani is very nice."
      c. [[dani]$_{DP}$ [[hu]$_{Infl}$ [mar yosef]$_{DP}$]$_{I'}$]$_{IP}$
              dani   Pron   mr yosef
          "Dani is Mr Yosef."

In (24a) I label the matrix small clause SC, as I did for the parallel *consider* complements. This captures the fact that the predicate AP *nexmad ad meod* is a maximal projection, and that the clause itself cannot be considered a projection of Infl or any other lexical or functional head.

8.3. *Analysis*

There are thus two major differences between Hebrew and English. First, a predicative sentence (but not an identity sentence) can do without a realisation of the copula, and second, when the copula is realised, it is realised in Infl, which does not necessarily select or govern a V. Doron (1983) relates both these facts about Hebrew to the defectiveness of the Hebrew tense system. She proposes that the tense system allows specification for [±tense] and [±past]. [−tense] is the specification for non-finite forms and [+tense] for finite forms. [+tense] automatically requires a specification of past features, where [+past] indicates past tense and [−past] indicates future tense. The present is not specified for either past or tense features. If it were specified as [+tense], then it would automatically require a specification for either [+past] or [−past], which would be inappropriate since it is neither, and if it were marked [−tense], then the present would be incorrectly classified as non-finite. Doron claims that it is tense features which force the projection of Infl, and thus in the present, Infl is optional and matrix small clauses are possible. An obvious reflection of this absence of tense or past features in Infl is the peculiar way in which the present tense forms of verbs are inflected; they bear only number and gender agreement features, and the morphological inflection is adjectival. Verbs have a morphological slot onto which Infl must be affixed, but when there is no lexical verbal predicate present, and no tense features forcing Infl to appear, agreement features can be deleted, or can be realised in Infl as the pronominal copula. However, as we saw in (2), the Infl node is not optional when a copular sentence is an expression of identity and both its maximal projections are referential.

Various explanations for the distribution of Pron have been proposed. Doron (1983, 1986) proposes that Pron may, but need not, theta-mark the subject and post-copula DP. In predicational sentences Pron will be optional, since the predicate itself theta-marks its subject. In identity sentences though, it will be obligatory since the post-copula expression is referential and cannot theta-mark the subject. Both major constituents thus need to be theta-marked, and the pronominal copula fills this theta-marking function. However, there are problems with this hypothesis. Conceptually, it undermines the content of the theta-marking relation. Theta-marking is by lexical heads, and the theta-marking properties of the head reflect the semantic function denoted by that head. It is conceptually wrong to allow Pron to assign theta-roles, since it is only a spell-out of formal agreement features in Infl and not a lexical head. Furthermore, Pron would have to be ambiguous between a theta-marking and non-theta-marking element, since while, according to Doron, it must theta-mark the constituents in identity statements, it does not do so in predicative constructions. Doron's account of the pronominal copula has the effect of assigning to Pron the semantic properties Russell assigns to the verb *be* (Russell 1919). Russell suggested that there are two verbs *be*, one of which denotes a two-place identity relation which, in government-binding terms, is a theta-assigner, marking both its subject and its complement, while the other is 'purely grammatical' and is a sign of predication. While it is plausible that a form of *be* does denote a two-place semantic relation, it is far less plausible to argue that a bunch of agreement features realised in Infl has this property. Further, because of the possibility of realising Pron in predicative sentences as in (22), where it cannot denote the identity function, we would have to posit 'ambiguous Pron', or at least to hypothesise that the bunch of agreement features optionally has this semantic property.

A third argument against this approach is that in a variety of identity sentences, Pron is not in fact obligatory. In (25a), with a pronominal subject, Pron is optional. In (25b), with the inflected negative particle *eyn*, which we will discuss in section 8.4, Pron is impossible. In (25c), the negative marker *lo* is used and Pron can optionally be dropped. Although the resulting sentence isn't perfect, it is much better than the ungrammatical result of dropping Pron without the negation marker.

(25) a. ani (hu)   mar yosef.
          I   (Pron) mr   yosef
          "I am Mr Yosef."
      b. dani (*hu)   eyno   mar yosef.
          dani (*Pron) not-m.s. mr   yosef
          "Dani is not Mr Yosef."
      c. dani ?(hu)   lo   mar yosef.
          dani ?(Pron) NEG mr   yosef
          "Dani is not Mr Yosef."

If Pron is a theta-assigner, then in these Pron-less sentences there would be exactly the same violation of theta-criterion as there is in the identity sentences without Pron in (2). While agreement features are realised in (25a/b), reflected in the fully inflected subject pronoun in the Pron-less version of (25a), and affixed onto *eyn* in (25b), it cannot be these features which themselves theta-mark, since they occur in every verbal sentence, where the theta-relations are taken care of by the verb itself. And in (25c), there are no agreement features visible at all.

In any case, the claim that Pron is inserted to save a structure from violating the theta-criterion is weakened by the fact that, as we have seen in the discussion in chapter 7:7.2.2, there are argument expressions which are licensed without being theta-marked:

(26) a. The book is [Op$_i$ [for you to read t$_i$]].
      b. John seems as if he is very tired. (Heycock 1991)
      c. The children are too sick [for Mary to go out tonight].

These examples were already discussed in chapters 2 and 5. (26a/b) involves a lexical head which is semantically an argument of a predicate CP which cannot theta-mark it. In (26c), as I claimed in chapter 5:5.2.2, the CP *for Mary to go out tonight* is not a predicate, as can be seen from the fact that it has no gap in it, but neither is it theta-marked as it is c-selected by the functional degree head *too*, which cannot assign theta-roles (see Rothstein (1991) for more discussion of these structures).

Another hypothesis about the obligatoriness of Pron is that it is due to the Case Filter. Purveyors of this approach note that in identity sentences such as (23) there are two argument DPs which need to be case marked, and suggest that Pron is inserted to assign them case. This makes the wrong prediction for the predicational sentences. Here too, the subject DP needs to be assigned case, and yet Pron is optional. One possibility is that Pron need not occur here since the subject DP is assigned case through agreement with the predicate. This would take care of the absence of Pron where the predicate is headed by an adjective which agrees in number and gender with the subject, but it would not account for sentences with PP predicates where there is no agreement and no Pron (see e.g. (1c)). Rapoport (1987) proposes a hybrid explanation, namely that the identity relation can be assigned at D-structure between two argument DPs which are sisters only under the government of a functional head which 'mediates' the relation. She assume that Infl is lexically realised as the pronominal copula at S-structure, since Infl is necessary for the assignment of case and the identity relation. The arguments against a case-theoretic explanation of the obligatoriness of the copula apply to her theory too, as well as to that of Sichel (1997), who presents an updated version of the Case Filter approach in the framework of Minimality Theory.

In place of these explanations, I argue that the correct way to view the role of Pron is not in terms of theta-roles or case assignment, but in terms of predication relations. As we have seen, a clause, small or otherwise, is an instance of a primary syntactic predication relation, where the subject and predicate form a constituent. Predication, as we have seen in the preceding chapters, is a primitive saturation relation between an open syntactic constituent, which, crucially, does not necessarily assign a theta-role, and a closed constituent. In small clauses, Pron is optional because the predicate can be directly predicated of the subject and there is no obligation for Infl to be present. I argue that in identity sentences, Pron is obligatory because we cannot form a instance of predication without it. Identity sentences do not contain a 'main predicate': if Infl projects an I' node, then it constitutes the predicate constituent of the clause, but if there is no Infl or I' node, then there is no predicate node either.

Reviewing here how the matrix small clauses work, we see that in each case the XP is inherently a syntactic predicate.

These are the small clause versions of (1):

(27) a. dani nexmad$_{AP}$.
        dani nice
        "Dani is nice."

b. dani rofe$_{NP}$.
   dani doctor
   "Dani is a doctor."
c. dani be-tel aviv$_{PP}$.
   dani in tel aviv
   "Dani is in Tel Aviv."

The small clause constituents have the structure [[DP] [XP]], where XP is a predicate and thus the clause is an instance of predication. The predication relation licenses both predicate and subject: the predicate is a monadic unsaturated constituent which requires, and finds, a subject, and the DP is an argument which can be, and is, licensed by saturating the open position in a predicate. Although, as we have seen, syntactic predication does not necessarily involve external theta-role assignment, it may do so, and where relevant, the predicate of the matrix small clause does theta-mark its subject. Thus small clauses are internally licensed by predication, and have the bare structure in (28):

(28) [[dani]$_{DP}$ [nexmad]$_{AP}$]$_{SC}$

In contrast, in an identity sentence neither of the two lexical constituents is a predicate and a Pron-less structure such as (29) is a string of two argument DPs between which no syntactic relation holds:

(29) *[[dani]$_{DP}$ [mar yosef]$_{DP}$]
     dani   mr yosef

However, Pron, a spell-out of agreement features in Infl, projects an I′ constituent. I′ is a syntactic predicate node, and the relation between I′ and Spec of IP is one of predication, as in any inflected sentence. An identity sentence will have the structure in (30):

(30) [dani [hu   [mar yosef]$_{DP}$]$_{I'}$]$_{IP}$
     dani Pron mr yosef
     "Dani is Mr Yosef."

The subject DP is licensed as the subject of I′, and the post-copula DP is licensed as the syntactic complement of Infl. In this case, there is no theta-marking relation between the predicate and the subject. Predictably, Pron is obligatory also when the second major constituent is a CP argument, since unless it is embedded under Pron as its syntactic complement, there will be no predicate in the sentence:

(31) haba'aya   *(hi)   Se ani roca la'azov.
     the problem *(Pron) that I   want to   leave
     "The problem is that I want to leave."

The role of Pron in these sentences is that of identifying the Infl node. This node is necessary to project the I′ constituent, and it must be syntactically marked or identified in some way – it cannot remain completely null. Normally,

Infl is identified since it is affixed onto the verbal head of its VP complement, but this is impossible here because the sentence is nominal. Pron is obligatory because there is no other syntactic way to identify the Infl node other than phonologically realising the appropriate agreement features in Infl.

The examples in (25), repeated here as (32), all support the claim that Pron is obligatory when Infl is required to create a predicate syntactically, and optional or impossible otherwise. The three different cases illustrate different ways of creating the necessary predicate structure:

(32)   a. ani (hu)   mar yosef.
          I   (Pron) mr yosef
          "I am Mr Yosef."
       b. dani (*hu)   eyno   mar yosef.
          dani (*Pron) not-m.sg. mr   yosef
          "Dani is not Mr Yosef."
       c. dani ?(hu)   lo   mar yosef.
          dani ?(Pron) not-m.sg. mr   yosef
          "Dani is not Mr Yosef."

Starting from the last example, in (32c), I′ is not necessary to create a predicate since the negative particle, marginally, can be treated as projecting a Neg Phrase which is a formal predicate and can be predicated of the subject. Infl is optional, but if realised, is filled by Pron. Evidence that *lo* projects a predicate phrase comes from the fact that it cannot be attached to a constituent which must be interpreted as an argument – either a theta-marked DP complement of a verb, or a CP argument or a matrix IP:

(33)   a. *dani ohev lo   bananot.
          dani likes NEG bananas
       b. *dani xoSev lo   Se-ha-SemeS zoraxat.
          dani thinks NEG that-the-sun shines
       c. *lo   dani holex.
          NEG dani goes

In (32a/b), where there is neither an inflected verb nor another predicate phrase, there is evidence that the Infl node is present although not realised via Pron. Let us assume that the set of features which Infl contains cannot just be abstract or null, but must be identified by a set of morphologically realised features or by a relation between Infl and such a set. This rules out the possibility of a simple null Infl, but makes possible a variety of identification mechanisms which coindex a phonologically empty Infl with some realised set of features. The most obvious mechanism for identifying Infl is where the features realised are attached to the verb via affixation, as in the normal case where Infl governs V. Pron is another mechanism for allowing the features to be realised directly in Infl without coindexing. (32b) shows another realisation mechanism: Infl governs the negative particle *eyn*, and the features that Infl contains are affixed onto it. (This makes *eyn* looks superficially as if it is a verb, though I shall argue below that this is not so.) *Eyn* thus differs from *lo*, which cannot be inflected. Further, *eyn* does not project a predicate phrase, otherwise inflection would not be required at all. Note that we can see that it does not project a predicate phrase from the fact that (i) if it is uninflected, it cannot licence an identity sentence, as (34a) shows, and (ii) it can attach to a matrix sentence, as in (34b). (I shall gloss *eyn* as EYN to avoid confusion with *lo*, which I have been glossing as NEG):

(34) a. *dani eyn   mar yosef.
          dani EYN mr   yosef
      b. eyn   dani ohev bananot.   (Doron p60)
          EYN dani likes bananas
          "Dani doesn't like bananas."

Thus the contrast between (32b/34a) shows that *eyn* must occur in the scope of Infl, which projects the predicate.

So the analysis of (32b) is that since *eyn* can be inflected, Infl features are lowered and cliticised onto the *eyn*, which is marked for person, number and gender, and there is nothing left in Infl for Pron to realise. Evidence for Infl-lowering in Hebrew comes from the placement of adverbs, as shown in the contrast between (14), repeated here as (35) and (36); inflected *eyn* follows rather than precedes adverbs, whereas the pronominal copula precedes an adverb and cannot follow it:

(35) a. dani (hu)   be-emet/ulay   ha- baxur Se-   raiti.
          dani (Pron) really/   perhaps the guy   that saw-I
          "Dani is really/perhaps the guy that I saw."
      b. *dani be-emet/ulay   hu   ha- baxur Se-   raiti.
          dani really/   perhaps Pron the guy   that saw-I

(36) a. dani be-emet/ulay   eyn + o   nexmad.
          dani really/   perhaps EYN + m.sg. nice
          "Dani really/perhaps isn't nice."
      b. *dani eyn + o   be-emet/ulay   nexmad.
          dani EYN + m.sg. really/   perhaps nice
          "Dani really/perhaps isn't really nice."

((36b) is marginal with *be-emet*, to the degree that it is possible to take the modifier as directly modifying *nexmad*. Such a reading is impossible for *ulay*.)

We saw that *hu*, which is in Infl, must precede the adverb. In (36a) the adverb *be-emet* precedes inflected *eyn*, indicating that *eyn* is not in Infl position and that Agr features lower to negation rather than that *eyn* raises to Infl. In (36b), where *eyn* does precede the adverb, *be-emet* is modifying the AP *nexmad*, and not the sentence. (Independent evidence for Infl lowering in Hebrew, in addition to V raising, is given in Borer's (1995) paper analysing the behaviour of the verbal copula in Hebrew.)

(32a), repeated in full in (37), shows another mechanism for licensing Infl, namely the relation between Infl and explicit nominative case. Here Pron is optional despite the fact that the post-copula constituent is an argument DP:

(37) a. ani mar yosef.
       I   mr yosef
    b. ani hu   mar yosef.
       I   PRON mr yosef
       both: "I am Mr Yosef."

In (37a), where there is no Pron, the fully inflected nominative subject pronoun *ani* identifies and licenses the Infl node. Here, Infl is coindexed through spec-head agreement with a full set of agreement features realised lexically in the pronoun which is located in [Spec,IP], and Pron need not occur since Infl is already identified. Pron itself consists only of number and gender features (Doron assumes that this is because the person feature in Infl is associated with the [±past] feature). However, licensing of a phonologically null Infl through coindexation with a non-verbal element is possible only when there is a full set of features there to identify the position. Thus Infl coindexed with *eyn* results in *eyn* inflected for person, number and gender. This means that in the situation illustrated in (37a), coindexation is with a fully inflected nominative pronoun. 'Bare' or Pron-less identity sentences, where the subject is a lexical DP, will not be acceptable, since non-pronominal DPs can be marked morphologically for number and gender, but not for person, and thus cannot license Infl.

This explains the version of (37a) where Pron does not occur. However, what about the case where Pron does occur, as in (37b)? In (32b) we saw that when *eyno* is present and Infl features are affixed onto it, Pron cannot occur, and we might expect that (37b), where Infl is coindexed with the subject pronoun, would be similarly ungrammatical. Further, we would expect that a subject pronoun cannot be coindexed with Infl when it contains Pron, since they are not identical bundles of features: the subject is inflected for person, number and gender, and Pron realises only number and gender.

The first point to make about this is that affixation onto V or *eyn* is different from simple coindexing, since when coindexing is between Infl and the head of its complement, the features actually move from Infl to the verbal/*eyn* element, while where we have simple coindexing between Infl and [DP,IP] through spec head agreement, the agreement features in Infl are not moved onto the subject pronoun. Pronouns project their own sets of features, as we can see from the fact that they occur in positions not governed by Infl, including object position, as objects of prepositions, and as single word emphatic utterances.

Second, if Infl is both licensed by coindexation with the subject pronoun, and features are lexically realised, then there is indeed a conflict, since the two bundles are not identical. In order to avoid the conflict, I hypothesise that the agreement features in Infl are lowered and are cliticised onto the post-copula argument DP, and agree with it in number and gender. Thus in (37b), if Pron is realised, it does not end up in Infl, but as a clitic on the DP *mar yosef.* I assume, since a syntactic lowering process is in any case necessary (see above), that this is an S-structure process. When the subject is not a pronoun, this rightward movement will be possible, but will not be forced, since there will be no feature conflict between DP and Pron.

There are various pieces of evidence which support this account of (37b). First, we look at when cliticisation occurs. Cliticisation classically involves coindexation with an argument. Usually in a sentence with Pron where the subject is a lexical DP, such as the versions of (1) where Pron appears, the clitic in Infl is coindexed with the subject. This has nothing to do with the licensing of Infl per se, but it has to do with the fact that clitics have to be 'attached' to something. Since non-pronominal subjects are marked only for gender and (possibly) for number, there is no conflict in this coindexing. In (37b), Pron is coindexed with the nominal following. Assuming that cliticisation does involve an argument DP, we predict that Pron can be cliticised rightward only if the post-Pron constituent is an argument. This is in fact the case: Doron (1983) pointed out that a subject pronoun followed by the pronominal copula is impossible in a predicational sentence, as (38) shows:

(38) *ani hu   rofe/ nexmad
       I   Pron doctor/nexmad

Pron cannot be coindexed with the subject pronoun since the latter contains a full array of features, and it cannot be cliticised rightward since it is followed not by an argument complement, but by a predicate expression. (38) contrasts with the sentences with Pron in (27), as well as with (37b).

If Pron can agree with the post-copula element only when cliticisation has taken place, then we correctly predict that in predicational sentences where Pron is possible, Pron will agree only with the subject and not with the post-copula predicate. The contrasting agreement facts in (39) (cited in Rapoport 1987) and (40) (from Doron 1983), support this prediction:

(39) sara   hi/   *hu   xamor
      sara(f) Pron-f./*Pron-m. donkey(m)
      "Sara is a donkey."

(40) ma Se dekart   katav hu/   hi   ha-hoxaxa
      what Descartes wrote Pron-m.sg./Pron-f.sg. def-proof(f)
      le-kiyum-o.
      to-existence-his
      "What Descartes wrote was the proof of his existence."

In (39), where the copula is followed by a predicative constituent *xamor*, 'donkey' which is masculine, Pron can agree only with the subject *sara*, a woman's name. (40) is an identity sentence with the structure of a pseudocleft, where the subject is a free relative, and the post-copula nominal is feminine. Here, Pron can agree with either the subject or the post-copula DP. If Pron is masculine singular, agreeing with the subject, the sentence can have either a predicational or identity reading, but when Pron is feminine singular, the sentence can have only the identity reading. The agreement features originating in Infl have cliticised onto the second DP so that spec-head agreement is not violated, but as a consequence, the post-copula nominal can only be interpreted as non-predicative. This analysis is further substantiated by the behaviour of the negative particle *lo*, as the contrasts in (41) show:

(41)   a. sara hi   lo   xamor
          sara Pron-f.sg. NEG donkey-m
          "Sara is not a donkey."
       b. ma Se dekart   katav hu/   / *hi   lo   ha- hoxaxa
          what Descartes wrote Pron-m.sg./Pron-f.sg. NEG the proof(f)
          le-kiyum-o.
          to existence-his.
          "What Descartes wrote wasn't the proof of his existence."

Normally, the negative marker appears between Pron and the post-copula XP as in (41a). But where cliticisation has taken place, the negative marker can no longer be inserted, as (41b) shows. (41b) is grammatical when the pronominal copula is the masculine singular form *hu*, since there is no cliticization to block the insertion of *lo*.

   However, 'real', as opposed to grammatical, gender agreement still plays a role. If I declare that I (a woman) am department chair, the pronominal copula has to be the feminine singular *hi* form, as in (42). Here, as in (39), Pron apparently agrees with the subject, rather than with the post-copula element, and thus it provides a problem for the claim that Pron cliticises onto the post-copula element.

(42)   a. ani hi   /*hu   rosh ha- maxlaka
          I   Pron-f.sg/*Pron-m.sg. head the department.
          "I am the department chair."
       b. at   hi   /*hu   rosh ha- maxlaka
          You-f.s Pron-f.sg/*Pron-m.sg. head the department.
          "You are the department chair."

But a closer look shows that *rosh hamaxlaka* is not inherently marked for gender, as can be seen from the fact that adjectival modifiers can be in either masculine or feminine form, depending on the sex of the department chair:

(43)   rosh ha-maxlaka   ha-noxaxi/   ha-noxaxit
       head the-department the-present-m/the = present-f

Thus in (42), there is no conflict between the gender features of the post-copula DP and Pron, and nothing to prevent the cliticisation. However, if the post-copula DP is genuinely marked for gender, and it does not match the actual gender of the referent of the subject, neither form of the pronominal copula is good. In identity sentences with pronominal subjects, the form of Pron must be compatible both with the 'natural' gender of the subject and the grammatical gender of the post-copula DP. Thus take a nominal like '(male) thesis advisor' *manxe*, which is marked masculine and requires a masculine-marked adjectival modifier, and has a feminine form *manxa*, requiring a feminine-marked modifier. In answer to the question *mi ha-manxe Selax*, 'who is your advisor(m)?' neither the (a) nor the (b) examples in (44) are acceptable if the advisor is a woman:

(44) a. *ani hu   ha-manxe.
          I   3.m.s. advisor-m
          "I am the advisor."
      a'. *at   hu   ha-manxe.
          you-f 3.m.s. advisor-m
          "You are the advisor."
      b. *ani hi   ha-manxe.
          I   3.f.s. advisor-m
          "I am the advisor."
      b'. *at   hi   ha-manxe.
          you-f 3.f.s. advisor-m
          "You are the advisor."

Thus it looks as if, while Pron must match the gender of the real world subject, it must also cliticise onto the post-copula DP, as I have suggested. And as predicted, when cliticisation results in a gender conflict, the result is ungrammatical. For some speakers, the (b) examples in (44) are marginally acceptable with a metaliguistic use in which they are being used with some irony to stress the fact that the post-copula DP is of the wrong gender. So I might use (44b) in response to the question who is X's (masculine) advisor, if I want to stress the fact that she has a woman advisor, and reject an implied presupposition that the advisor was a man. The use of Pron in identity sentences with pronominal subjects thus contrasts with its use in predictive sentences, and in identity sentences with non-pronominal subjects; in the first case agreement is only with the subject as (39) showed, and in the second, agreement is either with the subject or the post-copula DP as in (40).

8.4. A NOTE ON *EYN*

The properties of *eyn* are complex. I review them here because they support the account of the claims made above that there are a number of ways of identifying the Infl node in a sentence. The basic facts of distribution are as follows. *Eyn* can appear with sentences which are not marked [±past], in other words with present tense sentences. It appears sentence internally with verbal and non-verbal predicates, including referential DPs (i.e. in identity sentences) in which case it is inflected, as in (45). It can also appear sentence-initially, in which case it is uninflected, but only when the predicate of the clause is verbal as (46a-c) shows. As (46d) shows, *eyn* does not occur with past or future verbs.

(45) a. dani eyn+o   mar yosef.
       dani EYN-3.m.sg. mr yosef
       "Dani is not Mr Yosef"
     b. dani eyn+o   nexmad.
       dani EYN-3.m.sg. nice-m
       "Dani isn't nice."
     c. dani eyn+o   ohev bananot.
       dani EYN-3.m.sg. like bananas
       "Dani doesn't like bananas."

(46) a. eyn   dani ohev bananot.
       EYN dani likes bananas
       "Dani doesn't like bananas."
     b. *eyn   dani hu   nexmad.
       EYN dani Pron nice
     c. *eyn   dani (hu) mar yosef.
       EYN dani Pron mr yosef
     d. *eyn   dani haya/   yihye   nexmad.
       EYN dani be+PAST/be+PRES nice
       "Dani wasn't/will be nice."

I am not going to discuss the third usage of *eyn*, where it acts as the negation
of *yeS*, the existential particle:

(47) eyn   le-hoci   sefarim me- ha- sifria.
     EYN to take out books from-the-library
     "There is not take books out of the library." =
     "It is not allowed to take books out of the library."

The fact that there is a crucial relation between Infl and *eyn* is seen from
the fact, already mentioned above, that although Pron is usually obligatory in
identity sentences, it can be dropped when *eyn* occurs sentence internally. This
was illustrated in (32b) and in (45a). The question is what is the relation
between sentence internal *eyn*, which is clearly connected to Infl, and sentence
external *eyn* which cannot be inflected.

Doron (1983) shows that sentence initial and sentence internal *eyn* show
scope differences, and that each must be interpreted in situ:

(48) a. eyn rov   ha- talmidim maskimim iti.   (Doron p60)
       eyn majority the students agree   with-me
       "It is not the case that the majority of the students agree with me."
     b. rov   ha-talmidim eyn+am maskimim iti.
       majority the-students eyn-3.m.p. agree   with-me
       "The majority of the students do not agree with me."

Sentence intitial *eyn* cannot take just any IP as its complement. As (46) shows,
sentence-initial *eyn* can take as a complement only an IP which has a present
tense verb. It does not take as a complement a sentence in which Infl is marked

for [+past] (past tense) or [−past] (future tense). Also, *eyn* does not take a small clause complement where agreement features are not realised at all. The examples in (49) are ungrammatical:

(49) a. *eyn   dani nexmad
       EYN dani nice
    b. *eyn   rina mora
       EYN rina teacher
    c. *eyn   dani al ha-gag
       EYN dani on the-roof

Furthermore, though sentence-internal *eyn* can occur when the predicate is verbal, as in (46a), we have already seen that it cannot co-occur with Pron; both examples in (50) are ungrammatical:

(50) a. *dani hu   eyn+o   nexmad
       dani Pron EYN-3.m.sg. nice-ms.
    b. *dani hu   eyn+o   mar yosef
       dani Pron EYN-3.m.sg. mr yohen

Various possibilities for analysing *eyn* have been offered. It has been proposed that *eyn* is verbal (Borer 1981), that is generated in Tense or Infl (Déchaine 1993), and that it is generated adjoined to Infl (Doron 1983). My analysis will be closest in spirit to Doron's, though not identical. I suggest that *eyn* is generated either sentence initially or directly below Infl, and that its distributional properties follow from a condition that it must be coindexed with an Infl which has no [±past] features.

Let us first look at the problems with generating *eyn* in Infl. Déchaine (1993) argues that *eyn* is generated either there or in tense, but there is an immediate problem with this. *Eyn* does cooccur with verbal predicates, as (45c) shows, while the facts about the pronominal copula indicated precisely that a lexically filled Infl couldn't cooccur with verbs; Pron, which is clearly generated in Infl, (see section 8.2) cannot cooccur with V, as (10), repeated here, shows:

(51) *dani hu   holex
     dani Pron goes

Doron (1983) suggests that *eyn* is generated together with a clitic and that it is adjoined to Infl, as in (52):

(52) [eyn+cl] + Infl

The clitic may absorb the nominative case features which Infl can assign; in this Doron follows Jaeggli's (1980) analysis of clitics, where he suggests that a clitic always absorbs the case features of a head. Doron suggests that there is a problem with this: one would not expect to find inflected *eyn* cooccuring with nominative pronominals, since these presumably are assigned case features by Infl, and yet examples such as (53) are perfect:

(53)   ani eyn + eni   oxelet bananot.
     I   eyn + 1.sg. eat-f. bananas
     "I don't eat bananas."

However, if one assumes that Infl is coindexed with nominative pronouns, as we have been doing, then (53) is not a problem. What is a serious problem both for Doron's and Déchaine's analyses is that they predict the wrong word order for adverbs and *eyn*. As we saw in (35/36), repeated here, inflected *eyn* and Pron have different positions in relation to adverbs: inflected *eyn* follows rather than precedes adverbs, whereas the pronominal copula precedes an adverb and cannot follow it, indicating that, if Pron is in Infl position, *eyn* is not.

(35) a.   dani (hu)   be-emet/ulay   ha- baxur Se- raiti. (=(35))
          dani (Pron) really/ perhaps the guy   that saw-I
          "Dani is really/perhaps the guy that I saw."
     b. *dani be-emet/ulay   hu   ha- baxur Se- raiti.
          dani really/   perhaps Pron the guy   that saw-I

(36) a.   dani be-emet/ulay   eyn + o   nexmad. (=(36))
          dani really/   perhaps EYN + m.sg. nice
          "Dani really/perhaps isn't nice."
     b. *dani eyn + o   be-emet/ulay   nexmad.
          dani EYN + m.sg. really/   perhaps nice
          "Dani really/perhaps isn't really nice."

In fact, with respect to placement of adverbs, *eyn* behaves not as Infl, but as a copular verb. *h.y.y.* is the verb used in simple tensed copular sentences, and there is in addition a special copular use of *h.y.y.*, where it occurs in the past tense, and followed by a form of the present participial with which it agrees in number and gender. In this use it marks the past habitual:

(56)   pa'am, dani haya   oxel   bananot.
      once   dani be-PAST-3.m.sg. eat-m.sg. bananas
      "Once Dani used to eat bananas."

In these cases, the copula follows the adverb, exactly as inflected *eyn* does:

(57) a.   dani be-emet haya   ha- baxur   Se- raiti.
          dani really   be-PAST-3.m.sg. the young man that saw-I
          "Dani was really the guy that I saw."
     b. pa'am, dani be-emet haya   oxel   bananot.
          once   dani really   be-PAST-3.m.sg. eat-m.sg. bananas
          "Once Dani really used to eat bananas."
     c.   dani be-emet eyno   oxel   bananot.
          dani really   EYN-3.m.sg. eat-m.sg. bananas
          "Dani really doesn't eat bananas."

(58) a. ?dani haya   be-emet ha-baxur   Se   raiti.
         dani be-PAST-3.m.sg. really   the young man that saw-I
         "Dani was really the guy that I saw."
      b. ?pa'am, dani haya   be-emet oxel   bananot.
         once dani be-PAST-3.m.sg. really   eat-m.sg. bananas
         "Once Dani used really to eat bananas."
      c. ?dani eyno   be-emet oxel bananot
         dani EYN-3.m.sg. really   eat   bananas
         "Dani doesn't really eat bananas."

(Note the scope difference between (57c) and (58c).)
There is thus prima facie evidence that *eyn* is a verb, as Borer (1981) suggested.
But there are problems with this too. Only IP-internal *eyn* is inflected; if this
eyn is verbal, then it looks as if we would have to analyse sentence-initial *eyn*
as a different kind of element, since it is never inflected and appears in a
position where no other uninflected verb stem ever appears. Borer does try to
propose a uniform analysis of both forms of *eyn*. She posits a single verbal
element generated in Comp, directly giving us sentence-initial *eyn*. Sentence-
internal inflected *eyn* is derived by raising Infl to Comp, and the subject to
[Spec,CP]. However, this leaves too many unanswered questions. First, why
are no other verbal elements generated there? Second, if inflected *eyn* is also
generated in Comp and derived via Infl-raising, then we still have to explain
how uninflected *eyn* is possible, in other words, why Infl-raising doesn't always
happen. A more serious problem is that, if in (45c), repeated here as (59a),
eyno is in Comp with the subject raised to Spec of CP, then we predict that
there should be no place to put the question words. But, as (59b) shows, *eyn*
can occur in questions:

(59) a. dani eyn+o   ohev bananot
         dani EYN-3.m.sg. like   bananas
         "Dani doesn't like bananas."
      b. ma   dani eyno   ohev?
         what dani EYN-m.sg. like-m.s.
         "What does Dani not like?"

The problem is that aside from its inflectional properties in sentence-internal
position, *eyn* does not behave like a verb. And even these inflectional properties
are not good evidence for its being a verb, since, while it is inflected for person,
number and gender, it is clearly not semantically either past or future, and this
would make it the only present tense verb to be fully inflected.
    I propose that *eyn* itself isn't verbal, but that the inflectional markings on
eyn come from an association with Infl, as does inflection on a verb. (54b) and
(57c) indicate that *eyn* is neither in Infl nor above it; and I assume that it is
generated below Infl and above the VP projection – or XP projection if the
predicate is not verbal. I thus continue to assume (see section 8.3) that *eyn*
heads a (non-predicative) negative phrase, and selects a maximal projection as

complement, and that Infl features lower onto it. In sentence-initial position, *eyn* selects an IP, but of course, no Infl is lowered onto it. S-structures for identity and predicational sentences with sentence-internal *eyn* are given in (60a–c) and the S-structure for sentence initial *eyn* is given in (60d):

(60)   a. dani eyno   mar yosef.   (= 32b)
           dani EYN-m.sg. mr   yosef
           [dani [Infl [eyn + o [mar yosef]$_{DP}$]$_{NegP}$]$_{I'}$]$_{IP}$
           "Dani isn't Mr Yosef."
        b. dani eyno   nexmad.   (= 44b)
           dani EYN-m.sg. nice
           [dani [[Infl [eyn + o [nexmad]$_{AP}$]$_{NegP}$]$_{I'}$]$_{IP}$
           "Dani isn't nice."
        c. dani eyno   ohev bananot.
           dani EYN-m.sg. like   bananas
           [dani [Infl [eyn + o [ohev bananot]$_{VP}$]$_{NegP}$]$_{I'}$]$_{IP}$
           "Dani doesn't like bananas."
        d. eyn   dani ohev bananot.
           EYN dani like   bananas
           [eyn [dani [Infl [ohev bananot]$_{VP'}$]$_{I'}$]$_{IP}$]$_{NegP}$
           "Dani doesn't like bananas."

What is the relation between *eyn* and Infl which explains the distribution facts cited above? I suggest that *eyn* is licensed by a relation with the features in Infl which is minimally one of coindexing. When *eyn* appears below Infl, then the coindexing with the Infl which governs it means that Infl lowers onto the negative particle itself. This results in the inflected form that we see in (60a-c). This raises the question of how the verb following *eyn* gets its inflectional marking in sentences such as (60c). Either Infl lowers onto *eyn* and then lowers further, leaving an agreement marker in place of a trace, or Infl might simply lower to *eyn* and stay there. The verb would then agree with the fully inflected lexicalised head which governs it. The second seems plausible since such a process must presumably be available to account for agreement of the lexical non-copula verb in the habitual construction exemplified in (56). The fact that verb agreement here is due to feature matching between a verbal element and an inflected element that governs it explains why the only form of the verb that can follow either *eyn* or a copula in Hebrew is the 'defective' participial form which encodes the present and which is inflected only for number and gender and not person. Fully inflected verbs which are marked for person, number and gender, as well as [±past] can be inflected only through affixation and can thus occur only immediately dominated by Infl.

   In sentence-initial position such as (60d), I hypothesise that *eyn* is licensed because it takes an IP complement with which it is coindexed. Assuming feature percolation from Infl, IP will be marked for the features of its Infl (this is what allows *for* and *that* in English to distinguish between [−tense] and [+tense] IPs). Since *eyn* selects this IP, the relation to Infl will be close enough to license it. However, since the Agr features of Infl will already have been assigned or identified, sentence-initial *eyn* will not change its form. Sentence-initial *eyn* will thus govern Infl, and sentence-internal *eyn* will be governed by Infl; in either case the relation is close enough to license the negative particle.

We can now explain the other facts about the distribution of *eyn*. First, we can explain the ungrammaticality of (49), repeated here:

(61) a. *eyn   dani nexmad
          EYN dani nice
      b. *eyn   rina mora
          EYN rina teacher
      c. *eyn   dani al ha-gag
          EYN dani on the-roof

Since in these examples, *eyn* selects a small, and thus Infl-less, clause, it is not possible to coindex *eyn* with an IP, and license it through its relation with the head of its complement.

Second, since sentence-internal *eyn* bears the person, number and gender features lowered from Infl, it identifies the Infl node in the sentence, just as a nominative pronominal subject does. Thus, in an identity sentence such as (60a), the inflected *eyn* identifies the Infl node, and indicates the presence of the I′ predicate node. As we discussed in section 8.3, when Infl lowers onto *eyn*, we cannot have Pron, since there are no agreement features left for Pron to realise. This correctly rules out the examples in (50), repeated here:

(62) a. *dani hu   eyn + o   nexmad
          dani Pron EYN-3.m.sg nice-ms.
      b. *dani hu   eyn + o   mar yosef
          dani Pron EYN-3.m.sg mr yosef

In each case *eyn* is coindexed with a governing Infl and the agreement features lower onto it. The fact that coindexing Infl with a head that it governs necessarily involves affixation, rules out the ungrammatical (63), where the Infl is identified through the realisation of Pron and *eyn* is uninflected:

(63) *[dani [hu   [eyn   [nexmad]$_{AP}$]$_{NegP}$]$_{I'}$]$_{IP}$
           dani Pron EYN nice

When Pron is realised, only the features for number and gender are encoded, and we have a 'defective' Infl. If we assume that *eyn* has to be coindexed with a 'full' Infl or projection of Infl in which person, number and gender features are identified, we explain the unacceptability of the examples in (64):

(64) a. *eyn   dani hu   nexmad
          EYN dani Pron nice
      b. *eyn   rina hi   mora
          EYN rina Pron teacher
      c. *eyn   dani hu   al ha-gag
          EYN dani Pron on the-roof

The examples in (64) contrast sharply with those in (65), where the subject is a pronoun and Infl is not phonologically realised:

(65) a. eyn   hu nexmad.
       EYN he nice
       "He isn't nice."
     b. eyn   ani mora.
       EYN I   teacher
       "I am not a teacher."
     c. eyn   ata al ha-gag.
       EYN you on the-roof
       "you are not on the roof."

Here, *eyn* is apparently selecting a small clause, without a realised Infl. But, the discussion of Infl-identification here and in section 8.3 above predicts exactly these facts. The pronominals in (65) are all nominative pronoun subjects, and not Pron. (If they were instances of Pron, then the sentences would be subjectless. But we know independently that this is impossible since pro-drop is possible in Hebrew only when the verb has a [±past] feature and when the subject is not in the third person singular.) These subject pronouns must be fully coindexed with Infl for person, number and gender. Thus a full set of agreement features are identified and projected to IP level, and the clause is an appropriate complement for *eyn*.

We note also that the lowering of Infl onto *eyn* does not affect coindexation between Infl and a pronominal subject, and thus, as we saw, (66) raises no problems. (66) shows the two possible first person singular inflected forms which are available.

(66) ani eyn + eni/eyn + i oxelet bananot
      I   EYN-1.sg.   eat-f. bananas
      "I don't eat bananas."

Here, as well as lowering onto *eyn*, Infl must also be coindexed with the pronominal subject, and thus inflected *eyn* must agree in features with the pronoun. This leads to one further prediction. We saw above, in example (40), that in an identity sentence Infl may agree with the post-copula nominal. However, when that occurs, Pron moves out of Infl and cliticises onto the post-copula nominal, so that when Infl is coindexed with the subject, no clash of features occurs. One might think that *eyn* also could agree with a post-copula nominal. However, we argue that sentence-internal *eyn* is irrevocably coindexed with the Infl node, since Infl features lower onto it, and we know independently that Infl must be coindexed with the subject. Thus we predict that, in contrast with the pronominal copula in (40), *eyn* in identity sentences can agree in features only with the subject. (67) shows that this is indeed so:

(67) ma Se dekart   katav eyn + o/   *eyn + a   ha-hoxaxa
      what Descartes wrote EYN-3.m.sg./*EYN-3.f.sg. the-proof
      le-kiyum-o.
      to-existence-his
      "What Descartes wrote was not the proof of his existence"

The only problem left us is really with (46a), repeated here:

(68) eyn   dani ohev bananot
      NEG Dani likes bananas

If *eyn* selects an IP with a fully identified Infl, and if (64) is ungrammatical and the present tense is considered a defective form, then one might expect (68) to be ungrammatical, since here too the IP is a projection of a defective Infl which identifies only gender and number features.

The explanation of the contrast between (68) and (64) seems to lie in the nature of default realisation of Infl. I assume, following Doron (1983), that the present in Hebrew is defective because it lacks both a [±past] feature, which distinguishes it from the past and the future tense, and a [±tense] feature which distinguishes it not only from the [+tense] past and future, but also from the [−tense] infinitives. Infl in the present consists only of agreement features, but it must have a complete set of agreement features – person, number, and gender. We can see this because it assigns nominative case to a full complement of nominative pronouns, and because since, when it lowers onto *eyn* or similar sentence-internal inflected copular particles such as *hinehu*, these appear inflected for person, number and gender. The standard way of licensing, or identifying, an Infl is by affixation onto a verb which it governs. I assume that when this happens, as in (68), Infl is fully identified, even if all its properties are not fully encoded morphologically on the Hebrew present tense verb. The same thing happens in the present tense in English, where person features are morphologically represented only in the third person singular, but where we consider a full set of Inflectional features to be present. In a Hebrew present tense sentence, despite the fact that only number and gender are represented in the affixes of the present tense, Infl is normally fully identified. It is defective not because the person feature is missing, but because the tense feature is missing. Thus, in (68) Infl is fully projected and since it does not include a past feature, the IP can be the complement of *eyn*. When Pron occurs, as in (64), Infl is doubly defective. Not only does it lack tense and past features, but the agreement features which it does contain cannot be identified by affixation or agreement with the subject and have to be lexically represented by elements which encode only number and gender. It is this second defectiveness which means that it does not fully identify Infl, or project a full IP which can be the complement of *eyn*, and thus the examples in (64) are out.

8.5. Semantics

I assume that the semantic interpretation of Infl is the same as in English (see chapter 6:6.6); it is a function which takes a function from individuals into sets of events (i.e. $<d, <e,t>>$) and gives a possibly modified relation of the same type back again. Infl in English subcategories for a VP, but Hebrew Infl selects an XP and thus 'small' non-verbal inflected IPs are possible. Quite possibly this difference need not be represented in terms of subcategorisation relations: if we assume, following Doron (1983), that [±tense] must attach onto a V and that Hebrew differs from English in that a sentence does not require a tense feature, then the difference in the 'selectional properties' of Infl reduces to the fact that English Infl must include a tense feature which must immediately govern a verb for it to be affixed onto, while Hebrew IP does not require a tense feature and thus the Infl can take any XP as a complement. In any case, Hebrew Infl, like English Infl, is of type $<<d, <e,t>>, <d, <e,t>>>$. Infl adds a tense modifier to a predicate, and I assume that Pron or any other Hebrew Infl which does not contain a past or tense feature, is an identity function on predicates of the form $\lambda P.P$, (where 'P' is a variable of type $<d, <e,t>>$). So the semantic form of Infl the complement of Infl needs to be of the form in (69):

(69) $\lambda x \lambda e.\alpha(x)(e)$

Matrix small clauses and inflected matrix small clauses will be interpreted straightforwardly as in (70), using the same basic rules as in chapter 6

(70)   a. dani nexmad:

$$[\text{nexmad}]_A \rightarrow \lambda e.\text{NICE}(e) \wedge \text{Arg}(e) = x$$
$$[\text{nexmad}]_{AP} \rightarrow \lambda x \lambda e.\text{NICE}(e) \wedge \text{Arg}(e) = x$$
$$\text{(by Predicate Formation)}$$
$$[\text{dani nexmad}]_{SC} \rightarrow \lambda x \lambda e.\text{NICE}(e) \wedge \text{Arg}(e) = x \text{ (DANI)}$$
$$= \lambda e.\text{NICE}(e) \wedge \text{Arg}(e) = \text{DANI}$$
$$= \exists e[\text{NICE}(e) \wedge \text{Arg}(e) = \text{DANI}] \text{ (by } \exists\text{-closure)}$$

   b. dani hu nexmad:

$$[\text{nexmad}]_A \rightarrow \lambda e.\text{NICE}(e) \wedge \text{Arg}(e) = x$$
$$[\text{nexmad}]_{AP} \rightarrow \lambda x \lambda e.\text{NICE}(e) \wedge \text{Arg}(e) = x$$
$$\text{(by Predicate Formation)}$$
$$[\text{hu nexmad}]_{I'} \rightarrow \lambda P.P \ (\lambda x \lambda e.\text{NICE}(e) \wedge \text{Arg}(e) = x)$$
$$= \lambda x \lambda e.\text{NICE}(e) \wedge \text{Arg}(e) = x$$
$$[\text{dani hu nexmad}]_{IP} \rightarrow \lambda x \lambda e.\text{NICE}(e) \wedge \text{Arg}(e) = x \text{ (DANI)}$$
$$= \lambda e.\text{NICE}(e) \wedge \text{Arg}(e) = \text{DANI}$$
$$= \exists e[\text{NICE}(e) \wedge \text{Arg}(e) = \text{DANI}] \text{ (by } \exists\text{-closure)}$$

The question which we need to raise is: what about identity sentences? In (24c), repeated here as (71), we see that Infl takes a proper name of type d as its complement.

(71) $[[\text{dani}]_{DP} \ [[\text{hu}]_{Infl} \ [\text{mar yosef}]_{DP}]_{I'}]_{IP}$
          dani   Pron   mr yosef
       "Dani is Mr Yosef."

On the assumption that Infl takes an XP of any category as its complement, nothing needs to be said about the syntactic licensing of (71), but something does need to be said about how the interpretation takes place. I will discuss the interpretation of copular constructions in English at length in the next

/

chapter, and compare how the English and the Hebrew examples work, so this is only a preview. In brief, I assume that Infl triggers a type raising operation similar, but not identical to, the operation that Partee (1987) assumes is available for the individual type complement of *be* in English. She assumes an operation 'ident' that raises an individual to the property of being identical to that individual. $\lambda x.x = \alpha$ gives you the singleton set of individuals which are identical to α, where α is of type d.

(72) ident: $\alpha \rightarrow \lambda x.x = \alpha$

The ident function that is triggered by Infl in Hebrew needs to raise individuals to an expression of type $<d, <e,t>>$, which is the type of the complement of Infl. Intuitively, we want the rule to relate an individual α to the set of events E in which α is a participant, (where α is a participant in e if there is a thematic role which maps e onto α) and to pick out the set of individuals who are identical with α in the events which are members of E. The raising operation which does this is given in (73). (I'll discuss this operation in depth in the context of the parallel rule for English in chapter 9:9.2). 'R' is a variable over thematic roles, and 'Θ' denotes the set of thematic roles.

(73) Hebrew Ident: $\alpha \rightarrow \lambda x \lambda e. \exists R \in \Theta[R(e) = \alpha \wedge \alpha = x]$

Thus (73) gives a relation between an individual x and a set of events if the events are ones which demonstrate that α exists and that x is identical to α.

In the interpretation of (71), *MAR YOSEF*, the denotation of the DP, is raised from type d to type $<d, <e,t>>$:

(74) MAR YOSEF $\rightarrow \lambda x \lambda e. \exists R \in \Theta[R(e) = $ MAR-YOSEF $\wedge$ MAR-YOSEF $= x]$

The derivation is given in (75):

(75) [mar yosef]$_{DP}$ $\qquad \rightarrow$ MAR-YOSEF
$\quad$ [hu [mar yosef]$_{DP}$]$_{I'}$ $\quad \rightarrow \lambda P.P$ (ident(MAR-YOSEF))
$\quad = \lambda P.P (\lambda x \lambda e. \exists R \in \Theta[R(e) = $ MAR-YOSEF $\wedge$ MAR-YOSEF $= x])$
$\quad = \lambda x \lambda e. \exists R \in \Theta[R(e) = $ MAR-YOSEF $\wedge$ MAR-YOSEF $= x]$
$\quad$ [dani [hu mar yosef]$_{I'}$]$_{IP}$ $\rightarrow \lambda x \lambda e. \exists R \in \Theta[R(e) = $ MAR-YOSEF
$\qquad \wedge$ MAR-YOSEF $= x]$ (DANI)
$\quad = \lambda e. \exists R \in \Theta[R(e) = $ MAR-YOSEF $\wedge$ MAR-YOSEF $= $ DANI$]$
$\quad = \exists e \exists R \in \Theta[R(e) = $ MAR-YOSEF $\wedge$ MAR-YOSEF $= $ DANI$]$
$\qquad\qquad\qquad\qquad\qquad\qquad\qquad\qquad\qquad\qquad$ (by $\exists$-closure)

Since plausibly the requirement that Dani fills some role of some event can be seen as saying nothing more than the fact that Dani exists, this is eqivalent to MAR YOSEF = DANI. So, (71) is true if there is an event in which Mr Yosef is a participant in which Dani is identical to Mr Yosef, which is the result that we want.

8.6. GREENBERG'S (1998/1999) ANALYSIS

The analysis in this chapter has answered the question of why Pron is obligatory in identity sentences, but does not touch on the issue of why it is optional in predicative sentences. In Rothstein (1995b), I tried to distinguish between pairs of predicative sentences with and without Pron by assigning them two different syntactic structures. Sentences such as (1a), repeated here as (76a/c), were assigned the structures in (76b/d) respectively, with the subject moving to [Spec,IP] in (76b) to fulfill the predication requirement since I' had to be saturated.

(76) a. dani hu nexmad.
      b. [dani$_i$ [hu [t$_i$ [nexmad]$_{AP}$]$_{SC}$]$_{I'}$]$_{IP}$
      c. dani nexmad.
      d. [dani [nexmad]$_{AP}$]$_{SC}$

(76a) was assumed to differ in structure from identity sentences, where Infl takes a straight nominal complement and not a small clause. However, as I pointed out in Rothstein (1995b), it is not really possible to justify assigning such different syntactic structures to (76a/c). Worse, in a context in which we are assigning semantic interpretations to these sentences, (76b) gets us into trouble. Infl must be of type $<<d, <e,t>>, <d, <e,t>>>$, since in English, and in Hebrew non-small clauses, it takes a VP complement. Semantically, Infl maps expressions of the form $\lambda x \lambda e.R(x)(e)$ into expressions of the same form. We also introduced a type-raising rule to deal with identity sentences, which raised expressions of type d into $<d, <e,t>>$. But we have also argued in chapter 6 that a small clause – as well as an IP – is an expression of type $<e,t>$, denoting a set of events, or a function from events into truth values, having the form $\lambda e.E(e)$. If this is so, then a small clause will never be of the right type to be the complement to Infl. So if the pronominal copula had a small clause complement, we would have to assume either that it is a different type from other Infls, which is obviously undesirable, or we would have to posit some type-raising rule to take $<e,t>$ into $<d, <e,t>>$. But there isn't a plausible mapping from $<e,t>$ into $<d, <e,t>>$ and, unlike in the case of identity sentences, there is no good reason to suggest that Infl takes a complement which doesn't fit in the first place. I will continue to assume, as I have been assuming all along, that (76a) and similar predicative sentences have the same basic structure as an identity sentence, with Infl taking a maximal projection as its complement. The difference between (76a) and (76c), and the answer to the question 'why ever insert a Pron' if it is optional is not going to be answered in the syntactic domain.

Greenberg (1998, 1999) discusses the question of why Pron is sometimes present and sometimes not in identity sentences, and relates it to two other issues. The first is her observation that the analysis of obligatory Pron presented here – as well as Doron's (1983) analysis and Rapoport's (1987) analysis – assumes that Pron is obligatory only in identity sentences and that in all other predicational sentences it will be optional. As she shows, this prediction is wrong: there are various types of predicative sentences where Pron is obligatory. These include sentences with bare plural subjects, as in (77a) and assertions of fixed locations such as (77b):

(77) a. orvim *(hem) Sxorim.
      ravens Pron black
      "Ravens are black."
    b. tel aviv *(hi) be-yisrael.
      Tel Aviv Pron in Israel
      "Tel Aviv is in Israel."

(Rapoport mentions similar data, but it does not affect her analysis of obligatory Pron in identity sentences.) Greenberg's second point is to relate this data to the observation (Rubinstein 1968, Ben-David 1971, Borer p.c., Déchaine 1993) that, where Pron is optional in predicative sentences, its presence/absence often correlates with a difference in meaning: when Pron is present, the sentence has a more individual level reading, and when Pron is absent, it has more of a stage level interpretation. (78), from Ben-David (1971) and cited in Greenberg (1994, 1998), would be used to make different assertions depending on whether or not Pron is there:

(78) haSamaim (hem) kxolim.
      the sky   Pron blue
      "The sky is blue."

When Pron is present, the sentence is interpreted as asserting that the sky in general has the property of being blue, whereas without the Pron the sentence asserts that the sky is blue now, rather than grey or overcast or any of the other possibilities. Greenberg shows that this difference is quite general, and carries over to examples where the difference is much more subtle. Thus even in (79), she shows, a distinction can be made between the sentence with and without Pron:

(79) a. rina hi   tamid yafa.
        rina Pron always pretty
    b. rina tamid   yafa.
        rina always pretty
        both: "Rina is always pretty."

(79a) with Pron (which she claims is less acceptable than (79b)) is most appropriate if the assertion is that it is a characteristic property of Rina that she is always pretty, while (79b), without the Pron, is more likely to be used to assert that every time I see Rina, it is true that she is pretty. Greenberg (1999) argues that the pronominal copula in these sentence is best treated as indicating the presence of a generic operator binding the event variable. A generic operator, like markers for tense, is located in Infl but, unlike [±past], is not associated with a specific marker; when the generic operator is the only semantic feature to be associated with Infl, Infl is morphologically realised by the minimal Pron. When a generic reading is the only possible reading of a predicational sentence, Pron will be obligatory, and when a generic reading is impossible, for contextual or other reasons, Pron will be impossible.

It is tempting to try and explain the obligatoriness of Pron in identity sentences under the same rubric of genericity. Presumably being identical with oneself is about the most generic property that there is, and if Pron is an indication of genericity, then one would expect Pron to occur in identity sentences as in other generic sentences. But, as Greenberg herself points out, this cannot be the explanation for the obligatoriness of Pron in identity sentences. A characteristic of generic predication is that it is true at all (relevant) times and places and thus usually locative and temporal modifiers cannot be freely added. Thus, despite (79), (80b) is much more acceptable than (80a):

(80)   a. ???rina hi   yafa   ha-erev.
         rina Pron pretty tonight
       b.   rina yafa   ha-erev.
         rina pretty tonight
         both: "Rina is pretty tonight."

This is explained if (80a) is interpreted as a generic sentence, since if it is generically true that Rina is pretty, then it is odd to assert that the property 'pretty' holds of her tonight.

   In contrast to (80a), identity sentences which do not express permanent or generic identifications and which include temporal modifiers obligatorily require Pron and are fully acceptable. Greenberg offers (81) as an example, which she attributes to Edit Doron (p.c.):

(81)   hayom, ha-axot   ha-toranit *(hi)   rina (aval maxar   lo).
       today   the-nurse the-duty   Pron rina (but tomorrow no)
       "Today the duty nurse is Rina, but (tomorrow this is not so."

The property which the individual who is the duty nurse has of being identified with or identical to Rina is temporary, as the temporal adverbial shows, but nonetheless Pron is obligatory. This indicates that at least in these cases, the Infl node is required for reasons which have nothing to do with marking the generic/non-generic distinction.

   As I have argued, the explanation is to be found in the non-predicate status of the post-copula XP, and the consequent need to create a syntactic predicate at the I' level. Greenberg's account of (77)–(81) complements the account of identity sentence proposed in this chapter, rather than conflicting with it, and we have a different explanation for Pron in predicational and identity sentences. Infl can, but need not, be associated with semantic features. In identity sentences, Infl is required by the syntax to create a predicate structure and, as a semantic corollary, to trigger the type shifting required to interpret identity sentences. In generic predicational sentences, Infl is required to introduce the generic operator. The relation between Infl and the semantic features associated with it remains to be explored.

CHAPTER 9

COPULAR CONSTRUCTIONS IN ENGLISH

9.1. COPULAR CONSTRUCTIONS AND PREDICATION

This chapter looks at the structure of copular sentences in English. There are two basic issues which concern us. The first, which follows directly on from the discussion of Hebrew copular constructions in the previous chapter, is the fact that in English too, small uninflected clauses are possible, but not if the small clause is an expression of identity. In the previous chapter we saw that in Hebrew a semantically null Inflectional element is necessary in identity statements to create a syntactic predication structure, but not in small clauses, where the predication structure is created by the relation between the inherently predicative XP and the subject. In English, the same phenomenon occurs, but there are two major differences. First, we don't get the contrast in matrix sentences, since English doesn't allow uninflected matrix clauses, except in the 'echoic' questions and exclamations discussed in Akmajian (1984), and noted in chapter 2. Second, English requires Inflection to take a VP complement, and thus the contrast is not between small clauses and inflected small clauses, but between small clauses and IPs with infinitivally marked VPs, as illustrated in (1):

(1) a. I believe/consider Mary (to be) very clever/ a clever woman.
     b. I believe/consider Mary *(to be) Dr. Smith.

We see that, as in Hebrew matrix small clauses, the Infl + verbal copula is optional when the non-subject element in a small clause is a syntactic predicate, while in 'identity complements' the copula 'complex' is obligatory. This has led people to follow Russell (1919) in assuming that there are two copulas *be*, a *be* of predication and a *be* of identity. I shall begin the chapter by arguing against this approach, in part by showing that the post-copula DP in identity sentences does not have the properties of a direct object.

The second issue concerns the structure of simple copular sentences such as (2), and focusses on the properties of the post-copula element in (2b).

(2) a. Mary is a clever woman.
     b. Mary is Dr. Smith, (the dentist).

(2a) is a predicative sentence in which the DP *a clever woman* functions predicatively, like an adjective, and the sentence ascribes to Mary the property of being a clever woman. (2b) is an identity sentence in which the post-copula DP is a referential argument, as indicated by the fact that it is the subject of an appositional phrase, and the sentence asserts that the individual denoted by Mary and the individual denoted by Dr. Smith are identical. The problem is that while, as we shall see, the referential post-copula DP in (2b) does not behave like a direct object, it does not behave like a predicative DP either. In particular, we see that trying to extract from within the post-copula position is not possible in identity sentences, and in this respect, the post-copula DP has the properties of a subject rather than an object. This, together with other syntactic differences between (2a) and (2b), has led a variety of people (Williams 1983b, Longobardi 1984, Heggie 1988, Moro 1997) to propose that identity sentences are 'reverse copular constructions'. (Partee (1986), argues the same for pseudoclefts.) While in (2a) it is clear that [Spec,IP] is an argument and [XP,VP] is a predicate, this approach argues that in (2b) the higher DP is in fact a predicate and the lower one is an argument. There are a variety of different ways of working out the details of the approach: for example, Williams (1983b) and Partee (1986) suggest that *be* takes an argument and a predicate in either order, while Moro proposes that *be* takes a small clause complement and no subject, and that either subject or predicate move to fill [Spec,IP]. What is clear is that the kind of structures that these theories would produce are exactly what the structural theory of predication would predict should not occur. In a structure of the form in (3), we predict that *be* heads a predicate VP, and that [Spec,IP] will be filled by the subject of that predicate.

(3) $[[\alpha]_{[Spec,IP]} [Infl [be \beta]_{VP}]_{I'}]_{IP}$

If α in (3) is a predicate, then it cannot be correct to claim that IP is an instance of a structural predication relation in which the VP/I' constituent is predicated of the argument daughter of IP.

The goal of this chapter then, is to present an account of the structure of sentences in (2) which is compatible with the structural theory of predication and which seems a natural solution in the light of the discussion up till now. I will show that this account does explain why the post-copula DP in identity sentences behaves the way it does. After arguing against a 'two-verb *be*' approach in the next section, I will propose that *be* selects syntactically for the argument types of DP and small clause. (It will also select for the argument types IP and CP, but I won't do more than mention these here.) I will argue that in predicational sentences, *be* selects a small clause complement and the subject of the small clause raises to [Spec,IP] in order to satisfy the predication and case marking conditions, while in identity sentences, *be* takes a DP complement. The structures for (2) are as in (4):

(4)   a. [Mary$_i$ [is [t$_i$ a clever woman]$_{SC}$]$_{VP}$]$_{IP}$
      b. [Mary [is [Dr. Smith]$_{DP}$]$_{VP}$]$_{IP}$

I shall give an account of the interpretation of these structures which adheres to the rule of interpretation set out in chapter 6, and which makes use of

Partee's type-shifting account of the interpretation of nominals in Partee (1987). I'll then present the evidence in favour of and against the 'reverse copular construction' analysis, and having concluded that the evidence is overwhelmingly against, I'll show how the syntactic/type-shifting account that I have given allows us to explain the behaviour of the post-copula argument in identity sentences. The chapter concludes with some comments on the relation between NP and DP and the problem of predicative DPs.

9.2. Two verbs 'be'?

The evidence from the structure of complements of Exceptional Case Marking verbs like *consider* and *believe*, as in (1), repeated here, has led people to claim that there are two different verbs *be*, one used in predicational sentences and the other used in identity sentences.

(5) a. I believe/consider Mary (to be) very clever/ a clever woman.
     b. I believe/consider Mary *(to be) Dr. Smith.

It is claimed that predicational *be*, as illustrated in (5a) makes no semantic contribution to the sentence: it assigns no thematic roles and, unlike other verbs, it does not denote a relation. Its role is that of a grammatical formative, and it is a 'mark of predication'. It is obligatory in all but (predicational) small clauses in English because (in English) every matrix sentence and IP complement of CP is required to bear tense and inflection and the tense/Infl node can be affixed only onto a verb. If there is no lexical verb in the sentence, a copula must be added. 'Bare' predication is possible only where a small clause can be licensed as an argument. As we saw in chapter 2, a small clause can be an argument as the complement of an Exceptional Case Marking verb, in certain subject positions, and as an object of *with* in an absolutive adjunct phrase. In contrast, the *be* of identity, it is claimed, is a true transitive lexical verb denoting the relation that holds between two individuals if they are identical to each other. In the terms of government-binding theory, it assigns two thematic roles, one to its subject and one to its object. It thus cannot be deleted even in small clause contexts, as shown in (5b).

The "two verb" solution to the puzzle which the data in (5) represents, is inadequate for several reasons. First, as in pointed out in Rapoport (1987), this explanation makes it coincidental that in almost every language, the copula and verb of identity have the same phonological form. Second, we would expect the DP following the verb in identity sentences to behave straightforwardly as a direct object. However, as Longobardi (1984) and others point out, this is not the case. In particular, although the direct object position is one which it is usually easy to extract from, extraction is not always possible from the 'object' position following *be*. For example, moving an argument complement of *be* is not possible in relativisation contexts. The examples in (6) contrast with those in (7):

(6) a. *Mary, who his best friend is t, likes to go to the beach.
    b. *The woman that his best friend is t is here.
    c. *It is Mary that his best friend has been t.

(7) a. Mary, who his best friend met t yesterday for the first time, wants to invite him to a movie.
    b. The woman that his best friend invited t has arrived.
    c. It is Mary that his best friend has invited t.

We will return to a discussion of this data later.

The third issue which the "two verb" approach doesn't explain is that the same issue of obligatory vs optional copula elements turns up in Hebrew, where matrix small clauses are possible, as we saw in chapter 8. The data in (8) (from chapter 8) shows essentially the same pattern as (5): the pronominal copula *hi* is optional in the predicational sentence in (8a) and obligatory in the identity sentence in (8b):

(8) a. rina (hi)   nexmeda/mora.
      rina (Pron) nice-f.-sg./teacher-f.sg.
      "Rina is nice/a teacher."
    b. rina *(hi)   doktor cohen.
      rina Pron dr   cohen
      "Rina is Dr. Cohen."

The pattern is so similar to the contrast in English that it would seem that the same explanation should work for both sets of data. However, there is a difference between (8) and (5). In (5) the optional element is an infinitival verb. In modern Hebrew, as we saw in chapter 8, there is no present form of the copula *h.y.y.*, and the element which acts as a copula and is optional in predicational sentences is an expression of Inflection, and is not verbal at all. The contrast between a true verb and a grammatical formative that Russell proposes can work only in the verbal domain, since it relies on one of the elements (the one that cannot be omitted) denoting a genuine semantic relation, and it cannot deal with a contrast in the behaviour of inflectional elements. Inflection is by nature a grammatical rather than a lexical element, and it makes no sense to posit an inflectional element which denotes a semantic relation and assigns thematic roles. If essentially the same explanation is responsible for the patterns of data in English and in Hebrew, something other than an ambiguous verb *be* must be at the root of (5).

9.3. One 'be' + type-raising

The approach I am going to follow here is essentially that of Partee (1987), in which she assumes a single verb *be* whose meaning is 'apply function', and a theory of type-raising to explain how the identity sentences work. I shall give a syntactic account of these constructions, and show how Partee's semantic account can be adapted to take into account the event-framework and the theory of predication developed here. The semantic account will be revised further in the next chapter, when we look more closely at the meaning of predicational *be*.

I assume, following Stowell (1978), that *be* is a raising verb which takes a small clause complement, as shown in (9).

(9)   [John$_i$ is [t$_i$ tall]$_{SC}$]]

Be assigns no thematic roles, and thus is generated with an empty subject position. The subject of the small clause complement is raised to be the sentential subject, just like with *seems*. The subject of a predicational sentence is thus theta-marked indirectly by the small clause predicate since it heads a chain which ends in the theta-marked trace subject of the small clause predicate. (Stowell's main reason for proposing the raising analysis of *be* is that, under the assumption that existential *be* in 'there' insertion constructions selects a small clause (see also Keenan 1987, Safir 1987), existential *be* and copula *be* have the same subcategorisation frames. This particular aspect of the copula will not concern us here.) An advantage of this structure is that it explains intuitions about (10):

(10)   John [is [rich]$_{AP}$ and [proud of it]$_{AP}$]$_{VP}$.

(10) means that John is rich and proud of himself being rich. John is not proud of the property of richness, or even the property of being rich (in general) but rather the fact that he has that property, that richness is predicated of him. This should be captured in the dependency relations of the pronoun *it*. This pronoun cannot be dependent on a constituent which contains it, and thus it cannot be dependent on any constituent which includes the verb *be*, namely the VP or the I'. The obvious choice of antecedent is the AP *rich*, which, following the analysis in chapter 6, we would translate as $\lambda x \lambda e.\text{RICH}(e) \wedge \text{Arg}_1(e) = x$. But this gives the reading that we have said we don't want, namely that the antecedent of the pronoun is the richness relation itself. If we assume that *be* takes a small clause complement, then (10) has the structure in (11):

(11)   John$_i$ [is [t$_i$ rich]$_{SC}$ and [t$_i$ proud of it]$_{SC}$]$_{VP}$

The antecedent of *it* is now the small clause [t$_i$ rich], where rich is predicated of a variable which is dependent on John. The antecedent for *it* is the small clause which denotes $\lambda e.\text{RICH}(e) \wedge \text{Arg}_1(e) = j$. This gives the reading that we want: what John is proud of is the (stative) eventuality of being rich which has him as its argument. A reviewer notes that this predicts that it ought to be impossible to give *proud of it* a parallel interpretation in (12), since the conjunction *rich and proud of it* is the predicate of the small clause and there is therefore no appropriate small clause antecedent for *it*. I think that this prediction is indeed correct, and that this reading is not available.

(12)   I consider John rich and proud of it.

The idea presented in Partee (1987) is that *be* denotes the identity relation on predicates, translated as $\lambda P.P$ and that it thus gives as its value exactly the same property as it takes as its argument. With the syntactic structure in (9), and the conclusion from chapter 6 that a small clause denotes a set of events, we cannot adopt Partee's idea directly. If *be* is the identity function, it must be of type $<<e,t>, <e,t>>$ and denote the identity function on the set of events. I assume that this is the case, and that *be* denotes the function in (13):

(13)   Be $\rightarrow \lambda E.E$

Be takes a small clause complement, and assigns no thematic roles. This is how it works in (9), repeated here as (14):

(14)   [John$_i$ is [t$_i$ tall]$_{SC}$]

The original subject position of *be* is empty, and the subject of the small clause complement has raised to the subject of IP, where it is assigned case. The predicate of the small clause is predicated of the trace. The AP *tall* initially denotes a set of events, but, following the system developed in chapter 6, predicate formation at the AP level gives a function from individuals into sets of events. This is then predicated of the x variable denoted by the trace to give back the set of events which is the complement of *be*.

The derivation for (14) is as follows:

(15)   tall $\rightarrow \lambda e.\text{TALL}(e) \wedge \text{Arg}_1(e) = x$

    [tall]$_{AP}$ $\rightarrow \lambda x \lambda e.\text{TALL}(e) \wedge \text{Arg}_1(e) = x$

                                    (by Predicate Formation)

    [t tall]$_{SC}$ $\rightarrow \lambda x \lambda e.\text{TALL}(e) \wedge \text{Arg}_1(e) = x \,(x)$

                     $= \lambda e.\text{TALL}(e) \wedge \text{Arg}_1(e) = x$

    [be [t tall]]$_{V'}$ $\rightarrow \lambda E.E \,(\lambda e.\text{TALL}(e) \wedge \text{Arg}_1(e) = x)$

                     $= \lambda e.\text{TALL}(e) \wedge \text{Arg}_1(e) = x$

    [be [t tall]]$_{VP}$ $\rightarrow \lambda x \lambda e.\text{TALL}(e) \wedge \text{Arg}_1(e) = x$

                                      (by Predicate Formation)

    [is t tall]$_{I'}$ $\rightarrow \lambda x \lambda e.\text{TALL}(e) \wedge \text{Arg}_1(e) = x \wedge \text{PRES}(e)$

    [John is tall]$_{IP}$ $\rightarrow \lambda x \lambda e.\text{TALL}(e) \wedge \text{Arg}_1(e) = x \wedge \text{PRES}(e)(\text{JOHN})$

                     $= \lambda e.\text{TALL}(e) \wedge \text{Arg}_1(e) = \text{JOHN} \wedge \text{PRES}(e)$

      $= \exists e[\text{TALL}(e) \wedge \text{Arg}_1(e) = \text{JOHN} \wedge \text{PRES}(e)]$ (by $\exists$-closure)

Syntactically, the AP *tall* is a predicate, as is the VP *be tall*. Predicate absorption is not used here, since the complement of *be* is not a syntactic predicate but a small clause. The IP subject heads a chain which contains the theta-marked trace subject of the AP predicate, and thus is indirectly assigned the external theta-role of the AP. Partee assumes that *be* is obligatory because of the double requirement that tense is required and that tense must be affixed onto a verbal element. *Be* can be dropped in complement small clauses such as those in (1a) because in that environment tense is not required, and the AP can be directly predicated of its subject.

In contrast with predicate sentences, I assume that identity sentences do not involve a small clause or raising to IP, and that the syntactic structure of a sentence like (16a) is (16b) and not (16c):

(16) a. Mary is Dr. Smith.
      b. [Mary [Infl [be [Dr. Smith]$_{DP}$]$_{VP}$]$_{I'}$]$_{IP}$
      c. *[Mary$_i$ [Infl [be [t$_i$ Dr Smith]$_{SC}$]$_{VP}$]$_{I'}$]$_{IP}$

The reason why (16c) is impossible is that there is no way to license the small clause complement of *be*. The small clause remains a small clause although it has only a trace subject, and as such it is licensed only if it is an instance of predication. As I have been arguing all along, a small clause like [t$_i$ Dr Smith] cannot be possible because the referential DP *Dr Smith* is not a predicate and cannot be directly predicated of the trace, and thus the small clause cannot be an instance of predication. [t$_i$ Dr Smith] is as impossible as the matrix identity sentences without copulas in Hebrew that we examined in chapter 8.

   Heggie (1988), tries to argue that sentences such as (16a) are derived from a D-structure where *be* takes a small clause complement. She recognises the difficulty of licensing a small clause containing two referential expressions. Her analysis of equative sentences gives them the D-structure in (17):

(17)

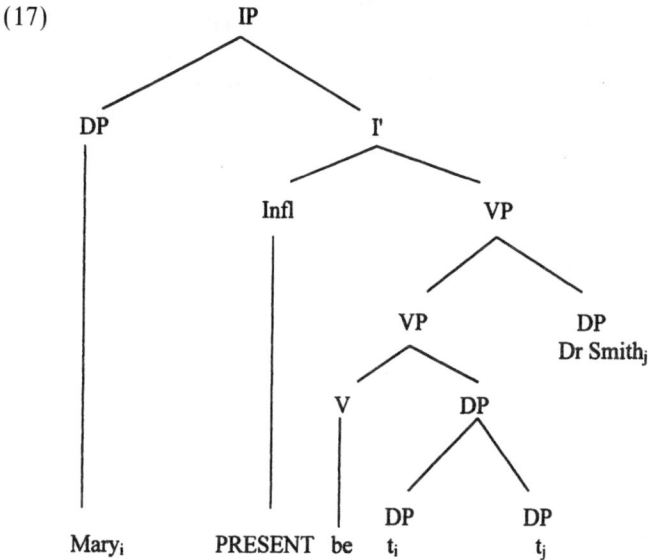

DP$_i$ moves to subject position as in any raising construction, while the second DP extraposes to be adjoined to VP because, she claims, it is focussed. She claims that the copula is obligatory in identity complements of verbs like *consider* and *believe*, as in (1b), for the following reason: assume that the second DP must always be extraposed because it is focussed. (This is necessary to justify moving it out of the small clause and thus out of predicate position.) Then, if the ECM verb complement is a small clause, the only VP available to adjoin it to is the matrix VP. But, since the subject of the small clause does not raise to [Spec,IP], this means that the subject of the small clause does not c-command its predicate, and so the sentence will be ruled out:

(18)   a. *Bill believes Mary Dr. Smith

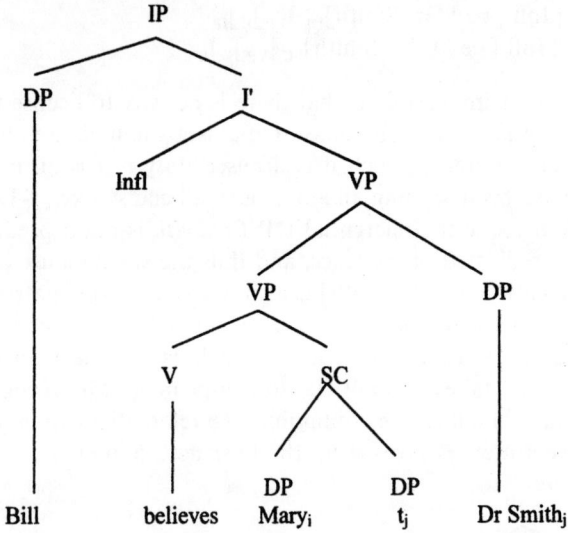

b.

```
                          IP
                  ┌───────┴───────┐
                 DP               I'
                  │          ┌────┴────┐
                  │         Infl       VP
                  │               ┌────┴────┐
                  │              VP         DP
                  │          ┌────┴────┐     │
                  │          V        SC     │
                  │          │      ┌──┴──┐   │
                  │          │     DP    DP   │
                 Bill     believes Maryᵢ  tⱼ  Dr Smithⱼ
```

Heggie argues that inserting *be* in the small clause provides a lower VP for the focussed DP to adjoin to, and a higher Spec of IP for the small clause subject to move to, so that the structure is saved:

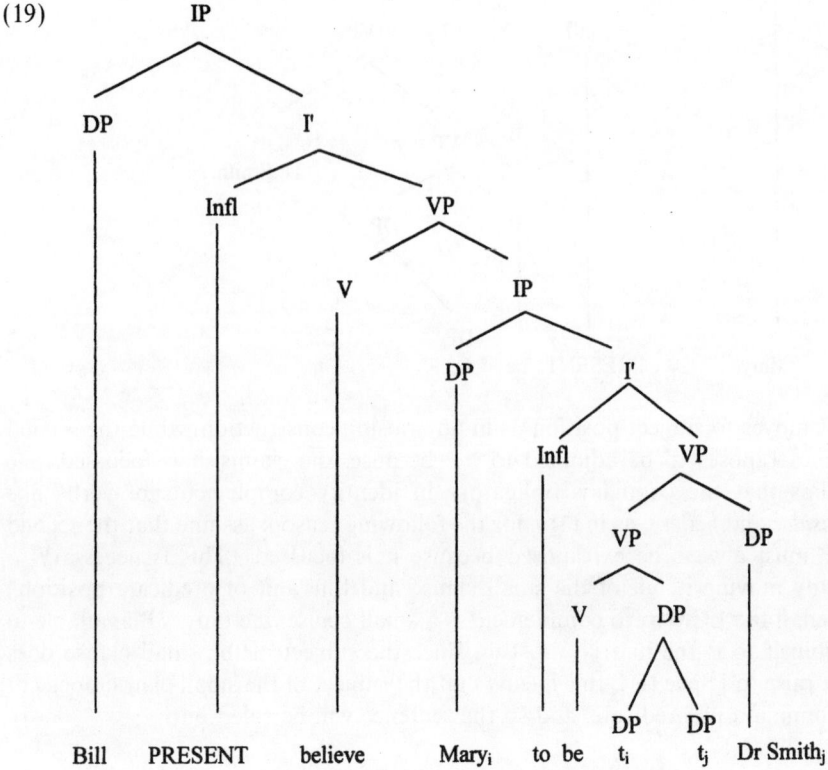

(19)

```
                           IP
                   ┌───────┴────────┐
                  DP                I'
                   │          ┌─────┴─────┐
                   │         Infl         VP
                   │          │      ┌────┴────┐
                   │          │      V         IP
                   │          │      │    ┌────┴────┐
                   │          │      │   DP        I'
                   │          │      │    │    ┌────┴────┐
                   │          │      │    │   Infl       VP
                   │          │      │    │    │    ┌────┴────┐
                   │          │      │    │    │   VP        DP
                   │          │      │    │    │  ┌─┴─┐        │
                   │          │      │    │    │  V   DP       │
                   │          │      │    │    │  │  ┌─┴─┐     │
                   │          │      │    │    │  │ DP  DP     │
                  Bill    PRESENT  believe Maryᵢ to be tᵢ   tⱼ  Dr Smithⱼ
```

There are various parts of the analysis that could be questioned, such as the basis for proposing that the second DP is indeed focussed. However, what is crucial here is the suggestion that the predication structure is saved because at S-structure DP_i c-commands DP_j. This explanation ignores the question of how the small clause complement of *be* is licensed. I have been arguing all along that argument nominals (which includes DP trace) are syntactically licenced by being subjects of predicates or by being selected as complements of heads. In particular, I have been arguing that the subject of a small clause can only be licensed as the subject of a primary predication relation. Such a relation cannot hold within the small clause complement of *be* since the constituent has two daughters, both of them nominal traces, neither of which can be predicated of the other. Heggie essentially accepts that a small clause containing two referential elements is not acceptable, but she tries to maintain the analysis of *be* in which it always takes a small clause complement for equative constructions too. She suggests raising both nominal constituents out of the small clause in which they are generated at D-structure. This cannot save her account, since the original small clause now containing only two DP traces (see 19) remains internally unlicensed, and there is no reason to think that a small clause doesn't need to be licensed just because it does not contain lexical material. We can see from this that identity, or equative, constructions in principle cannot involve a small clause complement of *be* because there is no way for that small clause to be licensed either at D-structure or at S-structure.   Assuming then that predicational copular constructions have the structure in (14) and identity, or equative, constructions have the structure in (16b), we conclude that *be* can select either an DP complement or a small clause. Since *be* can also select an IP and a CP complement, as (20a/b/c) show, we have the nice result that copula *be* subcategorises for all the inherent argument constituents:

(20) a. Mary is [t to head the delegation]$_{IP}$
      b. The problem is [that we are very late]$_{CP}$
      c. The difficult thing is [for us to convince him]$_{CP}$

Furthermore, *be* has the same subcategorisation frame as *believe* and *consider*, which also take any of the four possible argument constituents as their complements. Like the passive of forms of *believe* and *consider*, *be* does not assign an external theta-role, and thus does not assign accusative case, and when the complement is an IP or a small clause, the embedded subject is obligatorily raised to [Spec,IP] where it is assigned case. When *be* selects an DP or CP complement, however, no raising need take place, and we get the identity sentences in (16a) and (20b/c).

This raises some obvious syntactic and semantic questions about copular constructions. The syntactic issue is why equative sentences do not violate the theta-criterion or case theory. Assuming that there is a single verb *be*, and that it does not assign an external theta-role or accusative case, then in (16a), repeated here, neither DP is theta-marked, and only the DP in [Spec,IP] is case-marked.

(16a)   Mary is Dr. Smith.

That the [DP,IP] is not theta-marked seems the right conclusion, since *be* can take a pleonastic subject, indicating a non-theta-marked position, as we see in (21):

(21)   a. Look! It is John!
       b. Listen! It's the doorbell ringing!
       c. It is for you to do that.

The [DP,IP] is licensed as an argument, since it is the subject of the predicate projected by the V *be*, and it is assigned nominative case by Infl. On the assumption that *be* does not assign thematic roles, the post-verbal DPs in nominal identity sentences are neither theta-marked nor case marked. It seems reasonable to assume that *be* does not assign thematic roles: thematic roles are functions from events to their participants, and the properties of the thematic role give the nature of the participation. Since I am going to argue that the *be* defined in (13), namely the identity function on sets of events, is the same verb used in identity sentences, it would be implausible to suggest that it assigns thematic roles and thus adds participants in the identity cases. But then, if the DPs in identity sentences are not theta-marked, there is no reason for them to be case-marked, since the case filter applies only to thematic arguments, and, as we saw in chapter 7, such arguments are either theta-marked or subjects of predicates. By this definition, the complement of *be* isn't a thematic argument, and does not need to be assigned case. The argument complement of *be* in identity sentences thus contrasts with the subject of the small clause complement of *be* in predicational sentences; since this embedded subject is theta-marked, it also needs to be case-marked, and thus must raise out of the small clause to get case.

This leads us to the semantic question. If the post-copula elements in identity sentences are neither subjects of predicates nor theta-marked complements, then how are they interpreted? We will discuss this now, although, while recognising (20b/c) as genuine copular sentences, I am going to concentrate on the interpretation of nominal copular sentences of the kind in (16a).

I follow Partee (1987) in assuming that in order to interpret identity sentences, we need an operation of type-shifting. In her paper, Partee proposes that DP denotations are associated with a family of types and that a series of natural type-shifting principles map denotations from domain to domain. She assumes a principle which she calls "ident", which maps an entity of type d, and thus an individual, onto the singleton set of entities identical with the individual, which is of type $<d,t>$. (She uses 'e' and $<e,t>$, but we are reserving 'e' for the type of event). Thus JOHN is mapped onto the set of individuals who are identical with John:

(22)   a. ident: $\alpha \rightarrow <d,t>$; $ident(\alpha) = \lambda x.x = \alpha$
       b. $ident(JOHN) \rightarrow \lambda x.x = JOHN$

This operation is used when the complement of *be* is a non-predicative DP. Partee argues that *be* is the identity function on sets of predicates, and is of type $<<d,t><d,t>>$, and that the 'ident' operation is triggered by the type mismatch which occurs when *be* of type $<<d,t>,<d,t>>$ takes a complement of type d. So we lift α of type d to type $<d,t>$, denoting the set of individuals which are identical to **d**, and apply *be* to that.

(23)   BE(JOHN) $\rightarrow$ $\lambda Q \lambda x.Q(x)$ (ident(JOHN))
       $= \lambda Q \lambda x.Q(x)$ $(\lambda x.x = JOHN)$
       $= \lambda x.x = JOHN$

Partee argues that *be* is obligatory in identity sentences since it is necessary to induce the lifting operation; without it, the post-copula DP stays at type d and there is no functional relation, direct or indirect, between it and the subject. The difference, then, between sentences like (1a) and (1b), repeated here in (24), is that while a predicate like *very clever* in (24a) can be directly predicated of its subject, the referential post-copula element in (24b) cannot be directly predicated of the subject.

(24)   a. I believe/consider Mary (to be) very clever/a clever woman.
       b. I believe/consider Mary *(to be) Dr. Smith.

Be is obligatory in (24b) to trigger the raising.

Assuming the basics of Partee's account and the semantic framework developed in this book, we will need a more complex type-shifting rule, since in our event-based theory, *be* takes a set of events as its complement. The appropriate 'ident' rule will have to associate with an individual α the set of events in which α is a participant, and which are evidence for the fact that the individual α exists. We define an EXIST relation as in (25), which is the relation between an individual and the set of events for which that individual is the value of some thematic role (in other words, is a thematically defined participant in the events). 'R' ranges over the set Θ of recognised thematic roles (including those functions from adjectivally denoted events to participants which we have just called 'Arg'):

(25)   EXIST $=_{def} \lambda x \lambda e.\exists R[R \in \Theta \wedge R(e) = x]$

In other words, e is an existence event for α, or evidence that α exists, if α is the value of some thematic role for e.

We can now use EXIST(e,x) to define the necessary 'ident function' (although this will be revised in the next chapter where I argue that *be* is not in fact semantically empty):

(26) $ident(\alpha) \rightarrow \lambda e.EXIST(e,\alpha) \wedge \alpha = x$
       $= \lambda e.\exists R[R \in \Theta \wedge R(e) = \alpha \wedge \alpha = x]$

So ident maps an individual α onto the set of existence events for α in which $x = \alpha$.

Mary is Dr Smith then asserts that there is an existence event for Dr Smith in which Mary is identical to Dr Smith, which gives us the interpretation that we want. The derivation is as in (27):

(27)   Dr. Smith   → DR. SMITH

[be Dr. Smith]$_{V'}$ → $\lambda E.E$ (ident(DR. SMITH))
= $\lambda E.E$ ($\lambda e.$EXIST(e, DR. SMITH) $\wedge$ DR. SMITH = x)
= $\lambda e.$EXIST(e, DR. SMITH) $\wedge$ DR. SMITH = x

[be Dr. Smith]$_{VP}$ → $\lambda x \lambda e.$EXIST(e, DR. SMITH)
                                            $\wedge$ DR. SMITH = x
                                                            (Predicate Formation)
[is Dr. Smith]$_{I'}$ → $\lambda x \lambda e.$EXIST(e, DR. SMITH)
                                            $\wedge$ DR. SMITH = x $\wedge$ Pres(e)

[Mary is Dr. Smith]$_{IP}$ → $\lambda x \lambda e.$EXIST(e, DR. SMITH)
                                            $\wedge$ DR. SMITH = x $\wedge$ Pres(e)(MARY)
= $\lambda e.$EXIST(e, DR. SMITH) $\wedge$ DR. SMITH = MARY $\wedge$ Pres(e)
= $\exists e$[EXIST(e, DR. SMITH) $\wedge$ DR. SMITH = MARY $\wedge$ Pres(e)]
                                                            (by $\exists$-closure)

= [DR. SMITH = MARY]

I assume, as does Partee, that *Dr. Smith* starts off at type d and that type-shifting is triggered by the mismatch between *be* and the DP. We raise *Dr. Smith* from the type of individuals to $<e,t>$, at which it denotes the set of existence events for the denotation of *Dr. Smith*, in which x is identical to the denotation of *Dr. Smith*. At this stage, the x variable is free. It is bound by the λ-operator introduced at the VP level, and the result is applied to the subject argument. Finally we get the usual default existential closure.

Note here the relation between the English ident rule, given in (26) and the Hebrew ident rule, repeated from chapter 8 in (28a). This can be expressed as (28b) using the EXIST relation; it is the predicate expression derived from (26) by abstracting over the x variable, since Infl triggers raising to an expression of type $<d,<e,t>>$, the type of its complement.

(28)   a.   Hebrew Ident: $\alpha \rightarrow \lambda x \lambda e. \exists R \in \Theta[R(e) = \alpha \wedge \alpha = x]$ (8:(73))
         b. $\alpha \rightarrow \lambda x \lambda e.$EXIST(e,$\alpha$) $\wedge$ $\alpha = x$

(I assume that in fact Hebrew has both forms of ident available, since in past and future Hebrew identity sentence, the post-copula DP is the complement of the fully verbal *h.y.y.* copula, which takes complements of the form $<e,t>$.)

What is the relation between the type-shifting account of interpretation of identity sentences given in this section and the claim that Infl in Hebrew, and *be* in English are required to create a syntactic predicate? Let us look first at the type-shifting mechanism. It is important to stress, as Partee (1987) does, that the shifting rules in (26) and (28) are not the meaning of *be* and Infl respectively, but operations triggered by them. They cannot be the meanings of *be* and Infl since in the simple predicational *be* such as (29a) and Hebrew inflected small clauses as in (29b), no such operation is used.

(29) a. John is tall.
   b. dani [[hu]$_{\text{Infl}}$ nexmad]$_{\text{I'}}$
      dani Pron nice
      "Dani is nice."

Second, *be* and Infl must be syntactically expressed to trigger the type-shifting, as can be seen from the fact that the examples in (30) are not grammatical:

(30) a. *I believe Dr Smith Mary.
   b. *dani mar yosef
      dani mr yosef

In other words, type-shifting via the ident operations is not triggered by a simple mismatch of the type illustrated in (31), where neither sister is of a type which can be applied to the other:

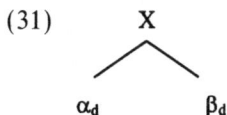

(31)   X

     α$_d$ β$_d$

If it were, then we would assume that β could be shifted to the type of a predicate, and that the constituent X in (30) would form an instance of predication, and be a legitimate small clause. The unacceptability of (30) shows that this is not possible.

   I suggest that what makes (31) unacceptable as the input to type-shifting is precisely the fact that the X node is not syntactically licensed as a small clause. I assume, following Klein and Sag (1985) and Partee and Rooth (1983) that semantic interpretation is type-driven. This means that if we have a node C, with two daughter nodes A and B, the constraint governing the application of one to the other is that the result must be an expression of the type of C. Type-shifting is similarly type-driven: if A or B must be shifted in order for application to take place, the constraint governing what shifts are possible is that they must enable application to result in an expression of the type C. The crucial thing is that it is the syntax which tells us what type C actually is. For example, look at a tree like (32), in which both AP and N are analysed as expressions of type $<d, <e,t>>$, and NP is also. (See the discussion in the final section of this chapter about the relation between nominals of type $<d,t>$ and predicate nominals.)

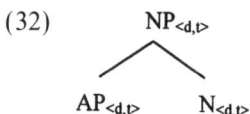

(32)   NP$_{<d,t>}$

     AP$_{<d,t>}$ N$_{<d,t>}$

Neither AP nor N can be applied to the other, since they are both of type $<d,t>$ so one will have to be shifted. Since we know that the node dominating the AP and N has NP properties rather than AP properties, the obvious move is to treat AP as a modifier and to shift it to $<<d,t>, <d,t>>$. What tells us that this move is the correct one is that we know independently that the dominating node is an NP, that NP expressions (bare nominals without determiners) denote expressions of type $<d,t>$, and that the result of application of one daughter to another must result in an expression of this type.

Two facts are crucial here. One is that we know independently that denotations of NPs are of type $<d,t>$. Second is the fact that we have independent syntactic evidence that the node in question is in fact an NP. This evidence comes at least in part, from X-bar theory, which dictates that the node dominating a nominal head must be a projection of that head, and from the way in which the node behaves with respect to a number of other syntactic tests. The important thing is that, as X-bar theory dictates, the syntactic properties of a node depend on the syntactic features projected up from its head; they are not determined by the relationship between its daughter nodes. (This is why it is possible for maximal XPs to dominate only non-branching nodes.)

Now we come back to (31). We have noted several times in the course of this book (e.g. chapters 2:2.3, 5:5.5) that small clauses are not projections of any lexical head. We saw that we had great difficulty choosing what to label the node dominating a small clause, since the syntactic label on a phrase is determined by the head of the phrase and small clauses lack such a head. Small clauses, as I already said, are, as far as I know, the only syntactic category which is exocentric (that is not projected from a head). As a consequence, a small clause is the only syntactic category which is defined and identified on the basis of the syntactic relation which holds between its daughters. A small clause is a syntactic primary predication relation unmediated by Infl, and can only be identified as such. The result is that a structure of the form in (30), repeated here in the tree in (33), consisting of two syntactic argument expressions, cannot form a small clause, since neither argument can be syntactically predicated of the other.

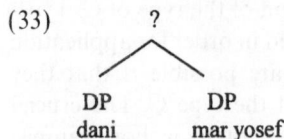

(33)   ?
         ╱‾‾‾‾‾‾╲
      DP   DP
      dani   mar yosef

But, if the syntactic structure in (33) is not syntactically licensed, and the node dominating the two DPs cannot be assigned to a syntactic category, then it also cannot be assigned a type. In such a case, there is no typal information to drive an APPLY operation at the level below. Both DPs denote expressions of type d, so there is no natural APPLY operation available, and since we do not have an output for functional application, there is nothing to drive type-shifting to apply to either of the expressions. Compare (32) with the inflected form in (34):

(34)

```
              IP
            /    \
         DP        I'
         |       /    \
         |     Infl     DP
        dani   hu     mar yosef
```

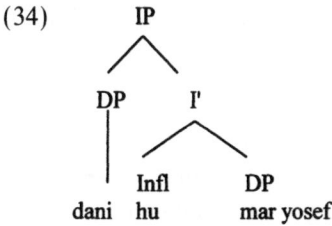

Here, we know independently that *hu* is an inflectional element of type $<<d, <e,t>>, <d, <e,t>>>$, that it must be dominated by an I' node, and that the type of I' is $<d, <e,t>>$. This gives the information, lacking in (33), necessary to trigger shifting the type of the complement of Infl to $<d, <e,t>>$.

In English, *be* performs the same function as Infl does in these examples. I argued in the previous chapter that the presence of Infl in matrix present tense identity sentences in Hebrew was essential in order to create a syntactic predicate node. I then argued that *be* has the same function in complements of *consider* type verbs. We see now how the syntactic-semantic interaction works. Infl, of type $<<d, <e,t>>, <d, <e,t>>>$, projects a predicate I' node of type $<d, <e,t>>$, while *be*, of type $<<e,t>, <e,t>>$, projects a V' node of type $<e,t>$, which is the input to predicate formation at the VP level. Each of them allows a DP complement in the syntax, and the resulting structural configuration triggers the type-shifting which allows the structures to be interpreted. What forces the use of *be* in English seems to be the fact that English Infl does not ever allow a non-verbal complement.

There is one use where what are normally assumed to be argument expressions of type d appear in predicative position. This is the so-called 'role' used discussed in Doron (1983), and already mentioned in chapter 8, in example (9):

(35) (Doron p116)
ha-yom dani (hu)   ben gurion ve roni (hu)   moSe Saret
the day dani (Pron) ben-gurion & roni (Pron) moshe sharet
"Today, Dani is Ben-Gurion and Roni is Moshe Sharet."

Doron (1983) points out that here a name is interpreted not as referring to an individual, but as expressing a role, and it can appear in a matrix small clause without a pronominal copula. (35) would be appropriate if parts are being assigned in a play. English displays the same use in (36):

(36) a. Jane is Ophelia in the new production of Hamlet.
      b. Today we will make Jane Ophelia.

Partee (1987) argues that these 'role' uses are intensional. Landman (in progress) argues that these intensional roles are in argument position and are not predicates. He suggests that in (35) and (36) the role-denoting DPs are complements of null prepositions; the apparent predicativeness of the role-denoting DP is due to the fact that the preposition of which they are the argument projects a predicative PP phrase.

Definite descriptions do appear to have a true predicative use, as in (37), and I'll come back to these at the end of the chapter.

(37)   a. I consider John the Mayor.
       b. ?I believe him the true owner of this land.

One further predicative usage of proper names that we find in English is illustrated in (38), where the proper name is being used as a common noun.

(38)   a. I consider the Mayor a real Gatsby.
       b. Winston is a real Churchill.

I assume that here there is a lexical rule mapping a proper name onto a nominal expression denoting a characteristic associated with it, and that the predicate nominals in (38) behave in the same way as any other indefinite.

One last point. Landman (in progress) argues that there is no lowering rule from $<<d,t>,t>$ into $<e,t>$: the examples in (39) are unacceptable because of an irreparable type mismatch, since *be* cannot take a complement of type $<<d,t>,t>$:

(39)   a. *Mary is every lawyer.
       b. *I consider Mary every lawyer.

Every lawyer is of type $<<d,t>,t>$, and as there is no natural way to get it to the type of sets of events, it cannot be a complement of *be*. Note that (39b) is much worse than (39a), which is surprising if they both have the same problem, namely a generalised quantifier in predicative position. But this brings us back to the issue of syntactic versus semantic licensing. (39a) can be assigned a legal syntactic structure, in which *be* takes a DP as its complement, but the semantic interpretation breaks down because of the type mismatch between *be* and its generalised quantifier complement. (39b), however, cannot even be assigned a legal syntactic structure, as discussed above, since we cannot form a small clause from *Mary* and the non-predicative *every lawyer*.

9.4. AGAINST PREDICATE RAISING ANALYSES OF IDENTITY SENTENCES

9.4.1. *The predicate raising approach*

There is a third approach to explaining the relation between identity and predicative sentences (aside from the 'two verb' approach which we have discarded and Partee's type raising approach which we have essentially adopted). This third approach I call the predicate-raising approach, and it has been argued for in particular in Moro (1991, 1997), Heggie (1988), and Heycock (1991, 1992) (although Heycock and Kroch (1999) presents arguments against predicate-raising). The approach seeks to maintain the principle that *be* has a single subcategorisation frame, and at the same time it tries to explain why a post-copula DP behaves differently when it is an argument and when it is predicative. The original impetus for the approach seems to come from a suggestion by Williams (1983b, 1994) who suggests that *be* selects for an argument and a predicate (i.e. is of type $<<d,t>, <d,t>>$) but is special in that it can take them in either order. The family of predicate raising theories (although not Williams') generally assumes that *be* subcategorises for a small clause complement and is a raising verb. However, unlike other raising verbs, either the subject of the small clause or the predicate of the small clause can raise. Thus a sentences like (40) can be derived from either of the two structures in (41):

(40)   My best friend is the mayor.

(41)   a. [e [is [my best friend the mayor]$_{SC}$]$_{VP}$]$_{IP}$
       b. [e [is [the mayor my best friend]$_{SC}$]$_{VP}$]$_{IP}$

If the D-structure is (41a) then the semantic subject of the predication is the DP in [Spec,IP], namely *my best friend*, but if the D-structure is (41b), then despite surface appearances, the DP *the mayor* is the semantic subject of the predication relation and *my best friend* is the predicate, and (40) is what is called a 'reverse copular construction'.

The idea that the [DP,IP] can be either the sentential subject or the sentential predicate was developed in Williams (1983b) and Partee (1986) to analyse the difference between specificational and predicational pseudoclefts, which is a topic that I am not going to go into here. But I am going to argue against that claims that (40) is structurally ambiguous in the way just outlined, and against the idea that the apparent subject of the copular construction may be its predicate.

Let us first look at the data that these theories want to explain.

Much of the original discussion about copular constructions comes from an unpublished paper by Longobardi (1984). Longobardi offers an analysis of Italian data and proposes a structure for identity sentence which is independently available in Italian for sentences with post-verbal subjects, but which is not a structure of English. He proposes that the subject of identity sentences is in the post-verbal subject position adjoined to VP, which Burzio (1986) argues is the position generally occupied by postposed subjects. Since postposed subjects are not a general phenomenon in English, and there is no post-verbal VP adjoined position available, I will assume that this analysis is not appropriate for the English data, and I will not try to comment on whether it is right for Italian. Longobardi's paper does, however, discuss differences between the post-verbal DP in predicative and identity sentences which also turn up in English. These are the main points to note:

(i) Longobardi (1984) notes that extraction out of a post-copula DP argument is much more difficult that from a post-copula predicative DP. He brings the contrast between the examples in (41) to support his point, and Moro (1997) makes the same point using the contrast between (43b) and (44b):

(42)   a. *The producer, who one of the soloists is the daughter of ...
       b.   The producer, who one of the soloists is a close friend of ...

(43) a. The picture of the president was the cause of the riot.
     b. Which riot was the picture of the president the cause of?

(44) a. The cause of the riot was the picture of the president.
     b. *Who was the cause of the riot the picture of?

(ii) Longobardi further notes that relativisation out of the post-copula position does not work if the position is filled by an argument, while relativisation out of the predicative post-copula DP is fine:

(45) a. *Mary, who his best friend is t, likes to go to the beach.
     b. *The girl that his best friend is t is here.
     c. *It is Mary that his best friend has been t.

(46) a. His best friend, which Mary is, is what Jane wanted to be.
     b. Mary is the scholar that Bill might have been.
     c. It is his best friend that Mary is/has always been, and not his lover.

(iii) Another test showing the difference between argument and predicative post copula DPs is the behaviour of clitics. Longobardi (1984) shows this in Italian, and Heggie (1988) shows how this works in French. I give the French examples here. The clitic *le* can replace a predicate XP (where XP can be DP) but not a referential or argument DP. Thus:

(47) a. Monsieur Ducros l'est, mon docteur.
        Mr   Ducros it is, my   doctor
        "Mr Ducros is my doctor."
     b. *Mon docteur l'est, Monsieur Ducros
        "My doctor it is, Mr   Ducros." (Heggie 3:100)

Furthermore, the clitic pronoun is clearly replacing a predicate nominal since it stays in the masculine singular and does not agree with the predicate:

(48) a. Jean et Marie sont les parents de Christine.
        John and Mary are the parents of Christine
     b. *Jean et Marie les   sont.
        John and Mary them are
     c. Jean et Marie le sont.
        John and Mary it are

(iv) Longobardi notes that the post-copula position in an equative appears to be a scope island:

(49) a. It is necessary that you call only Mary.
     b. I want you to call only Mary.

(50) A solution is to visit only Mary.

(49a) means either only Mary is such that it is necessary that you call her or it is necessary that only Mary is such that you call her, in other words, it is necessary that only Mary is called by you. Similarly (49b) means either only

Mary is such that I want you to call her or I want only Mary to be called by you. (50), on the other hand, can only mean a solution is to visit Mary and no-one else, and not that only Mary is such that visiting her constitutes a solution.

(v) Heggie (1988) brings an argument about properties of the putative subject. She claims that in apparent equative (identity) sentences, where the post-copula DP is an proper name, intensive reflexives like *himself* can, unusually, not attach to the apparent subject. She presents the following judgements about the distribution of *himself* in this use (but note that I shall argue in section 9.4.3 that (51c) should not be starred):

(51) a. John$_i$ himself$_i$ is the organiser of the group.
      b. John$_i$ is the organiser of the group himself$_i$.
      c. *The organiser of the group$_i$ himself$_i$ is John.
      d. The organiser of the group is John$_i$ himself$_i$.

Assuming that "himself" as an intensifier can adjoin only to definite arguments, Heggie suggests that the unacceptability of (51c) indicates that the organiser of the group is not a subject argument, but rather a raised predicate.

The line of explanation that the predicate raising approach gives for these facts is that the post-copula DP in identity sentences is in fact a subject, and is thus constrained by conditions on subjects, where conditions on extraction from subject position and from within subjects are particularly relevant.

9.4.2. *Details of the theories*

The central claim of predicate raising theories is that *be* takes a small clause complement, and that either the subject or the predicate of the small clause can raise to [Spec,IP]. I shall ask two kinds of questions about these theories. One is whether they are internally coherent, and the other is how they deal with 'true equatives'. We'll look at the second issue first. The general claim is that at D-structure, there is a structure like (52), and that the predication relation between subject and predicate holds locally within the small clause:

(52) [e PRES be [[John]$_{DP}$ [my best friend]$_{DP}$]$_{SC}$].

Now, in most of the examples in section 9.4.1, no more than one DP is a proper name and at least one DP is a definite description, which is in principle ambiguous between a referential and a predicative reading. Where there is only one definite description, the D-structure of the sentence is unambiguous. Both the examples in (53) must be derived from (52), (53a) by subject raising and (53b) by predicate raising, since *John* is presumably not the predicate of the small clause:

(53) a. John is my best friend.
      b. My best friend is John.

Where both DPs are definite descriptions there are two possible D-structures depending on which DP is analysed as a predicate nominal. Both (54a) and (54b) can be derived from either D-structure in (55), depending on whether the small clause subject or predicate are raised:

(54)   a. The Mayor is my best friend.
       b. My best friend is the Mayor.

(55)   a. [e PRES be [[the Mayor]$_{DP}$ [my best friend]$_{DP}$]$_{SC}$].
       b. [e PRES be [[my best friend]$_{DP}$ [the Mayor]$_{DP}$]$_{SC}$]].

Problems arise when we have an identity sentence where both DPs are proper names:

(56)   Mary is Professor Smith.

Doron (1983) has argued extensively that both DPs in (56) must be arguments. For example, they can both be modified by non-restrictive relative clauses:

(57)   a. Mary, who you know from the tennis club, is Professor Smith, who teaches maths at the university.
       b. The duty nurse, who is very efficient, is Rina, who I am very fond of.

On the raising theory, the D-structure for (56) would have to be either (58a) or (58b):

(58)   a. [e PRES be [[Mary]$_{DP}$ [Professor Smith]$_{DP}$]$_{SC}$]].
       b. [e PRES be [[Professor Smith]$_{DP}$ [Mary]$_{DP}$]$_{SC}$]].

In each case, we have at D-structure a small clause with a DP which cannot be a predicate in predicative position, and thus a predication relation which cannot be licensed. Predicate raising theories divide into strong and weak depending on how they deal with this question. 'Strong' forms of the hypothesis assume that the predicate raising account applies also to sentences like (56), and that the examples in (58) are legal D-structures. Moro (1997) is an example of this 'strong' approach. He analyses (56) as ambiguous between (59a) and (59b):

(59)   a. [Mary$_i$ PRES be [[t]$_{DPi}$ [Professor Smith]$_{DP}$]$_{SC}$]].
       b. [Mary$_i$ PRES be [[Professor Smith]$_{DP}$ [t]$_{DPi}$]$_{SC}$]].

In (59a), the subject of IP has been raised from the subject of the small clause and *Professor Smith* must be analysed as a predicate, and in (59b) *Mary* has been raised from the predicate position indicating that it and its trace are predicates. If we treat the proper names in (59) as potential predicates, then we have no explanation for the obligatoriness of *be* in small clause identity sentences such as (60a) and for Pron in the corresponding Hebrew small clauses, as in (60b), since it should be equally possible to have a small clause with a proper name in predicative position there:

(60)   a. *They consider/believe Professor Smith Mary.
       b. *rina doktor cohen.

If we do not analyse the proper names as potential predicates, then in both cases we have a small clause complement which does not consist of a predication structure, as we saw in (58) and (59). As we have seen, the theory of small clauses and predication that we have been developing means that these structures are unacceptable since there is no way of internally licensing the small clause.

'Weak' theories assume that (56) is a 'true equative' to which the predicate raising account does not apply. The most explicit weak account is that of Heggie (1988), who argues that predicate raising covers what she calls 'pseudo-equatives' in which we have at S-structure a definite description in [Spec,IP] and a proper name in post-copula position; the point of her analysis is to explain that in these case the post-copula DP behaves like an argument, and the pre-copula DP does not behave like a subject, as was illustrated in (51). Where both pre- and post-copula DPs have argument properties, she analyses them as true equatives. However, as we saw when we looked at her analysis of true equatives in examples (17–19) in section 9.3 above, her theory maintain the principle that *be* subcategorises for a small clause in true-equatives at the cost of assuming small clauses where both constituents are arguments, which are not internally licensed via the predication relation. The small clause in the structure that she proposed in (19) has the same problem as Moro's (59), notwithstanding the fact that in (19) the small clause consists of two traces.

The failure of any of the predicate raising analyses to deal with true equatives is a major flaw of the approach. As soon as it becomes clear that *be* cannot select a small clause in true equative constructions, and must thus select a single DP argument, the way becomes open to analyse so-called 'pseudo-equatives' as also taking a single DP argument complement. The post-copula argument complements in the examples in section 9.4.1 are then simply arguments without having to be analysed as 'stranded' subjects of small clauses, and a much simpler account of the construction can be given. Such an account is exactly what I gave in section 9.3, and I will show in section 9.4.3 below that it can explain the data given in examples (42)–(51). First, though, I want to examine the rest of the theory of predicate raising on its own terms.

The second way in which predicate raising theories differ from each other is the question of where the predicate raises to. When the subject of the small clause raises, we have a simple argument raising structure, as in (61):

(61) $[\text{Jane}_i \ [\text{Infl} \ [\text{be} \ [t_i \ \text{my best friend}]_{SC}]_{VP}]_{I'}]_{IP}$.

Moro (1991, 1997) and Heycock (1992) argue that the predicate also raises to [Spec,IP] and that the structure for (62a) is (62b):

(62)   a. The leader of the party is Mary.
       b. $[[\text{The leader of the party}]_{DP_i} [\text{is}_k [t_k \ [\text{Mary} \ t_i]_{SC}]_{VP}]_{I'}]_{IP}$.

There are a number of empirical problems with this claim – aside from the intuitive strangeness of having a non-argument in the most essentially argument position in the sentence (see also the discussion in Heycock and Kroch 1999).

First, as discussed in Heycock and Kroch (1999), we see that if [Spec,IP] can be filled by a predicate in a copular construction, there are very strong restrictions as to what predicate it can be. Although copular constructions can have a variety of constituents in predicate position, predicate raising – if it exists – applies only to definite DPs, and not to other XPs, nor even to indefinite DPs. (63b/d), where an AP and an indefinite DP have been raised, do not have the status of normal copular constructions, inverse or otherwise:

(63)   a. Mary is very clever.
  b. Very clever is Mary.
  c. Jane is a teacher.
  d. A teacher is Jane.

Note that constructions like (63b/d) do occur as stylistically marked, formal or literary uses, and appear to be a form of predicate topicalisation. (62a) is not marked at all – which means that predicate raising must be distinguished as an operation from predicate topicalisation illustrated in (63b/d). Second, the higher DP in (62) behaves as an argument with respect to raising to subject and clefting, and can be the subject of a small clause predicate in ECM complements. This is not the case with the topicalised predicates illustrated in (63). (64) contrasts with (65). And note also that the cleft in (64b) requires the argument relative pronoun *who* and not *that*, which is further indication that it is an argument and not a predicate:

(64)   a. The leader seems to be Mary.
  b. It is the leader who/*that is Mary.
  c. I consider the leader to be Mary.

(65)   a. *A teacher/Very clever seems to be Mary.
  b. *It is very clever/a teacher that/who is Mary.
  c. *I consider a teacher/very clever to be Mary.

It is interesting to contrast these example with locative PP subjects, where the same tests indicate that the locative PP does have some true subject properties. (66) and (67) contrast with (65). ((66) is based on Levin and Rappaport Hovav (1995); for further discussion see there, also Bresnan (1993)):

(66)   a. To this cone$_i$ seem [t$_i$ to adhere bushy twigs].
  b. It is to this cone$_i$ that [t$_i$ adhere bushy twigs].

(67)   a. Under this chair$_i$ seems t$_i$ to be a good place to hide.
  b. I consider under this chair a good place to hide.

I'm not going to discuss locative subjects at all here: I include the examples only to show that it is in principle possible for non-nominals to be subjects, but that then they do acquire genuine subject properties.

Third, on the same line of argument, the putative raised predicate behaves like a genuine subject argument with respect to agreement. (This is apparently not the case in Italian, but I am restricting the discussion to English copular constructions here.) The verb agrees with the subject in number, as long as the subject can be treated as an argument. In (68a) the subject is a conjoined [DP + DP] and the verb is plural. If a conjoined predicate is raised the verb does not become plural. Note also that locative PP subjects do induce agreement.

(68) a. The Prime Minister and the Minister of Defence in the 1992 Labour government were (both) Yitzhak Rabin.
      b. The leader of the group and the organiser of the party are both Mary.
      c. A teacher and educator is/*are John.
      d. Rich and famous is/*are John.
      e. In the chair and in the sofa are both comfortable places to sit.

We saw above, in (57), that argument DPs can be modified by non-restrictive relative clauses headed by *who*, binding a trace in an argument position. Predicate expressions can be modified by non-restrictives headed by *which*, where *which* binds a variable in a predicative position, as (69) shows.

(69) They think John mean, which is a horrible thing to be t.

Definite descriptions in the subject of identity sentences can only be modified by argument non-restrictives, as shown in (70). (70) shows that where the definite description can be interpreted as either predicative or referential, either type of modification is possible:

(70) a. *The murderer, which is a horrible thing to be, is John.
      b. The (alleged) murderer, who was acquitted yesterday, is John.

(71) a. John is the murderer, which is a horrible thing to be.
      b. It has just been revealed that John Smith is the alleged murderer, who was finally acquitted yesterday.

  A further point, noted by Heycock (1991) in a footnote on page 177, is that the definite description can introduce a discourse referent on which a later pronoun can be dependent, indicating that it is an argument and not a predicate:

(72) Now I realise that the murderer was John. He was wearing size 12 shoes and only John has feet that size.

  There is yet another problem with the predicate-raising analysis, and that is to do with restrictions on the post-copula DP. Kadmon (1987) has shown that cardinal DPs, instead of having their usual 'at least' reading, have an 'exactly' reading in this position:

(73) a. You get a group discount if you bring two children to the museum.
      b. The reporters are two children.

(73a) implies that you get a discount if you bring at least two children; I would not expect to be told that the discount was not available because I came with three children. (73b), on the other hand, has an exactly reading; Thus (74b) sounds contradictory (or a correction of an error) while (74a) does not:

(74) a. Can I have the discount please? I have brought two children – in fact I have brought three.

b. #The reporters are two children – in fact they are three.

Landman (2000) shows we should expect to get an 'exactly' reading when a cardinal DP is interpreted as a predicate and an 'at least' reading when it is interpreted as a generalised quantifier. The infelicity of (74b) is explained, then, if this is a position in which a cardinal DP can be interpreted only as a predicate. These facts about the interpretation of (73b) and (74b) are explained if *two children* is unambiguously in predicate position. But the predicate raising account of copular constructions requires *two children* in (73b/74b) to be either a predicate or an argument, depending on whether the structure of the sentence is analogous to (59a) or (59b):

(75) a. [The reporters$_i$ [are [t$_i$ two children]$_{SC}$]$_{VP}$]$_{IP}$.

b. [The reporters$_i$ [are [two children t$_i$]$_{SC}$]$_{VP}$]$_{IP}$.

It thus wrongly predicts that *two* children in (73b/74b) should be ambiguous between an 'exactly' and an 'at least' reading depending on whether the sentence is derived by subject raising, as in (75a) or predicate raising as in (75b). Since there is no 'at least' reading available, we have evidence that there is no predicate raising here, and that the cardinal DP is unequivocally in predicate position. (In principle, we can use the same argument to claim that, on the predicate-raising account, *two children* in (76) should have an 'exactly' reading, as well as an 'at least' reading, since it supposed to be analysed as either a raised subject or a raised predicate.

(76) Two children are the reporters (in fact three are).

But since, if there were a predicative 'exactly' reading, it would be a special case of the 'at least' reading anyway, it is not possible to show that this is an incorrect prediction.) Note that the discussion of (73b/74b) is particularly important, since, while the other tests we have discussed indicate that the apparent subject of the copular construction is genuinely an argument, this test shows that the post-copula expression is genuinely a predicate and cannot be analysed as a non-raised subject of a small clause.

This accumulated data leads to the conclusion that there is no reason to think the apparent subject in sentences like *The leader is Mary* to be anything but the subject. The predicate raising hypothesis would lead us to suppose that the structure of this sentence is basically such that *Mary* is the subject, and *is the leader* is in some sense predicated of it, but we have seen that the definite DP behaves as if it is [Spec,IP], and as if it is a perfectly normal argument there.

Heggie (1988) claims a different structure for 'reverse copular sentences'. She argues that the raised predicate is not in subject position, but in [Spec,CP] and that predicate raising is a form of topicalisation. She argues that "The leader is Mary" has the structure in (77):

(77) a. The leader is Mary.

b. [The leader$_j$ [is$_k$ [Mary$_i$ [t$_k$ [t$'_k$ [t$_i$ t$_j$]$_{SC}$]$_{VP}$]$_{I'}$]$_{IP}$]$_{C'}$]$_{CP}$.

However, as Heggie herself points out, the highest DP in the 'pseudo-equatives' behaves as if it is in [Spec,IP] and not as if it is in [Spec,CP] with respect to a number of syntactic tests. Heycock (1991) lists the following problems with the assumption that the apparent subject is not in [Spec, IP], some of which have already been mentioned in a different context. We have already seen in (64a) that the highest DP can be input to standard raising to subject, and that an apparent reverse copular construction can be the complement of ECM verbs, despite the fact that these take bare IPs and not CPs as complements. (77a) can also appear embedded under Comp, can be the input to subject-aux inversion, and, despite the implications of (77b) that only one aux can be raised to C, multiple auxiliaries are possible.

(78) a. I wonder whether the leader is Mary at the moment
      b. Is the leader Mary at the moment?
      c. The leader may have been John at that point.

All these imply that (77a) is a simple IP. Heggie suggests that (64a) and (78) are 'true equatives', where the highest DP is in [Spec,IP], but there seems to be no independent evidence that the core predication in (77a) is in any way different from those in the examples in (78). Furthermore, Heggie's analysis in (77) is open to exactly the same criticisms as those made above: we have already seen that in so-called pseudo equatives, there is plenty of evidence that a pre-copula definite description in [Spec,IP] behaves like an argument, which the structure in (77b) doesn't allow for. What remains now is to explain the data discussed in section 9.4.1, and to show that the account of copular constructions which I gave above is adequate to explain it.

9.4.3. *Solutions*

How can we explain the contrasts in (42–51) that predicate-raising accounts point out? I argued that *be* selects a small clause in predicative constructions and an argument DP in identity constructions and that the structures of typical predicational and identity sentences are as in (79), and the question is how these structures explain (42–51):

(79) a. [Jane$_i$ [is [t$_i$ polite]$_{SC}$]$_{VP}$]$_{IP}$.
      b. [Mary [is [Professor Smith]$_{DP}$]$_{VP}$]$_{IP}$.

  (i) The first problem was that relativisation,and other forms of extraction out of the argument post-copula DP was impossible, while extraction out of a post-copula predicate DP was fine. The relevant examples, (42)–(44) above, are repeated here:

(80) a. *The producer, who one of the soloists is the daughter of ...
      b. The producer, who one of the soloists is a close friend of ...
         (Longobardi (1984).

(81) a. The picture of the president was the cause of the riot.
      b. Which riot was the picture of the president the cause of?

(82)   a.   The cause of the riot was the picture of the president.
        b.   *Who was the cause of the riot the picture of? (Moro 1997).

Moro takes the ungrammaticality of (80a) and (82b) as indications that the post-copula positions here are subjects, since it is a well-known fact that it is not possible to extract out of subject position. But while these data may well be evidence that the post-copula position in identity sentences has some of the same properties as a subject position, that is a far cry from its actually being a subject.

It is a well known fact, going back to Ross (1967), that extraction out of complex DPs is difficult, and that the results are more or less degraded depending on a variety of different factors. Chomsky (1986b) argues that extraction out of a predicate is always possible (he argues that such extraction involves adjunction to the predicate on the way up, but the details need not bother us here), and that extraction out of an argument is possible if the argument is theta-marked by a properly governing, and thus lexical, head. (In Chomsky (1986b) he develops a closely related notion of 'L-marking' (for 'lexical marking'); again the details are not important). This means that extraction out of subject position will be impossible (i.e. the subject is a barrier for extraction), since the subject is governed by Infl, which is non-lexical; thus the subject position will never be properly governed. One possible reason why a theta-marked complement of a head is not a barrier for extraction is that reanalysis occurs, forming a complex predicate out of the head and its theta-marked complement. Reanalysis is a form of complex predicate formation, but one which, unlike predicate absorption, pays attention to the lexical content of the constituents to be reanalysed, and not just the formal syntactic relation between them. (See for example the discussion of reanalysis in Italian causative constructions in Rizzi (1982)). So in (83) extraction from the complex DP will be possible since the V and its theta-marked DP complement have been reanalysed as a complex predicate, and extraction is as simple as from any predicate:

(83)   What$_i$ do you [want a story about t$_i$]

A number of factors other than theta-marking influence whether extraction can take place, indicating that the reanalysis is constrained by a variety of factors. I bring the following data not to begin to embark on a theory of reanalysis, but to show how difficult it is to extract from argument DPs even in theta-marked complement positions. The data are as follows: (i) extraction is more acceptable from a DP adjacent to the verb, on the condition that the V takes a single complement. Thus (84a) is more acceptable than (84b), and (84c) is much less acceptable, if at all:

(84)   a.   Who$_i$ did you read [a new book by t$_i$]?
        b.   ?Who$_i$ did you send [Mary] [a new book by t$_i$]?
        c.   ??Who$_i$ did you send [a new book by t$_i$] to Mary?

(ii) extraction is more acceptable if the target is contained in an indefinite DP and least acceptable if the containing DP is a quantifier, as in (85):

(85) a.   Who did you read a new book by t?
      b.   ??Who did you read the new book by t?
      c.   ??Who did you read each new book by t?

  (iii) extraction is less good if it is from a direct object which is not a theme.

(86) a.   ?Which book did you send the review of t to the author?
      b.   ?Which book did you send the author the review of t?
      c.   ??Which book did you send the author of t the review?

  (iv) the combination of factors is cumulative. (87c), which is the least acceptable, involves extraction from a quantified DP which is not adjacent to the verb:

(87) a.   ?Who did you send Mary a new book by t?
      b.   ??Who did you send Mary the new book by t?
      c.   ???Who did you send Mary each new book by t?

I argued in section 3 that the best analysis of equatives is that they contain
a DP as the complement of *be*, but that *be*, the identity predicate on sets of
events, does not theta-mark them. In such a circumstance, where the argument
DP is not a lexical argument of the head, we would not expect to find the verb
and the DP reanalysed into a complex predicate, and we would therefore not
expect to find extraction from the DP. Note that if the nominal is predicative,
there is no problem extracting from it:

(88)   Which girl do you feel a sister to?

So, the solution to the data in (80–82) is that extraction is not possible from
a post-copula argument in (80a) and (82b), because extraction from within an
argument DP is generally ruled out, by subjacency, by the 'Complex NP
Constraint', or whatever name you want to give to the constraint. The mechanisms for circumventing the constraint cannot be used here because they
operates only on pairs of theta-assigning verbs and their theta-marked complements, and that situation doesn't hold here.
  The question is then not why extraction is impossible from (80a) and (82b),
but why it is possible in (80b) and (81b), despite the restrictions on extracting
from complex nominals. The answer is that these nominals, although definites,
are predicative and that they behave like any other predicate expression, also
with respect to extraction. We have already seen in example (38) that predicative
definites are possible, and what remains is to discuss when a definite nominal
can be a predicate and when not. It is the answer to this question which will
explain why extraction is possible out of *the cause of the riot* in (89a), but not
out of *the photograph of the president* in (89b):

(89) a.   Which riot was the picture of the president the cause of? (=81b)
      b.   *Who was the cause of the riot the picture of? (=82b)

I will return to this issue in section 9.5. In the meantime, here are two relevant
observations, which throw some light on these examples. First note that *the*

cause of the riot is a natural predicate in the sense that it has a verbal counterpart which is as good as synonymous. Extraction out of (90b) is of course also possible:

(90)   a. The photograph of the president was the cause of the riot.
       b. The photograph of the president caused the riot.
       c. Which riot did the photograph of the president cause t?

The photograph of the president has no naturally synonymous verbal counterpart. Even a noun like *picture*, presumably related to the verb *picture*, is not synonymous with that verb, nor are *destruction* and *destroy*. In all these cases, treating the nominal as a predicate and extracting out of it is difficult to impossible.

(91)   a.   The cause of the riot pictured the president.
       b.   The cause of the riot was the picture of the president.
       c.   *Which president was the cause of the riot the picture of?

(92)   a.   The cause of the riot was the destruction of the city.
       b.   The cause of the riot destroyed the city.
       c.   *Which city was the cause of the riot the destruction of.

Second, and more important, the semantic context makes it more or less easy to interpret a definite nominal as a predicate. Note that extraction out of *the picture of the president* is possible when the subject DP is naturally something which has the property of being such a picture. (89b) contrasts with the examples in (93), which are acceptable, and with (94) which shows that there are copular constructions with two definite arguments, either of which can be extracted out of in post-copula position.

(93)   a. Which president is that photograph the picture of t?
       b. Who is that photograph the picture of t?

(94)   a. Which film is this the book of?
       b. Which book is this the film of?

We predict that DPs which can be extracted out of in copular constructions should also be acceptable as bare DP predicates in small clause complements of verbs like *consider*. Thus, the examples in (95) are predicted to be acceptable.

(95)   a. I consider John the cause of the riot.
       b. The journalists think the picture of the president the (true) cause of the riot.

The examples in (96) are also predicted to be better than (97), and I think that this is indeed the case.

(96)   a.   I believe this photograph the picture of the president.
       b.   I consider this novel the (true) sequel to Gone With the Wind.

(97)   a. ??I consider the cause of the riot the photograph of the president.
       b. ??I consider the cause of the riot the destruction of the city.

A fuller exploration of the contrast that Moro brings between (89a) and (89b) will lead us deeper into a study of nominalisation and predication than there is space for here. What I have shown, however, is that difficulties with extraction out of post-copula arguments are because the argument is not theta-marked, and not because the position is in any way a subject position.

(ii) The second contrast between post-copula position in identity and predicative position shows up when relativisation is dependent on the post-copula position, as we saw in (44/45), repeated here:

(98) a. *Mary, who his best friend is t, likes to go to the beach.
     b. *The girl that his best friend is t is here.
     c. *It is Mary that his best friend has been t. (Longobardi 1984)

(99) a. His best friend, which Mary is t, is what Jane wanted to be t.
     b. Mary is the scholar that Bill might have been t.
     c. It is his best friend that Mary is/has always been t, and not his lover.

Direct questioning out of the post-copula position is possible in both identity and predicate sentences, showing that it is not the position of the trace which is the problem.

(100) a. I asked who his best friend is t.
      b. She wondered who the best student was t.
      c. I asked who had been his best friend t.

(101) a. I asked what Mary was t (to him).
      b. She wondered what kind of scholar Mary was t.

In particular, it is not extraction from a non-theta-marked argument position per se which is the problem, but rather something to do with the relativisation process. The problem stems from the fact that the relativisation context leads to a mismatch in types. In the grammatical examples in (99), the DPs *his best friend* and *the scholar*, which are modified by the relative clauses, are both predicative DPs; the trace in the relative clause dependent on them is also in a predicative position. If we assume that predicate nominals have the same denotations as adjectives, then the predicative DP will be of type $<d, <e,t>>$, and the traces will also be of this type. The relative clauses will be modifiers of type $<<d, <e,t>>, <d, <e,t>>>$, and thus appropriate modifiers for *his best friend* and *scholar*. Given a type-shifting account of identity sentences, then in (99) the traces in the relativised clauses are in a position where they have been raised to be complements of *be*, and they thus denote variables over sets of events; the relative clauses containing them will denote properties of sets of events, and will be of type $<<e,t>, <e,t>>$. But in (99a/c), the relative clauses are supposed to modify the referential *Mary* which is of type d, and in (99b) the relative clause modifies the common noun *girl*, which we are assuming is of type $<d, <e,t>>$. We have a type mismatch, and the modifications are ungrammatical.

(iii) The data about cliticisation, in (47/48), repeated here as (102/103), shows that there is a difference between the post-copula position in predicative and identity sentences. The clitic *le* can replace a predicate XP (where XP can be a predicate nominal) but not an argument DP:

(102)   a.   Monsieur Ducros l'est, mon docteur.
             "Mr   Ducros it is, my   doctor."
        b.   *Mon docteur l'est, Monsieur Ducros
             "My doctor it is, Mr   Ducros." (Heggie 3:100)

(103)   a.   Jean et   Marie sont les parents de Christine
             "John and Mary are the parents of Christine."
        b.   *Jean et   Marie les   sont
             "John and Mary them are."
        c.   Jean et   Marie le sont.
             John and Mary it are.

In terms of the theory I have presented here, the question is why, if the argument DP is raised to be a complement of *be*, it cannot be replaced by a clitic like any other predicate nominal. But the clitic and the raised argument phrase do not match in types. *Be* takes as its complement a set of events, and as we have seen, the argument DP which is the complement of *be* in identity sentences is raised to type $<e,t>$, the type of sets of events. Predicate nominals in predicative DPs are predicates of small clauses, and (after predicate formation) they are of type $<d, <e,t>>$. If we assume that the predicative clitic *le* is of type $<d, <e,t>>$ too, and that it binds a trace in position of the cliticised constituent, then it is clear that they can bind a trace of the same type in predicate nominal position, but that they can't bind a trace in the position of post-copula arguments that are of type $<e,t>$. What (103b) shows is that 'ordinary' argument clitics are of type d, and can't bind traces of type $<e,t>$ either.

(iv) The fourth point involved the contrast between (49/50), repeated here:

(104)   a.   It is necessary that you call only Mary.
        b.   I want you to call only Mary

(105)   A solution is to visit only Mary.

I have shown that the post-copula position, when it is nominal, is a position in which an argument of type d is raised to $<e,t>$. It would be too lengthy to try and discuss here what goes on in equative constructions when the post-copula argument is not nominal, but it is plausible to assume that type-raising is necessary here too, and that this will lead to the raised constituent behaving as a scope island. Note also that sentences like (105) behave more like pseudoclefts than like nominal identity sentences. We get the same kind of scope effects in pseudoclefts; in (106), *only* also has narrow scope, and thus contrasts with (104b):

(106)   What John wants is for you to call only Mary.

(v) Heggie (1988) argues that in equative (identity) sentences, where the post-copula DP is an proper name, intensive reflexives like *himself* can, unusually, not attach to the sentential subject; the data she discusses was shown in (51), repeated here as (107):

(107) a. John$_i$ himself$_i$ is the organiser of the group.
       b. John$_i$ is the organiser of the group himself$_i$.
       c. *The organiser of the group$_i$ himself$_i$ is John.
       d. The organiser of the group is John$_i$ himself$_i$.

This argument is different from the others, and important because, while the other four are all aimed at showing that the post-copula position is an argument position, the data about *himself* is supposed to show that in (107c) *the organiser of the group* is not an argument but a predicate. But the contrasts in (107) are a consequence of the pragmatic effects of using *himself* as an intensifier, and not evidence for the predicate status of the definite DP. In its intensifier use, the reflexive is attached to the most prominent discourse referent. In equative sentences, the effect of using an intensifier is to give the impression that the denotation of one DP, the one marked by the intensifier, is known, and that the pragmatic effect of the sentence is to fix the denotation of the second DP as being the same individual as the first. In (107a/107b/107d), the sentence asserts that the same individual is the denotation of the two DPs *John* and *the organiser of the group*. The intensifier tells us that the denotation of *John* is prominent, and this implies that we know which individual is the denotation of *John*, and that we are asserting that the denotation of the second DP is identical to him. Such an 'asymmetry' is not a necessary part of the assertion. (108) is an identity sentence where neither DP is particularly prominent:

(108) The leader of the group is the treasurer.

Here, an intensifying reflexive can be attached to either DP, unlike in (107b).

(109) a. The leader of the group himself is the treasurer.
       b. The leader of the group is the treasurer himself.

The contrasts in (107) follow, because it easy to use a definite description attributively, while the use of a proper name often indicates direct access to its referent. Both sentences in (110) are taken out of context as identifying the referent of *the leader of the group* as identical to the individual denoted by *John*, rather than the other way round, and this is not affected by which is in subject position:

(110) a. John is the leader of the group.
       b. The leader of the group is John.

It is this pragmatic effect which is reflected in the distribution of the intensifiers in (107). (This means that (107c) should be marked as infelicitous rather than starred.) If we can find a context where the process of identification is reversed, then the intensifier can be attached to the definite description and not the proper name, without there being any claim that the proper name is not an argument.

(111)   A. I'm looking for John but all I can find is a robot.
        B. That's right! The robot itself/himself is John.

(112)   A. I had a letter to get to John Smith, and I gave it to the leader of the group. Do you think he'll get it OK?
        B. Absolutely. The leader of the group himself is John.

9.5. Some discussion about predicate nominals

There are two obvious outstanding questions about predicate nominals. One is the question of what kind of constituent a nominal head denotes. The second is how the theory of syntactic predication deals with the fact that some nominals are ambiguous between a referential and a predicative reading.

The first question is the topic for a complete study in its own right. In the analysis of *be* that I have been proposing, *be* takes as its complement sets of events. I have been assuming (and we'll discuss this at length in chapter 10), that AP predicates have event arguments and denote expressions of the form $\lambda e.\alpha(e)$. If nominals behave like APs in these contexts, then presumably they have the same form. But presumably, nominals do not have an event argument in simple argument position, such as *the man*, in *the man left*. I have been tacitly assuming for the purposes of the discussion here that an N is ambiguous between $N(x)$ and $\lambda e.N(e,x)$, and that the first is the standard use and the second a derived predicative use, and I will continue to make this assumption. We will need a similar account of the denotations of adjectives, since it is implausible that an adjective has an event argument in attributive position as a modifier of nouns. This is very crudely put; it is not supposed to be an analysis, but a direction for pursuing an analysis, since saying anything else about the denotation of common nouns is impossible without an in depth study of nominals, and that would take us too far from the topic of this book. As we shall see in the next chapter, such a study will also require a more intensive look at the meaning of predicational *be*.

The second question is directly related to the main hypothesis of this book, and this is the issue of how to distinguish between argument and predicate DPs. The thesis that I presented in chapter 2 is that the grammar identifies certain syntactic constituents as predicates and requires that these be syntactically saturated. In the process of semantic interpretation, an operation of predicate formation is performed on the logical expressions which are the denotations of these syntactic predicates, prefacing them with λx. We saw in chapter 7 that the syntactic identification and the automatic λx-prefixation are crucial for ensuring that constituents whose denotation does not contain a free variable are nonetheless equipped with subjects, usually pleonastic ones. It is thus central to the hypothesis that the syntactic predicate constituent can be identified without reference to its interpretation. I argued in chapter 2 that lexical XPs are inherently predicates, and I argued in chapter 6 that automatic predicate abstraction applies to their denotations. In contrast, projections of functional heads cannot be unhesitatingly identified as predicative or non-predicative. CPs are inherently arguments which can be converted into predicates syntactically by using the operator-headed chain mechanism, where an appropriate operator in [Spec,CP] heads a licensed chain ending in a trace and introduces a syntactic (and corresponding semantic) variable. Since a predicate CP contains its own operator in [Spec,CP], which translates as a λ-operator binding the variable introduced by the trace, predicate formation as described in chapter 6 should not ever apply to CPs. Inflection is a predicate modifier, taking a predicate complement and projecting a predicate as the denotation of I'. Predicate formation does not apply to the I' node either.

We saw further, that there were some constituents which seemed to violate the claim that lexical projections are predicates, in particular locative PPs which seem to have an argument use as well as the standard predicative use:

(113)   a. John met Bill in the park.
        b. The child is hiding under the table.
        c. In the park is a good place to sit on Sundays.
        d. Under the table and behind the chair are both places where Dafna likes to hide.

But these have a restricted use; in (113a/b) the locative PP is introduced lexically as an argument, and the other PPs are subjects of copular constructions which have a 'quasi-equative' feel. Furthermore, they seem to be related to specificational pseudoclefts, which produce equative-type sentences where the two arguments are not necessarily nominal, and which I am not going to talk about here. Examples are given in (114):

(114)   a. Under the table and behind the chair are where Dafna most likes to hide.
        b. Muffins and potato chips are what she really likes to eat.
        c. Go to the beach is what we should do now.
        d. Tall is what she is going to be.

Unlike the kind of problem illustrated by (113/114), the relation between predicate and non-predicate nominals does seem to raise direct problems for the claim that the predicate/non-predicate status of a constituent can be determined without reference to the syntactic or semantic context in which it occurs. DPs can be arguments or predicates, and in some situations, one DP can be ambiguous between a predicative and a referential reading. Thus, a copular construction like (115a) is ambiguous between an equative reading where the structure is as in (115b) and a predicative reading where the structure in (115c):

(115)   a. Mary is the leader of the group.
        b. Mary [is [the leader of the group]$_{DP}$]$_{VP}$.
        c. Mary$_i$ [is [t$_i$ [the leader of the group]$_{DP}$]$_{SC}$]$_{VP}$.

As we saw, it is this ambiguity that is at the root of the 'reverse copular construction debate', for in a sentence like (115a), the post-copula can be equally well interpreted as a predicate or an argument. Furthermore, the contrast between (116a/b), which we noted in the previous section, makes it look as if the predicate/non-predicate status of a definite DP can be determined only by looking at the context of use and not by looking at the formal properties of the constituent.

(116)   a. *Which president was the cause of the riot the picture of? (=91c)
        b. Which president/Who is that photograph the picture of t? (=93)

The solution to this problem relies on clarifying the relation between determiners and DP expressions. I will make the by now uncontroversial assumption that determiners are functional heads which project maximal DP projections and which take maximal NP projections as their complements. I continue to assume that lexical XPs are predicative, and thus the inherent predicate constituents are the NP complements of determiners. Bare NP predicate complements occur either as complements of *be* or as primary predicates, in examples such as (117):

(117)   a. Mary is first violinist with the Israel Philharmonic.
        b. It is hard to believe John professor of linguistics; when I last saw him he was a high school student.

Since NPs are lexical predicates, automatic predicate formation applies to the denotation of the NP, and the complement of the D is thus of the form $\lambda x.\alpha(x)$. The question is what the denotation of DP is.

I assume that the basic relation between the determiner and the syntactic predicate NP complement is syntactic binding. The syntactic function of the determiner is to saturate syntactically the NP predicate (see Williams (1981), and also Higginbotham (1985)), and the semantic effect of the determiner is usually to bind the relevant semantic variable in the denotation of the NP expression. Paradigm examples are *the* and *every*. Assume that the NP is of the form $\lambda x.P(x)$; the definite determiner *the* is a function from predicates to expressions of type d, and *every* is a function from predicates into generalised quantifiers, as follows:

(118)   a. THE$(\lambda x.Q(x))$ $= \sigma x[Q(x)]$
        b. EVERY $(\lambda x.Q(x)) = \lambda P.\forall x[Q(x) \rightarrow P(x)]$

The DP in these cases are arguments, in (118a) of type d and in (118b) of type $<<d,t>,t>$. Since, as we have seen, quantifiers of type $<<d,t>,t>$ do not have a predicative use, we need say no more about *every* than is given in (118b). As far as *the* is concerned, the simplest solution is to assume that it is lexically ambiguous. In (118a) it denotes a function of type $<<d,t>,d>$. In addition, let there be a second meaning for *the* which yields a predicate as its output. This is Partee's (1987) suggestion to account for presuppositionless, predicative definite DPs. We could at the same type use the ambiguity of *the* as a possible solution to the question raised at the beginning of this section about the denotations of nominals and suggest that, while argument *the* is of type $<<d,t>,t>$, predicative *the* is of type $<<d, <e,t>>, <d, <e,t>>>$. Semantically, it is the identity function on relations between individuals and events if the number of individuals who can be the value of the argument function for this event-type is one, and is undefined otherwise.

(119) $THE(\lambda x \lambda e.P(e) \wedge Arg(e) = x) = \lambda x \lambda e.P(e) \wedge Arg(e) = x \wedge |x| = 1$

Thematic constraints on particular thematic argument relations will constrain when the predicative use is appropriate. In (120) it will be impossible to treat *the photograph of the president* as a predicate, because the subject of the sentence *the cause of the riot* cannot be the thematic argument of such a predicate.

(120)   The cause of the riot was the photograph of the president.

Thus the only possible reading of (120) is equative.

It is interesting to compare indefinite DPs of the form *a NP* with definite nominals. Indefinites are paradigmatic predicates, but they also occur in argument position. The crucial difference between indefinite DPs and definites is that when they appear in predicative position, for example in the complement of *be*, they can only have a predicative reading; the identity reading is just not available. (121) does not have a reading in which it asserts that the denotation of [Spec,IP] is identical to the denotation of the post-copula DP.

(121)   John is a tall man.

Thus, while *a tall man* can be modified by a non-restrictive modifier in argument position, this is not possible in post-copula position, showing that it really is not an argument:

(122)   a.   A tall man, who I often meet at the bus stop, stood at the door.
        b.   *John, who I had never been introduced to, is a tall man, who I often meet at the bus stop.

Assuming, Bittner's (1995) account of indefinite DP arguments, this difference falls out naturally. She argues that the indefinite determiner is an identity function on predicates, and yields an predicate as its value. A default raising rule raises the DP into a generalised quantifier if it is in argument position, which in our terms is either the subject of a predicate or a theta-marked argument of a head. This rule introduces the existential quantifier which will bind the variable. For example, the common noun *man* starts off denoting either $MAN(x)$ or $\lambda e.MAN(e) \wedge Arg(e) = x$. It projects an syntactic NP which is inherently predicative and predicate formation applies giving (123a/b).

(123)   a. $\lambda x.MAN(x)$
        b. $\lambda x \lambda e.MAN(e) \wedge Arg(e) = x$.

Bittner's type-shifting rule will be able to apply only to (123a), giving (124) in argument positions:

(124) $\lambda Q.\exists x[MAN(x) \wedge Q(x)]$.

In predicative positions, type raising will not apply, and thus only the predicative reading will be available. However, as predicative positions are those in which the indefinite has to be the daughter of a selected small clause, and as small clauses have to be arguments of type $<e,t>$, only (123b) will occur in predicative position. Of course, extending this to cardinal determiners raises all sorts of problems about downward entailing numerical indefinite DPs, but I am not going to go any further here.

PART IV

THE COPULA

CHAPTER 10

THE MEANING OF 'BE'

10.1. The problem

In the analysis of copula constructions that I have presented in the previous chapter, copula *be* adds nothing to the meaning of the sentence in which it occurs. It denotes the identity function on predicates, λE.E, and its semantic 'contribution' to the VP it heads is limited to the fact that if its complement is an argument DP, it triggers a type-shifting operation which raises the DP from type d to type $<e,t>$. Instead its contribution is structural. The copula is a V which heads a VP syntactic predicate, which is a constituent at which predicate formation occurs. The complement of *be* is interpreted as an expression with a free x variable, denoting a set of events. As we saw in the derivations in examples (15) and (27) in the previous chapter, predicate formation at the VP level introduces a λ-operator which binds the x variable (in both predicative and identity sentences), thus allowing the constituent to be predicated of the subject. The Hebrew inflectional copula, discussed in chapter 8, also need make no independent semantic contribution, and similarly denotes the identity function on expressions, but at type $<d,<e,t>>$. It also triggers a type raising operation from d → $<d,<e,t>>$ in its complement in identity (equative) sentences.

As we saw in chapters 8 and 9, this account explains why in predicative sentences the copula can on occasions be dropped, and why this is not ever the case in identity, or equative, sentences. The relevant examples are matrix tenseless small clauses in Hebrew, where the main predicate is not verbal, as illustrated in (1), and small clause complements of verbs like *consider* in English, as in (2).

(1) a. dani (hu)   nexmad me'od.
         dani Pron nice   very
         "Dani is very nice."
     b. ha- ax   Seli   *(hu) dani
         the brother of me   Pron dani
         "My brother is Dani."

(2) a. Mary believes/considers Jane (to be) very clever.
     b. I believe/consider the duty nurse *(to be) Rina.

The explanation for these facts is that, since APs (and other lexical predicates) are inherently syntactic predicates, and after predicate formation at the XP level are of type $<d, <e,t>>$, they can be directly predicated of the subject, without the predication being mediated by any copula. However, since proper names are of type d, the copula is necessary to raise them to 'usable' types. Infl triggers raising directly to $<d, <e,t>>$, while *be* triggers raising to $<e,t>$ and the expression of type $<d, <e,t>>$ is derived at the VP level.

The obvious question to ask is what, in English, is the relation between Inflection and the verbal copula. One the one hand, if there is a bare inflectional copula available in Hebrew, then why is there no inflectional copula in English; and on the other hand, if *be* is necessary to license the small clause in (2b), why does it have to be accompanied by inflection? In other words, if we examine the paradigm in (3), what rules out (3e/f)? And why, if we are asking such questions, are matrix small clauses impossible?

(3) a. I consider John smart.
    b. *I consider John Mr Smith.
    c. I consider John to be smart/Mr. Smith.
    d. *I consider John to smart/Mr Smith.
    e. *I consider John be smart.
    f. *I consider John be Mr Smith.

It is relatively easy to give an explanation for (3d) by comparing the Hebrew and English inflectional systems. In Hebrew, in the past and future tenses, the copula is verbal. It is only in the (so-called) present that it is inflectional, and can appear with a non-verbal complement, or can be dropped completely. It is clear that in Hebrew something 'odd' is going on with the present tense in general: while past and future verbal forms are fully inflected for person, number and gender, the present is inflected only for number and gender, and the morphological forms indicating inflectional features are the same as those used to mark agreement on adjectives. As we saw in chapter 8, Doron (1983) proposes that the tense system allows specification for $[\pm\text{tense}]$ and $[\pm\text{past}]$, where $[-\text{tense}]$ is the specification for non-finite forms and $[+\text{tense}]$ for finite forms. $[+\text{tense}]$ automatically requires a specification of past features, where $[+\text{past}]$ indicates past tense and $[-\text{past}]$ indicates future tense. The present is not specified for either past or tense features. Doron claims that it is tense features which force the projection of Infl; past and future tenses which are $[+\text{tense}]$ and $[\pm\text{past}]$ force a projection of Infl, while the so-called present, which is unspecified for these features does not require Infl to be projected. Thus in the present, matrix small clauses are possible, but since features other than tense can project Infl, inflected small clauses are possible.

Now, assume that while Infl is always of type $<<d, <e,t>>, <d, <e,t>>>$, and selects a maximal projection no matter what features it contains, it is the tense features in Infl which subcategorise for a Verb Phrase. This predicts correctly that whereas past, future and infinitival Infl in Hebrew will always take a verbal complement, inflected small clauses will be possible only in the present.

In English, Inflection always takes a verbal· complement. It is conventional to assume (Chomsky 1981 and many others) that while {[+tense], [+past]} in English is realised as past tense, {[+tense], [−past]} is realised as present tense. Assuming that the [−tense] feature indicates infinitivals, this means that infinitival, past and present inflection will require a verbal complement. But modals, including the modal auxiliary *will* used to mark future in English, also subcategorise for VPs, and are taken to be complements of Infl. As a result, inflected non-verbal clauses are not acceptable in English at all. Since non-inflected matrix assertions are not possible (except in the echoic 'Mad Magazine' constructions of Akmajian (1984)), this means that we can't get matrix clauses of either the form (4a) or (4b) in English, and an inflected copular construction will require both Inflection and a verbal element:

(4) a. *$[\text{DP } [\text{Infl } [\text{XP}]]_{\text{I}'}]_{\text{IP}}$ where XP is non-verbal.
     b. *$[\text{DP XP}]$ in matrix position

However, although we have explained why the structures in (4) are unacceptable, and why (3c), where Infl takes a non-verbal complement, is unacceptable, we still have not explained what is wrong with (3e/f), in the paradigm in (3) repeated here:

(3) a. I consider John smart.
     b. *I consider John Mr Smith.
     c. I consider John to be smart/Mr. Smith.
     d. *I consider John to smart/Mr Smith.
     e. *I consider John be smart.
     f. *I consider John be Mr Smith.

(3a) is the standard small clause complement to *consider*, which we have been arguing denotes a set of events, and (3b) is ruled out because the complement of *consider* does not form a small clause. (3c) is an infinitival complement, which is propositional, resulting from existential closure over a set of events (presumably the same set that is denoted by the small clause in (3a)). Assuming, as we have suggested above, that Infl selects a VP complement, we explain why both Infl and *be* appear in (3c) and why (3d) is unacceptable. The remaining problem is what is wrong with (3e/f). In (3e), the denotation of the VP *be smart* should be exactly the same as the denotation of the AP *smart*, namely $\lambda x \lambda e.\text{SMART}(e) \wedge \text{Arg}(e) = x$, as (5) shows:

(5)
$$\text{SC}, \lambda x \lambda e.\text{SMART}(e) \wedge \text{Arg}(e) = x \text{ (JOHN)}$$
$$= \lambda e.\text{SMART}(e) \wedge \text{Arg}(e) = \text{JOHN}$$

DP

VP, $\lambda x \lambda e.\text{SMART}(e) \wedge \text{Arg}(e) = x$
(Predicate Formation)

V', $\lambda E.E(\lambda e.\text{SMART}(e) \wedge \text{Arg}(e) = x)$
$= \lambda e.\text{SMART}(e) \wedge \text{Arg}(e) = x$

V

SC, $\lambda x \lambda e.\text{SMART}(e) \wedge \text{Arg}(e) = x \ (x)$
$= \lambda e.\text{SMART}(e) \wedge \text{Arg}(e) = x$

DP,x

AP, $\lambda x \lambda e.\text{SMART}(e) \wedge \text{Arg}(e) = x$

John$_i$ be t_i smart

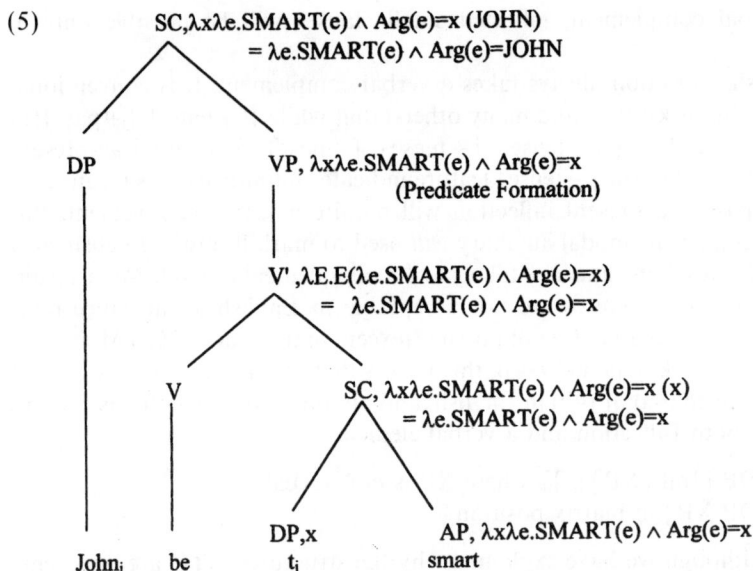

The denotation of the VP in (5) is exactly the same as the denotation of the predicate AP *smart*, namely $\lambda x \lambda e.\text{SMART}(e) \wedge \text{Arg}(e) = x$. Since in (3a), the AP can be predicated directly of the subject, then there should be no reason why *be smart* should not be directly predicated of the subject in (3e). The puzzle is all the greater because *make*, which also selects for a small clause, does allow a *be* + AP complement:

(6) a. I made John smart.
     b. I made John be smart.

Similarly, in (3f) *be Mr. Smith* should form a legal syntactic predicate with *be* inducing type-raising on *Mr. Smith* so that the small clause can be interpreted, and yet clearly, this is not grammatical.

On the assumption that *be* has no meaning, it is hard to see why (3e), which aparently has the identical meaning to (3a), should be ruled out, especially if (6c), is acceptable, and (3f) also remains a puzzle. We could simply stipulate that *consider* does not allow VP small clauses, but then the question is what is behind the stipulation, and that is tantamount to asking what the meaning of *be* is. I think that this is exactly the right question, and this chapter is an attempt to answer it.

One caveat. Since I am going to be talking almost entirely about predicative, as opposed to identity, constructions in this chapter, I am going to restrict the discussion to be + AP. I am assuming that the account of *be* can be extended to constructions where *be* has other constituents (NP, DP, PP) in its predicative complement, but since the semantics of each consituent is different and difficult, I will stick to *be* + AP examples here.

10.2. A MORE DETAILED LOOK AT THE DATA

First let us look in more detail at the problems with the hypothesis that *be* makes no semantic contribution to the sentence it appears in.

i. *ECM verbs*

On the approach given above, the two forms of (2a) repeated here in (7) should be synonymous:

(7) a. Mary considered Jane very clever.
     b. Mary considered Jane to be very clever.

Since the verb *be* is the identity function on predicates, the denotation of **very clever** and **be very clever** should be identical. And yet it has often been commented that small clauses like (7a) 'feel' more individual-level, inherent, or general than their inflected verbal counterparts in (7b). This cannot be related to the stage/individual-level distinction itself, since in a sentence like (8a), a temporary stage-level property is predicated of the subject in a bare small clause, while in (8b) the inflected form is used to make an individual-level predication:

(8) a. The doctor considers Mary quite sick/very fluish.
     b. I believe Mt. Everest to be the highest mountain in the world.

ii. *The distribution of bare infinitive clauses and bare AP clauses*

Here we look in more detail at the original problem raised in section 10.1. If *be* is the identity function on expressions of type $<e,t>$, then it should be possible to add it freely to any predicate clause. However, as we saw, in section 10.1, this is not true. The essential data is in (9):

(9) a. Mary considered Jane polite.
     b. *Mary considered Jane be polite.
     c. Mary made Jane polite.
     d. Mary made Jane be polite.
     e. Mary let Bill be rude.
     f. *Mary let Bill rude.

While *be* cannot be added in a small clause complement of *consider*, it can be added in the complement of *make*, and is obligatory in the small clause complement of *let*. (9b) might lead one to hypothesise that *be* is obligatorily a bearer of Infl, but (9d/e) show that the so called 'naked infinitive' form of *be* is frequently possible. (10) shows that in both these constructions *to be* is ruled out:

(10) a. *Mary let Bill to be rude.
     b. *Mary made Jane to be polite.

As (11) shows, the possibility of having a bare *be* correlates with the possibility in general of having a bare VP complement:

(11) a. Mary made Jane wash her face.
     b. Mary believes Jane *(to) need/want help.

The constraints on what the internal structure of non-tensed complement clauses can be is dependent on the selectional properties of the matrix verb. Assuming three different types of non-tensed clausal complements, *to* VP, bare VP or bare AP, there are seven different relevant selectional possibilities; a verb which takes a non-tensed clausal complement can select one of the above, any combination of two of the above or all three of the above. Five of these possibilities are realised:

1.   A verb may select a small clause with only a bare AP predicate. This kind is instantiated by *keep*:

(12) a.   Mary kept Jane polite.
     b. *Mary kept Jane be polite.
     c. *Mary kept Jane to be polite.

2.   A verb may select a small clause with only a bare VP predicate. *Let* and the perception verbs do this:

(13) a. *Mary let/saw/heard Jane polite.
     b.   Mary let/saw/heard Jane be polite.
     c. *Mary let/saw/heard Jane to be polite.

3.   A verb may select a complement with only *to* VP as predicate. *Cause* and *allow* behave in this way.

(14) a. *Mary caused/allowed Jane polite.
     b. *Mary caused/allowed Jane be polite.
     c.   Mary caused/allowed Jane to be polite.

4.   A verb may select a small clause with a bare AP or a bare VP complement. This class is represented by *make*.

(15) a.   Mary made Jane polite.
     b.   Mary made Jane be polite.
     c. *Mary made Jane to be polite.

5.   A verb may select a complement clause with a bare AP or *to* VP for a predicate. There are two groups here. One includes the ECM verbs *consider* and *find*, which do not allow a non-tensed CP complement nor a null embedded subject, as illustrated in (16), and the other includes the so-called 'subject control' verbs such as *prefer*, *want* and *like*, which do allow CP complements and null embedded subjects, as illustrated in (17).

(16) a.   Mary found/considered Jane polite.
    b.   *Mary found/considered Jane be polite.
    c.   Mary found/considered Jane to be polite.
    d.   *Mary found/considered (then) for Jane to be polite.
    e.   *Mary found/considered to be polite.

(17) a.   Mary prefers Jane polite.
    b.   *Mary prefers Jane be polite.
    c.   Mary prefers Jane to be polite.
    d.   Mary prefers/likes (now) for Jane to be polite.
    e.   Mary prefers/likes to be polite.

Note that *cause*, featured in (14) above, behaves with respect to these latter two properties like *consider* and *find*:

(18) a. *Mary caused/allowed (then) for Mary to be polite.
    b. *Mary caused/allowed to be polite.

Missing is a verb which selects a complement with VP or *to* VP as predicate and a verb which allows all three possibilities. Of course, if the first gap is non-accidental, and there is some principled reason why a verb does not allow both *Jane be polite* and *Jane to be polite* as a complement, then the second gap follows automatically.

(A possible counter-example to the claim that bare VP and inflected VP forms do not occur with the same verb is *help*:

(19) a. *Mary helped Jane polite.
    b.   Mary helped Jane be polite.
    c.   Mary helped Jane to be polite.

However, (19c) looks like an instance of an object control construction such as (20), where the object DP and the *to* VP do not form a constituent but are both sisters of the V:

(20)   Mary asked Jane to be polite.

Both (20) and (19c) entail the simple transitive of the form DP V DP. (20) entails (21a) and (19c) entails (21b), while, in contrast, *cause Jane to be polite*, *consider Jane to be polite* and *prefer Jane to be polite* do not entail the respective transitives in (22):

(21) a.   Mary asked Jane.
    b.   Mary helped Jane.

(22) a.   Mary caused Jane.
    b.   Mary considered Jane.
    c.   Mary preferred Jane.

It looks as if *help* selects a small clause with only a bare VP complement, while in (19c) the DP is the direct object and not within a small clause. The contrasts in (23) support this view:

(23) a. #The volcanic eruption helped the rain to fall.
      b.   The volcanic eruption helped the rain fall.

(23a) sounds a little odd because it treats *the rain* as a direct object of *help*, and to think of a 'help' relation holding between a volcanic eruption and a natural phenomenon such as rainfall is odd unless we ascribe some sort of agency to the rain. In (23b) the object of *help* is the small clause *the rain fall* and no direct relation between the rain and volcanic eruption is posited.

Help is, in any case, unusual among English verbs. Along with *dare*, it is the only verb, as far as I know, which can take a bare VP complement without an explicit subject, as in (24a). It is also the only verb that can take an infinitival complement with a null subject where the value of the subject is given contextually since (24a/b) clearly do not mean that Mary helped herself (to) build the house; however as was pointed out by the reviewer of a version of this chapter which appeared in NALS, the contrast in (24c/d) indicates that the situation is more complicated:

(24) a. Mary helped build the house.
      b. Mary helped to build the house.
      c. Mary helped convict herself.
      d. *Mary$_i$ helped convict her$_i$.

But there is no space for further discussion of this here.)

The question, then, is how to represent the selectional properties given above. We could assume that the features of the predicate of the small clause percolate to the dominating node, and that the three kinds of complements should be realised along the lines of (25). (Stowell (1983) suggests something like (25b/c) as the structure of small clauses.)

(25) a. [DP to VP]$_{IP}$
      b. [DP VP]$_{VP}$ (or VP′)
      c. [DP AP]$_{AP}$ (or AP′)

Feature percolation in (25a) is straightforward, since there is an explicit inflectional head. The verb selects a non-tensed IP complement (or, in the examples in (17), a non-tensed C complement). I assume that these denote propositions of a type distinct from those denoted by tensed CPs. (25b) and (25c) must involve feature percolation from the predicate of the small clause. (25b) resembles the type of the complements of auxiliary verbs such as *must* and *should*, as in *John must/should leave*, with the difference that in English auxiliary verbs take subject-less VP complements, while these verbs (with the exception of *help*, noted above) take small clauses with explicit lexical subjects. (25c) doesn't resemble any other construction, as far as I can tell.

(25b/c) raise a technical problem for an attempt to represent these head complement relations through syntactic subcategorisation. Normally, the features of a head percolate as far as the maximal projection of that head, and as we already argued in chapter 2:2.3, the predicate in (25b/c) is a maximal projection. As we saw, the small clause itself cannot be questioned, nor moved, while the predicate can, and this shows that it is the predicate AP or VP, and not the small clause, which is behaving like a maximal XP:

(26) a. *What did the witch consider/make? Mary very clever.
    b. *Mary very clever is what John considered/made.
    c. What did the witch consider/make Mary? Very clever.
    d. What the witch considered/made Mary was very clever.

Simliarly, we saw that when the predicate of the small clause is a possessive predicate DP, theta-marking indicates that the DP is indeed a maximal projection. The relevant example is (27), based on Stowell (1991) and Moro (1997):

(27) They considered that act the enemy's most serious violation of their sovereignty.

Here, the nominal small clause *that act the enemy's most serious violation of their sovereignty* constitutes the small clause complement of *consider*. However, the complete set of thematic roles that the derived nominal *violation* has to assign is assigned within the DP *the enemy's most serious violation of their sovereignty*, indicating that this constituent is the extended maximal projection of the nominal head.

It is obviously possible to find a technical mechanism which will allow percolation to take place so that distinctions between the complement types in terms of syntactic subcategorisation is possible. However, without an interpretation of the features involved, this is not very insightful. Turning to the semantic denotations of the complements under discussion, there are some obvious syntactic–semantic correlations. The bare VP complements can be analysed as denoting sets of events, following Vlach (1983) and others. The IPs are naturally given a propositional interpretation (though not of the same kind as tensed propositions). But if we want to explain the selectional restrictions in semantic terms then the bare AP complements must have a distinct interpretation also. I am going to argue in this chapter that they do. I shall propose that VPs, and small clauses with bare VP predicates, denote sets of locatable eventualities, while APs and their corresponding bare complement clauses denote sets of unlocatable states. We can sum up the selectional facts that we have discussed in the table in (28), where verbs are sorted according to possible forms of the verb in their complement phrases:

(28)	no verb	be	to be
keep	+	−	−
let/see/hear	−	+	−
cause/allow	−	−	+
make	+	+	−
consider/find	+	−	+
—	−	+	+
—	+	+	+
syntactic selection	selects [DP AP]$_{SC}$	selects [DP VP]$_{SC}$	selects [−tense] CP/IP
semantic selection	sets of states????	sets of events	propositions

This means that the meaning of *be* in the VPs of the form *be* + AP must be a function mapping from the unlocatable states denoted by the AP complements into sets of locatable eventualities denoted by VP. What this means, what this mapping operation is, and what these states and events are, is the subject of this chapter.

iii. *Agentive implications in bare infinitives*

We have discussed two problems for the 'no semantic contribution view', namely differences in meaning that *be* seems to introduce with ECM verbs, and accounting for the distribution of *be* in complement clauses. The third and fourth problems extend the discussion to the well known issues of agentivity effects in small clauses and in the progressive.   First, let's look at the agentivity effects in bare infinitives. It has often been noted that when an optional *be* is present, it seems to induce a meaning change. There is a contrast between the examples in (15a/b), repeated here; (15b) has strong implications that Jane is acting in an agentive way and performing some act of politeness, and this implication is missing in (15b). If *be* is a purely grammatical formative, then these two sentences ought to mean the same.

(15)   a. Mary made Jane polite.
        b. Mary made Jane be polite.

On the other hand, note that the meaning difference which seems to be introduced by *be* here is different from its effect in the *consider* complements in (7) above, where the bare AP complement had a more 'individual-level' feel to it. We expect the account of *be* to explain these differences in meaning.

iv. *'be' with the progressive*

Fourthly, there is the matter of the progressive. There are two issues here. First, *be* also seems to introduce agentive implications when it is the complement of the progressive. Out of the blue, (29a) implies that Jane is generally a polite person, while (29b) implies that she is consciously behaving in a polite way, and that she is actively responsible for her behaviour:

(29) a. Jane is polite.
      b. Jane is being polite (to her great aunt).

Second, when it is in the progressive, *be* can have only certain predicates as its complement. Lakoff (1970) distinguishes between active and stative APs and DPs and proposes that only the former can occur in the complement of progressive *be*.

(30) a. Mary is being noisy/mean/*awake/*healthy.
      b. John is being a nuisance/*a murderer.

Partee (1977) notes that as well as constraining properties of its complement predicate, *be* in the progressive also selects for properties of its subject. The examples in (31) seem to indicate that the subject must be animate. (Partee claims that (31d) is ungrammatical and stars it, but I will treat it as infelicitous, and explain the reasons for this later.)

(31) a. John is noisy.
      b. John is being noisy.
      c. The river is noisy.
      d. #The river is being noisy.

There is no general constraint restricting subjects of the progressive to animates, as we see in (32):

(32) a. John makes a lot of noise.
      b. John is making a lot of noise.
      c. The river makes a lot of noise.
      d. The river is making a lot of noise.

In fact, animacy is not enough. Partee shows from the examples in (33) that the subject of progressive *be* + AP must be a volitional participant in having the property denoted by the VP, and not merely animate. In (33), the children cannot be said to be volitional about being quiet if they are asleep. Again, (34) shows this is a constraint on progressive *be* and not on the progressive generally:

(33) a. The children are being quiet right now because they want a story.
      b. ?The children are being quiet right now because they are asleep.

(34) The children are making so little noise right now because they are asleep/want a story.

10.3. The agentive 'be' solution

Partee (1977) captures these intuitions in the claim that there is a distinct verb *be*, homophonous to predicative *be*, but marked [+active]. It combines with adjectives that allow an animate or volitional subject, and itself it requires an animate subject. Its meaning is like the meaning of the verb *act* as in *John is acting foolish*, and thus it is anomalous if the subject is not capable of acting to produce the property of the predicate. The subject of *be* is thus a thematic position, assigned the role of 'agent' by the verb, and the contrasts indicated above are predicted. In addition, Partee shows that the contrast in (35) is explained:

(35) a. John is easy to please.
      b. It is easy to please John.
      c. John is being easy to please.
      d. *It is being easy to please John.

Although *be easy to please* can usually take either a raised lexical subject or a pleonastic *it*, as in (35a/b), the progressive form can take only a lexical subject, strongly suggesting that it is a thematic position. This is predicted on Partee's account since *be* in the progressive must be the form which assigns an agent role to its subject.

Dowty's (1979) account of progressive *be* is based on the 'two-verbs-*be*' approach, and he also distinguishes agentive *be* from predicative *be*. His account is developed as part of a compositional analysis of predicates. He proposes that active verbs, but not statives, can be decomposed into a two-place abstract verbal predicate DO and an embedded sentential complement. *Look* is analysed as the active 'counterpart' of *see* and their lexical structures are compared in (36):

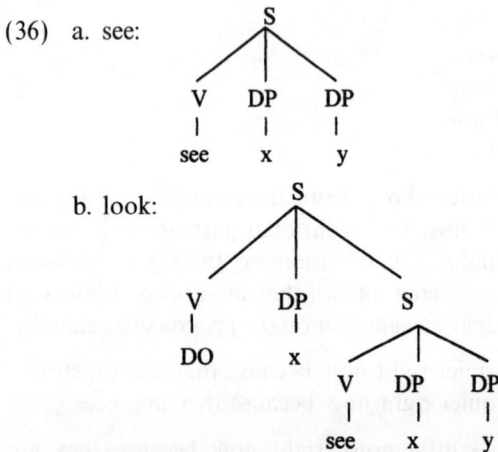

(36) a. see:

```
             S
          ／ |  ＼
         V   DP   DP
         |   |    |
        see  x    y
```

      b. look:

```
                  S
              ／  |   ＼
             V    DP      S
             |    |    ／  |  ＼
            DO    x   V    DP   DP
                      |    |    |
                     see   x    y
```

In the case of active verbs, the embedded verbal predicate is raised, and DO is absorbed into the lexicalised raised predicate. But, DO can also be independently lexicalised; it is realised as *do* in VP deletion constructions, as in (37a), and as *be* when the main predicate of its complement is an adjective (or nominal) as in (37b/c). In the latter case it is directly followed at S-structure by an AP or DP.

(37) a. John looked (at the view) and so did Bill.
     b. Jane is polite.
     c. Jane is a heroine.

Both forms of lexicalised DO can occur in the progressive, like any other verb:

(38) a. John is looking at the view, and Bill is doing so too.
     b. Jane is being polite/is being a hero.

There are some problems with this compositional account – in particular, the question of where the *do* comes from in VP deletion contexts involving non-active verbs, as in (39):

(39) a. John saw Mary and so did Bill.
     b. Jane knows the answer and so does Jill.

But I am not going to discuss these here. Rather, I am interested in the question of what the meaning of DO can be. As Dowty shows, pseudoclefts such as those in (40) indicate that DO does indicate some agentivity when it surfaces as *be*.

(40) a.   What I did then was be as polite as possible.
     b. ??What he did then was be a hero and refuse to budge.

But he goes on to point out that, while examples like (41a) indicate that progressive *be*+AP goes very naturally with expressions of intention, (41b) indicates that DO cannot be analysed as simply ascribing volitionality or intentionality to its subject. Nor can it indicate the occurrence of an action, where action is taken to involve some change of state, since there is no such change of state in, for example, (41c).

(41) a. John is deliberately/intentionally being obnoxious.
     b. John is unintentionally being impolite.
     c. John is being a hero by standing still and refusing to stir.

What the examples in (41b/c) show is that John may be being impolite or heroic by failing to do something, and that the failure to do something can be either deliberate or unintentional.

    Dowty proposes that DO + predicate indicates that the property denoted by the predicate can be "willed away" by the subject, and is "under the unmediated control of the agent". Going back to (29b), repeated here, we get the feeling not only that politeness is a property currently in evidence, but that it is an activity which is "in some sense under the control of the individual".

(42) Jane is being polite (to her great aunt).   (=29b)

We feel that if Jane is being polite even without noticing it, and "someone points it out to [him], [s]he can if [s]he so wishes, stop doing it at once." (p115). It is this implication of control by the subject which Dowty argues is contributed by DO, realised as *be*.

Dowty notes that some non-stative verbal predicates, such as *make a lot of noise*, in (32), pass the tests for activities or accomplishments and yet they do not necessarily imply control or agentivity by the subject, even though they too must have a DO component. So the proposal given so far cannot be complete. Dowty proposes distinguishing the verbs which do not involve agentivity on semantic grounds; though they have no agent, they all involve physical activity with either a change of position or internal movement which has results that can be perceived. He therefore gives a disjunctive definition of DO: (i) it implies unmediated controllability, which is relevant when the embedded complement is headed by nouns, adjectives or at least verbs like *ignore* and *refrain*, or (ii) if the complement is verbal it must express physical activity or movement, involving an "internal change of state that has visible, audible or tactile consequences." (p165). Partee's observation about the contrast between (31b/d) and (32d), repeated here, is explained:

(43)   a.   John is being noisy.   (=31b)
      b.   #The river is being noisy.   (=31d)
      c.   The river is making a lot of noise.   (=32d)

(43c) is felicitous because the complement *make a lot of noise* expresses a physical movement or action with (at least) audible consequences, thus satisfying (ii). (43b) is ungrammatical because, firstly, the complement of DO is the stative adjective *noisy*, and thus (ii) is not satisfied; and secondly, the property of noisiness is not under the unmediated control of the (non-animate) subject *the river*, and thus (i) isn't satisfied either. (43a) on the other hand is OK because, with an animate subject, it satisfies (i).

There are at least four problems with the 'two-verbs-*be*' solution:

i.   As Partee herself points out, there is a certain inelegance in solving the problem of progressive *be* – both its 'agentivity' effects and its apparent selectional restrictions on adjectival complements – by positing a second verb *be* in addition to predicative *be*. There is little supporting evidence for the existence of the homonym. Categorially, the two verbs *be* select AP (and other XP) complements. Agentive *be* exerts a further restriction on the complement, namely that the head of the AP assigns a [+animate] and maybe [+volitional] feature to its subject, but this is a selectional restriction of a very non-standard kind.

ii.   Dowty's weak notion of 'unmediated control' is still too strong to define the relation between the subject and the property expressed by the adjective, as the following examples show:

(44)   a. The baby is being difficult this evening; I think she is teething.
      b. The birds are being very noisy this morning.
      c. The pigeons in this square are being very obnoxious.
      d. The car is being very noisy this morning; I think we may need to buy a new muffler.

Each of the examples in (44) is acceptable, but in none of them is the property expressed by the adjective under the control (unmediated or not) of the subject. In asserting (44a), I make the suggestion that teething pains are causing the baby physical pain which leads to her being noisy and crying and being difficult to deal with, but I am not assuming or implying that, at a few months old, her behaviour is under her control or that she is able to control the crying or to stop being noisy or a bother. In (44b), the birds are particularly noisy, but this is not under their control; they are just behaving as birds are naturally wired to behave. Similarly, in (44c), if people drop chunks of bread in Trafalgar or some other square, the pigeons will react by swooping down and eating them: we may find this obnoxious behaviour, especially if we want to eat our own sandwiches, but it is not behaviour which we could call either volitional or under the control of the subject. (44d) is also felicitous, although the subject is not even animate.

iii. Partee and Dowty explain the meaning change when *be* occurs in small clause complements in terms of the selectional restrictions on agentive *be*. But, postulating a second agentive *be* doesn't explain why you can't use the **predicative** form of *be* in "Mary made Jane be polite" (= 8b). If *be* is ambiguous, there should be a second, non-agentive, reading in which predicational *be* is used, but it looks as if, when *be* is optional, it must be agentive *be* which is being used. One would equally expect predicative *be* to be available in all small clause complements, including those in (45), which, as noted above, are impossible:

(45) *Mary considered/found/kept Jane be polite.

One could try to argue that predicative *be* can only occur with inflection, and that it is banned in naked infinitive small clauses. But, this is a strange condition on a verb; even if its grammatical function is only to be the bearer of tense – as opposed to other verbs which have a lexical function as well – then untensed *be* should be redundant, but not ungrammatical; and we would expect the sentence in which it appears to be awkward, and maybe pragmatically inappropriate, but not ungrammatical, as the examples in (45) are.

iv. The agentive *be* theory leads us to expect that the distribution of agentive *be* should be the same in small clause and progressive constructions. Since implications of agentivity occur both with the progressive and with small clause complements, we would assume that a single explanation should account for this phenomenon in both contexts. (46) shows that things don't work this way:

(46)   a.   I made the children be ready at three.
       b.   #The children are being ready at three.
       c.   I made Jane be awake for the visit.
       d.   #Jane is being awake for the visit.
       e.   I made the river be noisy.
       f.   #The river is being noisy.

Partee claims that the anomaly of sentences like (46b/d/f) is because the subject of *be* is not capable of acting to produce the property of the predicate. But if the same *be* occurs in (46a/c/e), which is presumably the claim that one wants to make, then the identical combination of subject + *be* + adjective ought to be unacceptable there too. The fact that the set of adjectives which combine with *be* easily in one construction is not the same as the set which occur in the other indicates either that two separate constraints are involved – a solution we want to avoid as wasteful – or that the apparent selectional restrictions follow from the interaction of *be* with other properties of the two constructions. In that case, since syntactic and semantic selectional restrictions are not exercised by matrix verbs on the complements of their complements, the restrictions must be the result of semantic and pragmatic restrictions exercised by the environment in which they occur. This is the solution which we will come to in sections 10.9 and 10.10 of this chapter.

10.4.   VERBS AND ADJECTIVES

10.4.1.   *The theory*

The analysis of *be* which I shall propose is based on the hypothesis that there is a basic difference in the kinds of entities that verbs and adjectives denote, and that this is reflected in differences in their argument structure. AP and *be* + AP will denote different entities, and the distinguishing properties of VPs headed by copula *be* which we have discussed above will follow from this.

What I am going to propose is that the domain of eventualities is divided into two. The division is analogous to the division of the nominal domain into count and mass entities. Verbs have a "Davidsonian" event argument ranging over atomic, count-like eventualities, and they denote properties of these eventualities. I shall argue below that the domain of atomic count eventualities includes processes, such as those give by *sleep* and *dance*, and statives, such as those given by *know* and *love*, as well as the more obviously countable telic eventualities.

The domain of adjectives, on the other hand, is a set of non-atomic, mass, state-like eventualities. Strictly speaking, we should probably call the denotations of verbs 'c-eventualities' (for 'count-eventualities'), and the denotations of adjectives 'm-eventualities' (for 'mass eventualities'). But in order not to increase confusing terminology too much and to keep distinctions clear, I shall call the denotations of adjectives 'M-states' and use 'eventuality' in the restricted sense to refer to the denotations of verbs. On the rare occasions where I use 'eventuality' in the more general sense to cover the denotations of both kinds of lexical entities, it should be clear from the context.

Adjectives, then, have a state argument (represented by the variable 's') ranging over M-states, and they denote properties of M-states. Crucially, as we will see, M-states are non-countable, non-atomic entities, and thus differ from the countable, atomic, stative eventualities given by *know* and *love*.

As I will argue in section 10.5 below, the verb *be* denotes a function from the domain of M-states to the domain of Davidsonian eventualities, and has the effect of 'packaging' non-atomic M-states into atomic eventualities. 'Packaging' was the name given in Pelletier (1975) to the mechanism which allowes a nominal mass term to be used as a count term as in (47):

(47)   At the cafe, they ordered three beers, two teas, and ice-creams all round.

Be introduces a Davidsonian eventuality argument like any verb, but unlike lexical verbs, it does not express any property of that argument. Instead, it combines with an AP complement, as in *be polite*, in effect creating a complex verb where *be* introduces the eventuality argument and *polite* expresses a property of that eventuality, the M-state which it instantiates. The AP *polite* denotes the politeness property, and the VP expression *be polite* denotes the set of eventualities that instantiate the politeness property.

I will return below, in section 10.5.2, to the question of how exact the parallelism between the mass/count division in the nominal domain and in the verbal/adjectival domain is. At that point I will also discuss the relation between this proposal for structuring the domain of eventualities (in the wider sense of the term) with that of Bach (1986), who was, as far as I know, the first to make an explicit formal analogy between the mass/count distinction in the nominal and the verbal domains. Before getting to that, I want first to present evidence that the atomic/non-atomic distinction really does exist, and that *be* can be treated in the way I have just mentioned.

10.4.2. *The data*

What kind of distinctions between mass and count terms would we expect to find in the verbal domain? Presumably distinctions which parallel the differences in behaviour between mass and count nouns, taking into account the inherent grammatical differences between verbs and nouns. For example, many differences between mass and count nouns show up in the choice of determiners with which they may appear, but verbs don't appear with determiners. Also, count nouns do and mass nouns don't take plural morphology – but verbs don't show plural morphology anyway (except as a consequence of agreement). But both these tests, the syntactic and the morphological, are grammatical reflections of the basic fact that atomic entities can be counted, and we would expect to find some grammatical reflection of this in the verbal domain too. In the four tests below, I show four ways in which the denotations of verbs and of adjectives differ. All the tests indicate that the denotations of the verbs are sets of atomic entities, while the denotations of adjectives are not. In each case, the adjectival predicate is contrasted with a stative verb, since the latter is the least count-like of all verbal eventualities, and in each case the contrast shows up. As I said, I'll return to a more systematic comparison between the verbal and the nominal domain below.

i.   **test 1: the countability property – counting adverbials**: Count nouns do and mass nouns don't show up with numeral determiners. This countability property shows up in the verbal domain in the distribution of counting adverbials. In context, all verbs, including statives, can be modified by counting adverbials like *three times*, while adjectives cannot be modified by explicit counting adverbials. This is explained if verbs denote sets of atomic eventualities which can be counted, while adjectives denote non-atomic, mass-like entities. The contrast shows up clearly if we look at the behaviour of adverbials which explicitly count events in small clauses such as the complements of *make* and *see*:

(48)   a. I made Mary know the answer three times.
        b. I made Mary angry/clever (in class) 3 times.

(48a) is ambiguous. *Three times* can modify the matrix verb *make*, giving the reading that there were three acts of 'making Mary know the answer', but there is also the reading in which there was one event of 'making' which caused Mary to know the answer three times, for example if a witch gave her a magic potion which had as its effect that she could answer correctly in class three times. In this latter case, *three times* modifies the embedded verb, and we are counting instances of a stative eventuality type. (Note that it can but need not be the same answer that Mary knows in (48a); for example, I can, by careful coaching, make Mary know the answer to a particular question three times, though after that she forgets it again.) In contrast, (48b) has only the first reading, and *three times* cannot modify *clever*.

ii.   **test 2: temporal locatability**: What kinds of inherent properties do atomic entities have that non-atomic entities don't have? For eventualities it seems to be temporal locatedness: atomic eventualities are temporally located, while non-atomic M-states are not. This means that modifiers expressing temporal location cannot modify bare adjective phrases.

(49)   a. Yesterday the witch made John know the answer last night and forget it this morning.
        b. *Yesterday, the witch made John clever last night and stupid this morning.

This indicates that a crucial property of an eventuality is that it can be given a temporal location, while a state cannot be temporally located. Notice that temporal location doesn't necessarily mean temporally bounded. If the witch made John know the answer last night, it doesn't necessarily mean that he didn't know it either before or since; it might just mean that she made sure that he had the knowledge at some crucial point last night, leaving open what happened before or after. But then the relevant situation in which John has the property of knowing the answer is temporally locatable, though his having the property is not necessarily properly contained within that temporal location. So, while stative eventualities can be unbounded, they are still temporally locatable. In (50), John's knowing the answer may be an eventuality which is unbounded at each end (although, pragmatically, it seems likely to start and end at least with the beginning and ending of John). What the sentence asserts is that the witch made there be a relevant, possibly proper, sub-part of that eventuality which held at three o'clock.

(50)   The witch made John know the answer at three o'clock.

Returning to M-states, note that these may have a duration without being temporally located, as the contrast in (51) shows. *At three o'clock,* in (51b) must modify *made,* but *for three hours* in (51a) most naturally modifies *clever*:

(51)   a. Yesterday the witch made John clever for three hours.
      b. Yesterday the witch made John clever at three o'clock.

Small clause constructions such as those in (52) also show that adjectival predicates cannot be temporally located.

(52)   A. You saw Mary recently, in fact last night. How do you think she looked then?
      B. a. *I think Mary well-dressed last night (but less well-dressed this morning/now).
         b. I thought Mary well-dressed last night but less well-dressed this morning/*now.
         c. I think Mary looked well-dressed last night, and looks less well-dressed this morning.

Of the sentences in B, (a) is ungrammatical since *last night* cannot modify the adjective, and is incompatible with the matrix verb. (b) is acceptable with *last night* and *this morning* modifying the matrix verb. The contrast between *this morning* and *now* in the second conjunct shows this also; the acceptability of the sentence is dependent on the adverbial being compatible with the matrix verb. If the sentence is uttered later than this morning, the adverb *this morning* is compatible with *thought,* but *now* is always incompatible with a past tense verb. (53) also shows that temporally locating modifiers modify only the matrix verb and not the predicate within the small clause. *Last night* can only modify the matrix verb in (53a), and we can see this from (53b) which is unacceptable because the modifier *an hour ago,* which can also only modify the matrix verb, is incompatible with *last night*:

(53)   a. What did you believe Mary t last night?
      b. *An hour ago I believed her a genius last night, (but now I'm not so sure).

The fact that temporal locatedness is crucial follows from a theory of event individuation such as that of Parsons (1990). In this theory, events are individuated via the kind of event they are, the participants they have and their temporal location. An event of Jane running to the store today is distinguished from an event of Jane walking to the store today. It is also distinguishable from an event of John running to the store today at the same time as Jane and it is also distinguishable from an event of Jane running to the store yesterday. The first two of these individuating criteria – what kind of event it is and what participants it has – are dependent on the lexical properties of the head. The quality of occurring in time at a particular time is a property that events have independent of their lexical character, and the data in (48)-(53) support this.

iii.   **test 3: adverbial modification by event quantifiers**. Assuming that adverbials express properties of eventualities and/or states, we might expect some domain selection here. In other words, if there is a count domain of eventualities and a mass domain of M-states, then we might expect other adverbials, as well as the counting or temporally locating ones, to distinguish between them. Adverbial quantifiers over events in the 'every time' construction, discussed in Rothstein (1995c) do just that: they occur as modifiers of eventualities, but not with M-states. An instance of the normal case of the 'every time' construction is given in (54a). Rothstein (1995c) shows that (54a) is true if there are at least as many events of Mary opening the door as there are events of bell-ringing. I argue there that the correct representation of the meaning is the one in (54b):

(54)   a.   Mary opens the door every time the bell rings
       b. $\forall e[[\text{RING}(e) \wedge \text{Th}(e) = \text{THE BELL}] \rightarrow \exists e'[\text{OPEN}(e')$
            $\wedge \text{Ag}(e') = \text{MARY} \wedge \text{Th}(e') = \text{THE DOOR} \wedge \text{M}(e') = e]]$

The analysis argues that there is a 'matching function' (designated by 'M' in the representation), which maps from events in the set given by the matrix V onto the set of eventualities given by *time the bell rings*, where every event of bell-ringing must be the value of at least one argument of M, as illustrated in (55):

(55)   f: Door-openings ———→ Bell-ringings

Door-openings   Bell-ringings
  e'1.————————→ e1.
  e'2.————————→ e2.
  e'3.————————→ e3.
  e'4.—
  e'5.

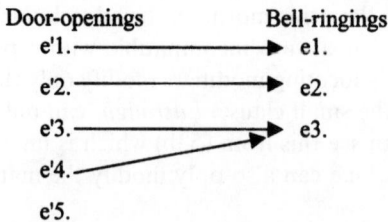

English does not allow matrix small clauses or small clauses immediately dominated by CP. Since *time* is modified by a CP relative clause, there is therefore no way to see whether a bare AP can give the range of the function as well as VP, though we predict that it can't. But it is possible to compare whether a small clauses with bare VP (stative for minimal contrast) and bare AP predicates can both give the domain of the function, and this is what we do in (56):

(56)   a.   I made Jane worry every time the bell rings.
       b.   *I made Jane nervous/excited every time the bell rings.

In (56a), *every time the bell rings* is an adverbial modifier of the embedded verb *worry* (stative in Dowty's (1979) classification), and the sentence asserts that there was an event of Jane's worrying for every event of the bell ringing. The adverbial cannot modify the matrix verb *make*, because, as I showed in Rothstein (1995), the tense of the matrix verb and the tense of the verb in the relative clause must be the same. (56b) is ungrammatical. Here too, the matching tense requirement means that the adverbial cannot modify the matrix verb, but it cannot modify the embedded adjective either. Note that if the tense of the verb in the relative clause matches that of the matrix verb, we get the previously unavailable reading where the adverbial modifies the matrix verb, mapping instances of making Jane nervous onto the set of events of bell-ringing. (56a) becomes ambiguous, and (56b) becomes grammatical but has only this one reading.

(57)   a. I made him worry every time the bell rang.
       b. I made him nervous/excited every time the bell rang.

Other stative verbs pattern with event verbs and contrast with adjectives:

(58)   a.   The witch made her feel fond of/love/hate the prince every time he drops in to visit.
       b.   *The witch made Mary fond of the prince/obnoxious to the prince, every time he drops in to visit.

iv.   **test 4: distributivity**: If eventualities are atomic and M-states are non-atomic, then we might expect a difference in whether they can distribute over their subjects. The occurrence of the 'floating quantifier 'each' shows that there is such a difference:

(59)   a.   The medicine made Jane and Mary each feel sick.
       b.   *The medicine made Jane and Mary each sick.

Together, these four tests provide clear evidence for the mass/count distinction I am proposing. The atomic, verbal domain can be counted (test 1). The entities in that domain have an individuating property, temporal locatedness, which entities in the domain of M-states don't have (test 2). There are linguistic functions, such as the matching function in the 'every time' construction, whose domain is restricted to the atomic eventuality domain (test 3). And the atomic entities can explicitly distribute over individuals, while the mass entities cannot (test 4). So the evidence given in this section shows that the kind of event argument introduced by even a stative verb, which intuitively is the most mass-like, has its denotation in a set of entities which are countable, individuable via the property of temporal location, and distributable, while M-states have none of these properties. In section 10.5, I'll discuss in greater depth what this data means, but first, I shall discuss some formal issues.

10.4.3. *The representation*

The formal framework for interpretation is what we set up in chapter 6. We assume a neo-Davidsonian theory of verbs, where verbs denote properties of eventualities and introduce a set of thematic roles (possible empty, as in the case of *snow*) denoting functions from e, whose value is given by the theta-marked syntactic argument. Arguments internal to VP are satisfied at the V′ level, and VP denotes a set of eventualities; the distinguished x variable which is the value of the external theta-role is bound by the λ-operator introduced by automatic predicate formation at the VP level. Simple Vs thus denote sets of events and are of type $<e,t>$; the lexical item associated with a V will include the event expression together with information about the thematic roles, conjunctively, and will be of a higher type, depending on the number and kind of arguments. In chapter 6 we showed that the schema for the translation of the verbal projection before predicate formation abstraction is (60a), and predicate formation is a gives (60b). (Θ is a variable over thematic roles):

(60)   a. $\lambda e.V(e) \wedge \Theta_1(e) = x$
       b. $\lambda x \lambda e.VP(e) \wedge \Theta_1(e) = x$

I restrict myself to a discussion of predicate adjectives. Adjectives (and APs) have a state variable and denote sets of M-states of type $<s_e,t>$, i.e. functions from state eventualities to type t. I have been assuming that adjectives introduce a set of 'argument-roles', parallel to the thematic roles introduced by verbs; I have been using 'Arg' as a variable expression over these argument roles, with "Arg_1" naming the external argument of the adjective, and Arg_2 name the complement. A difference between Arg and Θ now turns out to be that Θ-roles are functions from events to their participants and Arg-roles are functions from states to their participants. The adjectival schema parallel to (60) is thus (61):

(61)   a. $\lambda s.A(s) \wedge Arg_1(s) = x$
       b. $\lambda x \lambda s.AP(s) \wedge Arg_1(s) = x$

A natural proposal would be that the difference between verbs, denoting sets of events, and adjectives, denoting sets of M-states, is simply that the latter do not have the extra Davidsonian argument. We might hypothesise that the schema for the interpretation of an AP (before XP abstraction) is (62):

(62)   a. ADJ(x)   [or $\lambda x.ADJ(x)$ after Predicate Formation].
       b. TALL(x) [or $\lambda x.TALL(x)$ after Predicate Formation].

However, (62) doesn't work because of modification facts. Assume, following Davidson (1967) and Parsons (1990) that the Davidsonian argument is used in adverbial modification, as demonstrated in (63). (Two possible representations for the locative modifier are given in (63b) and (63c); the first is Parsons', and the second is based on a suggestion in Landman (1999)):

(63)   a. Anthony visited Cleopatra in Egypt
       b. $\exists e[VISITED(e) \wedge Ag(e) = A \wedge Th(e) = C \wedge IN(e) = EGYPT]$
       c. $\exists e[VISITED(e) \wedge Ag(e) = A \wedge Th(e) = C \wedge LOC(e) \sqsubseteq IN\ EGYPT]$

Adjectives too can be modified by durational and locative adverbials, as we saw in (51a), and as is shown by the examples in (64):

(64) a. The psychologist considers the child well-behaved/happy at school and badly-behaved/unhappy at home.
   b. The drug (immediately) made her quiet for hours.

In (64a) the locative adverbial *at home* can only be interpreted as modifying the adjectives in the predicate of the small clause and not the matrix verb, and similarly in (64b), the temporal *for hours* modifies *quiet*. I therefore assume that adjectives have a state argument, parallel to the eventuality argument, but whose value is in the mass rather than the count domain. The schema for the interpretation of adjective must be as in (61), and the representation of *quiet for hours* is given in (65):

(65) $\lambda s.\text{QUIET}(s) \wedge \text{Arg}_1(s) = x \wedge \text{DURATION}(s) = \text{HOURS}$

What the representation shows then, is that adjectives are very similar to verbs in that they both introduce sets of eventualities which have participants and which can be modified. The difference between them is in the properties these eventualities have. The data in 10.4.2 show that the eventualities introduced by verbs have properties that are associated with count entities, while the M-states introduced by adjectives lack these properties. This leaves open the question of what the crucial difference is between them which makes the verbally introduced eventualities atomic, and the M-states non-atomic. I'll show in the next section that the crucial property is temporal locatability.

10.5. 'BE' AND THE MASS/COUNT DISTINCTION

10.5.1. *'Be'*

Assuming then that there is a mass domain of M-states whose elements are the denotations of adjectival expressions and a count domain of eventualities whose members are the denotations of verbal expressions, what interests us next is the relations between the domains.

The relation between sets of M-states and sets of eventualities parallels the relation between mass-count nominal predicates proposed in Link (1983). Link basically assumes that both the count and the mass domain have the structure of a boolean semilattice, structured by a sum operation "⊔", and a part of relation "⊑", where the count structure is an atomic boolean semilattice of singular (atomic) and plural individuals. There is a function mapping from individuals to the stuff of which they are composed, which maps from the count domain (**C**) to the mass domain (**M**), mapping individual entities onto the join of their material parts. Lewis called this the **grinding** function, g, (cited in Pelletier 1975). The definition in (66) (and in (69) below) is the one used in Landman (1991):

(66) the **grinder** function is that function g: $C \rightarrow M$ such that for every $c \in C : g(c) = \sqcup \{x \in M: xKc\}$, where K is the relation 'material part of'.

This function is a homomorphism, preserving crucial ordering relations, so that if a is a part of the plural individual a ⊔ b, then the stuff making up a is a part of the stuff making up a ⊔ b. It is the function that we use in (67), where the count term *bicycle* is used as a mass term.

(67)   After he had been working for an hour, there was bicycle all over the garage floor.

Pelletier (1975) also discusses **packaging (p)**, which maps from the mass to the count domain, mapping quantities of stuff onto count individuals made from that stuff. It is used in sentences such as (47), repeated here as (68):

(68)   At the cafe, they ordered three beers, two teas and ice-creams all round.

Landman's formulation of the packaging operation, given in (69), characterises it by its crucial property; if you grind down the result of packaging, you get exactly the same stuff that you started out with.

(69)   the **packaging** operation is p: $M \rightarrow AT$ such that for every $m \in M$: $g(p(m)) = m$, where AT is the set of atoms out of which the count domain is built.

The packaging operation presents the mass stuff from a count perspective. Note that while grinding back down a packaged mass entity gives you the original stuff, the converse doesn't hold. Packaging a ground-down count entity does not necessarily give you back the individual that you started with. This is because mapping from the count to the mass domain is a function: grinding down a count element gives you only one possible result, namely the stuff that the count element is made of (although there are some problems, noted in Bach (1986), such as whether a snowman grinds into the snow that it is made of or the water that the snow is made of). Grinding is a many-to-one function, so, for example, the individual John and the sum of cells making up John are mapped onto the same chunk of stuff. Packaging is less predictable, and Link doesn't assume that it is a function; this is because the same chunk of stuff can be mapped onto the individual John and the sum of cells making up John. Chunks of stuff may also be packaged into something for which the language does not have a name: for example, the stuff making up John will be mapped onto the individual denoted by *John*, but the stuff which together makes up John's right leg and his left arm will not map onto any individual recognised and labeled by the language.

   Bach (1986), citing examples from Pelletier (1975), makes a further point, namely that packaging in English doesn't fully determine interpretation. Packaging does put stuff into units, but we rely on context to tell what the nature of the units is. In (70), the context tells us whether *three beers* means three portions of beer or three kinds of beer:

(70)   a. I drank three beers, and enjoyed them all.
         b. I tasted three beers and enjoyed them all.

I will assume that packaging is a function, but that instead of there being one packaging function p, we should assume a set of such functions P_C, with "C" a contextual variable. But nothing crucial rests on this assumption.

The packaging, or mapping from the mass to the count domain, that occurs in the nominal domain occurs in the verbal domain too. In the nominal domain, the use of a count determiner and/or a plural marker indicates that packaging has occurred. In the verbal domain, the packaging is explicitly introduced by the verb *be*.

Intuitively, what *be* + AP does is to package, or present from a count perspective, the set of M-states, or state type, denoted by AP. It does this by presenting it as a set of eventualities. The crucial property which is added when the M-states are packaged in this way is that like all other eventualities, they become temporally located (even if the temporal location is not explicitly mentioned in the sentence). Thus, *be* denotes a particular kind of packaging operation, namely, a locating function which maps from the domain of M-states to the domain of located eventualities. I call this locating operation 'instantiation'; it maps an M-state onto a located eventuality which displays an instance of the M-state. Formally, *be* denotes the relation INST (for instantiate). Let l be the locating function and 'S' a variable of type $<s_e, t>$. The instantiation relation denoted by *be* is given in (71):

(71) be $\rightarrow$ INST $= \lambda S \lambda e . \exists s \in S: e = l(s)$

Note that the domain of l is the set of M-states and its range is the set of events, i.e. l: $S \rightarrow E$. In other words, l(s) is not a location, but a located eventuality in E.

Compare (71) with the denotation of a verb like *walk*, which looks something like $\lambda e . WALK(e) \wedge Ag(e) = x$. We see that *be*, like any other verb, introduces a Davidsonian eventuality argument. Unlike other verbs, it doesn't tell us what kind of event it is, nor does it introduce thematic roles which tell us what participants it has. (This is what is at the root of the intuition that a 'copula' has no lexical content.) Instead, it selects a set of M-states and it denotes the relation between an eventuality and a set of M-states which holds if the eventuality instantiates a member of the set. Thus, while the AP has its denotation in the non-atomic, mass domain, *be* + AP has its denotation in the atomic, count domain. A VP headed by *be* denotes a set of atomic eventualities instantiating the set of states denoted by the complement of *be*; an eventuality e instantiates a set of states S if it is an eventuality in which some M-state s holds, where s is a member of S.

(72) a. clever $\rightarrow \lambda s . CLEVER(s) \wedge Arg_1(s) = x$
      b. be clever $\rightarrow \lambda e . \exists s [Clever(s) \wedge Arg_1(s) = x \wedge e = l(s)]$

Syntactically, *be clever* is a verb; it denotes a set of atomic eventualities with all the properties of count entities; we predict that *be* + AP should behave like any other verb with respect to counting, temporal location and adverbial modification. If we look again at the tests that we discussed in the previous section, we see that this is exactly what happens.

i.   **test 1: counting adverbials**: (73) is ambiguous, with *three times* modifying either the matrix verb or the embedded verbal predicate *be clever* in the small clause. In this, it is exactly like (48a), and contrasts with (48b) where *three times* can only modify the matrix verb and not the bare AP in the small clause.

(73)   I made Mary be angry/clever in classes 3 times. (ambiguous).

(48)   a. I made Mary know the answer three times.
       b. I made Mary angry/clever (in class) 3 times.

ii.   **test 2: temporal locatability**: (74) is acceptable, with *be clever* and *be stupid* each independently temporally located. In this (74) patterns like (49a), where the embedded predicate is a stative verb and unlike the unacceptable (49b), where the bare APs cannot be independently temporally located:

(74)   Yesterday, the witch made John be clever last night and be stupid this morning.

(49)   a.   Yesterday the witch made John know the answer last night and forget it this morning.
       b.   *Yesterday, the witch made John clever last night and stupid this morning.

Some speakers find (74) and (49a) less than perfect; as the NALS reviewer pointed out, events of causation usually only allow temporal adverbials that span both the causing event and the caused event, and this would mean that the temporal modifier of the matrix verb and the complement verb could not conflict. Nonetheless, even for these speakers, (49b) is much worse than either (74) or (49a).

iii.   **test 3: adverbial modification by event quantifiers**: in (75) *be nervous* can be modified by the event quantifier *every time the bell rings*. In this it behaves like the stative verb *worry* rather than the bare APs *nervous* and *excited*:

(75)   I made him be nervous/excited every time the bell rings.

(56)   a.   I made Jane worry every time the bell rings.
       b.   *I made Jane nervous/excited every time the bell rings.

Note also that the domain selection illustrated in (75/56) shows up in 'ordinary' adverbial modification too. In (76a), quickly can modify *made*, but not the AP *quiet*, but in (76b) it can modify either the verbal complex *be quiet* or the verb + particle *quiet down*:

(76)   a. Mary made the child quiet quickly.
       b. Mary made the child be quiet quickly/quiet down quickly.

iv.   **test iv: distributivity**: in (77) we see that the distributive adverbial can occur with predicates of the form *be* + AP. 'Each' thus treats *be* + AP like an ordinary verbal and not like a bare adjective.

(77) The medicine made Jane and Mary each be sick.

(59) a. The medicine made Jane and Mary each feel sick.
 b. *The medicine made Jane and Mary each sick.

We see then, that *be*, like any other verb, introduces an eventuality variable, 'e'. It presents a set of M-states from a count perspective, and allows us to treat M-states as members of the count domain. The fact that *be* essentially introduces a change of perspective is what is at the root of the intuition that *be* is a grammatical formative and not a 'content word' like other, lexical, verbs. Assuming the meaning for *be* given in (71), 'Jane was clever last Monday' will have the representation in (78):

(78) $\exists e \exists s [\text{CLEVER}(s) \wedge \text{Arg}_1(s) = \text{JANE} \wedge e = l(s) \wedge \text{PAST}(e)$
 $\wedge \text{ LAST MONDAY}(e)]$

(78) will be true if there was an eventuality which can be located in the past on last Monday and it was an eventuality in which Jane had the cleverness property.

Two further points about the nature of the locating function. First, I assume that finegrainedness in the Parsonian sense holds in the domain of eventualities, and that it extends, of course, to the eventualities in the denotations of VPs of the form *be* + AP. In the nominal domain, two atomic entities under different descriptions can be identical. But fine-grainedness as analysed by Parsons (1990) means that an eventuality – an entity from the domain of events – is not identical with an eventuality under another description. So while the event of Mary's passing a very difficult math exam may be the evidence for there being an event instantiating her being clever, Parsons would not analyse them as identical. The eventuality instantiating the state of Mary being clever is an independently individuated event; the instantiation relation sets up new eventualities and doesn't 'take a free ride' on already individuated eventualities. We can show this with an argument from Chierchia (1984).

Chierchia (1984) argues that every selling event is matched with a buying event. If John sold Bill the book, then Bill bought the book from John. The selling event talked about has the same participants as the buying event, namely John, Bill and the book, and it took place at the same time. Nonetheless, they must be two separate events, since they can have different properties, indicated by the fact that in each sentence different modifiers can appear. Thus, if Bill bought the book with a credit card, it doesn't follow that John sold the book with a credit card. Parsons (1990) gives a different example: suppose that in a billiards game, with one stroke, John hit the 8-ball into the corner pocket and the 9-ball into the side pocket. We would want to say that two different hitting events have occurred distinguished by their participants, each with a different theme. Again, each event can be modified independently; for example the hitting of the 8-ball into the corner pocket was gentle and unintentional, and the hitting of the 9-ball into the side pocket was violent and intentional.

By the same criteria, an event which is the output of the locating operation is not going to be identified with any other event. For example, if we assert that Jane is helpful, we assert that there is an event instantiating Jane having the helpfulness property. Suppose that the evidence for our assertion is that she helpfully drove her aunt to the shops, then is the instantiating event that we talk about the same as the event of her taking her aunt to the shops? The modification argument indicates that these are two separate events. Suppose that Jane is happy about being helpful to her aunt, but reluctant about driving her to the shops (maybe it's rush hour and the traffic is appalling). Then the event instantiating the state of Jane's being helpful is one she has happy relation with while the event of driving to the shops is one she has a reluctant relation with. So the instantiating event and the driving to the shops event cannot be identical.

Second, the locating operation must be a function because of the abstract nature of events. An M-state, being a mass entity, is dense (each subpart of a state s is also a state s). It is mapped by the locating operation onto the temporal location at which it holds (while it may itself be a proper subpart of a bigger state of the same type). Since this new located eventuality has no inherent properties other than those provided by the state, then if a state were mapped onto more than one event there would be no way of distinguishing them, and they would de facto be identical. This emphasises the fact that the locating function is a linguistic construct expressing primarily a change of perspective on the state. Two states which are members of the denotation of a single lexical expression will be identical if they hold at exactly the same time. Because a state is dense (and time also) there will be an infinite number of instantiation functions (though their values may overlap). This parallels the way that an operation maps water onto quantities of water. While there are an infinite number of ways of dividing a mass up into smaller quantities, any two quantities which occupy the same space-time location must be the same 'chunks of stuff'.

One might ask whether verbs can be lexically decomposed analogously to the way in which *be clever* can be decomposed into the meaning contributed by *be* and the meaning contributed by *clever*. This would give *walk*, for example, a lexical representation like that in (79a), in which the verb is analysed as denoting an instantiation relation between an eventuality variable and a state WALK. But this implies that the meaning of the verb can be broken down into the elements in (79b):

(79)   a. $\lambda e.\text{WALK}(e) = \lambda e.\exists s[\text{WALK}(s) \land e = l(s)]$
        b. $\lambda S\lambda e.\exists s[S(s) \land e = l(s)](\lambda s.\text{WALK}(s))$

This decomposition would not be visible in either the syntactic or the semantic representations. If this decomposition were typical, then all verbal meanings would have the function expressed in (79b) as an element of their meaning, and they would differ in the set of states to which this function was applied. This function is exactly the meaning we gave to *be* in (71). So, the meaning of *be* would then be the same as the non-varying part of the meaning of a lexical verb. And the difference between *be* and lexical verbs would be that the functional application which takes place covertly in the construction of the lexical meaning in the case of (79) takes place explicitly in the syntax in the case of *be*. Whether verbal meanings can ultimately be analysed in this way is a question which I leave open.

10.5.2. *A comparison between the mass/count distinction in the nominal and verbal domains*

I have been arguing that the denotations of APs are sets of mass states (M-states) and that the denotations of VPs are sets of atomic eventualities (and sums of atomic eventualities) and that we can therefore find in the verbal/adjectival domain a count/mass distinction which parallels the distinction within the nominal domain. In this section I want to look more closely at how exact this parallelism is.

The relation between mass and count which I am assuming is that set out in Link (1983) in his discussion of the relation between mass-count nominal predicates. Link argues for a structured domain of individuals which includes a domain (i-domain) of singular individuals denoted by count predicates: these include the denotations of *Mary* and *Jane* and *my ring*, and also plural individuals such as those denoted by *Mary and Jane, my two wedding rings*, and *Fred's and my wedding rings*. He argues also for a d-domain of quantities of 'stuff' such as the silver that my rings are made out of and the gold that my rings are made out of and the stuff which is the join of these two portions of matter, in other words the denotation of *the silver and gold that my rings are made out of*. The count domain forms an atomic boolean semilattice structure, with the singular individuals being the atoms, while the mass domain of stuff forms a non-atomic (and possibly atomless) boolean semilattice structure. There are mappings between the domain of individuals (atomic and plural) and the domain of stuff; a 'packaging' operation maps quantities of stuff onto individuals made up of the stuff, and a 'grinding' operation maps individuals onto the stuff of which they are made up. The mapping relations between the two structures show that a particular spatio-temporally located entity can appear as "stuff" in the mass domain and, under a different description, as the denotation of a count term in the atomic domain: the distinction between mass and count is thus a distinction between predicates, or entities under a particular description, and not a distinction between kinds of entities.

The semantic properties that Link's structure is intended to capture are two: countability and homogeneity. Countability is self-explanatory: a countable domain is one in which one can count the elements; this occurs when the elements of the domain occur in units – the atoms. This means that addition preserves the structure: if one puts two units together one can see in the result that it has two parts. If you put one dog together with another dog, then you can see that the result has two elements, the two dogs, and count them. In a non-atomic, homogenous domain, putting two entities together is not 'structure-preserving'. If you pour two glasses of water into a bigger glass, the result is a glass of water. The elements which contribute to it are 'lost' in the operation and you cannot count them. This is what we might call 'upward homogeneity'. There is also a property which we can call 'downward homogeneity': it is a characteristic of a quantity of mass 'stuff' like water that if you split it into two parts, both parts can still be called water (as long as you don't split too small). This does not hold generally of count nouns. Normally, if you split a dog or table, you won't get two dogs or two tables. (We ignore the reproductive processes of amoebae here.) There are two caveats about the splitting of denotations of count nouns; one is that if one takes a small enough part out of a dog or a table, one will still be left with a dog or a table. But this is because the small enough part is 'too small to be important', and the original count term will apply only to the larger entity that one is left with. This means that the contrast with mass stuff still holds. When we split water into parts, we are interested precisely in the cases in which all parts are 'big enough'; in these situations, there are no constraints on the relative sizes of the parts and all resulting parts are called water. A second, and more important, issue is that there are count nouns denoting entities which can be split in the same way that water can be split. This observation is attributed to Mittwoch (1988) in a footnote (fn24), and to Barbara Partee, in a p.c. to Krifka, who discusses it in Krifka (1989). Mittwoch points out that *line* and other mathematical terms are downward homogeneous; a line can be broken into two parts, both of which are lines, with exactly the same caveat as for mass terms, namely that both parts must be big enough. Krifka (1989) and Zucchi and White (1996) discuss Partee's observation that nouns such as *sequence, twig* and *quantity of milk* may have proper parts which are sequences, twigs and quantities of milk respectively. Examples like these will be central in our discussion of the comparison between the nominal and verbal domain, and we'll return to them below.

Ignoring them for the moment, however, we see that the differences in 'downward homogeneity' in the mass and count domains are related to the fact that the count domain has a set of atoms as its minimal elements, while the mass domain is atomless. Thus while part of a quantity of water is still water, a part of a unit of dog is not a dog. So, the nominal count domain is countable and non-homogenous and the nominal mass domain is non-countable and homogenous, and this follows from the fact that the count domain is atomic and the mass domain non-atomic.

Predicates are count or mass depending on what domain they find their denotation in. A singular count predicate is one that has its denotation in the set of atoms; for example, the predicate *dog* can apply to Spot and to Max. It is non-homogenous, because it does not apply to parts of Spot or Max, nor does it apply to the sum of Spot and Max. For that we need a plural predicate, *dogs. Water* is a mass term. It does not apply only to atoms of water, but to non-countable quantities, and it is homogenous: if you split the water in a bucket into two, both will be water, and if you take two bodies of water, then the predicate *water* will apply to their sum. That the mass/count distinction is a distinction in the way linguistic terms work is shown by the existence of near synonyms such as *coins/change, shoes/footwear* (see Pelletier 1979 and references there).

These semantic properties have grammatical reflexes. Chierchia (1998a) lists ten well-known "main empirical properties that jointly characterise the different behaviour of mass and count nouns" and which "appear to be tendentially universal i.e. they turn up whenever such a contrast can be detected" (his section 1.2). We have, in section 10.4.2, identified a number of linguistic properties which distinguish adjectival from verbal predicates, and I claimed that these differences followed from a mass/count distinction. It is interesting to look at these properties and see how they match with the empirical properties which Chierchia, in his summary, expects to see characterise any mass/count contrast.

The first three properties that Chierchia mentions clearly reflect the countable/non-countable (i.e. atomic/non-atomic) contrast. Count nouns take plural morphology, can co-occur with numeral determiners and do not (usually) occur with classifiers. Mass nouns, on the other hand, do not pluralise (except as a result of packaging), do not occur bare with numeral determiners, and require classifiers if they are to be counted:

(80) a.   chair, chairs   a'.   furniture, *furnitures
      b.   three chairs   b'.   *three furnitures
      c.   *three pieces of chair(s) c'.   three pieces of furniture

(80c) can be interpreted as applying to parts of a chair that can be put together or parts of a broken chair, but on this reading, 'chair' has undergone grinding, and that's not the reading we are interested in here.) Pluralisation is a morphological operation applying to nouns, which doesn't work in English in the verbal count domain – verbs denoting plural eventualities are not morphologically marked as plural – so in English, the first property cannot have a parallel in the domain of eventualities and M-states. (There may well be cross linguistic variation here, since there may be inflectional affixes on verbs, marking such things as iteration, which one would want to count as pluralisers. This would be a place to look for contrasts between adjectives and verbs.) The second property is realised in the verbal domain: the parallel to numeral determiners can reasonably be assumed to be the counting adverbials we discussed in test 1 above in section 10.4.2, which distinguishes between verbal and adjectival predicates exactly as Chierchia would predict. The question of classifiers is slightly more complicated. If classifiers are seen as inherently nominal elements, then again independent restrictions on the distribution of nominals would rule out classifiers with either verbs or adjectives. This is because nominal classifiers are restricted to taking as their complements (and thus to classifying) expressions which have the form [of DP]$_{PP}$. Neither adjectives nor verbs will fit into this form. However, if we see classifiers as lexical elements introducing some form of packaging function, then we might want to identify *be* itself as essentially a classifier.

The second group of properties that Chierchia talks about revolve around the determiner system. Determiners can select for only count nouns (singular or plural), only mass nouns, mass nouns and plurals, or can be unrestricted. The four possibilities are illustrated in (81):

(81) a. each/every/a book; several/few/many books; *every/several water
      b. little/much water; *little/*much book(s)
      c. a lot of/plenty (of) water; a lot of/plenty (of) books; *a lot of/*plenty (of) book.
      d. the/some book(s); the/some water

I just suggested that counting adverbials have the function in the verbal/adjectival domain which numeral determiners such as those in (80b) have in the nominal domain. Carrying this through, we might expect to find adverbial modifiers which exert selectional restrictions parallel to those illustrated in (81). Since there is no lexical distinction between verbal expressions denoting singular and plural eventualities, we might expect to find adverbials selecting only mass expressions, adverbials selecting only count expressions and adverbials which are unrestricted. We have seen that expressions of temporal location, and also adverbials such as *'every time ...'*, and the floating adverbial quantifier *each*, modify only count expressions. This is what we would expect since temporal locatedness is, by hypothesis, only a property of count expressions, and the quantifier *each*, as a distributor, should occur only in an atomic domain.

We have also seen that there are adverbial expressions which are unrestricted, for example, adverbials which are expressions of temporal duration like *for two hours* (see examples (51) and (64)). The NALS reviewer suggests that some differences may be seen in intensifiers and degree modifiers. So, the degree modifier *a bit* seems to modify both adjectives and verbs (with the modifier preceding the adjective and following the verb), while *a lot* seems to modify only verbs. In (82e), where the modifier follows the adjective, it modifies only the matrix verb.

(82) a. We made/let Mary sleep a bit.
      b. We made/kept Mary a bit sleepy.
      c. We made/let Mary sleep a lot.
      d. *We made/kept Mary a lot sleepy.
      e. We made/kept Mary sleepy a lot.

There are also degree expressions which seems to modify only adjectives, and some of these have 'pseudo-adverbial' forms:

(83) a. The birthday party made Dafna extremely/very happy.
      b. *She laughed extremely.

Also, while *enough* as a verbal degree modifier can have either a temporal reading or a reading as an intensifier, it seems that as an adjectival modifier it has only a use as an intensifier. (84a) easily has a reading in which they made the quantity of Mary's sleeping or laughing sufficient in duration or frequency, and, also (especially with *laugh*) in intensity, but (84b) has only the reading in which her sleepiness or happiness is sufficient in intensity. (Both, of course, have a reading where *enough* modifies the matrix verb.)

(84)   a. They made Mary sleep enough/laugh enough.
       b. They made Mary sleepy enough/happy enough.

So taking into account the syntactic categorial differences, there does seem to be some evidence that lexical items can select for mass or count elements in the verbal/adjectival domain also.

Chierchia's last three tests concern the relation between nouns and their denotata. Crucially, the mass/count distinction is independent of the structure of matter, and this is demonstrated by the fact that even within languages, and certainly across languages, the same items can be denoted by either mass or count expressions. Chierchia cites the following as near-synonyms in English *shoes* vs. *footwear*, *clothes* vs. *clothing*, *coins* vs. *change*, and *carpet* vs. *carpeting*. The tests that Chierchia discusses involve the relation between mass predicates and count predicates as expressed by the packaging and grinding functions. These are correlations of the fact that the linguistic distinction is independent of the structure of matter: since the mass/count status of the lexical noun is a linguistic property and is not reflected in the structure of matter, the language can easily allow the change of perspective which is expressed in the grinding and packaging operations.

The first two of these properties clearly show up in the verbal-adjectival domain. The independence of the count-mass distinction in the eventuality-M-state domain is independent of the structure of 'the world', and must be so because of the abstract nature of events. Eventualities and states are ways of organising the world into entities. The fact that there is a function mapping from the mass domain of M-states to the count domain of eventualities shows that the difference is one of perspective, of the way we classify situations. As for packaging, I have argued that it clearly exists in the form of the locating function. It is less obvious that there is a grinding function, mapping events onto unlocated states. Hoever, there are two places where we might look for it. One is in lexical decomposition operations such as the one involved in the decomposition in (79). The other we will come back to below in our discussion of the mass-like properties that Bach argues that activities/processes display.

So we see that the kinds of differences that we have seen between adjectives and verbs are of the kind that we expect to find at the mass-count fault, and parallel the differences between mass and count nominals. The two categories, adjectives and verbs, denote entities from sortally different domains, and linguistically represented functions (denoted by adverbials) recognise and distinguish between these domains. Counting adverbials and adverbial 'floating quantifiers' like *each*, which modify only verbs are the clearest indication that verbs denote atomic, countable entities, while adjectives don't.

However, Chierchia's tests don't tell us anything about how the property of homogeneity is realised in the domain of eventualities and states. This is because the property that really indicates whether the domains are homogenous for nominals is plurality, and this is a morphological property which doesn't apply outside the nominal domain. We saw above that the evidence that *water* or *wine* denote homogenous entities is that the term applies equally to a chunk of stuff, to subparts of the chunk of stuff and to sums of two or more chunks of stuff. And crucially, these chunks can be discontinuous. So, I can easily say things like the examples in (85):

(85) a. The wine for dinner is in the fridge and on the balcony.
      b. The water in both lakes is fresh water.

We can see that the count domain is non-homogenous because of the requirement that terms which apply to sums of atoms are marked as plural. We can only say (86a) or (86b) and not (86c):

(86) a. Spot is a dog and Max is a dog.
      b. Spot and Max are dogs.
      c. *Spot and Max are a dog.

The fact that counting adverbials modify verbs and do not modify adjectives shows that we do have pluralities of eventualities, and strongly implies that we don't have pluralities of M-states, and therefore that the domain of the first isn't homogenous and the domain of the second is. This means that in the domain of eventualities, when we put together instances to make a sum, the sum should in essence be 'different thing' from the singular entity; indeed we should be able to see that they are sums of atoms, and to have access to their atomic structure. In the domain of states, this should be impossible.

It is very difficult to test for this because neither verbs nor adjectives are marked for plurality. Thus the standard test in the nominal domain, illustrated in (85/86), namely whether or not the same predicate applies to the singular and plural entity, is just not relevant. Plural markers on verbs indicate agreement with plural subjects, but this does not necessarily mean that a verb marked plural denotes a plurality of events because a singular event can have a plural subject, as in the example in (87):

(87) The boys carried the piano upstairs together (once).

Discourse anaphora doesn't help either, since the plural pronoun *they* never has its denotation in the domain of events. (I gather that this is different in American English; a reviewer offers *they* in (88b) as grammatical, but in my dialect, and for other speakers of British English, only *it* is possible, as indicated in the diacritics.)

(88) a. The three girls each jumped once. It/*They happened between three and four o'clock.
      b. I had a difficult afternoon: the dishwasher overflowed. The cat had kittens. The lights fused. And it/*they all happened at once.

What we do see is that in examples like (89), we can make reference to a sum of eventualities and still have access to the atomic structure. (89a) is an example with an activity verb and (89b) with an accomplishment. I am interested in the non-cumulative reading of (89b), where there was a plurality of events of eating three apples, and each girl ate three.

(89) a. The girls ran in turn. It happened over a period of an hour at five minute intervals.
      b. There were three girls. In turn they ate three apples. It took half an hour.

In (89a) *it* makes reference to the sum of running events which lasted an hour and the adverbial *at five minute intervals* makes use of the atomic structure. In (89b) we see that the telic predicate *eat three apples* applies to the singular atomic events of which the sum denoted by *it* is composed. The plural event is an event in which nine apples are eaten. Both of these examples are indications that eventualities are not upwardly homogenous. However, there is one point at which upward non-homogeneity seems to break down. In the examples given above, the atoms of a sum can be distinguished by the fact that they have different agents and occur at different times. Suppose that there are two non-telic events (where the same predicate applies to a singular and a plural event) which have the same agent and which are temporally contiguous. If the two running events that I refer to are temporally adjacent, then they may be treated as a single event. If Dafna runs in the park and then she runs in the park some more, then whether we count one event of Dafna's running or two seems to depend on whether the two runnings are temporally separated or temporally connected. So it looks as if two events of Dafna's running, if they are temporally contiguous can be treated as a singular event, with each of the subevents and the sum event falling under the event description *Dafna run once*. This partial upward homogeneity ('partial' because it depends on the extra condition of temporal contiguity) occurs with atelic predicates. With a telic predicate such as *eat two apples*, if there is an event of eating two apples and then another event of eating two apples, the only way we can label them as a single event is to call them an event of eating four apples.

It turns out to be very difficult to prove that M-states are homogenous, independent of showing that they are non-countable. Since, as we have seen, the pronoun *it* can always make reference to sums of non-individual entities as well as singulars, and since there is no syntactic way of predicating properties of parts of states, we are essentially forced to treat M-states as upwardly homogenous for independent reasons. But there are at least some indications that M-states are different from eventualities in this respect.

First, suggested to me by Fred Landman (p.c.), is the effect of using the expression *it lasted x time*. This expression seems to give the duration of a single eventuality or state. As we said above, pluralities of eventualities may always be combined into a single abstract eventuality, but some contexts make this less plausible. If we find a context in which it is inappropriate to treat a number of eventualities as a sum, but we find that in the same context, a number of M-states are treated as a sum, then we have some evidence that pluralities of non-distinguishable M-states must be treated as single entities. In (90), the adverbial **independently** stresses that there were two events of 'making', and thus two events which were caused.

(90)   Independently, Jane and Mary made the child run. It lasted two hours.

In this circumstance, *it* naturally refers to the process of Jane and Mary making the child run, and the second sentence asserts that this process lasted for two hours and not that the combined events of running lasted for two hours. In contrast, in (91) *it* most naturally refers to the state of being angry which was the combined result of both Mary and Jane's actions (although the other reading is also available):

(91)   Independently, Jane and Mary made the child angry. It lasted two hours.

If M-states are upwardly homogenous, then this is explained: the result of each action must have been a state of the child being angry, and the result of both their actions is a single state of the child being angry, which we can assign a duration. As we would predict, (92) patterns like (90) and not like (91):

(92)   Independently, Jane and Mary made the child be angry. It lasted two hours.

Another indication of upward homogeneity is use of the expression *the same*. If I make Dafna happy on Monday morning and on Tuesday morning, I can say (93); there is an intuitive sense that she is in the same state.

(93)   On both Monday and Tuesday, I made Dafna be in the same state.

Of course, there also are two occurrences of the state, and crucially, it is these occurrences that we count, and not states themselves; but (93) seems to make reference to a single state, part of which is instantiated by an event located on Monday, and part of which is instantiated by an event located on Tuesday. However, if I make or see her run twice, then I haven't made or seen the same event occur twice, but rather, I have made or seen two instances or occurrences of the same kind of event. (94a) implies that I watching a video with a rewind button, and not that I saw two running occurrences. If I want to say that I saw two tokens of the same kind of event, I'll say (94b):

(94)   a. I saw the same event (Dafna run) twice.
       b. I saw the same thing/?event happen twice.

Testing for downward homogeneity, it is impossible to make any distinctions along the M-state/eventuality line, and the crucial distinction becomes telic vs non-telic. The distinction that downward homogeneity draws is essentially the one captured by Krifka (1992) when he uses the notion of "Set Terminal Point" to distinguish between quantized (telic) and non-quantized (non-telic) predicates. A 'set terminal point' is the externally given point which dictates when the eventuality ends. The point at which the two apples disappear indicates the end of an event of eating two apples. An atelic predicate like *run* has no set terminal point because the predicate itself gives no information about when the event it denotes ends. A telic predicate like *run a mile* has a set terminal point because it dictates how long the event it applies to lasts, namely until the mile is run. It follows that a subevent of 'run a mile' is not also an event of 'run a mile' while a subevent of 'run' is also an event of running. In this respect, M-states are like any other non-telic predicate. If I make Jane happy, then the any subpart of that state is also a state of Jane being happy.

The line between atelic predicates and telic predicates drawn by downward homogeneity is essentially the same division between verbal predicates that Bach (1986) draws; however, Bach argues that atelic verbal predicates denoting processes should be considered mass terms, while telic verbal predicates have their denotation in the count domain. Bach (1986) was the first, to my knowledge, to propose applying Link's distinction between mass and count to the verbal domain, and he distinguished between events and processes rather than between eventualities and states. He argued that events are count entities, and that the mass 'stuff' of which events are made are processes. This hypothesis is based on contrasts such as those in (95/96), which show that adverbial expressions for counting events like *three times*, contrast in their distribution with 'mass' adverbials like *a lot*, and with adverbials based on *much*:

(95) a. John slept a lot/too much last night.
       b. (*)John found a unicorn a lot/too much last night. (Bach; ex.2)

(96) a. John fell asleep three times during the night.
       b. (*)John slept three times last night. (Bach; ex.4)

The analysis that I am proposing here predicts that all eventualities are in principle countable, and that alongside the examples in (95/96), there must be sentences which indicate that verbally expressed processes also denote countable events. This seems to be correct. In context, (97a) is acceptable, and has different truth conditions from (97b), since if I fell asleep but was woken after two minutes, it would count as an event of falling asleep, but not, in my experience, as an event of sleeping.

(97) a. I slept only three times last week.
       b. I fell asleep only three times last week.

Bach claims that examples like this are instances of packaging stuff into count entities, and that temporal boundaries are all that is needed to package processes, while I claim that processes (and states, which Bach doesn't talk about) are inherently countable entities, and that no particular packaging process is going on. The counting of processes is a frequent and non-marked linguistic operation, as (98) shows, as is the modification of processes by adverbials which individuate events, as in (99a), and of course there is no problem temporally locating processes, as (99b) shows:

(98)   a. Truus has already walked several times since the operation on her hip.
       b. We have danced many times since then.
       c. Jane has been building a house three times since I met her. Once she got as far as putting up the walls, once she only dug some of the foundations, and once she got no further than getting the planning permission.

(99)   a. Every time she walks/dances/runs, she is glad that she had the operation.
       b. She walked yesterday for the first time.

The easy acceptability of these examples contrasts with impossibility of modifying adjectives with counting expressions, modifiers of temporal location and the 'every time' modifier which we saw in section 10.4.2, and makes it seem that it is adjectives which do not have their denotation in the domain of individuable events.

However, if we consider that non-countability and homogeneity are the hallmarks of mass expressions, then, as Fred Landman pointed out (p.c.), there is an apparent conflict here, which Bach's account of eventualities and Krifka's discussion of telicity brings out. Assume that (97/98), together with (48a), repeated here, shows that the denotations of even process and state verbs are in the count domain:

(48)   a. I made Mary know the answer three times.

By the criterion of countability, these atelic predicates are clearly count predicates, and non-mass. However, the same predicates are clearly downward homogenous, and partially upward homogenous (if contiguous constituents are added together), and are thus mass. Landman suggests that this indicates that in the verbal domain, homogeneity and countability are separable. This would constitute a difference between the mass/count distinction in the verbal domain and the nominal domain: in the nominal domain mass predicates are homogenous and non-atomic (= non-countable) and count predicates are atomic and non-homogenous, while in the verbal domain true mass predicates are homogenous and non-atomic, but count predicates are divided into one group which is atomic and non-homogenous, the telic predicates, and one which is atomic and homogenous. If this distinction is correct, then it would be an interesting distinction between the verbal/adjectival and nominal domains, but it would weaken the claim that the verb/adjective distinction is strongly analogous to the distinction between count and mass nominals. I shall argue in a moment that the strong analogy does not break down, and that the problem of countable but partially homogenous predicates occurs in the nominal domain as well, but first let us raise another question. If there are countable but partly homogenous predicates, then these presumably denote sets of atoms (or sums of atoms). But what is atomicity for a homogenous predicate? The notion of a partly homogenous, but atomic, predicate requires us to think differently about what atoms might be.

Normally, we think of atoms as being unbreakable small units. The atoms of the set of individuals denoted by *dog* are the individual dogs, none of whose subparts are dogs, and the atoms of the set of events denoted by *eat three apples* are the events of eating three apples none of whose subparts are events of eating three apples, and these are the things we count. But when we count events such as events of running, or, walking or being happy, then intuitively we are counting not the smallest units which have no subparts of the same type, but rather large temporally bounded units. If I say "Truus has walked three times since her operation", I am counting three 'big' events of walking. Each can be subdivided into smaller events of walking, but each is temporally bounded by a period of time which was not a walking event, as in the diagram in (100):

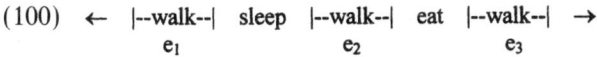

(100)   ← |--walk--| sleep |--walk--| eat |--walk--| →
          e_1 e_2 e_3

So the atoms, in this case, are not indivisible units, but atomic constructs; they are constructed not in terms of the relation between an event and its parts, but rather in terms of the relation between an event and the events that it may or may not be part of. Landman (p.c.) suggests the definitions in (101–103), restricting our attention to singular eventualities (where E_s is the domain of singular eventualities, I is the set of intervals and τ is the function mapping an event onto its running time).

(101)   e is an atom in E_s iff $\tau(e) \in I \wedge \neg \exists e' \in E_s: e \sqsubset e' \wedge \tau(e) \sqsubset \tau(e')$

Thus an atomic event, be it telic or atelic, is one which is not a proper part of a bigger event of the same kind. Atelic events are homogenous if they belong to a homogenous event type, where the latter is defined as follows:

(102)   Let $X \sqsubseteq E_s$:
        X is homogenous iff
        (i) if $i = i_1 + i_2 \wedge e \in X \wedge \tau(e) = i$,
            then $\exists e_1 e_2 \in X: e_1, e_2 \sqsubset e \wedge \tau(e_1) = i_1 \wedge \tau(e_2) = i_2$
        (ii) if $i = i_1 + i_2 \wedge e_1, e_2 \in X \wedge \tau(e_1) = i_1 \wedge \tau(e_2) = i_2$,
            then $\exists e \in X: e_1, e_2 \sqsubset e \wedge \tau(e) = i$.

Run denotes a homogenous event type:

(103) $\forall d \in AT: \{e \in RUN: Ag(e) = d\}$ is homogenous (if defined).

This means that for every event of Mary running holding at interval i, if we can reasonably split i into two subintervals i_1 and i_2, we find events of Mary running going on at i_1 and i_2 as well. Also, if a process of running goes on at i_1 and i_2 and they are adjacent, then an event of Mary running is going on at

$i_1 + i_2$. ('Adjacent' has to be defined in such a way as to allow single events to have pause stages, as defined in Landman (1992)). Thus events are allowed to be atomic and homogenous, with downward homogeneity being complete, and upward homogeneity being restricted to essentially temporally contiguous constituents. This would mean that if Jane made Betty run from one to two and Mary made Betty run from two to three we might consider there to be one extended event of Betty running, but if Jane made Betty run from one to two and Mary made Betty run from five to six, then there would be two events of Betty running. (Presumably there could also be contextual factors which would cause what would normally be considered a single event of running to be analysed as consisting of several atomic events, but I won't go into this here.)

Atoms, on this account, are not inherently indivisible, small units, but the smallest individuable units out of which count structures can be built. Verbal predicates access these units, adjectival ones do not.

Is this any different in the nominal domain? Is it the case that while the mass and count domains are distinguished by two properties in the nominal domain, namely countability and homogeneity, only the first is relevant in the verbal domain? And are atoms any more 'real' and less constructed in the nominal domain?

I think that the answer is perhaps slightly surprising: the verbal and nominal domains are parallel even with respect to homogeneity, but it is the verbal domain which gives a truer indication of how homogeneity and atoms work.

First, homogeneity **is** relevant in the verbal domain for distinguishing count eventualities from mass M-states. This is because, despite the apparent homogeneity of atelic events, there is a crucial distinction between the mass and count domain which makes use of upward homogeneity: events e_1 and e_2 can be part of a singular event e only if e_1 and e_2 are temporally connected in an appropriate way. True upward homogeneity, with mass predicates like *water* and, I would argue, M-states, like the state of Mary being happy, involves putting together chunks of stuff which are not necessarily contiguous, either temporally or spatially. The difference shows itself in the fact that if I put together contiguous events of, say, Dafna running, I will end up with an atomic unit, but if I collect together temporally non-contiguous events of the same kind, I will get a plurality.

Second, the property of downward homogeneity and partial upward homogeneity which we find in the verbal count domain can be found in the nominal count domain too. It is much rarer, although not as rare as some previous discussions of 'atelic' count predicates may lead one to think. As noted earlier, Mittwoch (1988) mentions the problem of mathematically defined terms such as *line*, and Krifka (1989) and Zucchi and White (1996) discuss the problem of *sequence*, *twig* and *quantity of milk*. The issue arises with a larger number of non-mathematical concrete terms; for example, predicates like *wall*, *fence*, *lawn* and *hedge*, which pass the obvious tests for count predicates: they pluralise, and they occur with count determiners and numeral determiners:

(104) a. fence/fences, wall/walls, lawn/lawns.
       b. two fences, three walls, four lawns.
       c. every fence, few walls, each lawn.

These predicates are homogenous in exactly the same sense that an event type like 'Mary run' is homogenous; they are downward homogenous and upward homogenous with respect to contiguous constituents, although contiguity is determined spatially rather than temporally. Suppose there is a square field and each side borders onto a different farmer's land. Each farmer builds a fence along the side which borders her land. Now imagine the situations in (105a/b), and the assertions in (105c–f):

(105) a. ┌──────┐   b. ──────
          │ The │   │ The │
          │ Field│   │ Field│
          └──────┘   ──────

       c. Four farmers have each built a fence.
       d. Four fences have been built.
       e. There is a fence surrounding The Field.
       f. There are four fences surrounding The Field.

Clearly, the assertions in both (105c) and (105d) can be true in both the pictured situations, since both pictures can support the assertions that there were four fence-building events, each with a different agent, and a different fence as theme. But, if the situation is as in (105a), we can also make the assertion in (105e), while it would be much less appropriate to use (105f). By contrast, if the farmers have built their fences so they looked liked (105b) we would not say that the field had a fence around it, and we might well say that there were four fences surrounding it or bordering it. So we don't have true upward homogeneity, and *fence* can be distinguished from true mass terms which apply to discontinuous constituents. Note, that we do have downward homogeneity. If the farmers take a piece of the fence out of the fence pictured in (105a) and put it around a tree, we can easily say that there is a fence around part of the field and a fence around the tree.

What makes it possible for *fence* to behave in this way is that there is no inherent unit of 'fence' as there is a well-defined unit or entity of 'dog'. Intuitively, a piece of fence is an atom iff there is no other piece of fence of which it is a proper part. If we assume that individuals are assigned a spatial location, or (assuming they are movable) a spatio-temporal location, then we can define homogeneity in the count domain and atomicity for homogenous count entities of the 'fence' variety parallel to the way we did it for count eventualities.

(106) Assume that L is a set of spatial locations and Loc(d) is a function from individuals into pairs of locations and intervals, assigning a spatial location to d at i: then d is an atom in D iff
       $Loc(d) \in LxI \land \neg \exists d' \in D: d \sqsubset d' \land Loc(d) \sqsubset Loc(d')$.

Homogeneity will occur whenever the entities involved do not have an inherent structure dictating what a unit of stuff is; the units will be defined contextually by looking for the maximal boundaries which an element has. I have suggested that the boundaries of events are defined temporally, and that the boundaries of noun-denotations are defined spatio-temporally; presumably boundaries of the mathematical concepts and abstract nouns will be defined in other terms, but the principle will be the same.

Note that this strengthens the well known claim that the mass/count distinction is independent of the structure of matter; it is well-known that a mass predicate like *furniture* can apply to stuff made up out of individuable units, and we now see the converse too: count predicates can apply to entities that do not consist of inherently individuable units. Atoms are not the 'smallest' elements in any ontological sense, but semantic constructs that we use as the basic units in constructing the count domain, and count terms force us to make such a construction. The fact that, in the case of dogs and cups and forks, the semantic atoms correspond to real-world units in the world is no doubt to do with the fact that the way the world is broken into units influences the way we construct our count domains, but it only influences it. I suspect that the problem of twigs and sequences, which I have extended to fences, walls and such like, is much more widespread.

There is clearly much more to say about the structure of the mass/count domains, and the importance of the property of homogeneity, both in the domain of individuals and in the domain of eventualities. I am not going to say it here. What I am interested in is two crucial points. One is that what I have hypothesised to be a mass/count distinction in the domain of eventualities shows the same kind of semantic properties as the distinction in the domain of individuals, and essentially the same grammatical properties – taking into account the categorial differences between nouns, verbs and adjectives. The second is that the crucial semantic property in both the domain of individuals and the domain of eventualities is the property of atomicity. In order to use homogeneity, one must test for upward homogeneity with discontinuous entities, since it is this which is an indication of a mass expression. Downward homogeneity and upward homogeneity between contiguous constituents is not a test for a mass term in either the nominal or the verbal domain.

Finally, note that since mass terms are completely homogenous both upwardly and downwardly, it is not surprising that those count terms which are partially homogenous feel more 'mass-like' that those which are not, and we would expect it to be easier to 'grind' such partially homogenous count entities. The kind of events which Bach categorises as mass are the partially homogenous ones; the fact that process verbs can be easily modified by modifiers like *a lot* while accomplishments can not, may be because there is a grinding operation which applies easily to the downwardly homogenous predicates. For at least some speakers (especially of British English), there is a correlation in the nominal domain; it easier to treat downwardly homogenous count terms as mass than it is to 'grind' non-homogenous ones. So, if I am painting the walls of a room, (107a) is much more natural than (107b);

(107)   a. Don't worry; there is enough wall for everyone to paint some.
        b. Don't worry; there is enough room for everyone to paint some.

But this is just the tip of the iceberg in a discussion of the properties of downwardly homogenous count terms.

10.6. HOW A DERIVATION WORKS

Let us go back to *be*, and look at how a derivation works. Remember that we argued in chapter 9, following Stowell (1978), that *be* selects a small clause complement and that the subject of the small clause raises to [Spec,IP], as in (108):

(108)   Mary$_i$ is [t$_i$ clever]

Up till now, we have adapted Vlach's (1983) and Parsons' (1990), analysis and treated small clauses generally as denoting sets of events. Now we will continue to assume that small clauses where the predicate is headed by a verb denote sets of events, but we will assume, in contrast, that small clauses where the predicate is headed by an adjective denote sets of M-states. This will give (109) as the derivation for (108):

(109)   [clever]$_A$ $\rightarrow$ λs.CLEVER(s) $\wedge$ Arg$_1$(s) = x
        [clever]$_{AP}$ $\rightarrow$ λxλs.CLEVER(s) $\wedge$ Arg$_1$(s) = x
                                                                    (Predicate Formation)
        [t clever]]$_{SC}$ $\rightarrow$ λxλs.CLEVER(s) $\wedge$ Arg$_1$(s) = x (x)
            = λs.CLEVER(s) $\wedge$ Arg$_1$(s) = x
        [be [t clever]]$_{V'}$ $\rightarrow$ λSλe.$\exists$s $\in$ S: e = l(s)(λs.CLEVER(s) $\wedge$ Arg$_1$(s) = x)
            = λe.$\exists$s $\in$ λs.CLEVER(s) $\wedge$ Arg$_1$(s) = x: e = l(s)
            = λe.$\exists$s[CLEVER(s) $\wedge$ Arg$_1$(s) = x $\wedge$ e = l(s)]
        [be [t clever]]$_{VP}$ $\rightarrow$ λxλe.$\exists$s[CLEVER(s) $\wedge$ Arg$_1$(s) = x $\wedge$ e = l(s)]
                                                                    (Predicate Formation)
        [is clever]$_{I'}$ $\rightarrow$ λxλe.$\exists$s[CLEVER(s) $\wedge$ Arg$_1$(s) = x
                    $\wedge$ e = l(s) $\wedge$ PRES(e)]
        [Mary is clever]$_{IP}$ $\rightarrow$ λxλe.$\exists$s[CLEVER(s) $\wedge$ Arg$_1$(s) = x
                    $\wedge$ e = l(s) $\wedge$ PRES(e)] (MARY)
            = λe.$\exists$s[CLEVER(s) $\wedge$ Arg$_1$(s) = MARY $\wedge$ e = l(s) $\wedge$ PRES(e)]
            $\rightarrow$ $\exists$e$\exists$s[CLEVER(s) $\wedge$ Arg$_1$(s) = MARY $\wedge$ e = l(s) $\wedge$ PRES(e)]

So, the sentence asserts that there is a present event which packages some state of Mary having the clever property.

Here is a summary of the proposal so far:

V (and VP)   denotes sets of count eventualities.
A (and AP)   denote sets of mass states.
Predicative *be* denotes the function INST defined as follows:
$\quad\quad\quad\quad\quad$ INST $= \lambda$Sle.$\exists$s $\in$ S: e $= $l(s).

10.7. SELECTIONAL RESTRICTIONS

We are now in a position to go back to the problems raised in section 10.2. These can be divided into two groups. One set concerns the semantic selection by matrix verbs, and the second involves the apparent change in meaning caused by the introduction of *be*.

It becomes quite straightforward to express the selectional restrictions that matrix verbs exert on non-tensed complements in semantic terms once we see that small clauses with VP predicates denote different entities from small clauses with AP predicates. Small clauses with VP predicates – and no inflection – denote sets of events, and crucially, the lack of inflection means that existential quantification over the event argument isn't triggered. Thus an IP will denote a proposition, and a bare verbal small clause will denote a set of events. Following the analysis in sections 10.4 and 10.5, small clauses with AP predicates will denote sets of states, and here too there will be no existential quantification over the state argument.

I assume the semantics proposed in Vlach (1983), and extend it to apply to complements denoting sets of states as well as those denoting sets of events:

(110)   V(x,Y) is true if x stands in the V relation with a member of the set (of events or states) Y.

Vlach uses this rule to interpret perception verb complements, such as (111):

(111)   Mary saw John leave.

See denotes a relation between an event, an experiencer (in this case Mary) and a set of events of John leaving. The assertion in (111) is true if Mary stands in the seeing relation with at least one member of the set of events of John leaving, that is if there is at least one event of John leaving which Mary saw. I assume that this extends naturally to other verbs with small clause complements. *Mary let John leave* will be true if there is at least one member of the set of events denoted by *John leave* which Mary allowed to happen, and so forth.

When the small clause has a bare AP predicate, things will work basically the same way, but with some important caveats. The matrix verb will denote a relation between an individual and a set of states, and parallel truth conditions will hold. So, using (110), (112a/b) will be true if there is a state in the set of states of politeness holding of Jane which Mary has the 'consider' and the 'make' relation with respectively:

(112)   a. Mary considered Jane polite.
$\quad\quad$ b. Mary made Jane polite.

What exactly the relation is with a state depends on the meaning of the matrix verb. One crucial difference between verbs selecting event complements and those selecting state complements is that while the former are extensional with respect to their complements, the latter are not always extensional with respect to their state complements, although I think they sometimes are. Suppose Jane has the politeness property when and only when she is happy. If Mary considers Jane polite, it need not follow that she considers her happy (she might not know of the constraints on Jane's politeness), but I think that if Mary made or kept Jane polite, then it follows that she made or kept Jane happy. I don't have strong intuitions about this, and it would be easier (and maybe more interesting) if it could be argued simply that verbs are extensional with respect to event complements and intensional with respect to state complements. But for the moment, I'll assume that the extensionality/intentionality follows from the properties of the matrix verb and not the nature of the complement.

If states are fully homogenous, as I argued in the last section that they are, then a set of states will either have one member (the 'biggest' state S which is the sum of its parts) or no members. So you have a 'consider' relation with a set of states $\lambda s.\text{POLITE}(s) \wedge \text{Arg}_1(s) = \text{JANE}$ iff you consider that the set is non-empty, i.e. that Jane has the politeness property. And, roughly, you have a 'make' relation with a set of states if you act in such a way as to guarantee that the relevant set of states isn't empty. Then (112a) is then true roughly under the conditions in (113a), and (112b) will be true roughly under the conditions in (113b):

(113)   a. $[\![\text{Mary considers } [\lambda s.\text{POLITE}(s) \wedge \text{Arg}_1(s) = \text{JANE}]]\!] = 1$
           iff $[\text{Mary considers } \exists s \, [\text{POLITE}(s) \wedge \text{Arg}_1(s) = \text{JANE}]]$
        b. $[\![\text{Mary made } [\lambda s.\text{POLITE}(s) \wedge \text{Arg}_1(s) = \text{JANE}]]\!] = 1$
           iff $\exists s \, [\text{Mary made } s: s \in \lambda s.\text{POLITE}(s) \wedge \text{Arg}_1(s) = \text{JANE}]$

There is no specification as to how big the state is: the truth conditions require only that there be such a state and don't specify any state-part or properties of a state part as being particularly relevant, and thus, unless the context implies otherwise, the maximal available state will be the witness for (113) being true. In this particular case, this will give an 'individual-level' flavour to the complement. Because of the way in which people tend to have the politeness property, the biggest available state will, out of context, be the one in which Jane has the politeness property in what Condoravdi (1992) calls a 'tendentially stable' way; the effect will be to assume that the state of politeness that has Jane as a participant is stable, and that we are therefore dealing with an individual-level predication. But this is context dependent, and may be overridden by many factors, including the context in which the sentence is uttered, and the nature of the participants in the state. (The NALS reviewer suggested *I consider that remark polite* as a stage-level predication: I would rather say that the state of politeness with 'that remark' as a participant is not stable because remarks don't usually have a continuing existence in time and space.)

We can now go back to the problems that we looked at in section 10.2.

First, How can we account for the distribution of small clause complements? As soon as we phrase the selectional restrictions in semantic terms, the problem resolves itself. The constituents we are interested in denote different semantic entities in each case:

(114)   [DP VP] denotes a set of events: $\lambda e.E(e)$
       [DP AP] denotes a set of states: $\lambda s.S(s)$
       [DP I′] denotes a proposition: $\exists e[\alpha]$

The selectional restrictions of the matrix verb have to be stated in semantic terms. ECM verbs may subcategorise for (non-tensed) IPs and/or small clauses, and can select semantically for propositional complements, for sets of events as complements or for sets of states as complements. I repeat here the crucial examples that we discussed in section 10.2, summed up in (115), while (116) gives an update of the original table (28), which sums up the data and the explanation. (Remember that 'proposition' is the denotation of a non-tensed IP (or CP) of the form [DP to VP]$_{IP}$. I ignore 'that' clauses entirely.):

(115)   a.   Mary made Jane (be) polite.
      b.   Mary let/helped Jane *(be) polite.
      c.   Mary considers/found/kept Jane (*be) polite.
      d.   Mary considered/found/helped Jane to be polite.
      e.   *Mary saw/made/kept/let Jane to be polite.
      f.   Mary caused/allowed Jane *(to be) polite.

(116)	[DP AP]$_{SC}$	[DP VP]$_{SC}$	[DP to VP]$_{IP}$
keep	+	−	−
let/see/hear	−	+	−
cause/allow	−	−	+
make	+	+	−
consider/find	+	−	+
—	−	+	+
—	+	+	+
semantic selection	sets of states	sets of events	propositions

What looks like an optional *be* in a complement, as in (115a), shows up in the table as the effect of a V selecting for either a set of states or a set of events. What looks like an obligatory *be* in (115b) is the effect of a matrix V selecting only for a set of events and not a set of states, and what looks like an obligatorily absent *be* in (115c) is the effect of V selecting only a set of states and not a set of events. Some, but not all, verbs which allow a small clause complement allow an untensed IP, and these are the ones which select for a propositional complement. Of course, this leaves open the question of how the meanings of the matrix verbs dictate their selectional restrictions, but I am not going to discuss this here. What we have is a semantic characterisation of the selectional restrictions which allows us terms in which to ask this question. Note that these selectional restrictions are assumed to be a grammatical property of the verbs, and thus a violation of table (116) results in an ungrammatical construction marked by "*", and not just an infelicity.

Now we can look at the question of subtle meaning differences between minimally different complements of ECM verbs. First, we asked with respect to *consider* and the paradigm in (117) why it was that the small clause and the infinitival complement feel as if they do not mean the same.

(117)   a.   Mary considers Jane to be polite.
      b.   Mary considers Jane polite.
      c.   *Mary considers Jane be polite.

(117) reflects the selectional properties given for *consider* in the chart in (116): it selects a proposition and a set of states but not a set of events.

The representations of the meanings of (117a/b) will be roughly as in (118a/b) respectively:

(118)   a.   Mary considers $\exists e[\exists s[\text{POLITE}(s) \wedge \text{Arg}_1(s) = \text{JANE} \wedge e = 1(s)]]$
      b.   Mary considers $[\lambda s.\text{POLITE}(s) \wedge \text{Arg}_1(s) = \text{JANE}]$

As I suggested above, (118b) will be true if Mary considers that the set of states of politeness with Jane as participant is not empty. This is essentially equivalent to asserting that Mary considers that Jane has the 'polite' property. (120a) asserts that Mary is in the 'consider' relation with a proposition that there is an event which instantiates Jane having the 'polite' property. But this adds the information that Mary considers that there is a individuable and temporally locatable eventuality which is evidence for asserting that Jane has the 'polite' property, which is more than is asserted in (117b/118b). In (117b) Jane's having the politeness property is not associated with any instantiating eventuality; rather, as I suggested above, the 'witness' state for this sentence will be the maximal available state, which, out of context, will be a tendentially stable one. The assertions thus 'feels' more 'inherent' than in (117a), where tying the state to a locatable individuable eventuality gives a less inherent 'feel'. But these implications are easily overridable, as we saw in section 10.2.

10.8. Aspectual classification of 'be + AP'

The third question that we raised in section 10.2 is why *be* seems to introduce agentive implications in examples like (119b) which are absent from (119a):

(119)   a.   Mary made Jane polite/nice to her family.
      b.   Mary made Jane be polite/nice to her family.

I am going to argue that these agentive implications follow from the way in which a VP of the form *be* + AP gets assigned to an aspectual class. In order to do this, we need first to review some features of the aspectual classification of VPs, and look at some differences between lexical VPs and *be* + AP with regard to aspectual classification.

It is a well-known semantic fact that verbs, or more properly VPs, can be classified into aspectual classes according to the kind of eventualities they denote. A familiar classification, which I shall use here, is that of Vendler (1967), which was analysed in depth in Dowty (1979). This divides eventualities into states, activities, accomplishments and achievements, where states and activities are atelic, while accomplishments and achievements are telic.

Stative verbs, such as *know* and *love*, are (downwardly) homogenous and if they hold over a period of time, they hold at any instant at that time. Activities are typically 'under the control of' the subject, although, as noted in section 10.3, Dowty (1979) points out that there is also a group of non-agentive activities involving physical activity or movement, and an "internal change of state that has visible, audible or tactile consequences." (see the discussion of Dowty's theory of 'DO' in section 10.3). While activities are atelic and hold over an interval i, they hold at sufficiently large subintervals of i, where 'sufficiently large' is contextually defined. Thus if John ran for an hour, he ran at any sufficiently large subinterval of that hour, but not necessarily at the moment he stopped to cross a road or the instant after he started to run and so on. Achievements are typically punctual, and involve a near-instantaneous change of state from a situation where $\neg$ P is true of the subject to a situation in which P is true of the subject. This change of state may or may not be under the control of the subject, as in (120):

(120)   a. John arrived at the station.
         b. The letter arrived after three days.

Accomplishments are often thought of as distinguished from the other classes since they are often treated as complex eventualities while the others are treated as simple eventualities. An event-based interpretation of Dowty's (1979) theory treats accomplishments as consisting of two subeventualities, an activity and a resultant change of state, where the change of state gives the natural stopping point for the activity. While the eventuality in (121a) is an atelic activity, the one in (121b) is a telic accomplishment.

(121)   a. Mary was cooking for hours last night.
         b. Mary cooked pasta for dinner last night.

In (121b) the state brought about by the pasta becoming cooked provides the culmination or natural stopping point of the cooking activity.

Formally, I assume event-based schemas for the representation of aspectual properties, based on Dowty (1979), as in (122), with examples in (123). 'DO' is Dowty's activity operator which introduces both the agentively based-activities and the non-agentive physical activities involving internal changes of state as discussed above. 'BECOME' is the operator expressing the punctual change of state involved in achievements, and, by hypothesis, in the culmination of accomplishments:

(122) a. *States*: $\lambda P \lambda e.P(e)$

        b. *Activities*: $\lambda P \lambda e.(DO(P))(e)$

        c. *Achievements*: $\lambda P \lambda e.(BECOME(P))(e)$

        d. *Accomplishments*: $\lambda P \lambda e.\exists e_1 \exists e_2 [e_1 \sqsubset e \wedge e_2 \sqsubset e \wedge (DO(P))(e_1)$
$\wedge (BECOME(P'))(e_2) \wedge Cul(e) = e_2]$

(123) a. 'love' $\rightarrow \lambda e.LOVE(e)$

        b. 'run' $\rightarrow \lambda e.(DO(RUN))(e)$

        c. 'arrive' $\rightarrow \lambda e.(BECOME(AT\ A\ LOCATION))(e)$

        d. 'write the paper' $\rightarrow \lambda e.\exists e_1 \exists e_2 [e_1 \sqsubset e \wedge e_2 \sqsubset e$
$\wedge (DO(PAPER\text{-}WRITE))(e_1)$
$\wedge (BECOME(THE\ PAPER$
$WRITTEN))(e_2) \wedge Cul(e) = e_2]$

While it is VPs, or the denotations of VPs, which are assigned to a particular aspectual class, the denotations of verbs also have aspectual properties, and can be assigned to a basic aspectual class, although the VP which they head may ultimately be assigned to a different class. The trickiest classification in terms of basic classes is probably that of accomplishments, since, as is well known, they seem to move between the activity or the accomplishment class depending on whether the direct object of the V contributes information about when the end point of the activity is – in Krifka's (1992) terminology, determining whether or not it is 'quantized'. This is illustrated in (124):

(124) a. This morning Dafna ate cheerios/apples.

        b. This morning Dafna ate 35 cheerios/three bowls of cheerios/two apples/the apple I gave her.

In (124a) the direct object of *eat*, and thus the VP, is not quantized, and the VP denotes an activity, and in (124b) the direct object, and thus the VP, is quantized, and the VP denotes a accomplishment. However, rather that say that a verb like *eat* is ambiguous between an activity and an accomplishment, I think it is more proper to see this sensitivity to the quantized status of the direct object as a characterising property of accomplishments, and to contrast (124) with transitive activity verbs such as *push* which are not aspectually sensitive to the quantized status of the direct object. Thus both the examples in (125) are activities, and *push* is squarely in the activity class:

(125) a. The child pushed an apple around.

        b. The child pushed apples around.

Although verbal predicates do get assigned to a basic class, aspectual shifting may be forced by interaction with modifiers and other operators. For example, directional PPs may have a 'quantizing' effect, as (126) shows.

(126) a. The children are running in the park.
        b. The children are running to the swings.

In (126a) *run in the park* denotes a set of activity eventualities, but in (126b), the directional PP provides a 'natural end' to the running activity, and the VP is understood as denoting a set of accomplishments. Modifiers may cause aspect shift between other classes too, as illustrated in (127), from Zucchi (1998). The predicate *resemble her mother* is inherently a state. It is a downwardly homogenous predicate, and it is inappropriate in a pseudo-cleft construction with *do*, like (127a), and progressives, such as (127b), but, as Zucchi (1998) shows, in conjunction with the operator *more and more* it can occur in the progressive, as in (127c).

(127) a. *What Mary did was resemble her mother.
        b. *Mary is resembling her mother.
        c. Mary is resembling her mother more and more every day.

Resemble is naturally stative, while the progressive operator cannot apply to a stative predicates but only to activities or accomplishments. But, Zucchi argues, the progressive operator can force *resemble DP more and more* to be reanalysed as a non-agentive process or activity, and thus to become an appropriate complement of the progressive operator. (See Zucchi (1998) and Moens and Steedman (1988) for discussion). Other linguistic elements may also cause aspectual shift; for example plural DPs may interact with achievements to get an iterative activity reading for *spot trains* and *notice pictures*, but I won't go into this further here. What we see in general is that verbs can be assigned to a basic aspectual class, with interaction with modifiers and other operators causing a shift between the class of the V and the class of the VP. Some of these modifiers, such as the directional PP in (126b) are probably best analysed as functions from sets of eventualities of one class into sets of eventualities of another class, and others, such as the progressive operator in (127c) seem to trigger an aspectual shift analogous to type-shifting; the exact analysis of each is not important for our purposes.

The point that I want to make is that with expressions of the form *be* + AP the situation is much freer, so much so that I want to suggest that these expressions are not inherently assigned to a particular aspectual class. 'Lexical' Vs of the kind discussed above are assigned to a particular class and can be reanalysed as belonging to a different class in the context of an appropriate operator. But *be* + AP seems to move quite freely between at least two classes, often between three classes and sometimes (arguably) between all four, depending on contextual factors; the relevant contextual factor may be the semantic effect of a particular linguistic operator in whose scope the V occurs, but it may also be purely pragmatic, based on the discourse. The evidence for this is that sentences with $[be + AP]_{VP}$ can easily be analysed as stative, activity or achievement (we'll come back to accomplishments below). First, they are often ambiguous between different aspectual readings, as in (128); (128a) is ambiguous between an stative and an activity reading, and (128b) between a stative and an achievement reading, asserting either that Jane was in the awake state at three o'clock (stative reading) or that there was a punctual change of state in which Jane moved from being not awake to being awake, and that this took place at three o'clock.

(128)   a.   I met Mary and John yesterday. Mary was pleasant and John was obnoxious. (stative or activity).
        b.   Jane rested for half an hour. At three o'clock she was awake just as she had said she would be.

Second, aspectual classifications which are provoked by modifiers give a much more natural reading with $be + AP$ than with shifted or coerced lexical verbs. Thus, *be obnoxious* easily has an achievement reading in (129a), which we don't get if we use a typical verbal state or activity in the same construction as in (129b/c):

(129)   a.   It took Mary only three minutes to be obnoxious to her brother.
        b.   ?It took me ten years to own a house.
        c.   ?It took Bill half an hour to run.

Context also pushes $be + AP$ into particular aspectual classes much more easily than it can shift a verb. So although *suddenly* can provoke an achievement-like reading for *know the answer*, as in (130a), it is difficult, if not impossible, to get an activity-like reading for the same VP, as in (130b). In contrast, *be tall*, which most naturally has only a stative reading, can be given achievement and activity readings as in (130c/d), even without *suddenly* in (130c) (although the presence of the adverb rules out the stative reading).

(130)   a.   When Alice ate the mushroom, she ?(suddenly) knew the answer.
        b.   *Since she ate the mushroom, she has been knowing the answer all the time.
        c.   When Alice ate from the right side of the mushroom, she was (suddenly) tall, and when she ate from the left side she was short again.
        d.   Since she put on those high heels, she has been being tall.

Not all aspectual classes are available for all lexical choices of AP – for example, *be ready* does not have natural activity reading. I assume that which aspectual classes are readily available for a particular $be + AP$ is dependent on the meaning of the adjective, but I don't have anything to say at the moment about how this might work. The point that I want to make is that there is a real contrast between how these 'derived' $be + AP$ verbs work aspectually and how lexical verbs work. What I'd like to suggest is that *be* itself is not assigned to a particular lexical class, and that the result of applying *be* to an AP is not determined with respect to aspectual class; rather, it can fit into any lexical class if it is pragmatically appropriate, taking into consideration the meaning of the adjective and the context in which *be* + AP occurs. More precisely, we can think of the schemas in (122) as being possible forms that an eventuality can take. We know from the fact that verbal predicates can shift from one aspectual class to the other that these schemas are not just formulae abstracted from existing lexical predicates and representing what members of groups of predicates have in common, but also independent schemas representing forms that verbal predicate meanings can be shifted or coerced into. It is reasonable to assume that they are available also for the 'aspectually unclassified' meanings of *be* + AP to shift into. We can think of the schemas in (122), repeated here, as functions, any of which can apply to the meaning of *be* + AP freely according to the needs of the context (although so far we have not seen any examples of accomplishments).

(122)   a. *States*: $\lambda P \lambda e . P(e)$
      b. *Activities*: $\lambda P \lambda e .(DO(P))(e)$
      c. *Achievements*: $\lambda P \lambda e .(BECOME(P))(e)$
      d. *Accomplishments*: $\lambda P \lambda e . \exists e_1 \exists e_2 [e_1 \sqsubset e \wedge e_2 \sqsubset e \wedge (DO(P))(e_1)$
                              $\wedge (BECOME(P'))(e_2) \wedge Cul(e) = e_2]$

The effect of applying (122a–c) to *be obnoxious* will give the results in (131):

(131)   **be obnoxious**: $\lambda e . \exists s [OBNOXIOUS(s) \wedge Arg(s) = x \wedge e = l(s)]$
      a. *state*:
        $\lambda P \lambda e . P(e) (\lambda e . \exists s [OBNOXIOUS(s) \wedge Arg(s) = x \wedge e = l(s)])$
        $= \lambda e . \exists s [OBNOXIOUS(s) \wedge Arg(s) = x \wedge e = l(s)]$
      b. *activity*:
        $\lambda P \lambda e .(DO(P))(e) (\lambda e . \exists s [OBNOXIOUS(s) \wedge Arg(s) = x \wedge e = l(s)])$
        $= \lambda e .(DO(\exists s [OBNOXIOUS(s) \wedge Arg(s) = x \wedge e = l(s)]))$
      c. *achievement*:
        $\lambda P \lambda e .(BECOME(P))(e) (\lambda e . \exists s [OBNOXIOUS(s) \wedge Arg(s) = x$
        $\wedge e = l(s)])$
        $= \lambda e .(BECOME(\exists s [OBNOXIOUS(s) \wedge Arg(s) = x \wedge e = l(s)]))$

I suggest then that the an instance of *be* + AP is not inherently marked as belonging to a particular aspectual class, and it can shift into any of the aspectual classes under contextual pressure. Because it is not aspectually classified, shifting into a particular class does not mean shifting out of another class, and thus the contextual pressure can be much, much weaker than that required for aspect shift with lexical verbs. Further, since the stative function is the identity function, as (131a) shows, the stative reading will be the unmarked or default class for all *be* + AP meanings. Activities and/or achievement forms are available depending on the meaning of the AP. The one missing, of course, is the accomplishment reading. If we look at what the representation of *be obnoxious* as an accomplishment would be, we can see why accomplishment *be* + AP is problematic:

(132) **be obnoxious** – *accomplishment*:
$$\lambda P\lambda e.\exists e_1 \exists e_2 [e_1 \sqsubset e \wedge e_2 \sqsubset e \wedge (DO(P))(e_1) \wedge (BECOME(P'))(e_2)$$
$$\wedge\; Cul(e) = e_2]\; (\lambda e.\exists s[OBNOXIOUS(s) \wedge Arg(s) = x \wedge e = l(s)])$$
$$= \lambda e.\exists e_1 \exists e_2 [e_1 \sqsubset e \wedge e_2 \sqsubset e \wedge (DO(\exists s[OBNOXIOUS(s)$$
$$\wedge\; Arg(s) = x \wedge e_1 = l(s)]))$$
$$\wedge\; (BECOME(\exists s[OBNOXIOUS(s) \wedge Arg(s) = x$$
$$\wedge\; e_2 = l(s)]')) \wedge Cul(e) = e_2]$$

The problem is that (132) requires there to be an activity of obnoxiousness performed by the subject, which culminates in a change of state in which the subject changes from non-obnoxious to obnoxious. This is prima facie contradictory, since it requires the subject at the point immediately prior to the culmination of the accomplishment to be lacking the property which s/he has had during the activity stage. The only way in which an accomplishment of this kind could not be self-contradictory would be if one could engage in an activity of kind P without directly displaying property P until the culmination. I think that *be obnoxious* does in fact have an accomplishment reading in this way, although it is very unusual in doing so. The scenario which would allow this reading would be the one in (133):

(133) John has an obnoxious habit of drawing people into conversations by first being initially charming and then, as their defenses drop, by becoming more and more unpleasant and trapping them into embarrassing and uncomfortable situations. At a party, I see John collar some unsuspecting person and put into action stage one of his habit, the charming and gracious stage. I register what is going on, perhaps because he is never charming except in this context or maybe because he has some tic whenever he practices this game.

I can later report on what was happening at this stage with the imperfect and I can say: "John was being obnoxious last night". But, if because of some unforeseen circumstance, such as his being interrupted by an earthquake or a fire alarm or some helpful friend, he never gets to the stage of being explicitly unpleasant, "John was obnoxious last night" will not be true, and the victim may never even realise what was going on. This means that we have an instance of the imperfective paradox, in which "John was being obnoxious last night" does not entail "John was obnoxious last night", and this is a good indication of an accomplishment reading. Note that this of course depends on the use of the progressive. If he was interrupted in time, then (134) is infelicitous:

(134) Last night I watched/saw John be obnoxious, though he was interrupted before he got to the stage of being really unpleasant.

So, the general picture is that instances of *be* + AP are not firmly anchored in a particular aspectual class, but move relatively freely between different aspectual classes. There are constraints, apparently dependent on the meanings of the adjective, and as a result adjectives do not allow the *be* + AP in which they occur to surface in all aspectual classes, but in comparison with lexical Vs, they do not seem to have a single inherent aspectual characterisation.

The kind of underdeterminedness that we see here parallels the underdeterminedness that Bach (1986) noticed in the output of the packaging operation in the nominal domain: "if we start with a count meaning and derive the non-count meaning, there seems to be a regular and predictable meaning ... going in the other direction, the connection seems to be much less systematic. A beer may be a serving of beer or a kind of beer." (p11) The packaging operation which allows *three beers* gives three units of beer, and the context determines what the units are. Something similar seems to be going on here. *Be*+AP the verbal equivalent of the packaging operation, gives a set of eventualities which instantiate a set of states, but it does not give any information about the aspectual properties that those eventualities have. The aspectual properties of *be*+AP depend on how we choose to analyse the eventuality; and how we choose to analyse it depends on the interaction of the meaning of the adjective with contextual factors.

10.9. AGENTIVITY EFFECTS WITH BE IN SMALL CLAUSES

I argued above that for reasons of finegrainedness, the two examples in (135) are truth conditionally equivalent: if we can assert that there is a state of Jane's having the politeness property, then there is an eventuality instantiating it and vice versa.

(135) a. Mary made Jane polite.
       b. Mary made Jane be polite.

In the light of the discussion in the previous section, this statement is too strong. If there is a state of Jane's being polite, it will follow that there is at least an eventuality instantiating it. However, if the eventuality is assigned to an aspectual class other than that of stative eventualities, then there will be additional information in (135b) not present in (135a). With this, and with some basic Gricean maxims, we can get the meaning differences that we discussed in section 10.2.

I assume two Gricean pragmatic maxims:

(i) the maxim of *quantity*: the injunction not to say more than is required;
(ii) the maxim of *manner*, the injunction to avoid obscurity and to say things briefly, simply and not in an unnecessarily complex way.

The first maxim, the maxim of quantity, tells us that if an eventuality must be assigned to an aspectual class, then all things being equal, assign it to the simplest class with the least additional information. This means that in (136), the maxim of quantity will force us to treat the eventuality as a stative eventuality, which is identical with the input to the packaging function:

(136) Jane is polite.

And indeed 'out of the blue' (136) will be taken as asserting that there is an eventuality instantiating Jane having the 'polite' property, and no more. We shift the eventuality to a different aspectual class only if there is some good reason, given either by lexical material or context, to do so, as, for example, in (137):

(137)   a. Jane was polite to a lot of people last night.
        b. Dafna tried hard to be polite to all the visitors.

The maxim of manner, which enjoins us to be straightforward and not unnecessarily complex in our communications, tells us that if (135a/b) are truth-conditionally equivalent, then there has to be some good reason to introduce a set of eventualities in (135b) rather than just making use of the set of states already available in (135a). We then have an apparent conflict between these two instructions. The maxim of quantity tells us that we should assign the set of eventualities denoted by *Jane be polite* to the class of stative eventualities. But, if we assign the set of eventualities denoted by *Jane be polite* to the set of stative eventualities, then these are so minimally different from the set of states denoted by *Jane polite* that we shouldn't use the packaging function at all. This situation doesn't arise in (136) because English requires the sentence to have a tense, and tense can be attached only to predicates of eventualities. Thus the maxim of manner can't rule out the introduction of stative eventualities, since the conditions on tense require an eventuality argument and make the use of bare states unavailable.

If we look more closely, we see that the two maxims work together to get us exactly the subtle meaning differences that exists. In (135b), Mary stands in the 'make' relation to a set of eventualities which instantiate the set of states of Jane being polite. This set must be assigned to an aspectual class. The maxim of quantity tells us to assign it, out of the blue, to the set of stative eventualities. The maxim of manner tells us not to use a set of stative eventualities unless there is good reason to do so. Assume the maxim of manner wins out; the result will be that small clause complements will not be interpreted as denoting sets of stative eventualities, unless this is justified. (We will come back to what might justify it in a moment.)

This means that in order to satisfy manner and quantity, the sets of eventualities in these complements must be assigned to one of the other three classes. Suppose that the denotation of $be + AP$ is interpreted as denoting a set of **activities** (or, much less likely, **accomplishments**). This would involve a change of perspective which justifies introducing the eventuality argument. But, as we saw in the discussion of Dowty's analysis of activities, the operator DO implies (though it does not entail) that its animate subjects are in some sense agents of or in control of the activity. As Dowty showed, the strength of the control is determined pragmatically by the nature of the activity. We would expect to find just these agentivity or control implications where $be + AP$ is assigned to the activity or accomplishment class in small clause complements, and the subject is animate.

If the denotation of *be* + AP is assigned to the class of **achievements**, the relation between an animate subject argument and the event may but need not be agentive. Some predicates allow, but do not force, an agentive reading, as in (138a/b), but in other cases, an agentive reading is basically out, as in (138c/d).

(138)   a. Dafna proudly reached the top of the flight of stairs alone.
        b. Dafna reached the top of the stairs in her father's arms.
        c. She realised that she had to be careful.
        d. She arrived home fast asleep.

In the non-agentive cases, an animate subject is typically an active and sentient participant in the event, unless this is explicitly ruled out as in (138d). We get the same effect in achievement uses of small clause *be* + AP.

(139)   a. I made her be awake for the visit.
        b. We made the children be ready before us.
        c. They made the dog be quiet by giving it a tranquillizer.

This makes several correct predictions:

i.   If the subject of an activity, accomplishment, or achievement eventuality denoted by *be* + *AP* does not naturally have an agentive relation to the eventuality, then there are no agentive implications. This explains our examples such as (139) above and (140):

(140)   a. They made the pigeons be obnoxious by teasing them with food.
        b. They can make the river be very noisy by opening the dam.

ii.   Stative eventualities are possible in bare infinitive small clauses if the addition of the event argument is justified. This occurs when the introduction of an eventuality argument is necessary to allow adverbial modification, temporal locating of the eventuality and so on.

(141)   a. They made her be afraid of dogs when she meets them.
        b. They made/had the children be ready/awake at three.
        c. They had/made the music be particularly noisy last night.

iii.   If a matrix verb allows only a set of events as a complement and not a set of states, then it will be much easier to get a stative eventuality as a small clause since there can be no 'competition' from the bare state reading. Thus (142b) is better than (142a), since the interaction between the eventuality argument and the modifying 'when' clause justifies using the stative eventuality, but (142c) is much better than (142a). Since *let* does not allow for a set of bare states, justification of the eventuality argument by the introduction of a modifier isn't necessary. (Note that in (142) *when they arrived* modifies *be untidy* and not the matrix verb.)

(142) a. ?She made the room be untidy.
      b. She made the room be untidy when they arrived.
      c. She let the room be untidy.

Notice that in many of these cases (except (139, 141, 142b)) the aspectual shift to an activity or an achievement is not provoked by the need to allow a compositional rule to operate, but is a the result of less local contextual factors and pragmatic constraints.

10.10. AGENTIVITY EFFECTS WITH 'BE' IN THE PROGRESSIVE

The facts to be accounted for here are as follows:

i. When predicative *be* occurs in the progressive, there are very strong implications of agentivity which can, but need not be present in simple tensed sentences. This shows in the contrast between (143a), where the subject is, out of context, not assigned an agentive relation to the eventuality, and (143b) in which the subject is preferentially a causing agent with respect to the eventuality in which she displays the polite property.

(143) a. Dafna is polite.
      b. Dafna is being polite (to our guests).

These agentivity restrictions are so strong that they appear to rule out progressives where the subject is not capable of being agentive, as in Partee's contrasts, repeated here as (144):

(144) a. John is being noisy.
      b. #The river is being noisy.

As we saw above, the subject of *be* + AP in a small clause doesn't have to be animate. The contrast between (145a) and (145b) is sharp.

(145) a. She made the room be tidy when they arrived.
      b. #The room was being tidy when she arrived.

ii. Independent of whether the subject can be an agent, there are restrictions on what predicates can occur with progressive *be*. These restrictions do not occur with matrix sentences or small clauses.

(146) a. The children are awake/ready.
      b. I made the children be ready/awake.
      c. #The children are being ready/awake.

Be + AP combinations which are odd in small clauses are completely unacceptable in progressives. This is particularly clear where the subject is inanimate. The generalisation seems to be that if *be* + AP doesn't naturally have an activity (or accomplishment) reading, it doesn't occur in the progressive. The unacceptable examples in (145) and (146) are bad precisely because it is not possible to interpret the verbal *be* + AP as denoting an activity or accomplishment. The agentivity effects that occur so strongly in (145b) do so because *be polite* must be interpreted as an activity and, as we have seen above, it is the activity operator *DO* which introduces the implications that the subject has an agentive relation to the predicate. In order to give a precise statement of how this works, I shall explore how *be* + AP interacts within the account of the progressive given in Landman (1992). I'm going to use Landman's theory because it is intensional, and because (unlike Dowty's 1979 account) it makes explicit use of a Davidsonian eventuality variable, treating the progressive operator as introducing a relation between two sets of eventualities.

Landman treats the progressive operator as a VP operator relating a set of events to the set of events denoted by the lexical VP as in (147):

(147)   BE ING(VP) $\rightarrow \lambda e.\text{Prog}(e, \lambda e'.\text{VP}(e') \wedge \text{Ag}(e') = x))$.

The central problem for any theory of the progressive is how to treat the imperfective paradox. Clearly the truth value of a sentence like (148) is dependent in some way on events of building a tower (out of lego).

(148)   Dafna is building a tower out of lego.

The question is what this dependence is. If Dafna gets interrupted in her tower building, then while (148) is true, there will never be an actual event of the type denoted by *build a tower* to justify using the predicate in (148).

Landman's theory crucially introduces the notion of event stages. An event e is a stage of an event e' if it grows or develops into e'. Thus the relation 'stage of' is a much closer relation than the more familiar 'part-of' relation. My frying onions and my listening to the radio may both be part of the event of my making fried rice, but only the first is a stage of it. Landman argues that the progressive introduces a relation between two events if one is a stage of the other. A sentence like (148) asserts that there is an event going on which is a stage of a 'build a tower' event. The problem of the imperfective paradox occurs with accomplishments because the progressive is an intensional operator. We are allowed to assert that an event such as the one which we are talking about in (148) is a stage of an event of tower-building even if the event in which the tower is built doesn't occur in this actual world. What we assert in a progressive sentence like (148) is that there is an event going on which, on the basis of evidence internal to the event itself, we judge very likely to turn into an event of the type denoted by *build a tower*. If Dafna is left alone for long enough and she is sufficiently concentrated, then the event which warrants the assertion in (148) will turn into an event of the type denoted by *build a tower* in the actual world. If Dafna gets interrupted in her tower-building by external circumstances – she is suddenly hungry and stops to eat, or another kid knocks the tower down, or someone tells her to put the lego away – then the event e warranting the assertion in (148) won't be a stage of an actual event of the build-a-tower type. But, Landman claims, there is an event of building a tower in a near enough world of which we can say that e is a stage.

In order to explain the intuition that an event e in this world can be a stage of an event e' in another world, and also to give content to the notion 'near enough world' in this context, Landman develops the notion of a 'continuation branch' of an event. Landman's idea is that when checking the truth value of a sentence like (148), we take the event stage that warrants the assertion and follow through its development. If it turns into an event of the right kind in this world (in our case an event of building a tower), then the sentence is true. If the event is interrupted before this happens, we jump to the closest world to this one where the event was not interrupted, and we follow through its development there. If there is another interruption, we jump to the next closest world and carry on following through the development of the event. Sooner or later, either we find that the original event stage does turn into an event of the desired type, in which case the sentence is true, or we decide we are too far from the original world and the sentence is deemed false. The line which traces the development of the event through the worlds is called its continuation branch.

Landman's rule for interpreting (147) is given in (149):

(149) $\llbracket PROG(e, VP)) \rrbracket_{w,g} = 1$, iff $\exists f \exists v$: $<f,v> \in CON(g(e),w)$
and $\llbracket VP \rrbracket_{v,g}(f) = 1$,
where $CON(g(e),w)$ is the continuation branch of $g(e)$ in w.

So, *x is VPing* is true iff there is an event going on which gives every indication that, in the absence of interruptions, it will turn out to be a stage of an event of type VP.

Landman's paper discusses explicitly only how activities and accomplishments work in the progressive. Activities have stages, and accomplishments must also, since they have an activity part and a culmination. What then about statives and achievements? And how does this question relate to our problem of trying to explain the agentivity implications in *being* + AP and the restrictions on what AP can occur there?

It is clear that Landman's theory predicts correctly that the progressive operator should not apply to stative verbs. The progressive denotes a relation between two sets of events where the first is a stage of another. States are by definition downwardly homogenous and since a state which holds at interval i holds at every subinterval of i, no stages can be distinguished. So, it is inherently contradictory to analyse them as having stages, and the progressive operator just cannot apply to a stative VP. Since it denotes a relation 'be a stage of', there will be type-mismatch if PROG applies to verbs which do not have stages.

This means that we can explain the contrast in (143) above, repeated here:

(150) a. Dafna is polite.
       b. Dafna is being polite.

As we argued in the previous section, the maxim of quantity, forbidding excess or unnecessary information, will leave the eventuality in (150a) in a form equivalent to a stative, unless there is good contextual reason not to. In the absence of such contextual justification, there will be no agentive implications. But, if (150b) is to be felicitous, the progressive operator must have as its complement a set of non-stative eventualities, in fact, for reasons that we'll see below, a set of activities or accomplishments. Thus, *be polite* will be assigned to one of these classes. But this will mean that *be polite* is analysed as the complement of a DO operator, and thus, if the subject is animate, it will be assigned an agentive relation to the eventuality.

This predicts that non-animate, non-agentive subjects of *being* + AP should be OK as long as it is acceptable to interpret the eventuality as an activity, in Dowty's second sense of a physical activity or movement, involving an "internal change of state that has visible, audible or tactile consequences." (Dowty 1979, p16). The relevant examples from above are repeated here in (151):

(151)   a. #The river is being noisy. (= 144b)
        b. #The room was being tidy when she arrived. (= 145b)

These examples are infelicitous to the degree to which the predicates *be noisy*, and *be tidy (when she arrived)*, cannot be interpreted as activities (and even less as accomplishments) as the progressive requires. To the degree to which the predicates can be interpreted as activities under Dowty's second definition of activity, the sentences improve. It is possible to find a context in which (151a) is acceptable, since we can think of the river as being noisy as a result of an activity of internal movement; (151a) improves in the context given in (152a), since this indicates that the river's being noisy is to be considered as a stage of an activity, in this other sense.

(152)   The river is being very noisy this evening; it must be breaking through the dam.

Since it is impossible (as far as I can see) to find any way in which *tidy* can have an activity reading with an inanimate subject, shifting to the activity reading of *be tidy* will be impossible, and the progressive will have an inappropriate complement and will be infelicitous. Of course, with an animate subject the progressive is fine.

The fact that the progressive operator cannot apply to statives is a semantic fact, and the examples in (151) are thus semantically uninterpretable if *be* + AP is assigned to the class of stative eventualities. (But they are marked infelicitous, rather than ungrammatical, because they could in principle have an activity reading – it's just that the activity reading isn't very plausible.) In the small clause examples discussed in the previous section, the constraint against having stative eventualities in small clause constructions was pragmatic, and if it could be shown that the maxim of manner was not violated, they were quite acceptable. This explains why felicity violations in (151) are much stronger than in the corresponding small clause examples in (153):

(153)   a. They made the river be very noisy by opening the dam.
        b. She made the room be untidy ?(when they arrived).

An obvious question is whether an achievement reading of *be* + AP is acceptable as complement to the progressive, and this brings us back to the second fact that we need to explain, namely, why do expressions like *be ready* and *be awake* not have progressive readings at all, as (154) shows:

(154)   a. #The children are being ready/awake. (= 146c)
          b. #She is being afraid.

The adjectives in these examples are those which do not naturally have an activity reading, and where the non-stative reading of *be* + AP is naturally an achievement one. But, as with (151a), if these examples are to have any reading at all, the predicates have to be assigned to the activity class. The reading we get is the usually inappropriate one that the children are ostentatiously displaying awake or ready behaviour, and this is odd because we don't associate behaviour or activity with these predicates, except in ironic sentences like (155).

(155)   Dafna has been ready to go to kindergarten for some time. She has found her shoes and her bag and she has gone to stand by the door where she is very ostentatiously being ready.

What we don't get or 'Dafna is being ready' is an achievement reading.

If we could believe the often-repeated generalisation that achievements don't occur in the progressive, then we would not expect to get an achievement reading for (154). And it would make sense. Landman's paper doesn't talk about the progressive and achievements, but on the plausible assumption that achievements, being punctual, do not have stages, we would expect that achievements do not occur in the progressive any more than stages do. Classic examples like (156) seem to bear this out, since they have only a 'slow-motion' reading where we assign stages to a slowed-down version of the eventuality introduced by *notice*. (I believe this observation is due to Sandro Zucchi).

(156)   John is noticing that Mary has cut her hair.

However, it is not possible to maintain the claim. Achievements do occur, with a non-slow motion reading, in the progressive:

(157)   a. Dafna is reaching the top of the ladder.
          b. The kids are arriving at the station.

(157) is reasonably interpreted as asserting that there is some preparatory eventuality going on which, if not interrupted, will turn into an eventuality in which Dafna reached the top of the ladder, and (157b) has an analogous paraphrase.

If this is the case, then why isn't there an acceptable progressive reading for *Dafna is being ready*? Neither the 'preparatory' activity nor the 'slow motion' reading are available. We can't interpret *Dafna is being ready* as asserting that there is an eventuality which, if not interrupted, will turn into an eventuality in which Dafna becomes ready. If we could, then (158a/159a) would have readings parallel to the sentences with 'true' verbal predicates in (158b/159b).

And the slow motion reading is not possible either. (158a/159a) can only have the odd 'pseudo-activity' reading, which we saw illustrated in (155).

(158)   a. #Dafna is being ready.
       b. Dafna is getting ready.

(159)   a. #She is being awake.
       b. She is waking up.

Since we know that the progressive triggers aspect shift (see (125) above), that it applies to achievements, and that very little is required to trigger shift of $be + AP$ into an achievement, why is the progressive not acceptable with the achievement use of $be + AP$ here?

Rothstein (1998) proposes that what makes it possible for verbal achievements to occur in the progressive is also a type-shifting process. In a sentence like (160), the progressive operator cannot normally apply to the VP since it requires the eventuality denoted by the VP to have stages, while achievement VPs like *arrive at the bakery* denote punctual events which do not have stages.

(160)   Dafna is arriving at the bakery.

I argue in that paper that, in a number of ways, progressive achievements are different from progressive accomplishments, and we do not want simply to shift the achievement into a corresponding accomplishment form. What we want is for the progressive to associate with an achievement a set of event stages which will plausibly develop into the achievement event, without actually being part of that event. I propose there that when the progressive operator applies to a punctual VP, it triggers the type-shifting process given in (161), which raises the denotation of the VP into the structure of an accomplishment whose culmination is given by the lexical VP.

(161) $\text{SHIFT}(\text{VP}_{\text{punctual}})$:
$$\lambda e.(\text{BECOME}(P))(e) \rightarrow$$
$$\lambda e. \exists e_1 \exists e_2 [e_1 \sqsubset e \wedge e_2 \sqsubset e \wedge \text{DO}(\alpha))(e_1)$$
$$\wedge (\text{BECOME}(P))(e_2) \wedge \text{Cul}(e) = e_2]$$

If this type-shifting operation applies to the VP in (160), then (161) asserts that there is an event e_1 which is a stage of an event e which has an arrive-at-the-bakery event e_2 as its culmination, without being part of the arrive-at-the-bakery event. The output of (161) is an 'abstract accomplishment' which does not correspond to any lexical item. I suggest that what is going on with the examples is (154/158a/159a) is that the normal aspectual shift rule cannot apply. Suppose that (161), being a rule of aspectual shift, applies only to lexical predicates. In order for $be + AP$ to be the input to this rule, it would already have had to shift into the achievement class, and (161) would have to apply to an already shifted predicate, and this is ruled out. The 'slow motion' reading is not available for similar reasons. I assume that the slow motion reading of *Dafna is noticing the new picture* is derived by slowing down the change of state so much that it can be assigned stages and treated as an accomplishment. In these cases, an achievement is genuinely being treated as an accomplishment. But here too, the shift must be from a lexical achievement to an accomplishment and not from an achievement which is itself the result of aspectual shifting.

11. SOME LOOSE ENDS

10.11.1. *Progressive 'be' vs copula 'be'*

An obvious question is whether we can assimilate progressive *be* to the copula *be* we have be examining above, especially because of the much discussed idea that the progressive is a stativizer. The simple answer is no. Progressive *be* takes a VP as a complement and VP denotes a set of eventualities, while copula *be* takes a set of M-states as a complement. They must thus be of different types:

(162)   a. copula *be*: $<<s_e,t>\ <e,t>>$
        b. progressive *be*: $<<e,t>\ <e,t>>$

This difference in types reflects the very different semantic functions that they perform. Copula *be* takes sets of unlocated states into sets of eventualities of an unspecified aspectual class which locate or instantiate the states; progressive *be* takes sets of eventualities into the sets of activity stages out of which they are (partially) composed.

10.11.2. *'be' in identity sentences*

In the light of this chapter we need to adapt the type-shifting rule which operates in identity sentences. On the assumption that there is one copula *be* which operates in predicative and identity sentence and which takes a set of states as a complement, the type-shifting operation which is used in identity sentences will have to raise a complement of type d to $<s_e,t>$. Instead of EXIST (defined in chapter 9:(25)), which gives us a set of existence events, we will have EXIST* as in (162), which will give us á set of existence states.

(163) $EXIST^*(s,x) =_{def} \lambda x \lambda s. \exists R[R \in \Theta \wedge R(s) = x]$

In other words, s is an existence state for α, or evidence that α exists, if α is the value of some thematic role for s. The 'ident' function function will be as in (164):

(164) $ident(\alpha) \rightarrow \lambda s.EXIST^*(s,\alpha) \wedge \alpha = x$
        $= \lambda s.\exists R[R \in \Theta \wedge R(s) = \alpha \wedge \alpha = x]$

(165a) will have the interpretation in (165b):

(165)   a. Mary is Dr Smith.
        b. There is an event which instantiates a state which is an existence state for Dr Smith, whose argument is Mary.

The derivation is given in (166):

(166)   Dr. Smith   → DR SMITH
        [be Dr. Smith]$_{V'}$ → $\lambda S \lambda e. \exists s \in S: e = l(s)(ident(DR\ SMITH))$
        $= \lambda S \lambda e. \exists s \in S: e = l(s)\ (\lambda s.EXIST^*(s, DR\ SMITH) \wedge DR\ SMITH = x)$
        $= \lambda e. \exists s \in \lambda s.EXIST^*(s, DR\ SMITH) \wedge DR\ SMITH = x: e = l(s)$
        $= \lambda e. \exists s[EXIST^*(s, DR\ SMITH) \wedge DR\ SMITH = x: e = l(s)]$
        [be Dr.Smith]$_{VP}$ →
        $\lambda x \lambda e. \exists s[EXIST^*(s, DR\ SMITH) \wedge DR\ SMITH = x: e = l(s)]$
                                                        (Predicate Formation)
        [is Dr. Smith]$_{I'}$ →
        $\lambda x \lambda e. \exists s[EXIST^*(s, DR\ SMITH) \wedge DR\ SMITH = x: e = l(s)] \wedge Pres(e)$
        [Mary is Dr. Smith]$_{IP}$ →
        $\lambda x \lambda e. \exists s[EXIST^*(s, DR\ SMITH) \wedge DR\ SMITH = x: e = l(s)] \wedge Pres(e)$
        (MARY)
        $= \lambda e. \exists s[EXIST^*(s, DR\ SMITH) \wedge DR\ SMITH = MARY:$
        $e = l(s)] \wedge Pres(e)$
        $= \exists e[\exists s[EXIST^*(s, DR\ SMITH) \wedge DR\ SMITH = MARY:$
        $e = l(s)] \wedge Pres(e)]$ (by $\exists$-closure)

10.11.3. *Adjunct predicates revisited*

We saw in chapter 6 that adjunct predicates are interpreted via conjunction with the predicate headed by the denotation of V. The rule for general event-based conjunction given in chapter 6:(26) is repeated here:

(167) $\alpha_{<d, <e,t>>} + \beta_{<d, <e,t>>} := \lambda y \lambda e. \exists e_1 \exists e_2[e = e_1 \sqcup e_2 \wedge \alpha(e_1, y) \wedge \beta(e_2, y)]$

This rule was used for interpreting sentences like (168):

(168)   The police arrested John drunk

The rule takes α as the denotation of *arrest* and β as the denotation of *drunk*, and yields the complex predicate in (169) as the output which is then applied to *John*:

(169) $\lambda y \lambda e. \exists e_1 \exists e_2[e = e_1 \sqcup e_2 \wedge ARREST(e_1) \wedge Ag(e_1) = x \wedge Th(e_1) = y$
        $\wedge DRUNK\ (e_2) \wedge Arg_1(e_2) = y]$

A consequence of this chapter is that the denotation of *drunk* is not a set of events, but a set of states. Generalised event conjunction will then be an operation that has the option of conjoining sets from both the count and the mass domain. This is very natural since in the nominal domain the sum operation sums across the mass-count division, as illustrated in (170):

(170)   In the shop I bought milk and two oranges.

So, while the version of event conjunction (more properly, eventuality conjunction) given in (167) may well be the rule used in verb conjunction, there will also be a version where α is of type $<d, <e,t>>$ and β of type $<d, <e_s,t>>$, as in (171a). Its output will be (171b) rather than (169):

(171) a. $\alpha_{<d,<e,t>>} + \beta_{<d,<e_s,t>>} := \lambda y \lambda e_1 . \exists e \exists s [e_1 = e \sqcup s \wedge \alpha(e,y) \wedge \beta(s,y)]$
       b. $\lambda y \lambda e_1 . \exists e \exists s [e_1 = e \sqcup s \wedge ARREST(e) \wedge Ag(e) = x \wedge Th(e) = y$
       $\wedge DRUNK (s) \wedge Arg_1(s) = y]$

The modifications made here will generalise unproblematically to the other rules for interpreting secondary, absorbed, resultative and complement predicates given in chapter 6.

10.11.4. *A note on Hebrew adjectives and possible cross-linguistic variation*

Although AP predicates in small clauses in English cannot be temporally modified, in Hebrew matrix small clauses, non-inflected adjectival predicates can be temporally modified, as in (172):

(172) a. ha- ben Seli hole ha-yom/axSav.
           the son my sick today/ now
           "My son is sick today/now."
       b. rina gevoha haerev (ki   hi al akevim gvohim).
           rina tall   tonight (because she on high   heels)
           "Rina is tall this evening because she is wearing high   heels."
           (Greenberg 1996)
       c. dani xaxam ha-boker   (ki   hu haya etzel ha-maxSefa
           dani clever this morning (because he was with the witch
           etmol).
           yesterday).
           "Dani is clever this morning (because he visited the witch yesterday)."

There are several possible reasons for this difference. One possibility is to introduce a null inflection which introduces an event argument in these sentences, but I already argued in chapter 8 that there is no evidence for this in these sentences. Furthermore, we would have to prevent the null inflection from appearing in identity sentences, since otherwise Pron-less identity sentences ought to be possible.

Another possibility is that adjectives in Hebrew have an event argument. This may well be the case, since Hebrew adjectives pass other 'eventuality' tests. As predicates of matrix small clauses they can be modified in the 'every time' construction, as in (173), and in colloquial Hebrew they can be modified by adverbs of temporal location, as in (174):

(173) dani me'od nexmad kol   pa'am Se- dafna ba'a.
       dani very   nice   every time that dafna comes
       "Dani is very nice every time that Dafna comes."

(174)   dani texef   Sikor axSav, ki   hu lokeax trufot.
        dani immediately drunk now   because he takes   medicines
        "Dani gets immediately drunk now, because he is taking medicine."

The idea that adjectives in Hebrew are 'verb-like' is the more intuitively plausible because, as we have already observed, 'present tense' verbal forms in Hebrew have adjectival properties – in particular they are inflected only for number and gender with typically adjectival morphological markings. This leads to the feeling that the verb-adjective distinction in Hebrew is less a contrast and more a continuum. Be that as it may, the data raises the possibility of cross linguistic variation in syntactic-semantic categorial mappings. Chierchia (1998b) has suggested that NPs may be of different types in different languages; specifically, he suggests that Italian NPs (as opposed to DPs) are of type <d,t> and denote predicates, while English NPs are of type d and denote individuals, and he derives from this differences in references to kinds in the two languages. If there is cross-linguistic categorial variation of this kind with respect to nominal predicates, then whether adjectives denote mass states or count eventualities may well also be a parameter along which differences can occur.

BIBLIOGRAPHY

Abney, S.: 1987. *The English Noun Phrase in its Sentential Aspect*. Ph.D. dissertation, MIT.

Akmajian, A.: 1984. Sentence types and the form-function fit. in: *Natural Language and Linguistic Theory* 2, pp1–24.

Andrews, A.: 1982. A note on the constituent structure of adverbials and auxiliaries. *Linguistic Inquiry* 13, pp313–317.

Aristotle, *The Basic Works*, edited R. McKeon, Random House (1941).

Authier, J-M.: 1991. V-governed expletives, case-theory and the projection principle. *Linguistic Inquiry* 22, pp721–740.

Bach, E.: 1979. Control in Montague grammar. *Linguistic Inquiry* 10, pp515–533.

Bach, E.: 1982. Purpose clauses and control. In: P. Jacobson and G. Pullum (eds.), *The Nature of Syntactic Representation*, Kluwer: Dordrecht.

Bach, E.: 1986. The algebra of events. *Linguistics and Philosophy* 9, pp5–16.

Baker, M.: 1988. *Incorporation: A Theory of Grammatical Function Changing*, University of Chicago Press: Chicago.

Baltin, M.: 1995. Floating quantifiers, PRO and predication. *Linguistic Inquiry* 26, pp199–248.

Ben-David, A.: 1971. *Lashon ha-Mikra ve-Lashon Xaxamim*. Dvir: Tel Aviv.

Berman, R. and A. Grosu: 1976. Aspects of the copula in Modern Hebrew. In: P. Cole (ed.), *Studies in Modern Hebrew Syntax and Semantics*. North Holland: Amsterdam.

den Besten, H.: 1977. On the interaction of root transformations and lexical deletive rules. In: W. Abraham (ed.), *On the Formal Syntax of the Westgermania*. Benjamins: Amsterdam. pp47–131.

Beukema, F.: 1984. Extractions from 'with' constructions. *Linguistic Inquiry* 15, pp698.

Beukema, F. and T. Hoekstra: 1988. 'Met' met PRO of 'met' zonder PRO: een absolute constructie. *De Nieuwe Taalgids*, 76, pp 532–548.

Bittner, M.: 1994. Cross-linguistic semantics. *Linguistics and Philosophy* 17, pp57–108.

Bolinger, D.: 1977. *Meaning and Form*. Longman: London.

Borer, H.: 1981. *Parametric Syntax*. Foris: Dordrecht.

Borer, H.: 1986. I-subjects. *Linguistic Inquiry* 17, pp375–416.

Borer, H.: 1995. The ups and downs of Hebrew verb movement. *Natural Language and Linguistic Theory* 13.

Bresnan, J.: 1973. Syntax of the comparative clause construction in English. *Linguistic Inquiry* 4, pp274–344.

Bresnan, J. (ed.): 1982a. *The Mental Representation of Grammatical Relations*, MIT Press: Cambridge, Mass.

Bresnan, J.: 1982b. Passive. In: Bresnan 1982a.

Bresnan, J.: 1994. Locative inversion and the architecture of universal grammar. *Language* 70, pp72–131.

Browning, M.: 1987. *Null Operator Constructions*. Ph.D. dissertation, MIT.

Burzio, L.: 1986 *Italian Syntax*. Kluwer: Dordrecht.

Butt, M.: 1995. *The Structure of Complex Predicates in Urdu*. CSLI Publications: Stanford, CA.

Carrier, J. and J. Randall, 1992. The argument structure and syntactic structure of resultatives. *Linguistic Inquiry* 23, pp173–234.

Cattell, R.: 1978. On the source of interrogative adverbs. *Language* 54, pp51–77.

Chierchia, G.: 1984. *Topics in the Syntax and Semantics of Infinitives and Gerunds*. Ph.D. dissertation, University of Massachusetts, Amherst.

Chierchia, G.: 1986. Predication. *Linguistic Inquiry* 17, pp417–443.
Chierchia, G. and R. Turner: 1988. Semantics and property theory. *Linguistics and Philosophy* 11, pp261–303.
Chierchia, G.: 1989. A semantics for unaccusatives and its syntactic consequences. Unpublished manuscript, Cornell University.
Chierchia, G.: 1995. Individual-level predicates as inherent generics. In: G. Carlson and F.J. Pelletier (eds.), *The Generic Book.* Chicago University Press: Chicago.
Chierchia, G.: 1998a. Plurality of mass nouns and the notion of 'semantic parameter', In: S. Rothstein (ed.), *Events and Grammar*, Dordrecht: Kluwer.
Chierchia, G.: 1998b. Reference to kinds across languages. *Natural Language Semantics* 6, pp339–405.
Chomsky, N.: 1981. *Lectures on Government and Binding.* Foris: Dordrecht.
Chomsky, N.: 1982. *Some Concepts and Consequences of the Theory of Government and Binding.* MIT Press: Cambridge Mass.
Chomsky, N.: 1986a. *Knowledge of Language.* Praeger: New York.
Chomsky, N.: 1986b. *Barriers.* MIT Press: Cambridge, Mass.
Cinque, G.: 1989. Ergative adjectives and the lexicalist hypothesis. *Natural Language and Linguistic Theory* 8, pp1–40.
Condoravdi, C.: 1992. Individual level predicates in conditional clauses. Unpublished manuscript. Yale University.
Davidson, D.: 1967. The logical form of action sentences. In *Essays on Actions and Events*, Oxford University Press: Oxford.
Déchaine, R.: 1993. *Predicates Across Categories: Towards a Category Neutral Syntax.* Ph.D. dissertation, University of Massachusetts, Amherst.
Doron, E.: 1983. *Verbless Predicates in Hebrew.* Ph.D. dissertation, University of Texas at Austin.
Doron, E.: 1986. The pronominal copula as agreement clitic. In: H. Borer (ed.), *The Syntax of Pronominal Clitics.* Syntax and Semantics 19, pp313–332. Academic Press: New York.
Dowty, D.: 1979. *Word Meaning and Montague Grammar.* Kluwer: Dordrecht.
Dowty, D.: 1982. Grammatical relations and Montague grammar. In: P. Jacobson and G. Pullum (eds), *The Nature of Syntactic Representation*, Kluwer: Dordrecht.
Dowty, D.: 1985. On recent analyses of the semantics of control. *Linguistics and Philosophy* 8, pp1–41.
Dowty, D.: 1989. On the semantic content of the notion of thematic role. In: G. Chierchia, B. Partee and R Turner (eds.), *Properties, Types and Meaning* (Volume 2), Kluwer: Dordrecht.
Dowty, D.: 1991. Thematic proto-roles and argument selection. *Language* 67, pp547–619.
Dummett, M.: 1973. *Frege: Philosophy of Language.* Harvard University Press: Cambridge, Mass. (citation from second edition, 1981)
Frege, G.: 1891. Function and concept. In: P. Geach and M. Black (eds.), *Translations from the Philosophical Writings of Gottlob Frege* (1980 edition). Rowman and Littlefield: New Jersey.
Frege, G.: 1892. Concept and object. In: P. Geach and M. Black (eds.), *Translations from the Philosophical Writings of Gottlob Frege* (1980 edition). Rowman and Littlefield: New Jersey.
Fukui, N.: 1986. *A Theory of Category Projection and its Applications.* Ph.D. dissertation, MIT.
Fukui, N. and M. Speas: 1986. Specifiers and projections. In: *MIT Working Paper in Linguistics* 8, pp128–172. Department of Linguistics and Philosophy, MIT, Cambridge, Mass.
Gazdar, G., E. Klein, G. Pullum and I. Sag: 1985. *Generalized Phrase Structure Grammar.* Blackwell: Oxford.
Geach, P.: 1962. *Reference and Generality.* Cornell University Press: Ithaca, New York (reprinted 1980).
Greenberg, Y.: 1994. *Hebrew Nominal Sentences and the Stage-Individual Level Distinction.* MA thesis, Bar-Ilan University.
Greenberg, Y.: 1998. An overt syntactic marker for genericity. In: S. Rothstein. (ed.), *Events and Grammar.* Kluwer: Dordrecht.
Greenberg, Y. 1999. The pronominal copula in Hebrew as a realization of a generic operator. Unpublished manuscript. Bar-Ilan University.

Grimshaw, J.: 1979. Complement selection and the lexicon. *Linguistic Inquiry* 10, pp279–326.

Gruber, J.: 1965. *Studies in Lexical Relations*. Ph.D. dissertation, MIT.

Halliday, M.: 1967. Notes on transitivity and theme in English (Part I). *Journal of Linguistics* 3, 37–81.

Hegarty, M. 1992.: Adjunct extraction without traces. In: *Proceedings of the 10th West Coast Conference in Formal Linguistics*. Stanford, California: CSLI Publications.

Heggie, L.: 1988. *The Syntax of Copular Constructions*. Ph.D. dissertation, University of Southern California.

Heller, D.: 1999. *The Syntax and Semantics of Specificational Pseudoclefts in Hebrew*. MA thesis, Tel Aviv University.

Heycock, C.: 1991. *Layers of Predication: the Non-Lexical Structure of the Clause*. Ph.D. dissertation, University of Pennsylvania, Philadephia.

Heycock, C.: 1992. Layers of predication and the syntax of the copula. *Belgian Journal of Linguistics* 7, pp95–123.

Heycock, C. and A. Kroch: 1999. Pseudocleft connectedness: implications for the LF interface level. *Linguistic Inquiry* 30: pp365–397.

Higginbotham, J.: 1985. On semantics. *Linguistic Inquiry* 16, pp547–593.

Higginbotham, J.: 1987. Indefiniteness and predication. In: A. ter Meulen and E. Reuland (eds.), *The Representation of (In)definiteness*. MIT Press: Cambridge, Mass.

Hoekskma, J.: 1991. Complex predicates and liberation in Dutch and English. *Linguistics and Philosophy* 14, pp661–710.

Jaeggli, O.: 1980. *On Some Phonologically Null Elements in Syntax*. Ph.D. dissertation, MIT.

Jackendoff, R.: 1972 *Semantic Interpretation in Generative Grammar*. MIT Press: Cambridge, Mass.

Jackendoff, R.: 1977. *X-bar Syntax*. MIT Press: Cambridge, Mass.

Jacobson, P.: 1990. Raising as function composition. *Linguistics and Philosophy* 13, pp423–477.

Jones, C.: 1991. *Purpose Clauses*. Kluwer: Dordrecht.

Kadmon, N.: 1987. *On Unique and Non-Unique Reference and Asymmetric Quantification*. Ph.D. dissertation, University of Massachusetts, Amherst. Published 1992 by Garland: New York.

Kayne, R.: 1984. *Connectedness and Binary Branching*. Foris: Dordrecht.

Keenan, E.: 1976. Towards a universal definition of "subject", In: C. Li (ed.), *Subjects*. Academic Press: New York.

Keenan, E.: 1987. A semantic definition of 'indefinite NP'. In: A. ter Meulen and E. Reuland (eds.), *The Representation of (In)definiteness*. MIT Press: Cambridge, Mass.

Klein, E. and I. Sag: 1985. Type-driven translation. *Linguistics and Philosophy* 8, pp163–202.

Koster, J.: 1977. Subject sentences don't exist. In: S.J. Keyser (ed.), *Recent European Studies in Transformational Grammar*. MIT Press: Cambridge Mass.

Kratzer, A.: 1994. Aspect. Unpublished manuscript, University of Massachusetts at Amherst.

Krifka, M.: 1989. Nominal reference, temporal constitution and quantification event semantics. In: R. Bartsch, J. van Bentham, and Peter van Emde Boas (eds.), *Semantics and Contextual Expressions*. Foris: Dordrecht.

Krifka, M.: 1992. Thematic relations as links between nominal reference and temporal constitution. In: I. Sag and A. Szabolcsi (eds.), *Lexical Matters*, Stanford University: CSLI Publications.

Lakoff, G.: 1970. *Irregularity in Syntax*. Holt, Rinehart and Winston: New York.

Landman, F.: 1991. *Structures for Semantics*. Kluwer: Dordrecht.

Landman, F.: 1992. The progressive. *Natural Language Semantics* 1, pp1–32.

Landman, F.: 1995. Advanced Semantics. Unpublished manuscript, Tel-Aviv University.

Landman, F.: 1996. Plurality. In: S. Lappin (ed.), *Handbook of Contemporary Semantics*. Blackwell: Oxford.

Landman, F.: 1999. *Events and Plurality*. In press, Kluwer: Dordrecht.

Landman, F.: 2000. Argument-predicate mismatches. Paper presented at NP-DP Conference, University of Antwerp.

Lappin, S. 1983. The theta-criterion and pronominal binding. *Proceedings of NELS 13*, 121–128. GLSA, University of Massachusetts, Amherst.

Larson, R.: 1985. Bare NP adverbs. *Linguistic Inquiry* 16, pp595–621.

Lasersohn, P. 1992. Generalized conjunction and temporal modification. *Linguistics and Philosophy* 15, pp381–411.

Lasersohn, P.: 1995. *Plurality, Conjunction and Events.* Kluwer: Dordrecht.

Levin, B. and M. Rappaport (Rappaport Hovav): 1986. The formation of adjectival passives. *Linguistic Inquiry* 17, pp623–662.

Levin, B. and M. Rappaport Hovav, 1995. *Unaccusativity.* MIT Press: Cambridge, Mass.

Link, G.: 1983. The logical analysis of plurals and mass terms: a lattice theoretical approach. In: R. Bäuerle, C. Schwarze and A. von Stechow (eds.), *Meaning, Use and Interpretation of Language.* Berlin: de Gruyter.

Link, G.: 1987. Algebraic semantics of event structures. In: J. Groenendijk, M. Stokhof, and F. Veltman (eds.), *Proceedings of the Sixth Amsterdam Colloquium.* ITLI, Amsterdam.

Lobeck, A.: 1991. Phrase structure of ellipsis in English. In: S. Rothstein (ed.), *Perspectives on Phrase Structure: Heads and Licensing.* Syntax and Semantics 25. Academic Press: New York.

Longobardi, G.: 1984. Copular constructions. Unpublished manuscript, University of Venice (revised 1991).

Longobardi, G.: 1994. Reference and proper names. *Linguistic Inquiry* 25, pp609–665.

Marantz, A.: 1984. *On the Nature of Grammatical Relations.* MIT Press: Cambridge, Mass.

McCloskey, J.: 1991. *There, it,* and agreement. *Linguistic Inquiry* 22, pp563–567.

McNally, L.: 1997. *A Semantics for the English Existential Construction.* Garland: New York.

McNulty, E.: 1988. *The Syntax of Adjunct Predicates,* Ph.D. dissertation, University of Connecticut, Storrs.

Mittwoch, A.: 1988. Aspects of English aspect: on the interaction of perfect progressive and durational phrases. *Linguistics and Philosophy* 11, pp203–254.

Moens, M. and M. Steedman: 1988. Temporal ontology and temporal reference. *Computational Linguistics* 14, pp15–28.

Montague, R.: 1970. Universal Grammar. *Theoria* 36, pp373–398. Reprinted in *Formal Philosophy: Selected Papers of Richard Montague,* R.H. Thomason (ed.), New Haven: Yale University Press, 1974.

Montague, R.: 1973. The Proper Treatment of of Quantification in English. In: J. Hintikka, J. Moravcsik, and P. Suppes (eds.), *Approaches to Natural Language: Proceedings of the 1970 Stanford Workshop on Grammar and Semantics.* Kluwer: Dordrecht. Reprinted in *Formal Philosophy: Selected Papers of Richard Montague,* R.H. Thomason (ed.), New Haven: Yale University Press, 1974.

Moro, A.: 1991. The raising of predicates: copula, expletives and existence. *MIT Working Papers in Linguistics* 15.

Moro, A.: 1997. *The Raising of Predicates: Predicative Noun Phrases and the Theory of Clause Structure.* Cambridge: Cambridge University Press.

Napoli, D.J.: 1988. Subjects and external arguments clauses and non-clauses. *Linguistics and Philosophy* 11, pp323– 354.

Neeleman, A. 1994. *Complex Predicates.* Ph.D. dissertation, Utrecht University. OTS, Utrecht.

Parsons, T.: 1990. *Events in the Semantics of English.* MIT Press: Cambridge, Mass.

Partee, B.: 1977. "John is easy to please," In: A. Zampolli (ed.), *Linguistic Structures Processing.* North Holland: Amsterdam.

Partee, B. and M. Rooth, 1983. Generalised conjunction and type ambiguity. In: R. Bäuerle, C. Schwarze and A.von Stechow (eds.), *Meaning, Use and Interpretation of Language.* Berlin: de Gruyter.

Partee, B.: 1986. Unambiguous 'be' in ambiguous pseudoclefts, *Proceedings of NELS* 16.

Partee, B.: 1987. Noun Phrase interpretation and type shifting principles. In: J. Groenendijk and M. Stokhof (eds.), *Studies in Discourse Representation Theory and the Theory of Generalized Quantifiers.* GRASS 8. Dordrecht: Foris.

Pelletier, F.J.: 1979. Non-singular reference. In: F.J. Pelletier (ed.), *Mass Terms: Some Philosophical Problems.* Kluwer: Dordrecht.

Perlmutter, D. (ed.): 1983. *Studies in Relational Grammar 1.* University of Chicago Press: Chicago.

Perlmutter, D. and C. Rosen (eds.), : 1984. *Studies in Relational Grammar 2.* University of Chicago Press: Chicago.

Postal, P. and G. Pullum., 1988. Expletive noun phrases in subcategorised position. *Linguistic Inquiry* 19, pp635–670.

Pullum, G.: 1987. Implications of English extraposed irrealis clauses. *ESCOL 4*, The Ohio State University, Columbus.

Rapoport, T.: 1987. *Copular, Nominal and Small Clauses*: a study of Israeli Hebrew. Ph.D. dissertation, MIT.

Rapoport, T.: 1991. Adjunct predicate licensing and D-structure. In: S. Rothstein (ed.), *Perspectives on phrase structure: heads and licensing.* Syntax and Semantics 25. Academic Press: New York.

Rappaport (Rappaport Hovav), M. and B. Levin: 1988. What to do with theta-roles. In: Wendy Wilkins (ed.), *Thematic Relations.* Syntax and Semantics 19. Academic Press: New York.

Rappaport Hovav, M. and B. Levin, 1999. Events and resultatives. Unpublished manuscript, Bar-Ilan University and Northwestern University.

Reinhart, T.: 1981. Pragmatics and linguistics: an analysis of sentence topics *Philosophica* 27, 53–94.

Reinhart, T.: 1983. *Anaphora and Semantic Interpretation.* University of Chicago Press: Chicago.

Reinhart, T.: 1991. Non-quantificational LF. In: A. Kasher (ed.), *The Chomskyan Turn*, Blackwell: Oxford.

Rizzi, L.: 1982. *Issues in Italian Syntax.* Foris: Dordrecht.

Rizzi, L.: 1986. On chain formation. In: H. Borer (ed.), *The Syntax of Pronominal Clitics.* Syntax and semantics 19, Academic Press: New York.

Rizzi, L.: 1990. *Relativized Minimality.* MIT Press: Cambridge, MA.

Roberts, I.: 1988. Predicative APs. *Linguistic Inquiry* 19: pp703–710.

Rosen, C.: 1984: The interface between semantic roles and initial grammatical relations. In: D. Perlmutter and C. Rosen (eds.), 1984.

Ross, J.R.R.: 1967. *Constraints on Variables in Syntax.* Ph.D. dissertation, MIT.

Rothstein, S.: 1983. *The Syntactic Forms of Predication.* Ph.D. dissertation, MIT. Published Indiana University Linguistics Club 1985.

Rothstein, S.: 1984. On the conceptual link between clauses I and II of the Extended Projection Principle, *Proceedings of the Meeting of the Berkeley Linguistics Society.*

Rothstein, S.: 1991. Clausal licensing and subcategorisation. In: S. Rothstein (ed.), *Perspectives on Phrase Structure: Heads and Licensing.* Syntax and Semantics 25. Academic Press: New York.

Rothstein, S.: 1992a. Case and NP licensing. *Natural Language and Linguistic Theory* 10, pp119–139.

Rothstein, S.: 1992b. Predication and the structure of clauses. *Belgian Journal of Linguistics* 7, pp155–169.

Rothstein, S.: 1995a. Pleonastics and the interpretation of pronouns. *Linguistic Inquiry* 26, pp499–529.

Rothstein, S.: 1995b. Small clauses and copular constructions. In: A. Cardinaletti and T. Guasti (eds.), *Small Clauses*, Syntax and Semantics 28, Academic Press: New York.

Rothstein, S.: 1995c. Adverbial quantification over events. *Natural Language Semantics* 3, pp1–31.

Rothstein, S.: 1998. Progressive achievements. Unpublished manuscript, Bar-Ilan University.

Rothstein, S.: 1999. Secondary predication and aspect. talk presented at the Oslo Conference on Adjuncts, Norwegian Academy of Sciences, September 1999.

Rothstein, S.: 2000. Secondary Predication and Aspectual Structure. To appear in C. Fabricius-Hansen, E. Lang, and C. Maienborn (eds.). *Adjuncts*, ZAS Papers in Linguistics.

Rubinstein, E.: 1968. *Ha-Mishpat Ha-Shemani.* Kibbutz Hameuchad.

Russell, B.: 1919. *Introduction to Mathematical Philosophy.* London: Allen and Unwin.

Safir, K.: 1983. On small clauses as constituents. *Linguistic Inquiry* 14, pp730–735.

Safir, K.: 1987. *Syntactic Chains.* Cambridge University Press: Cambridge.

Sag, I.: 1976. *Deletion and Logical Form.* Ph.D. dissertation, MIT.

Sag, I.: 1982. NP-movement dependencies. In: P. Jacobson and G.Pullum (eds.), *The Nature of Syntactic Representation*, Kluwer: Dordrecht.

Schein, B.: 1995. Predication. In: A. Cardinaletti and T. Guasti (eds.), *Small Clauses, Syntax and Semantics* 28, Academic Press: New York.

Sichel, I.: 1997. Two pronominal copulas and the syntax of Hebrew non-verbal sentences. *Texas Linguistics Forum 38: Proceedings of the 1977 Texas Linguistic Society Conference*, University of Texas at Austin.

Simpson, J.: 1983. Resultatives. In, L. Levin, M. Rappaport and A. Zaenen (eds.), *Papers in Lexical-Functional Grammar*. Indiana University Linguistics Club.

Speas, M.: 1986. *Adjunctions and Projections in Syntax*, Ph.D. dissertation, MIT.

Steedman, M.: 1990. Gapping as Constituent Conjunction. *Linguistics and Philosophy* 13, pp207–263.

Stowell, T.: 1978. What was there before there was there. *Papers from the Fourteenth Regional Meeting, Chicago Linguistics Society*, 458–71. Chicago Linguistics Society, University of Chicago, Chicago.

Stowell, T.: 1981. *The Origins of Phrase Structure*. Ph.D. dissertation. MIT.

Stowell, T.: 1983. Subjects across categories. *The Linguistic Review* 2, pp285–312.

Stowell, T.: 1991a. Small clause restructuring. In: R. Frieden (ed.), *Principles and Parameters in Comparative Grammar*, pp182–218. MIT Press: Cambridge, Mass.

Stowell, T.: 1991b. The alignment of arguments in adjective phrases. In: S. Rothstein (ed.), *Perspectives on Phrase Structure: Heads and Licensing*. Syntax and Semantics 25. Academic Press: New York.

Strawson, P.F.: 1950. On Referring, *Mind* 59, pp320–244. Reprinted in: Strawson (1971) *Logico-Linguistic Papers*. Methuen: London..

Strawson, P.F.: 1964. Identifying reference and truth values. *Theoria*: 96–118. Reprinted in P.F. Strawson (1971) *Logico-Linguistic Papers*. Methuen: London.

Strawson, P.F.: 1970. The asymmetry of subjects and predicates, In: H.E. Kiefer and M.K. Munitz (eds), *Language, Belief and Metaphysics*, SUNY Press, N.Y.: reprinted in P.F. Strawson (1971) *Logico-Linguistic Papers*. Methuen: London.

Strawson, P.F.: 1974. *Subject and Predicate in Logic and Grammar*. Methuen: London.

Stump, G.: 1985. *The Semantic Variability of Absolute Constructions*. Kluwer: Dordrecht.

Vendler, Z.: 1967. *Linguistics in Philosophy*. Cornell University Press: Ithaca, N.Y.

Vlach, F.: 1983. On situation semantics for perception. *Synthese* 54, pp129–52.

Wechsler, S.: 1997. Resultative predicates and control. *Texas Linguistics Forum 38: Proceedings of the 1977 Texas Linguistic Society Conference*, University of Texas at Austin.

Williams, E.: 1977. Discourse and logical form. *Linguistic Inquiry* 8, pp101–140.

Williams, E.: 1980. Predication. *Linguistic Inquiry* 11, pp203–238.

Williams, E.: 1981. Argument structure and morphology. *The Linguistic Review* 1, pp81–114.

Williams, E.: 1983a. Against small clauses. *Linguistic Inquiry* 14, pp287–308.

Williams, E.: 1983b. Semantic vs. syntactic categories. *Linguistics and Philosophy* 6, pp423–446.

Williams, E.: 1984. *There*-insertion. *Linguistic Inquiry* 15, pp131–153.

Williams, E.: 1987. NP trace and theta-theory. *Linguistics and Philosophy* 10, pp203–238.

Williams, E.: 1994. *Thematic Structure in Syntax*. MIT Press: Cambridge, Mass: .

Zaenen, A., J. Maling and T. Thrainsson., 1985. Case and grammatical functions: the Icelandic passive. *Natural Language and Linguistic Theory* 3, pp441–483.

Zimmermann, T.E.: 1992. On the proper treatment of opacity in certain verbs. *Natural Language Semantics* 1, pp149–180.

Zubizaretta, M. L.: 1987. *Levels of Representation in the Lexicon and in the Syntax*. Ph.D. dissertation, MIT.

Zucchi, A. 1998. Aspect shift. In S. Rothstein (ed.), *Events and Grammar*. Kluwer: Dordrecht.

Zucchi S. and M. White: 1996. Twigs, Sequences and the Temporal Constitution of Predicates," *Proceedings of SALT VI*.

Index

99, 119, 120, 182, 184, 213, 250, 255, 256, 257, 259
Higginbotham, J.   30, 31, 37, 42, 85, 101, 103, 111,135, 268
higher-order equative construction   56
homogeneity   301, 302, 306–314
Hoekstra, T.   54

Icelandic   18, 186
identity relation   63, 213, 214, 240
identity relation on predicates   119, 240
identity sentences   xii, 205, 206, 211–214, 218, 220–222, 228, 230–246, 249–264, 273, 335, 337
   predicate raising approach to   250–259
indexing   103–105, 145
individual level   233, 277, 282, 317
individuals, domain of   136, 179, 190, 191, 301, 314
infinitivals   69, 96, 109, 116–118, 167, 238, 274, 275, 280, 319
Infl   28, 30, 41, 48, 75,76, 79, 99, 134, 141, 148, 149, 154, 163, 166, 205–237, 241, 242, 244, 246–249, 255, 260
   defective   229
inflection   ix, xii, 12, 20, 39, 41, 50, 76, 155, 163, 167, 207, 212, 217, 225, 237, 274, 275, 287, 316, 337
inherent predicates   59, 118, 129, 145
instantiate INST   289, 297, 316, 326, 327, 335
intensifier   253, 265, 304, 305
intransitive resultatives   128, 157, 159
intransitivisation   14, 82
Italian   12, 102, 182, 251, 252, 256, 260, 338

Jackendoff, R.   11, 35, 107
Jacobson, P.   23, 54, 82, 93
Jaeggli, O.   223
Jones, C.   116, 128

Kadmon, N.   190, 257
Kartunnen, L.   168, 171
Kayne, R.   53, 124
Keenan, E.   ix, 239
Klein, E.   ix, 39, 168, 171, 174, 247
Koster, J.   81, 83
Kratzer, A.   135, 139
Krifka, M.   302, 308, 310, 312, 321
Kroch, A.   56, 250, 255, 256

Lakoff, G.   283
lambda abstraction   xii, 86, 97, 119, 136, 168, 171, 173–175, 178, 179
Landman, F.   23, 26, 31, 45, 56, 137, 150, 155, 170, 191, 193, 249, 250, 258, 294–296, 307, 310, 311, 312, 330, 331, 333

Lappin, S.   90, 184
Larson, R.   188
Lasersohn, P.   150
Levin, B.   30, 37, 49, 156, 158, 74, 102, 127, 128, 156, 158, 256
Lewis, D.   295
lexical decomposition   305
lexical heads   xi, 19, 28, 39, 43–45, 47, 58, 59, 72, 77, 78, 113, 129, 133, 134, 137, 149, 150, 174, 180, 212
licensing,
   DP   185
   identity sentences   217
   Infl   217–219, 229
   function application   139, 177
   pleonastics   80, 187, 250
   predicates   47, 49, 95, 103
   small clauses   241, 255
   subject   63, 70, 71
   syntactic   42, 63, 75, 90, 97,184, 230
Link, G.   136, 137, 147, 191, 295, 296, 301, 309
lo   171, 209, 210, 213, 216, 217, 220, 226, 227, 229, 234
Lobeck, A.   13, 24
locality   29, 47, 48, 62, 80, 100, 106, 113, 114
locating function   297, 299, 300, 305
locatives, see adverbials, locative
Longobardi, G.   58, 236, 237, 251, 252, 259, 263

Marantz, A.   135, 139
mass property   136, 288–290, 292, 293, 295, 296, 297, 300–305, 309–316, 336, 338
mass nouns   136, 289, 290, 304
mass/count distinction   289, 293, 295, 301, 303, 305, 310, 314
matching   169, 189, 190, 191, 226, 292, 293
matching function, M   292, 293
McCloskey, J.   168, 182
McNulty, E.   125, 127
Mittwoch, A.   110, 302, 312
Minimality Theory   214
Moens, M.   322
Montague, R.   ix, 36, 45, 46, 164
Moro, A.   63, 236, 250, 251, 254, 255, 260, 263, 281
M-states   288–309, 312, 315, 335

Neeleman, A.   50, 101, 104
non-atomicity   136, 288, 289, 290, 293, 295, 297, 301–303, 310

object control   279

348

Studies in Linguistics and Philosophy

1.   H. Hiż (ed.): *Questions*. 1978   ISBN 90-277-0813-4; Pb: 90-277-1035-X
2.   W. S. Cooper: *Foundations of Logico-Linguistics*. A Unified Theory of Information, Language, and Logic. 1978   ISBN 90-277-0864-9; Pb: 90-277-0876-2
3.   A. Margalit (ed.): *Meaning and Use*. 1979   ISBN 90-277-0888-6
4.   F. Guenthner and S.J. Schmidt (eds.): *Formal Semantics and Pragmatics for Natural Languages*. 1979   ISBN 90-277-0778-2; Pb: 90-277-0930-0
5.   E. Saarinen (ed.): *Game-Theoretical Semantics*. Essays on Semantics by Hintikka, Carlson, Peacocke, Rantala, and Saarinen. 1979   ISBN 90-277-0918-1
6.   F.J. Pelletier (ed.): *Mass Terms: Some Philosophical Problems*. 1979
                                                                ISBN 90-277-0931-9
7.   D. R. Dowty: *Word Meaning and Montague Grammar*. The Semantics of Verbs and Times in Generative Semantics and in Montague's PTQ. 1979 ISBN 90-277-1008-2; Pb: 90-277-1009-0
8.   A. F. Freed: *The Semantics of English Aspectual Complementation*. 1979
                                                                ISBN 90-277-1010-4; Pb: 90-277-1011-2
9.   J. McCloskey: *Transformational Syntax and Model Theoretic Semantics*. A Case Study in Modern Irish. 1979   ISBN 90-277-1025-2; Pb: 90-277-1026-0
10. J. R. Searle, F. Kiefer and M. Bierwisch (eds.): *Speech Act Theory and Pragmatics*. 1980
                                                                ISBN 90-277-1043-0; Pb: 90-277-1045-7
11. D. R. Dowty, R. E. Wall and S. Peters: *Introduction to Montague Semantics*. 1981; 5th printing 1987   ISBN 90-277-1141-0; Pb: 90-277-1142-9
12. F. Heny (ed.): *Ambiguities in Intensional Contexts*. 1981
                                                                ISBN 90-277-1167-4; Pb: 90-277-1168-2
13. W. Klein and W. Levelt (eds.): *Crossing the Boundaries in Linguistics*. Studies Presented to Manfred Bierwisch. 1981   ISBN 90-277-1259-X
14. Z. S. Harris: *Papers on Syntax*. Edited by H. Hiż. 1981
                                                                ISBN 90-277-1266-0; Pb: 90-277-1267-0
15. P. Jacobson and G. K. Pullum (eds.): *The Nature of Syntactic Representation*. 1982
                                                                ISBN 90-277-1289-1; Pb: 90-277-1290-5
16. S. Peters and E. Saarinen (eds.): *Processes, Beliefs, and Questions*. Essays on Formal Semantics of Natural Language and Natural Language Processing. 1982   ISBN 90-277-1314-6
17. L. Carlson: *Dialogue Games*. An Approach to Discourse Analysis. 1983; 2nd printing 1985
                                                                ISBN 90-277-1455-X; Pb: 90-277-1951-9
18. L. Vaina and J. Hintikka (eds.): *Cognitive Constraints on Communication*. Representation and Processes. 1984; 2nd printing 1985   ISBN 90-277-1456-8; Pb: 90-277-1949-7
19. F. Heny and B. Richards (eds.): *Linguistic Categories: Auxiliaries and Related Puzzles*. Volume I: Categories. 1983   ISBN 90-277-1478-9
20. F. Heny and B. Richards (eds.): *Linguistic Categories: Auxiliaries and Related Puzzles*. Volume II: The Scope, Order, and Distribution of English Auxiliary Verbs. 1983 ISBN 90-277-1479-7
21. R. Cooper: *Quantification and Syntactic Theory*. 1983   ISBN 90-277-1484-3
22. J. Hintikka (in collaboration with J. Kulas): *The Game of Language*. Studies in Game-Theoretical Semantics and Its Applications. 1983; 2nd printing 1985
                                                                ISBN 90-277-1687-0; Pb: 90-277-1950-0
23. E. L. Keenan and L. M. Faltz: *Boolean Semantics for Natural Language*. 1985
                                                                ISBN 90-277-1768-0; Pb: 90-277-1842-3
24. V. Raskin: *Semantic Mechanisms of Humor*. 1985   ISBN 90-277-1821-0; Pb: 90-277-1891-1

Volumes 1–26 formerly published under the Series Title: Synthese Language Library.

Studies in Linguistics and Philosophy

25. G. T. Stump: *The Semantic Variability of Absolute Constructions.* 1985
     ISBN 90-277-1895-4; Pb: 90-277-1896-2
26. J. Hintikka and J. Kulas: *Anaphora and Definite Descriptions.* Two Applications of Game-Theoretical Semantics. 1985   ISBN 90-277-2055-X; Pb: 90-277-2056-8
27. E. Engdahl: *Constituent Questions.* The Syntax and Semantics of Questions with Special Reference to Swedish. 1986   ISBN 90-277-1954-3; Pb: 90-277-1955-1
28. M. J. Cresswell: *Adverbial Modification.* Interval Semantics and Its Rivals. 1985
     ISBN 90-277-2059-2; Pb: 90-277-2060-6
29. J. van Benthem: *Essays in Logical Semantics* 1986 ISBN 90-277-2091-6; Pb: 90-277-2092-4
30. B. H. Partee, A. ter Meulen and R. E. Wall: *Mathematical Methods in Linguistics.* 1990; Corrected second printing of the first edition 1993   ISBN 90-277-2244-7; Pb: 90-277-2245-5
31. P. Gärdenfors (ed.): *Generalized Quantifiers.* Linguistic and Logical Approaches. 1987
     ISBN 1-55608-017-4
32. R. T. Oehrle, E. Bach and D. Wheeler (eds.): *Categorial Grammars and Natural Language Structures.* 1988   ISBN 1-55608-030-1; Pb: 1-55608-031-X
33. W. J. Savitch, E. Bach, W. Marsh and G. Safran-Naveh (eds.): *The Formal Complexity of Natural Language.* 1987   ISBN 1-55608-046-8; Pb: 1-55608-047-6
34. J. E. Fenstad, P.-K. Halvorsen, T. Langholm and J. van Benthem: *Situations, Language and Logic.* 1987   ISBN 1-55608-048-4; Pb: 1-55608-049-2
35. U. Reyle and C. Rohrer (eds.): *Natural Language Parsing and Linguistic Theories.* 1988
     ISBN 1-55608-055-7; Pb: 1-55608-056-5
36. M. J. Cresswell: *Semantical Essays.* Possible Worlds and Their Rivals. 1988
     ISBN 1-55608-061-1
37. T. Nishigauchi: *Quantification in the Theory of Grammar.* 1990
     ISBN 0-7923-0643-0; Pb: 0-7923-0644-9
38. G. Chierchia, B.H. Partee and R. Turner (eds.): *Properties, Types and Meaning.* Volume I: Foundational Issues. 1989   ISBN 1-55608-067-0; Pb: 1-55608-068-9
39. G. Chierchia, B.H. Partee and R. Turner (eds.): *Properties, Types and Meaning.* Volume II: Semantic Issues. 1989   ISBN 1-55608-069-7; Pb: 1-55608-070-0
     Set ISBN (Vol. I + II) 1-55608-088-3; Pb: 1-55608-089-1
40. C.T.J. Huang and R. May (eds.): *Logical Structure and Linguistic Structure.* Cross-Linguistic Perspectives. 1991   ISBN 0-7923-0914-6; Pb: 0-7923-1636-3
41. M.J. Cresswell: *Entities and Indices.* 1990   ISBN 0-7923-0966-9; Pb: 0-7923-0967-7
42. H. Kamp and U. Reyle: *From Discourse to Logic.* Introduction to Modeltheoretic Semantics of Natural Language, Formal Logic and Discourse Representation Theory. 1993
     ISBN 0-7923-2403-X; Student edition: 0-7923-1028-4
43. C.S. Smith: *The Parameter of Aspect.* (Second Edition). 1997
     ISBN 0-7923-4657-2; Pb 0-7923-4659-9
44. R.C. Berwick (ed.): *Principle-Based Parsing.* Computation and Psycholinguistics. 1991
     ISBN 0-7923-1173-6; Pb: 0-7923-1637-1
45. F. Landman: *Structures for Semantics.* 1991   ISBN 0-7923-1239-2; Pb: 0-7923-1240-6
46. M. Siderits: *Indian Philosophy of Language.* 1991   ISBN 0-7923-1262-7
47. C. Jones: *Purpose Clauses.* 1991   ISBN 0-7923-1400-X
48. R.K. Larson, S. Iatridou, U. Lahiri and J. Higginbotham (eds.): *Control and Grammar.* 1992
     ISBN 0-7923-1692-4
49. J. Pustejovsky (ed.): *Semantics and the Lexicon.* 1993
     ISBN 0-7923-1963-X; Pb: 0-7923-2386-6

Studies in Linguistics and Philosophy

Further information about our publications on *Linguistics* is available on request.

Kluwer Academic Publishers – Dordrecht / Boston / London